W0018182

SAGE was founded in 1965 by Sara Miller McCune to support the dissemination of usable knowledge by publishing innovative and high-quality research and teaching content. Today, we publish over 900 journals, including those of more than 400 learned societies, more than 800 new books per year, and a growing range of library products including archives, data, case studies, reports, and video. SAGE remains majority-owned by our founder, and after Sara's lifetime will become owned by a charitable trust that secures our continued independence.

Los Angeles | London | New Delhi | Singapore | Washington DC | Melbourne

ARREST AND DETENTION IN INDIA

Thank you for choosing a SAGE product!
If you have any comment, observation or feedback,
I would like to personally hear from you.

Please write to me at **contactceo@sagepub.in**

Vivek Mehra, Managing Director and CEO, SAGE India.

Bulk Sales

SAGE India offers special discounts
for purchase of books in bulk.
We also make available special imprints
and excerpts from our books on demand.

For orders and enquiries, write to us at

Marketing Department
SAGE Publications India Pvt Ltd
B1/I-1, Mohan Cooperative Industrial Area
Mathura Road, Post Bag 7
New Delhi 110044, India

E-mail us at **marketing@sagepub.in**

Subscribe to our mailing list
Write to **marketing@sagepub.in**

This book is also available as an e-book.

ARREST AND DETENTION IN INDIA

Law, Procedure and Practice

Edited by
DIPA DUBE
SHRUTI BEDI

Los Angeles | London | New Delhi
Singapore | Washington DC | Melbourne

First published in 2022 by

SAGE Publications India Pvt Ltd
B1/I-1 Mohan Cooperative Industrial Area
Mathura Road, New Delhi 110 044, India
www.sagepub.in

SAGE Publications Inc
2455 Teller Road
Thousand Oaks, California 91320, USA

SAGE Publications Ltd
1 Oliver's Yard, 55 City Road
London EC1Y 1SP, United Kingdom

SAGE Publications Asia-Pacific Pte Ltd
18 Cross Street #10-10/11/12
China Square Central
Singapore 048423

Published by Vivek Mehra for SAGE Publications India Pvt Ltd and typeset in 10.5/13 pt Bembo by AG Infographics, Delhi.

Library of Congress Cataloging-in-Publication
Names: Dube, Dipa, editor. | Bedi, Shruti, editor.
Title: Arrest and detention in India : law, procedure, and practice / [edited by] Dipa Dube, Shruti Bedi.
Description: Thousand Oaks : SAGE Publications India Pvt Ltd, 2021. | Series: Sage law | Includes
    bibliographical references and index. |
Identifiers: LCCN 2021043958 | ISBN 9789354792441 (hardback) | ISBN 9789354792458 (epub) |
    ISBN 9789354792465 (ebook)
Subjects: LCSH: Arrest—India. | Detention of persons—India. | Preventive detention—India.
Classification: LCC KNS4654 .A97 2021 | DDC 345.54/0527—dc23/eng/20211004
LC record available at https://lccn.loc.gov/2021043958

ISBN: 978-93-5479-244-1 (HB)

SAGE Team: Aarooshi Garg, Syed Husain Naqvi and Rajinder Kaur

Contents

Part I: Arrest and Detention: Constitutional Perspectives

Part II: Legislative Perspectives on Arrest and Detention

Part III: Arrest and Detention: A Global Perspective

Part IV: Judicial Interventions, Legal Reforms and the Way Ahead

List of Illustrations

TABLES

FIGURES

Foreword

I am incredibly pleased that the authors and the editors of this book have shown interest in writing about Article 22 of the Indian Constitution as well as covering various other facets of arrest and detention in the country, which has become a subject of heated debates in recent times. I have read a draft of this book and have found its content to be interesting, informative, and educational. The book at hand eloquently examines the nuances of law and practice of preventive detention in the constitutional backdrop.

Article 21 of the Indian Constitution, which falls in the Chapter 'Fundamental Rights', guarantees that the right to life and personal liberty to every person is not limited to the Indian citizens only (in contradistinction to some other fundamental rights which are guaranteed only to citizens of India) but to non-citizens as well. It amply signifies the universal character of this valuable human right. There are two dimensions to Article 21. In the first place, the expression 'personal liberty' occurring therein is meant to be of the widest amplitude and covers a variety of rights which go to constitute the personal liberty of man, and some of them have been raised to the stature of distinct fundamental rights and given additional protection under Article 19.[1] Second, it ensures that personal liberty of only those persons who have committed some offence which is proscribed by the law would be taken away. This refers to those persons who are found guilty of committing an offence by a court of law and are given the sentence of imprisonment. Of course, it also includes those persons who are accused of committing an offence against whom investigation is in progress or are undertrials. Here also, the arrest of such persons can be

---

[1] Maneka Gandhi v. Union Of India, (1978) 1 SCC 248.

only according to the procedure established by the law, and Code of Criminal Procedure and the likes provide sufficient protection against indiscriminating arrests. These laws contain provisions which duly safeguard the interest of such undertrials, and courts are empowered to give bail during the trial. In order to balance the personal liberty of such persons and the public interest, the Apex Court has laid down extensive principles for grant of bails to undertrials with clear motto 'bail is the norm and jail is the exception' in such cases. The challenge lies in the enforcement of these principles in particular cases.

In contrast, the Constitution recognizes detention of certain persons under certain circumstances even if no offence is committed, but there is propensity to commit an offence. However, it does not include any or all types of offences but is limited to those acts which may pose a threat to the independence and national security of the nation or the economy of the country. This is known as 'preventive detention' where a person is imprisoned without any trial. Here, paramount consideration is the public interest which outweighs individual freedom. Obviously, a person is detained as a preventive measure and is not punitively treated. Notwithstanding, harsh reality is that such a person is also deprived of their personal liberty. Though in such cases safeguards mentioned in Clauses (1) and (2) of Article 22 do not apply, such persons are given protections under Clauses (4)–(7) which provide for the protection in accordance with preventive detention.

Undoubtedly, protecting the limited resources alongside preserving the peace and order is essential for a developing country. Public interest demands that those posing threat to the independence and national security of the nation or the economy of the country by resorting to white-collar crimes at mass scale have to be strictly dealt with. This need is to be balanced with the constitutional ethos enshrined in Articles 21 and 22 of the Constitution, which demands that preventive detention laws have to be fair and reasonable and also demands that these laws are not abused.

When the character of detention is 'preventive' and not 'punitive', the safeguards given to such persons under the Constitution as well as the statute relating to preventive detention have to be zealously guarded. More important is to check the abuse of such laws, recognizing the harsh reality of frequent misuse at the hands of the executive for oblique motives. In this context, role of judiciary assumes paramount significance. The responsibility for upholding the Rule of Law and the Constitution, thereby protecting the constitutional democracy, lies with the judiciary. It is for the judiciary to check the arbitrary exercise of powers on the part of the authorities and to ensure that freedom of individual is not taken away on specious grounds. Swift action by the judiciary in habeas corpus matters pertaining to preventive detention by striking down wrongful detention, wherever it is so found, becomes paramount as that would ensure that all persons are able to live securely under the rule of law. After all, liberty is the characteristic of social contract on the basis of which nation states have been formed, and the Constitutions of these States recognize the principles of liberal democracies. This notion of liberty demands that personal liberty of individuals is duly protected and is taken away only under limited circumstances.

The judiciary in India has laid down certain norms/principles in this behalf. The courts have, in umpteen number of judgements, given a message to the executive that infringement upon the personal freedom of an individual in the form of preventive detention cannot be on a drop of a hat, that is, an easy-going way. Whereas the constitutional and statutory provisions as well as judicial pronouncements give a profound message of safeguarding the personal liberty, there are also instances where infringement of liberty at the hands of executive is condoned. Here also, the challenge lies in curbing the misuse in specific cases, which onus is put on the judiciary.

In the aforesaid backdrop, undertaking the task of assessing the contours of preventive detention laws, and how far such laws have subserved the public interest or caused depravation of liberty of individuals unjustifiably, becomes imperative, and this task is remarkably accomplished in the various essays appearing in this book.

Taking the above note in consideration, I wish the authors of the book good luck. The contents of each of the chapters do not suffer from any legalistic approach. The book can easily be understood even by laymen. Students studying law, legal practitioners, judges and professors should add this to their library to gain insight on the law and regulation of arrest, detention, remand, etc.

I wish the authors good luck!

Justice A. K. Sikri
Former Judge, Supreme Court of India
Presently, International Judge, SICC Singapore

Preface

The world is passing through an extraordinary crisis. The pandemic has highlighted the existing weaknesses in our health systems as well as other basic institutions of a democracy. In such a situation, the maintenance of law and order assumes a higher imperative in ensuring the security and safety of the most vulnerable and the precarious. While applauding the untiring humanness and grit of the frontline warriors in ensuring the best implementation of government protocols, incidents of misuse or abuse of powers during these trying times have come to the fore. Not long ago, the brutal death of father and son in custody for allegedly failing to abide by lockdown rules sparked a nationwide furore, compelling the judiciary, Human Rights Commission and intelligentsia to delve into the issue of arbitrary exercise of police powers.

The death of Bennicks and Jayaraj is not an isolated incident. The last few years have posed innumerable questions on the legalities of exercise of powers by the police. The dramatic, yet unfortunate, death of Vikas Dube while being transported from one state to another, the arrest of Munawar Faruqui, a stand-up comedian for allegedly hurting Hindu sentiments, the arrest of Disha Ravi, a climate activist, on charges of sedition—are just a few noteworthy incidents of recent times, not to mention the innumerable others which have eluded the public memory. Interestingly, such impunity is not confined within the geographical boundaries of our nation. Protests under the *Black Lives Matter* banner rocked the streets of the USA in June 2020 when the police killed George Floyd, a black man. 'There is a George Floyd in every country', said Lynsey Chutel, a South African journalist, and that is the truth that the citizens of the free nations have to live by.

Such incidents across the world have captured the attention of millions and are a source of modest inspiration for the present book. The constitutional commitment to ensure justice and liberty to our democratic polity provides the basic framework for this volume on the law of arrest and detention. Respect for a person's autonomy demands that the measures taken for restricting it must pursue a proportionate and legitimate aim. The police have been endowed with wide preventive and investigative powers under the laws. These powers allow them to arrest people on suspicion, detain them for interrogation, conduct search and seizures, etc. While the exercise of these powers stands validated on the ground of security of the nation and its people, the limits to the same pose a difficult task, in both theory and practice.

The international instruments, beginning with Universal Declaration of Human Rights (UDHR) and International Covenant of Civil and Political Rights (ICCPR), have paved the path for securing the life, liberty and security of the people. The deprivation of these values by way of arbitrary arrest and detention has been proscribed by the international order. In the same spirit, the Constitution of India upholds the supreme values of life and liberty and outlines the confines within which they may be curtailed by procedure established by law. Such procedure must be 'just, fair and reasonable' and in accordance with 'morality, public order and general welfare in a democratic society'. It is in this backdrop that a plethora of criminal legislations, conferring various powers to the law enforcement officers, must be tested and validated. The Code of Criminal Procedure (CrPC), Narcotic Drugs and Psychotropic Substances Act, 1985 (NDPS), Armed Forces (Special Powers) Act, 1958 (AFSPA), Unlawful Activities (Prevention) Act, 1967 (UAPA) and a host of similar legislations lay down the law and procedure by which denial of liberty may be secured for larger societal interests. However, such deprivations must be absolutely necessary, legally permissible and minimalist in nature so as to uphold the rights and dignity of the person. Any violation of the standards needs to be dealt with stern action against the offenders.

The present offering is a unique amalgam of scholarly essays demonstrating the diverse facets of the law of arrest and detention based on the vast area of comparative constitutional and criminal jurisprudence. It is a compilation of contributions from law experts, including jurists, advocates, police and academia, both national and international. It encompasses recent and analytical reflections on a wide range of issues on the subject, not previously discussed in legal literature. The book constructs a comprehensive narrative of the arrest and detention provisions, seeking to provide a critical analysis under the constitutional mandate.

The book has been divided into four sub-themes for the convenience of the readers: Constitutional Perspectives; Legislative Powers of Arrest and Detention; Global Perspectives on Arrest and Detention; and Legal and Judicial Reforms and the Way Forward. Various laws pertaining to arrest and detention, commencing with the emerging constitutional dimensionality of the fundamental protection under Article 22, proceeding to CrPC, NDPS and AFSPA, including the modalities of arrest, such as inter-state arrests, juvenile arrests and remand, have been penetratingly analysed. Judicial decisions, law commission recommendations as well as developments in countries such as Canada, Nepal and Indonesia find a relevant dwelling in the book. It provides a deep insight on the subject of arrest and detention to policymakers, police, legislators, judges, academicians, students and people involved in analytical research.

In the end, the editors would like to acknowledge the contributions of all the authors whose collective efforts have resulted in this book. The authors are people who have been involved with the subject of arrest and detention at various levels in their professional and academic capacities and have helped in moulding the procedure and practice of the law. We could not have hoped for a more eminent set of contributors. We are deeply grateful to Justice A. K. Sikri for writing an insightful and thoughtful foreword to the book. Blessed with the attributes of an academician, he continues to deliver justice, humbly and elegantly. We would also like to place our gratitude on record to Mr Sidharth Luthra, senior advocate, Supreme Court of India, for a succinct and brilliant epilogue. We are sincerely thankful to the publisher, SAGE Publications, for allowing us to express ourselves on this subject and bringing this work to fruition.

PART I

Arrest and Detention: Constitutional Perspectives

Chapter 1

Arrest and Detention
The Umbrella of Constitutional Protection

Shruti Bedi

INTRODUCTION

Of all the rights available to the people of India, the right to life and personal liberty has been understood to be the 'most precious right'.[1] 'Without such sanctity of life and liberty, the distinction between a lawless society and one governed by laws would cease to have any meaning'.[2] Article 21 assimilates this principle as a fundamental right in the Constitution. The right cannot be denied 'except in accordance with procedure established by law' and this procedure must be 'just and fair', as held in *Maneka Gandhi v. Union of India*.[3] By consequent inference, we conclude that the procedure denying personal liberty cannot be arbitrary or oppressive.[4]

---

[1] Suhrith Parthasarthy quotes Justice Tashi Rabstan in his article, *Liberty at the Government's Whim*. THE HINDU, 11 February, 2020, https://www.thehindu. com/opinion/lead/liberty-at-the-governments-whim/article30785807.ece (last visited 1 February, 2021).

[2] A.D.M. Jabalpur v. Shivakant Shukla, (1976) 2 S.C.C. 521, para 530 (Justice H.R. Khanna's dissent).

[3] (1978) 1 S.C.C. 248.

[4] An administrative officer, while lawfully depriving any person of his life or personal liberty, must have authority by law to do so and must act strictly according to the procedure which he has been authorized by law to follow. Makhan Singh v. State of Punjab, (1951) S.C.J. 835; Ram Narayan Singh v. State of Delhi, (1953) S.C.J. 326.

While exhorting on the interplay between the Constitution and criminal procedure, Aparna Chandra and Mrinal Satish highlight the lingering classic debate between protecting 'personal liberty' and subserving 'public good'.[5] Public good legitimizes the State's use of its coercive powers in the interest of the critical issues of State security and public order through investigation and prosecution of a crime. Contrarily, the protection of an individual's 'liberty' necessitates a circumscription of the State's power through constitutional limitations.[6] Therefore, fundamental rights available against the State dictate constraints on the State's powers such as those of arrest and detention.[7] The guarantees of criminal due process rights ensure that a State validly justifies every denial of liberty.[8] In pursuance of the 'sacrosanct purpose' of a fair trial, it is imperative that 'the accused should not be prejudiced'.[9] This demands a deeper scrutiny of the interface between Articles 20, 21 and 22. However, for the purpose of this chapter, only Article 22 Clauses (1) and (2) will be examined in the context of the rights of an accused under an ordinary arrest. An attempt is made to trace the emerging dimensionality of the three fundamental immunities of Article 22.

The fortification of Article 21 provides protection against legislative authority, as a person may only be deprived of his personal liberty in accordance with a procedure which must conform to the requirements of Article 22 and guarantees to an arrested person the right to be informed of the grounds of arrest, to not be denied the right to consult and to be represented by a counsel of their choice and to be produced before the nearest Magistrate within 24 hrs of being arrested. These safeguards, however, are not available in instances where the arrest or

---

[5] Aparna Chandra & Mrinal Satish, *Criminal Law and the Constitution*, *in* THE OXFORD HANDBOOK OF THE INDIAN CONSTITUTION 794–96 (Choudhry, Khosla & Mehta eds, Oxford University Press, 1st ed. 2016).

[6] Also see *Constituent Assembly Debates*, vol. 7 (Lok Sabha Secretariat 1986) 853, Dec. 6, 1948 (Alladi Krishnaswami Ayyar). See generally, Herbert Packer, *Two Models of the Criminal Process*, 113 UNIV. PA. LAW REV. 1–68 (1964).

[7] Erik Luna, *The Models of Criminal Procedure* 2 BUFFALO CRIM. LAW REV. 389, 402 (1999).

[8] Chandra & Satish, *supra* note 5, at 795.

[9] Rattiram v. State of Madhya Pradesh, (2012) 4 S.C.C. 516, para 39.

detention is of an enemy alien or is under any law relating to preventive detention. Both parts of Clause (1) of Article 22 come into play as soon as any person is arrested.[10]

RIGHT TO BE INFORMED OF THE GROUNDS OF ARREST

Article 22(1) provides that *no person who is arrested shall be detained in custody without being informed, as soon as may be, of the grounds of such arrest.* The objective behind the two requirements of Clause (1) of Article 22 is to 'afford the earliest opportunity to the arrested person to remove any mistake, misapprehension or misunderstanding in the minds of the arresting authority and, also, to know exactly what the accusation against him is so that he can exercise the second right, namely, of consulting a legal practitioner of his choice and to be defended by him'.[11] Section 50, Code of Criminal Procedure (CrPC), also provides for the right to be informed of the grounds of arrest, 'Every police officer or other person arresting any person without warrant shall forthwith communicate to him full particulars of the offence for which he is arrested or other grounds for such arrest'.

To enable the arrested person to analyse his position after the arrest, whether to apply for habeas corpus or bail or to prepare his defence, he must be disclosed the grounds of arrest. The Supreme Court in *re Madhu Limaye*[12] held that the authorities had failed to inform the grounds of arrest to Madhu Limaye, the then member of Lok Sabha who had been arrested and kept under preventive detention, which would lead to his release.[13] The court ordered his release on the ground of violation of the provisions of Article 22(1) *and remand order* which did not reflect the application of mind of the Magistrate.[14]

In *Kanu Sanyal* v. *District Magistrate, Darjeeling*,[15] a writ petition challenging the legality of his detention in the Central Jail was filed,

---

[10] A.K. Gopalan v. State, (1950) S.C.R. 88 at 325 (*per* Das J.).

[11] Madhu Limaye, In re, (1969) 1 S.C.C. 292 at 298, para 10.

[12] *Id.*

[13] *Id.* para 11.

[14] Id. para 12 (emphasis mine).

[15] (1974) 4 S.C.C. 141.

praying for a writ of habeas corpus to set him at liberty forthwith. Of the three grounds raised for challenging his arrest, one was that his detention was in violation of Clause (1) of Article 22 of the Constitution, as he was not informed of the grounds for his arrest. However, the Supreme Court held that there was no need to go into the legality of the initial detention, as the earliest date with reference to which the legality of detention challenged in a habeas corpus proceeding may be examined is the date on which the application for habeas corpus is made to the Court.[16]

However, it is pertinent to note here that both *Madhu Limaye* and *Kanu Sanyal* pertain to preventive detention of the petitioners and are not cases where the arrest is of a person accused of an offence punishable under IPC or under any other special law.[17] This difference between the two types of detention was specifically considered by the Delhi High Court in a recent matter under the Prevention of Money Laundering Act, 2002 (PMLA), *Moin Akhtar Qureshi v. UOI*[18] where the issue was whether he had been informed of the grounds of his arrest and whether there was sufficient compliance of Article 22(1). The court pointed out that there exists a basic and fundamental difference between detention under preventive detention and detention for the commission of an offence. In a situation where the person is arrested on accusation of commission of an offence, he is required to be produced before the Magistrate within 24 h. Moreover, he has the right to consult and to be defended by a legal practitioner. The objective of such provisions being that the arrestee is able to apply for his release on bail when he is produced before the Magistrate. Accordingly, the court held that decisions of matters under preventive detention under Article 22(5) cannot be relied upon for determining the scope and ambit of right to be informed of the grounds of arrest under Section 50, CrPC (or Article 22(1)).[19]

---

[16] *Id.* para 4.

[17] Chhagan Chandrakant Bhujbal v. Union of India, (2016) S.C.C. OnLine Bom 9938, para 47.

[18] (2017) S.C.C. OnLine Del 12108.

[19] *Id.* para 65.

Manner of Communication of Grounds

The manner of communication of grounds of arrest should enable easy comprehension[20] and it should be in the language which the arrested person understands as to why he has been arrested. In *Harikishan v. State of Maharashtra*,[21] it was held by the Supreme Court that if the detained person is not conversant with English then, 'the detenue must be communicated the grounds in a language which he can understand and in a script which he can read'.[22] The same position was reiterated by C. J. Madan B. Lokur of Guwahati High Court in *Firoz Khan v. State of Manipur*[23] that if the detenue is literate or semi-literate, the grounds ought to be communicated in the language that he could read.[24]

On the issue of the necessity of communication of the grounds in writing, the Bombay High Court has also differentiated between detention under preventive detention and detention on an accusation. In *Sunil Chainani v. Inspector of Police*,[25] the court stated that in a preventive detention case, the detenue only has the right to representation as opposed to the various other rights available to an arrestee under Article 22(1) and (2). Relying on this judgement, *Moin Akhtar* also states that communication under Section, 50 CrPC, need not be in writing.[26] What was more important was the 'communication, or knowledge, or information regarding the particulars of the offence for which the arrest is made, or the grounds for such arrest'.[27]

---

[20] Tarapada De v. West Bengal, A.I.R. 1951 S.C. 174. Also see Alan Gledhill, *Life and Liberty in the First Ten Years of Republican India* 2 J. IND. LAW INSTT. 251 (1960).

[21] 1962 Supp (2) S.C.R. 918.

[22] *Id.* para 8. Also see Mrs. Tsering Dolkar v. The Administrator, Union Territory of Delhi, (1987) 2 S.C.C. 69; Hadibandhu Das v. District Magistrate, Cuttack, A.I.R. 1969 S.C. 43.

[23] (2010) 6 Gau LR 576.

[24] *Id.* at 579.

[25] (1987) S.C.C. OnLine Bom 424.

[26] Moin Akhtar, *supra* note 18, para 65.

[27] *Id.*

Time of Communication of Grounds

Article 22(1) further provides that the grounds of arrest should be communicated *as soon as may be*. This condition was clearly acknowledged as a necessary requirement by the Supreme Court in *Tarapade De v. State of West Bengal*,[28] though the court did not find any such laxity on the part of the authorities for disclosing the grounds of arrest to the appellants in the matter. The obligation to 'forthwith communicate to him full particulars of the offence for which he is arrested' under Section 50, CrPC, 'can be said to be discharged if it is done with all reasonable dispatch and without avoidable delay. It can also be interpreted to mean, as soon as possible, without any delay'.[29] In *Sunil Chainani,* a case under the Narcotic Drugs and Psychotropic Substances Act, 1985 (NDPS), this obligation was held to be discharged when the accused were apprehended while attempting to flush the white powder (suspected to be heroin) in the toilet and the police officer had orally communicated the reason of their arrest to the accused.[30] In *Moin Akhtar,* the court held that the accused was duly informed of the grounds of arrest as required under Section 19(1), PMLA, when he was served the *Arrest Memo* at the time of arrest as well as the day after when the remand application was moved before the special judge.[31] Even in the *Leachinsky's case,*[32] Lord du Parcq observed that 'The omission to tell a person who is arrested at, or within a reasonable time of, the arrest with what offence he is charged cannot be regarded as a mere irregularity'.[33]

Grounds of Arrest

J. Desai in *Vimal Kishore v. State of U.P.*[34] examines the words 'grounds of arrest' under Article 22(1), in the context of two situations, one where a person is arrested on a warrant and the other, without a

---

[28] Tarapada De, *supra* note 20.

[29] Sunil Chainani, *supra* note 25, para 12; Moin Akhtar, *supra* note 18, para 65.

[30] Sunil Chainani, *supra* note 25, para 12.

[31] Moin Akhtar, *supra* note 18, para 77–78.

[32] Christie v. Leachinsky, (1947) 1 All E.L.R. 567.

[33] *Id.* at 600.

[34] (1955) S.C.C. OnLine All 407.

warrant. If the arrest is on a warrant, the reasons are contained in the warrant. Therefore, when the warrant is read over to the accused, it complies with the requirement of arrest. If the arrest is without a warrant, then 'he must be told that he has committed a certain offence for which he would be placed on trial. In order to inform him that he has committed a certain offence, he must be told of the act done by him which amounts to the offence'.[35] This does not lead to an inference that technical or precise language needs to be used to communicate the reasons for arrest. Professor Glanville, L. Williams states that 'Indeed, the precise charge need not be formulated, provided that the accused is told the act for which he is arrested'.[36] In *Vimal Kishore*, the authorities had simply informed the arrestee that he had been arrested under Section 7 of the Criminal Law Amendment Act. According to the Allahabad High Court, this communication did not sufficiently comply with the requirement of Article 22(1).

Detention, When Illegal

Article 22(1) states that no person arrested shall be detained in custody without informing him or her as soon as may be of the grounds of such arrest. Consequently, if the person is not informed as soon as, 'his further detention may become invalid or unlawful. But it cannot be said that his initial arrest itself becomes illegal'.[37] In *Vimal Kishore*, J. Desai has also emphasized that 'the very nature of the right indicates that if he is not informed, his detention after the arrest is illegal'.[38] Because of fundamental right, no detention can be sustained without sufficient compliance of the requirement under Article 22(1), and consequently, the detention becomes illegal, which must naturally lead to the release of the arrested person on a habeas corpus application. In *Moin Akhtar*, the Delhi High Court held that there was no illegality in the initial arrest of the petitioner as there was sufficient compliance of Article 22(1), when he was permitted to read the grounds of arrest.

---

[35] *Id.* para 48.

[36] Glanville L. Williams, *Requisites of a Valid Arrest* 16 CRIM. LAW REV. (1954).

[37] Sunil Chainani, *supra* note 25, para 12.

[38] Vimal Kishore, *supra* note 34, para 56.

Furthermore, in *Vimal Kishore*, the court was of the view that since non-communication of the grounds of arrest makes the detention unlawful, a later communication of the grounds to remedy the previous mistake would not make the detention legal. The detention 'would remain unlawful notwithstanding the communication'.[39]

Due to the lack of precedential expertise from the Apex Court, it is to the decisions of the high courts that we look for a clarification on various issues arising out of this right to be informed of the grounds of arrest under Article 22(1). It is apposite to note that Article 22 itself draws a distinction between the manner in which detention under preventive detention and under ordinary arrest is dealt with. The safeguards provided to the arrestee/detenue in both circumstances are diverse. Conclusively, it may not be expedient to interpret the safeguards provided in respect of preventive detention, similarly to the safeguards provided for ordinary arrest. Article 22 conspicuously uses the expression *informed* in Clause (1) in contraposition to *communicate* in Clause (5). This divergence in the two expressions must be interpreted in the context of its usage. *Moin Akhtar* removes the ambiguity by elucidating that a person may be *informed* of the 'grounds of arrest' through any mode of communication.[40] Information could be derived upon hearing or 'upon viewing/reading/seeing'. The transference of the information is complete when it is received by the person, which in turn enables him to consult his legal counsel.[41] Furthermore, the production of the

---

[39] *Id*. para 72. It has been contended that *Vimal Kishore* was overruled by Bal Mukund Jaiswal v. Superintendent, District Jail, (1997) S.C.C. OnLine All 960: 1998 All LJ 1428, a full bench decision of the same high court. However, *Bal Mukund* simply pointed out that *Vimal Kishore* did not deal with a situation where a particular person's detention at a subsequent stage had been legalized by a valid order of remand. In *Vimal Kishore*, the Court had only restricted the decision to the question whether the grounds of arrest were communicated to the petitioner 'as soon as may be', and since it was found that the grounds were not communicated forthwith, the Bench found that the detention of the petitioner was rendered illegal [para 7]. The issue before the Full Bench in *Bal Mukund* was whether an accused person who is under judicial custody on the basis of a valid remand order passed under Section 209 or 309 of CrPC by the Magistrate pending committal proceedings or trial should be set at liberty by issuing a writ of habeas corpus on the ground that his initial detention was violative of Articles 21 and 22.

[40] Moin Akhtar Qureshi, *supra* note 18, para 69.

[41] *Id*

arrestee before the Magistrate ensures the examination of the legality of the arrest. Conversely, these safeguards are not available to the person detained under preventive detention wherein the *communication* of the grounds must necessarily be more seriously executed, as the only redress available is the right to immediate representation under Article 22(5).[42]

The division bench judgements of both Delhi (*Moin Akhtar*) and Bombay (*Chhagan Chandrakant*) High Courts along with the single bench decision (*Sunil Chianani*) of the Bombay High Court have placed due emphasis on the relevance of the constitutional safeguards present under Article 22 and the existing contradistinction between the safeguards under Clauses (1) and (5). Though the decisions do not trivialize the right to be informed of the grounds of arrest, there does arise a prospect of misuse of the police authority under Clause (1) of Article 22 in a situation where the officer makes an assertion of fulfilment of the condition, without actually informing the arrestee of the grounds of arrest. The statutory law, therefore, needs to take into account such a manifestation by raising the degree of commitment to the constitutional protection through an effective solution to attenuate misuse. The need to avert such occurrences acquires a greater implication in a constitutional democracy which promotes the rule of law.

RIGHT TO LEGAL COUNSEL

Under Article 22(1), the Constitution guarantees a safeguard against abuse of executive authority by giving the accused a *right to consult and to be defended by a legal counsel of his choice*. The expansion of the scope of Article 21 in *Maneka Gandhi* recognized the unenumerated right to counsel in Article 21, which was broader than the right guaranteed under Article 22(1).[43] As Sekhri rightly states that, 'while Article 22(1) granted a right to counsel *of choice*, Article 21 carried a *right to* counsel,

---

[42] See *Sunil Chianani, supra* note 25; *Chhagan Chandrakant, supra* note 17 and *Moin Akhtar, supra* note 18, para 70.

[43] Recently a three-judge bench of the Supreme Court in Subedar v. State of U.P., (2020) S.C.C. Online SC 1084, while directing the Allahabad High Court to hear a criminal appeal held that the 'right of being represented through a counsel is part of due process clause and is referable to the right guaranteed under Article 21 of the Constitution of India' (para 8).

thus prohibiting deprivation of life and personal liberty made in absence of legal assistance'.[44] The Supreme Court, thus, extends the right to legal aid to any and every person who is economically incapable of engaging a legal counsel.[45]

Right to Counsel During Interrogation

The examination of the scope of the right to counsel projects the issue as to whether the counsel can be present during interrogation or not. Section 41D, CrPC, is a provision parallel to Article 21 which reads as follows: 'When any person is arrested and interrogated by the police, he shall be entitled to meet an advocate, though not throughout the interrogation'. Therefore, the right to counsel is available to a person immediately upon his arrest, to assist him in the process of interrogation. Unlike the Code, the Constitution does not impose any limitation on the time that the advocate spends with the arrested person during interrogation. The framers presumably understood the ramifications of such a limitation on a vulnerable arrestee and his right against self-incrimination under Article 20(3) and, accordingly, provided for a wider constitutional protection in the form of Article 22(1).

The Supreme Court relied on the *Miranda*[46] decision in *Nandini Satpathy v. P.L. Dani*[47] and recognized the need for a lawyer's presence during interrogation, in the context of Article 20(3) as an 'observance of the right to silence'.[48] Though the mere presence of a lawyer is not a panacea for the problem of 'involuntary self-incrimination',[49] the absence of one allows the interrogating officer to employ coercive measures to extract confessions. Consequently, the court held that if the accused so

---

[44] Abhinav Sekhri, *Article 22: A Constitutional Paradox* in INDIAN CONSTITUTIONAL LAW AND PHILOSOPHY BLOG (Gautam Bhatia, 16 November, 2018), https://indconlawphil.wordpress.com/2018/11/16/guest-post-article-223-a-constitutional-paradox/ (last visited 7 February 2021).

[45] Hussainara Khatoon (IV) v. Home Secretary, State of Bihar, (1980) 1 S.C.C. 98, para 6–9.

[46] Miranda v. Arizona, (1966) 16 L Ed 2d 694: 384 US 436.

[47] (1978) 2 S.C.C. 424.

[48] *Id.* para 63.

[49] *Id.* para 64.

desires, he should not be denied this facility.[50] Recognizing that it was the emergence of the accused's 'right to counsel' that gave meaning to his 'right to silence' in *Selvi*,[51] the court adopted a similar view. The court held the intrusive interrogation method of the narcoanalysis test as unconstitutional on account of the accused's inability to access legal advice when the 'subject has no conscious control over drug-induced revelations or substantive inferences'.[52] These judgements assiduously rely upon the personal liberty perspective while mandating the access to legal counsel during interrogation.

However, the enactment of Section 41D, portraying a narrower view, diminishes the progressive protection afforded by the unlimited constitutional right to legal counsel under Article 22(1). The harmonization of the statutory provision with the fundamental right becomes difficult to fathom. After all, when would an accused require legal advice, if not at the time of interrogation when the fear of self-incrimination is the highest? The absence of a lawyer during interrogation sanctions the use of excessive force as an interrogating technique, thereby rendering the role of a legal counsel superfluous.

The varied decisions of the court on the issue of right to counsel have led to further complications. In *Senior Intelligence Officer, Director of Revenue Intelligence v Jugal Kishore Samra*[53] *a case under the Narcotic Drugs and Psychotropic Substances (NDPS) Act, 1985*, the court held that the lawyer cannot be present during the interrogation but can 'watch proceedings from a distance or from beyond a glass partition but … not within hearing distance'.[54] With the imposition of such barriers between the accused and his lawyer, the constitutional right to counsel under Article 22(1) turns symbolic, bereft of any substance.

Conversely, in *State (NCT of Delhi) v. Navjot Sandhu*,[55] the court relied on the view expressed in *Nandini Satpathy* that Article 22(1)

---

[50] *Id.* para 63.
[51] Selvi v. State of Karnataka, (2010) 7 S.C.C. 263.
[52] *Id.* para 247.
[53] (2011) 12 S.C.C. 362.
[54] *Id.* para 29.
[55] (2005) 11 S.C.C. 600.

was complementary to Article 20(3). The interpretation given by the court was that the constitutional guarantee under Article 22(1) implied that the suspect would 'not be denied the right to meet and consult his lawyer even at the stage of interrogation'.[56] However, the court acknowledged that to reach such conclusion, it had to rely on Section 52(2), Prevention of Terrorism Act, 2002 (POTA). Section 52(2), POTA, casts an imperative on the police officer to inform the person arrested of his right to consult a legal practitioner, soon after he is brought to the police station. Consequently, the court's decision is not based on an effort to expand the scope of the fundamental right to counsel but is an outcome of the specific direction under Section 52(2), POTA.

Finally, in *Mohd. Ajmal Amir Kasab v. State of Maharashtra*,[57] the Supreme Court severely restricted the right to counsel to court proceedings. The need for a lawyer, as per the court, arose only during the stage of framing charges and for the trial and was 'not based on the *Miranda* principles'.[58] Though the court emphasized on the constitutional requirement to provide a counsel to an indigent person, 'failure to provide a lawyer to the accused at the pre-trial stage' would not vitiate the trial unless it results in some 'material prejudice' to the accused.[59]

The narrow interpretation of the fundamental right to counsel, stemming from the lack of understanding of the higher law and the inability to harmonize the statutory provision with the constitutional right, has restricted its scope. The significance of access to counsel is lost if the accused is unable to protect himself against involuntary self-incrimination at the pretrial stage. There is an emergent need to amend the text of the Code to bring it in line with the constitutional provision.[60]

---

[56] *Id*. para 160.

[57] (2012) 9 S.C.C. 1.

[58] *Id*. para 475.

[59] *Id*. para 478.

[60] Shivjeet Parthasarthy, 'Constitutional Failures of the CrPC: An Analysis of S. 41D and An Accused's Right to Legal Counsel' *The Criminal Law Blog* (1 September, 2020), https://criminallawstudiesnluj.wordpress.com/2020/09/01/constitutional-failures-of-the-crpc-an-analysis-of-s-41d-and-an-accuseds-right-to-legal-counsel/#_ftn1 (last visited 8 February 2021).

RIGHT TO BE PRODUCED BEFORE NEAREST MAGISTRATE

Article 22(2) of the Constitution provides that the arrestee is to be *produced before the nearest Magistrate within 24 hours of such arrest and no such person shall be detained without the authority of the magistrate.* This safeguard ensures the applicability of a judicial mind to the arrest to determine its legality and pronounce upon the regularity of the procedure adopted. It provides for a constitutional injunction that a person arrested cannot be detained in custody without being produced before a Magistrate within a prescribed time. Except in instances where the Magistrate has dispensed with the personal attendance, the accused must be produced before the Magistrate. Thereafter, he 'may either be released on bail or be remanded into custody. If he is released on bail, the bail bond ensures his attendance at the trial'.[61]

Arrest and detention in contravention of this provision is illegal.[62] In *State of U.P. v. Abdul Samad*,[63] the foreigners who were directed to leave the country were arrested for the purpose of deportation and were not produced before the nearest Magistrate within 24 h.[64] The constitutional bench of the Supreme Court found the detention to be illegal and ordered their immediate release.[65] That a person is in another jail in a different state for another offence is not considered as a justification for not producing him before a Magistrate in an arrest in a different case.[66]

In *State of Punjab v. Ajaib Singh*,[67] it was observed by the constitutional bench of the Supreme Court that the language of Article 22(1) and (2) indicates that the fundamental protection is provided for an arrest made without a warrant.[68] This is because arrests made without warrants demand a greater protection as the legality of the arrest is yet

---

[61] State of M.P. v. Shobharam, A.I.R. 1966 S.C. 1910, para 24.
[62] State of U.P. v. Abdul Samad, A.I.R. 1962 S.C. 1506.
[63] *Id.*
[64] *Id.* para 20.
[65] *Id.* para 22.
[66] Manoj v. State of M.P., (1999) 3 S.C.C. 715.
[67] 1953 S.C.R. 254.
[68] *Id.* para 20.

to be judiciously evaluated. Conversely, when an arrest is made under a warrant, the judge has already applied his mind to the matter to a material extent.

Application of Mind

Article 22(2) aims to ensure the application of a *judicial mind* to the arrest and also scrutinize as to whether there is sufficient compliance with the procedural formalities required under law. Such non-application of mind and the lack of scrutiny of the legality and propriety of the procedure by the Magistrate himself compelled the division bench of the Allahabad High Court in *Swami Hariharanand Saraswati v. Jailor I/C Dist. Jail*[69] to conclude that the detention was 'illegal and unconstitutional'.[70] The same reasoning was also adopted by the Supreme court in *Madhu Limaye* while ordering the release of the detenue where it was found that the Magistrate had passed the remand order mechanically and without due application of his mind.[71]

The requirement of production before a Magistrate is not a mere 'formality', it is 'to enable the person arrested and detained to be released on bail or other provision made for his proper custody pending the investigation into the offence with which he is charged or pending an enquiry or trial'.[72] In a matter of gross violation of the constitutional rights of the person under Article 22 (1) and (2), the Supreme Court in its wisdom ordered the payment of monetary compensation to the arrestee by the State.[73]

To Be Produced Within 24 Hours

Article 22(2) specifically postulates that the arrestee is to be produced before the nearest Magistrate *within 24 hours of his arrest*. Section 57, CrPC, which is in consonance with Article 22(2) provides that 'no

---

[69] (1954) S.C.C. OnLine All 87.

[70] *Id.* para 33.

[71] *Supra* note 18, para 12.

[72] *Supra* note 62, para 12.

[73] Bhim Singh v. State of J&K, (1985) 4 S.C.C. 677. Since the arrestee in the case had already been released, the court ordered ₹50,000 to be paid to him.

police officer shall detain in custody a person arrested without warrant for a longer period than under all circumstances is reasonable and such period shall not in the absence of a special order of a Magistrate under S. 167 *exceed 24 hours* exclusive of the time necessary for the journey from the place of arrest to the Magistrate's Court'. In *Satyajit Ballubhai Desai v. State of Gujarat*,[74] the Supreme Court has held that whenever any person is arrested under Section 57, CrPC, he should be produced before the nearest Magistrate within 24 h. It is irrelevant whether 'such Magistrate may or may not have jurisdiction to try the case'.[75]

In *Jeevakhan v. Officer-in-charge of 'Q' Branch of Tamil Nadu police*[76] the accused was taken into police custody on 23 September 1981 at around 6.30 am. He was produced before the Magistrate on 28 September 1981 at around 5 pm. The court held that this was an illegal detention which was in complete violation and disregard for the provisions of the Constitution.[77]

Nearest Magistrate

The precise connotation of the expression 'nearest Magistrate' requires interpretation. Recently, in *Vachhalabai v. State of Maharashtra*,[78] the Bombay High Court observed that the safeguards under Article 22 need to be strictly followed while effecting arrest. Upon arrest, if the accused is not taken before the nearest Magistrate and he is 'taken far away from that place for production before the concerned Magistrate, the moment the accused is taken out of the jurisdiction of nearest Magistrate, his detention becomes unauthorized and illegal'.[79] Such detention will not

---

[74] (2014) 14 S.C.C. 434.

[75] *Id.* para 12. CBI v. Anupam J. Kulkarni, (1992) 3 S.C.C. 141, para 13. The alleged encounter of the dreaded criminal Vikas Dubey also displayed a critical lapse on the part of the police authorities, who did not produce him before the nearest Magistrate. See Chittarvu Raghu, *Police Must Function Within Law* TELANGANA TODAY (28 July 2020), https://telanganatoday.com/police-must-function-within-law (last visited 13 February, 2021).

[76] (1982) S.C.C. OnLine Mad 190.

[77] *Id.* para 20.

[78] (2019) S.C.C. OnLine Bom 2937.

[79] *Id.* para 56.

gain legality subsequently in case the accused is produced before the Magistrate having jurisdiction to try or inquire into the offence within 24 h of the actual arrest.[80]

The question whether the 'nearest Magistrate' means the Magistrate nearest to the place where the arrest is made or where he is produced by the police within 24 h, was raised before the Supreme Court in *Rajinder Prasad Aggarwal v. Chief Metropolitan Magistrate.*[81] However, the Court did not decide the query, as the accused had already been released, and that the question required in-depth consideration. Such an interpretive disposition reflects the lack of a judiciary shepherding the rule of law.

While the Constituent Assembly was mulling over the draft Article 15A (Article 22), an amendment was proposed by Shri Pataskar who wanted the word 'First Class' to be added as a prefix to 'Magistrate'. This was opposed by Dr Ambedkar.[82] Evidently, the expression 'nearest Magistrate' was introduced as a constraint on the power of the police authorities to detain a person beyond 24 h, seeking to justify such detention on the ground that the Magistrate having jurisdiction to try the case was not available within the limited period. The apparent intention was to ensure a protection through a scrutiny of the legality of arrest by a judicial mind rather than conceding a lacuna to the police allowing them to escape the requirement of production of the arrestee before a Magistrate who *had jurisdiction and was unavailable* within the prescribed time.

The person arrested must be produced before *the nearest Magistrate* within 24 h of *such arrest*. Conspicuously, the expression 'nearest Magistrate' is preceded by the word *the* and succeeded by the expression *such arrest* which suggests that 'the nearest Magistrate' has to be a *Magistrate nearest from the place of arrest*. Such interpretation

---

[80] *Id.*

[81] (1985) Supp S.C.C. 607: 1985 S.C.C. (Cri) 570.

[82] *Constituent Assembly of India Debates* – Vol. IX (16 September 1949), http://loksabhaph.nic.in/writereaddata/cadebatefiles/C16091949.html (last visited 10 February 2021).

fundamentally fosters liberty of the individual and insulates citizens from any imperious exercise of powers by securing them against illegal arrests. Ultimately, the interpretive posture of the courts should be to eschew arbitrary arrests and negate any perversion of police powers.

CONCLUSION

Article 21 of the Constitution prohibits any arbitrary deprivation of life and personal liberty. It further provides that life and liberty can only be taken away in accordance with the procedure established by law. Consequently, no authority whether legislative, executive or judicial can deprive a person of life or liberty unless it is justified by a procedure established by law. The Constitution and our statutory laws provide for general and specific protections against unjustified arrest. Additionally, judicial interventions have prominently contributed towards ensuring these constitutional and procedural safeguards against arbitrary arrest.[83] However, such unjustified arrests are inevitable in every society. The effort to minimize such anomalies must reflect the willingness to adopt additional telling checks. A narrow interpretation or absence of interpretation on certain concerns surrounding the rights of the arrestee displays a lack of judicial insight, which in turn has contributed to legislative laxity. This is evident in the interpretive attitude adopted by the judiciary on the right to be *informed* of the grounds of arrest. Though it situates the right emphasis on the distinction between preventive detention and ordinary arrest, it has failed to demand a higher level of executive and legislative subscription to the practical aspects of execution of the right. The omission of insistence on the right to counsel *during interrogation* renders the constitutional protection inconsequential. Lastly, the insufficient interpretation of the right to be produced before the *nearest Magistrate* does not reflect a decisive demeanour.

---

[83] B. Deepthi, *Judicial Analysis of the Constitutional and Procedural Safeguards Against Arbitrary Arrest and Detention* 2(2) CULJ 39 (2013).

The role of courts in the current times is challenging in view of the continual confrontation between liberty and the necessity for effective law enforcement. Undoubtedly, the deportment of the Indian judiciary fortified by the decisions of the Supreme Court has solidified its role as a consummate scene stealer in safeguarding the liberty of citizens. However, it must forge ahead with its efforts to resolve every interpretive bottleneck through a purposive reading of the constitutional guarantees. This will further regulate the arrests by the police on a systemic level. After all, fundamental justice demands that there should be an existence of a good cause to interfere with an individual's liberty and security interests.

Chapter 2

Arrest
Necessity and Justification

Nitish Nawsagaray

INTRODUCTION

Arrests lie at the core of our way of thinking about police and law enforcement agencies. We often measure the success of criminal justice system by the number of arrests made by police officers during investigation. Most critics of the criminal justice system agree that arrests are important to ensure public safety and order, thus arguing that the power of police to arrest is largely sacrosanct.[1] All those who criticize arrest are making a point about abuse of arrest power by the police.[2] However, we are not concerned about whether such power needs to be given to the executives in a liberal society.

It is necessary to analyse whether the costs of arrests are proportionate to the ends it serves. Many laws which authorize arrest largely

---

[1] See R. V. Kelkar, *Law of Arrest: Some Problems and Incongruities* 22(3) J. IND. LAW INSTT. 314–21 (1980); S. R. Sankaran, *Curbing the Power to Arrest* 44(10) ECON. POLIT. WKLY. 12–14 (2009); S. R. Sankaran, *Amendment to an Amendment: To Arrest or Not to Arrest* 45(17) ECON. POLIT. WKLY 17–18 (2010).

[2] See N. S. Kamboj, *Police Custodial Death: A Growing Abuse to Human Rights in India* 36(3) J. ID. LAW INSTT. 372–77 (1994); M. Afzal Wani, *Tracheotomy of Infernality in Arrest and Detention Laws: A Gender Perspective* 53(2) J. ID. LAW INSTT. 227–53 (2011).

remain unexamined. Maybe because of the constitutional doctrines which regulate arrests, the power to arrest is taken for granted. In considering the issue of arrest, we assume that arrests are not too costly; rather, arrests are crucial to meet the law enforcement goals. However, these assumptions are preposterous and far from truth. Arrests are more harmful than they seem, not only to the individuals who are arrested but also to their communities and to the society as a whole.

WHAT IS ARREST?

The word 'arrest' is derived from the French word 'arrêter' which means 'to stop' or 'stay' and signifies a restraint on a person's movement. In common parlance, the word 'arrest' means the 'apprehension or restraint or the deprivation of one's liberty'.[3] It is 'some kind of stopping of a person by authority of law', primarily made 'for the purpose of bringing a prosecution against the person arrested'.[4] In arrest, a person is deprived of his freedom, at least, until there is a judicial review of the arrest. In 1964, a study conducted by the Human Rights Committee on the rights of a person free from arbitrary arrest, detention and exile defined arrest as

> The act of taking a person into custody under the authority of the law or by compulsion of another kind and includes the period from the moment he is placed under restraint up to the time he is brought before an authority competent to order his continued custody or to release him.

There was no specific definition of 'arrest' under the Indian legal system. However, the Supreme Court defined the term 'arrest' occurring in Article 22 of the Constitution of India in *State of Punjab* v. *Ajaib Singh*.[5] The Court defined it as 'indicating physical restraint of a person under the authority of the law in respect of an alleged accusation or

---

[3] B. Uma Devi, Arrest, Detention and Criminal Justice System (Oxford University Press 2012).

[4] Glanville Williams, *When is an Arrest?* 54 Mod. L. Rev. 408, 408 (1991).

[5] A.I.R. 1953 S.C. 10.

default or violation of the law'.[6] In *State of Haryana* v. *Dinesh Kumar*,[7] the Supreme Court held that the term 'arrest' means restraining liberty of a person, and hence, submitting a person in custody amounts to arrest. An element of coercion by the State can be inferred as inherent in the idea of arrest. The fact that the arrested person is sent to a jail or detention facility, and his identifying information is taken, is in conformity with the element of coercion.[8] The key aspects of an arrest are significant deprivation of liberty by use of State power and some formal steps towards criminal prosecution.

LAW OF ARREST IN INDIA

The general law of arrest is found in Chapter 5 of the Code of Criminal Procedure (CrPC), 1973. CrPC does not purport to be an exhaustive or unqualified law on arrest. There are two types of arrest as designed in CrPC: arrests made in pursuance of a warrant issued by a Magistrate and arrests made without such warrant but made in accordance with some legal provision permitting such arrest. Apart from CrPC, various provisions for arrest without warrant can be found in other legislations also. Police Act, 1861, Arms Act, 1959, Explosives Act, 1884, and Indian Railways Act, 1989, are few examples wherein an arrest could be made without a warrant.

A warrant of arrest involves a written order which is issued and signed by a Magistrate, thereby commanding a police officer or some other person specifically named, to arrest the accused person named in it. In case of arrest without warrant, the decision to make the arrest is made by persons other than Magistrates, that is, by police officers or private citizens. Many times, these people do not have the judicious mind and detached outlook. Yet, the Code allows them to make the arrest-related decisions themselves without obtaining warrants of arrest from the Magistrates, looking into the exigencies of the situation.

---

[6] *Id.*

[7] A.I.R. 2008 S.C. 1083.

[8] Rachel A. Harmon, *Why Arrest?* 115 MICH. L. REV. 307 (2016).

Extensive powers have been conferred on the police for making arrests without a warrant under circumstances mentioned in Sections 41[9] and 42 of the Code, 1973. Section 41 is the main section providing for situations when police may arrest without a warrant.

---

[9] Section 41, CrPC, 1973 reads as:

'41. When police may arrest without warrant.—(1) Any police officer may without an order from a Magistrate and without a warrant, arrest any person—

(a) who commits, in the presence of a police officer, a cognizable offence;

(b) against whom a reasonable complaint has been made, or credible information has been received, or a reasonable suspicion exists that he has committed a cognizable offence punishable with imprisonment for a term which may be less than seven years or which may extend to seven years whether with or without fine, if the following conditions are satisfied, namely:—

(i) the police officer has reason to believe on the basis of such complaint, information, or suspicion that such person has committed the said offence;

(ii) the police officer is satisfied that such arrest is necessary—

(a) to prevent such person from committing any further offence; or

(b) for proper investigation of the offence; or

(c) to prevent such person from causing the evidence of the offence to disappear or tampering with such evidence in any manner; or

(d) to prevent such person from making any inducement, threat or promise to any person acquainted with the facts of the case so as to dissuade him from disclosing such facts to the Court or to the police officer; or

(e) as unless such person is arrested, his presence in the Court whenever required cannot be ensured, and the police officer shall record while making such arrest, his reasons in writing:

[Provided that a police officer shall, in all cases where the arrest of a person is not required under the provisions of this sub-section, record the reasons in writing for not making the arrest.]

(ba) against whom credible information has been received that he has committed a cognizable offence punishable with imprisonment for a term which may extend to more than seven years whether with or without fine or with death sentence and the police officer has reason to believe on the basis of that information that such person has committed the said offence;]

(c) who has been proclaimed as an offender either under this Code or by order of the State Government; or

(d) in whose possession anything is found which may reasonably be suspected to be stolen property and who may reasonably be suspected of having committed an offence with reference to such thing; or

(e) who obstructs a police officer while in the execution of his duty, or who has escaped, or attempts to escape, from lawful custody; or

In 2008, many new provisions were introduced in CrPC by way of the Criminal Procedure Code (Amendment) Act. Most of these provisions were from the Supreme Court's decisions in *D.K. Basu v. State of West Bengal*[10] and *Joginder Kumar v. State of Uttar Pradesh*[11] and from the recommendations given by the Law Commission in its 177th Report. Section 41 was amended by CrPC (Amendment) Act, 2008, which broadened the meaning of arrest. Clauses (a) and (b) of Sub-section (1) have been amended to provide that the police officer must exercise the powers of arrest only after reasonable care and justification. Such officer must be satisfied that such arrest is necessary and required under the said section. Sub-section (2) of Section 41 has been amended to provide that subject to the provisions of Section 42 relating to arrest on refusal to give name and residence, a person shall not be in a non-cognizable offence except under a warrant or order of a Magistrate. Prior to the 2008 Amendment, Sub-section (2) of Section 41 dealt with arrest powers in preventive scenarios, but this was felt to be unnecessary since Section 151 already existed in the Code.

(f) who is reasonably suspected of being a deserter from any of the Armed Forces of the Union; or

(g) who has been concerned in, or against whom a reasonable complaint has been made, or credible information has been received, or a reasonable suspicion exists, of his having been concerned in, any act committed at any place out of India which, if committed in India, would have been punishable as an offence, and for which he is, under any law relating to extradition, or otherwise, liable to be apprehended or detained in custody in India; or

(h) who, being a released convict, commits a breach of any rule made under sub-section (5) of section 356; or

(i) for whose arrest any requisition, whether written or oral, has been received from another police officer, provided that the requisition specifies the person to be arrested and the offence or other cause for which the arrest is to be made and it appears therefrom that the person might lawfully be arrested without a warrant by the officer who issued the requisition.

[(2) Subject to the provisions of section 42, no person concerned in a non-cognizable offence or against whom a complaint has been made or credible information has been received or reasonable suspicion exists of his having so concerned, shall be arrested except under a warrant or order of a Magistrate.]'

[10] (1997) 1 S.C.C. 416.
[11] (1994) 4 S.C.C. 260.

As per Section 41 (1) (a) of CrPC, police officers can arrest a person without a warrant when someone commits a cognizable offence in the presence of a police officer. More so, Section 41 divides the cognizable offences in two categories: offences where punishment is up to 7 years of imprisonment and offences where punishment is more than 7 years of imprisonment or death sentence. In India, as a rule of thumb, offences where the maximum punishment is up to 7 years are not viewed as 'heinous' crimes, and therefore, someone accused of such offence is seen as posing a lower risk to society. As per Section 41 (1) (b) of CrPC, 1973, 'if a reasonable complaint has been made, or credible information has been received, or a reasonable suspicion exists' of the commission of a 'cognizable offence punishable with imprisonment for a term which may be less than seven years or which may extend to seven years with or without fine',[12] the arrest of an accused person cannot be effected by the police officer only on his satisfaction that such person had committed the offence punishable as aforesaid. Before making the arrest, a police officer must further satisfy himself that such an arrest is necessary

1. 'To prevent such person from committing any further offence; or
2. For proper investigation of the case; or
3. To prevent such person from causing the evidence of the offence to disappear; or tampering with such evidence in any manner; or
4. To prevent such person from making any inducement, threat or promise to any person acquainted with the facts of the case so as to dissuade him from disclosing such facts to the court or the police officer; or
5. As unless such person is arrested, his presence in the court whenever required cannot be ensured'.[13]

Thus, even if the police officer is satisfied about commission of an offence, still he cannot arrest a person if there is no pressing need to arrest the accused. The Code has listed out five circumstances which should be considered by the police officer before arresting an accused in a cognizable offence punishable with less than 7 years imprisonment.

---

[12] See, Section 41 (1) (b) CrPC, 1973.
[13] *Id.*

The 2008 Amendment inserted Section 41 A in CrPC, which was further amended in 2010 to replace the word 'may' with 'shall'. As per Section 41 A of CrPC, if any police officer requires the participation of any individual who is not required to be arrested under Section 41 (1) of CrPC, the police officer is duty-bound to issue a notice to that individual to appear before him. The individual to whom the notice is served is obliged to show up at the specified place and time. The individual confirming the notice will not be arrested, except if in any case considered fit by the police for which the official is duty-bound to record reasons in writing. In *Arnesh Kumar case*,[14] the Supreme Court directed that issuing a notice of appearance under Section 41A was thoughtfully implemented. Police officers should not arrest an individual unnecessarily without any justifiable grounds, and the Magistrate should not authorize detention in a casual and mechanical manner.

While the measures introduced in CrPC in 2008 were hailed as being progressive, some provisions of the amendment could not be brought into force till 2010 due to protests. While an earlier amendment required the recording of reasons for making an arrest, the 2010 amendment requires justification for not arresting a person as well. It has been argued that to say that reasons should be recorded for not arresting a person is to treat arrest as a normal requirement and not as an exception. It would defeat the entire objective of amending the law on arrest in 2008.[15]

As per Section 41 (1) (ba), CrPC, in instances where credible information is received by the police of commission of cognizable offence punishable with more than 7 years of imprisonment or with death sentence and the police officer has reason to believe on the basis of such information that such person has committed the said offence, they can arrest the accused without a warrant. The police power to arrest is much easier to exercise when it comes to someone accused of cognizable offences where the maximum punishment is more than 7 years imprisonment. In such cases, the police must have 'credible information' that the person has committed such an offence; beyond that, there are no further preconditions for arrest.

---

[14] (2014) 8 S.C.C. 273.

[15] Sankaran, *supra* note 1.

The 2008 Amendment also inserted Sections 41A, 41B, 41C and 41D. Section 41A dealt with notice of appearance to the accused where arrest was not required; 41B laid the procedure of arrest and the duties of the police officer making the arrest; 41C discussed about the establishment of a control room where information about arrests could be recorded; and 41D made provisions for an accused to meet his lawyer during interrogation. These provisions were directly based on the guidelines given by the Supreme Court in *D.K Basu*.[16] A proviso to Section 46(1) was added which provided that a male police officer should not touch any female 'unless the circumstances indicated to the ordinary'.

There are several other situations covered in Section 41 where a police officer can arrest without a warrant. This includes when someone is declared a proclaimed offender, who has some stolen property in their possession, is a deserter from Armed Forces, or is a convict who has breached the terms of their parole, etc.

Section 42 specifies yet another situation where a police officer can arrest a person. If a person commits a non-cognizable offence in the presence of a police officer or where he has been accused of committing a non-cognizable offence and refuses, on demand being made by a police officer, to give his name and residence or gives false name or residence, such person may be arrested but such arrest shall be only for the limited purpose of ascertaining his name and residence. Section 43 speaks of a situation where an arrest can be made by a private person and the procedure to be followed on such arrest. Section 44 lays down the power of arrest by a Magistrate where a person commits an offence in his presence. The Magistrate can himself proceed to arrest the person, or alternatively direct another person to do so. Section 47 enables the police officer to enter a place if he has reason to believe that the person to be arrested has entered into that place or is within that place. Section 48 empowers the police officers to pursue a person, whom they are authorized to arrest without a warrant, into any place in India beyond their jurisdiction.

---

[16] Harmon, *supra* note 8.

Apart from the powers of arrest endowed under the Code to apprehend a person who has committed an offence, the Code also encapsulates arrest as a preventive mechanism. Under Section 149, every police officer may interpose for the purpose of preventing the commission of a cognizable offence and shall do so to the best of his ability. Furthermore, a police officer receiving information of a plan to commit any cognizable offence is required to communicate such information to another police officer whose duty it is to prevent such commission. Such police officer may arrest a person, without orders from a Magistrate and without a warrant, if it appears to such officer that the commission of the offence cannot be otherwise prevented.[17] When a person is arrested without a warrant under Section 151(1), all the provisions of the Code applicable to arrest without warrant, for example, informing the arrested person of the grounds of arrest, informing his family, friends, production before Magistrate within 24 h, etc. would as far as apply to the arrested person.

WHAT DOES AN ARREST COST?

In Indian criminal justice system, arrests are essentially a police activity. Neither scholars nor reformers have asked why police need to make arrests. Arrests are often humiliating and degrading. Apart from loss of liberty, a person may also lose his job and livelihood for not showing up for a job. Apart from paying fees to a lawyer, if he hires a lawyer for the first appearance, he also ends up paying for bail if granted by the court. He can be thrown out of his residence, if arrested, as also abandoned by family at times. An arrest might also affect his/her child custody rights; it can trigger deportation of foreigners. People with arrest records have worse employment and financial prospects.[18] All of this could happen even if a person arrested is never convicted of a crime.

---

[17] Section 151, Code of Criminal Procedure, 1973.

[18] Christopher Uggen et al., *The Edge of Stigma: An Experimental Audit of the Effects of Low Level Criminal Records on Employment* 52 CRIMINOL. 627 (2014); Benjamin D. Geffen, *The Collateral Consequences of Acquittal: Employment Discrimination on the Basis of Arrests Without Convictions* 20(2) UNIV. PA. J L. SOC. CHANGE. 82 (2017).

Arrests greatly enhance the possibility that a suspect will be detained prior to trial. A consultation paper by the Law Commission of India in 2001[19] suggested that nearly about 60 per cent of the arrests made are quite unnecessary and uncalled for and account for more than 40 per cent of the jail expenditures arising due to such arrests which may easily be avoided. While the law relating to arrest has certainly become more progressive through the years, the major hurdle has always been implementation of the law. Illegal arrests and prolonged detention in violation of provisions under the law continue to be reported. Seven in 10 of the 478,600 people in Indian jails are under trials, according to the National Crime Records Bureau data on prisons released in August 2020.[20] India ranks 15th out of 217 countries on the basis of its undertrial population.[21]

Arrest involves a serious invasion of the life and privacy of individuals. Arrested individuals are likely to be photographed and fingerprinted; also, after arrest, their clothing and personal belongings are taken by the authorities. They are often subjected to body search[22] and medical examination[23] after arrest.

Once a police officer attempts an arrest, he is authorized to use force to effect an arrest. Arrest always entails risks and sometimes leads to injury or death. Law authorizes police officers to use all means necessary to effect the arrest.[24] If an individual is to be arrested for an offence punishable with death or imprisonment for life, the use of force can extend to the causing of death of the accused. Thus, though the arrest and the force used to ensure it are legally authorized, arrest costs injuries and deaths. Post-arrest an individual may also be subjected to physical violence in police custody, which may further result in the death of the person. During the lockdown, a trader P. Jayaraj and his

---

[19] Law Commission of India, Govt. of India, *One Hundred and Seventy Seventh Report on Law Relating to Arrest* (2001).

[20] *Prison Statistics India 2019*, Published by National Crime Records Bureau, New Delhi.

[21] https://www.prisonstudies.org/sites/default/files/resources/downloads/world_pre-trial_list_4th_edn_final.pdf

[22] See Section 51, CrPC, 1973.

[23] See Sections 53 and 54, CrPC, 1973.

[24] Section 46(2), CrPC, 1973.

son J. Bennicks were arrested and detained by Tamil Nadu Police for allegedly violating COVID-19 lockdown rules. They were subjected to custodial violence and, thereafter, admitted in hospital. Three days after the arrest, Bennicks died in hospital and Jayaraj died the next day. They had allegedly endured hours of beating and torturing by police. Nine Tamil Nadu police officials are booked by CBI for the alleged murder of Jayaraj and Bennicks and an amount of ₹10 lakhs has been announced as ex-gratia to the family of the deceased.[25] Again, in Thiruvananthapuram, Udayakumar, picked up in a theft case, died in police custody. A CBI probe and prosecution led to death sentence of two police personnel and imprisonment for others, after a protracted 13-year battle.[26] According to a report by a rights group, a total of 1,731 people died in custody in India in 2019. This works out to almost five such deaths daily. The report further states that 1,606 of the deaths occurred in judicial custody while 125 in police custody.[27] According to the report, deaths in police custody occur primarily as a result of torture. Out of the 125 deaths studied by National Campaign Against Torture (NCAT), 93 persons, which accounts for 74.4 per cent, died during police custody due to alleged torture/foul play; another 24 persons (19.2%) died under suspicious circumstances in which police claimed they committed suicide. Most of the victims of police torture were part of the poor and marginalized of the society who are often the soft targets because of their socio-economic status.

Some who are unsympathetic to recent critiques of criminal justice might be tempted to discount the arrests on the grounds that they accrue largely to criminals who, after all, deserve them. However, several arrests are effected for frivolous and trivial acts of violations wherein the crimes are so minor that the harms of arrest far outweigh the purpose of punishment if they were imposed for a retributive or deterrent purpose. People

---

[25] https://thewire.in/rights/tamil-nadu-protests-thoothukudi-custodial-deaths (last visited 5 March, 2021).

[26] https://indianexpress.com/article/what-is/what-is-the-udayakumar-custodial-death-case-5275619/

[27] National Campaign Against Torture, *India: Annual Report on Torture 2019* (26 June, 2020). See http://www.uncat.org/wp-content/uploads/2020/06/INDIATORTURE2019.pdf

are arrested for loitering, gambling, begging, money dispute, family dispute, water dispute and similar incidents. Also, the consequence of arrests simply cannot be waived away on the ground that they are deserved. It is hard to say that these criminals 'deserve' the harms that come from arrests. 'Out of the deaths of 125 persons in 124 cases of deaths in police custody documented by NCAT in 2019, 76 persons or 60.8 per cent belonged to the poor and marginalized communities. These included 13 victims from Dalit and tribal communities, 15 victims from Muslim minority community, 37 victims were picked up for petty crimes such as theft/burglary/cheating/selling of liquor illegally, gambling, etc., three were farmers, one was labourer, one was a refugee and two worked as drivers',[28] which indicate their economic status.

When a person is arrested, his family also suffers along with him. His family faces humiliation and contempt from society. They might be deprived of the decent means of livelihood as it is likely that the only breadwinner of the family is in jail or police custody. Sometimes, police threaten the family members of suspected accused or take a family member or friend into custody and use them as a bargaining tool. Though such type of custody without significant reasons amounts to a serious illegality on the part of police, still one private individual cannot compete alone against a well-shielded state machinery. The arrest of a parent or other family member can have deleterious effect on the physical and mental well-being of children. Children exposed to arrest of parents or other family members exhibit higher levels of mental health difficulties compared to peers not exposed.[29]

CONSTITUTIONALITY OF ARREST

Under Article 21 of the Indian Constitution, personal liberty of an individual can be deprived only in accordance with the procedure established by law. Post *Maneka Gandhi* v. *Union of India*,[30] now it is

---

[28] *Id.* at 80.

[29] Yvonne Humenay Roberts et al., *Children Exposed to the Arrest of a Family Member: Associations with Mental Health* 23(2) J. CHILD FAM. STUD. 214–44 (2014). https://doi.org/10.1007/s10826-013-9717-2

[30] A.I.R. 1978 S.C. 597.

a settled principle of law that the 'procedure' established by law must be 'right and just and fair' and not arbitrary, fanciful or oppressive. *Maneka Gandhi* has practically imported the concept of 'due process of law' from the American Constitution into Indian jurisprudence. Article 22 of the Constitution lays down a safeguard against arbitrary arrest and detention by mandating production of an accused before a Magistrate within 24 h, being informed of the grounds of his arrest and being afforded the opportunity of consulting a legal practitioner. The Draft Constitution did not have protections against arbitrary arrest; they were added later. Article 22, therefore, became the provision which would ensure that 'procedure established by law' would have some element of the 'due process'. The draft of Article 22 borrowed from the Criminal Procedural Code of 1898 which was in force at the time. Post-independence, CrPC, 1973, was enacted, which remedied some of the problems of the 1898 Code. Under the 1898 Code, Section 173(4) mandated the police officer to furnish to the accused, 'a copy of the charge-sheet, first information report etc.' 'before the commencement of the inquiry or trial'. This was found to be vague, and therefore, to ensure implementation of the constitutional mandate, under Section 50 of the 1973 Code, the police officer must 'forthwith communicate' to the accused full particulars of the offence for which he is arrested or other grounds for such arrest'. The 1898 Code had provisions which dealt with the production of a person who was either arrested with a warrant (Section 81) or without a warrant (Sections 60 and 61). Analogous provisions exist in the 1973 Code too, with the former being incorporated under Section 76 and the latter under Sections 56 and 57. Thus, it is evident that the 1973 Code improved upon the 1898 Code in furthering the protection provided by the Constitution under Articles 21 and 22.

We often assume that an arrest, in compliance with the Constitutional safeguards, is legal and if legal, it is justified. People suffer because of arrest, not only when it is illegal or arbitrary, but also in instances where it is legal and without excessive force. As arrests result in deprivation of liberty, it is important that they should be imposed only when they serve a significant state interest. Section 41 of CrPC, 1973, empowers a police officer to arrest without a warrant of court on 'reasonable suspicion'. Section 151 permits arrest 'if it appears' to a police officer that a person is likely to commit a cognizable offence. Is it justifiable to subject the liberty of an individual on subjective satisfaction of a police officer? What are the objective rounds on which such suspicion or belief can be measured? The 2008 Amendment to CrPC imposes duty on the police officer to record in writing the reasons for making an arrest or not making an arrest. While granting remand, the Magistrate should examine the police case diary to satisfy himself that the police officer was justified in making an arrest. However, this is only in those cognizable cases where the punishment extends to 7 years of imprisonment or fine. In *Arnesh Kumar* v. *State of Bihar*,[31] the Supreme Court observed that:

> Before a Magistrate authorised detention under Section 167 CrPC, he has to be first satisfied that the arrest made is legal and in accordance with law and all the constitutional rights of the person arrested are satisfied. If the arrest effected by the police officer does not satisfy the requirements of Section 41 of the Code, Magistrate is duty-bound not to authorise his further detention and release the accused....[32]

The court directed that when a person is arrested and produced before a Magistrate for authorizing detention, he needs to investigate the reasons recorded by the police officer and prima facie whether those reasons are relevant. To this limited extent, the Magistrate makes a judicial scrutiny. *Arnesh Kumar* judgement includes a direction that a failure to comply with the procedure by the police will lead to departmental action and make them liable for contempt of court. Is a Magistrate who authorizes detention without the procedure being complied with liable for departmental action as well?

Even if a person is arrested as per the procedure established by law and is produced before the Magistrate within 24 h, still the question persists as to whether there is a larger state interest to arrest a person compared to the probable costs of arrest suffered by the individual. Is not it that the power of arrest should be granted by law only when the risk of harm is not grossly disproportionate to State interest? If the State

---

[31] *Supra* note 12.
[32] *Id.* at 279.

can perform its functions without arresting an individual, unless there is a larger interest in arresting an individual, should it not be taken into consideration. Police officers have many roles to play. They exist both to protect life and property and to maintain public order and safety. Public safety and public order are preconditions of any free society. Towards achieving those goals, the state requires to control individuals who threaten them, even by use of force, especially through arrests. However, if police cannot do the job of maintaining law and order in society without arrests, then our practice of arrests might well be justified, despite the harm it causes. Arrests have long been the first step in initiating criminal proceedings and bringing criminals to justice. The question is how significant are arrests in investigating and adjudicating criminal cases as well as punishing the guilty? Not all criminal cases mandate an arrest. In fact, many criminal cases start with some form of summons issued to an accused. A summon equally demands that an individual answer criminal charge.

CONCLUSION

Constitutional restrictions on the state power to arrest have limited bearing on whether the current scenario to heavily rely on arrest as a tool of policing is appropriate and legitimate. Our traditional justification for arrests, that it is essential in criminal investigation and for maintaining public order, at best supports very few arrests than we currently permit. Constitutional safeguards guaranteed to individuals set a minimum rather than best standards for State conduct. They may not adequately take into account the aggregate effects of state coercion. Though with judicial activism, the criminal law jurisprudence has evolved dynamically, citizens should not only be satisfied with mere compliance of constitutional standards but should demand reorienting the criminal jurisprudence in light of liberty, equality and fraternity.

The colonial hangover of criminal jurisprudence as regards the role of police should be refuted. Police should be looked upon with trust and as a friend of common citizens. This has been discussed a lot many times, but as long as the police powers are not curtailed, the police force would not be able to change as a 'service' to citizens. Now the final question from a colonial hangover mindset, 'How do police deter if not by arresting criminals?' The answer is, police deter a potential criminal by persuading him that they will not succeed, rather than by arresting some criminals to make others afraid of future arrests. Police deter as 'sentinels', not as 'apprehension agents'. Police need not make arrests to stop crime; rather, they should set such high standards of policing that people would be naturally inclined towards following law. In terms of CrPC, the definition of cognizable[33] and non-cognizable offences[34] could be changed, wherein an investigation could be conducted by police officials without any order or direction of Magistrate, but police cannot arrest a person without a warrant of a Magistrate. The additional conditions imposed on Section 41 (1)(b) that have to be satisfied before an arrest can be made in case of offences where the punishment extends to 7 years of imprisonment and should equally be made applicable for all cognizable offences irrespective of the quantum of punishment for an offence. If those conditions are not satisfied, then the police cannot make an arrest without a warrant. These changes may help to bring about a positive impact.

---

[33] See Section 2(c) and Sections 156(1) and 157 CrPC, 1973. In case of a cognizable offence, a police officer can arrest the alleged offender without warrant and can investigate into such cases without any orders or directions from Magistrate. Also, offences generally punishable with imprisonment for more than 3 years are categorized as cognizable offences.

[34] See Section 2(l); Offence punishable with imprisonment for less than 3 years or with fine only, are generally categorized as non-cognizable offences.

Chapter 3

Arrest by Police
Power, Procedure and Impact on Fundamental Rights

Amiya Kumar Samanta

INTRODUCTION

For centuries in India, the common man used to avoid the sight of a policeman for fear of being arrested as the police hardly required any excuse to arrest a person. Once a man is arrested, he may be insulted, assaulted and detained and he may be totally clueless as to when he would be free. With the introduction of a new criminal procedure in the 1970s, arrest and detention were systematized and brought within the framework of law, but abuse of arrest and detention continued to plague the law enforcement scenario.

Law has given the officers the power to arrest a person under certain circumstances, relating to the commission of a crime. But at the time of arrest, the officer may not know for certain whether the man has committed the crime—he is arrested primarily on suspicion that he may have committed or will commit a crime in the future. In both cases, if the suspicion is based on strong material grounds, the arrest will stand the scrutiny in the court of law. But if the suspicion is subjective and is not based on objective facts, it will be a case of violation of human rights. This chapter presents a detailed discussion on the scope and ambit of police powers of arrest under the present Code, its impact on fundamental rights, and the probable areas of misuse which have been sought to be addressed by guidelines of authorities from time to time.

ARREST AND CUSTODY

Arrest in a layman's language means restraint and detention and consequently, the deprivation of personal liberty of a person who has done something against the law. But restraint or detention is not arrest unless done by an authority empowered by law and following the legally established procedure. Ironically, the Code of Criminal Procedure, 1973, nowhere attempts to define the word 'arrest;' nor does any other substantive or procedural laws. According to Black's Law Dictionary[1], the term 'arrest' means 'to keep a person in lawful custody. A warrant, crime, or statute can authorize this'. The most common definition of the term 'arrest' is the physical restraint of a person sanctioned by legal authority resulting in the loss of personal liberty. As stated by the Supreme Court in *State of Haryana v. Dinesh Kumar*,[2]

> the question whether a person is under arrest or not, depends not on the legality of the arrest, but on whether he has been deprived of his personal liberty to go where he pleases. When used in the legal sense in the procedure connected with criminal offences, an arrest consists in the taking into custody of another person under authority empowered by law, for the purpose of holding or detaining him to answer a criminal charge or of preventing the commission of a criminal offence. The essential elements to constitute an arrest in the above sense are that there must be an intent to arrest under the authority, accompanied by a seizure or detention of the person in the manner known to law, which is so understood by the person arrested.

Often arrest is confused with custody, but both these words carry different meaning. An arrest is done prior to appearance before a Magistrate while putting a person in custody refers to the Magistrate's orders indicating that a person should be kept under supervision either within the authority of a police officer or in district prison. This means that

---

[1] B. A. GARNER, BLACK'S LAW DICTIONARY (Thomson Reuters 2004)
[2] (2008) 3 S.C.C. 222, at p. 229, para 21.

all arrests constitute custody. However, the reverse does not stand true since there is no need to necessarily arrest a person to constitute *custody*. In the case of *Roshan Beevi v. Joint Secretary, Govt. of Tamil Nadu*,[3] a full bench of the Madras High Court after examining the meaning of the term 'arrest' expressed the view that the terms custody and arrest are not identical. In all circumstances, custody does not necessarily amount to an arrest. For instance, if a person submits to the Magistrate or voluntarily confesses about committing a crime, there is no requirement of making an arrest. The person will be kept in custody. In *Directorate of Enforcement v. Deepak Mahajan*[4], the Supreme Court held that as enumerated in the Code, the powers of arrest are exclusive not only to the police officer but also extends to Magistrates and private persons under circumstances mentioned in the Code. Thus when a person appears before a Magistrate or simply surrenders to him, the Magistrate is empowered to directly take him to custody to deal with him according to law. However, it is instinctive that the custody of an individual is followed after the arrest by the Magistrate on appearance or surrender. If custody and arrest are transcribed as synonymous, the court held that 'it is nothing but an ultra-legalist interpretation which if under all circumstances accepted and adopted, would lead to a startling anomaly resulting in serious consequences'.[5]

POWER OF ARREST BY POLICE

For the purpose of attaining the attendance of an accused during the time of trial, an arrest is of utmost importance. It acts as a pre-emptive and deterrent measure for an individual planning to commit a cognizable offence, or a habitual offender or an ex-convict, or a person found under doubtful circumstances[6]. It is sometimes essential to obtain the correct name and address of a person committing a non-cognizable offence[7]. A person may be arrested instantly if he interferes and obstructs a police officer in due discharge of his duties.

[3] 1984 CrlJ 134 (Mad).
[4] (1994) 3 S.C.C. 440.
[5] Niranjan Singh v. Prabhakar Rajaram Kharote, (1980) 2 S.C.C. 559, at 562.
[6] See, Sections 151 and 41, Code of Criminal Procedure, 1973.
[7] See, Section 42, Code of Criminal Procedure, 1973.

According to the Code of Criminal Procedure, an arrest can be of two types. One, in the execution of a warrant issued by a Magistrate; and two, arrests without a warrant. In the case of the former, the Magistrate issues and signs a written order directing the police officer to arrest the accused person. The order contains the name of the accused. The decision to issue a warrant or otherwise by a magistrate involves a balancing of social interests with those of the accused. The Code correctly postulates that the contradictory claims can be resolved if the decision concerning arrest is made by an unbiased judge with adequate prowess[8].

It is in case of arrest without a warrant that most critical situations arise. Under the Code, arrests can be made by police officers, private persons, as well as Magistrates. In the case of private persons and Magistrates[9], the Code lays down specific conditions whereby such arrest can be affected, like the commission of a non-bailable and cognizable offence in the presence of a private person or a proclaimed offender or committed in the presence of a Magistrate, etc. On the other hand, the Police have been given extensive powers of arrest. Though the police may not be judicious or balanced in their approach or known for their impartiality, yet the exigencies of the situation require the law to accord powers of arrest when the situation arises. As Pillai asserts[10], in cases of serious cognizable offences, there exist high possibilities of offenders escaping unless instantly arrested. Thus, it would be imprudent if arrests are made subsequent to obtaining a warrant from the Magistrate. Preventive action also, at times, may require the exercise of the power of arrest to avert the danger of a sudden outbreak of crime, and immediate arrest of the trouble maker may be an important step in such preventive action.

Apart from other provisions, Sections 41 and 42 enumerate the conditions under which arrests may be made. A police officer may make an arrest in case of commission of a cognizable offence[11], either

---

[8] K. N. C. PILLAI, R.V. KELKAR'S CRIMINAL PROCEDURE (Eastern Book Co. 2014).

[9] See, Sections 43 and 44, Code of Criminal Procedure, 1973.

[10] PILLAI, *supra* note 8, at 49.

[11] See, Section 2 (c) Code of Criminal Procedure, 1973.

in his presence[12], or where there is credible information or reasonable suspicion of its commission[13], or in other situations specified in the sections. Notably, vide amendment Act 5 of 2009, certain conditionalities have been laid down to effectuate the arrest for a cognizable offence. One, he/she must have reason to believe the information received, and two, he must be satisfied that the arrest is absolutely necessary under the circumstances. Such necessity is to be determined on grounds such as prevent further offences, the disappearance of evidence or manipulations, or for proper investigation. The officer is mandated to record his reasons for making the arrest and in case it is challenged, the burden is on the police officer to explain his grounds of belief[14]. It may be noted that malicious and excessive exercise of powers of arrest under the section would be a punishable offence under Section 220 Indian Penal Code, 1860.

The use of the word 'may' in the section signifies that arrest is a matter of discretion for the police[15]. They are required to be satisfied with the circumstances under which they exercise the power, and it is not obligatory for police to make arrest in every case. However, the Allahabad High Court[16] maintained that

if an arrest is made, it does not require any, much less strong, reasons to be recorded or reported by the police. So long as the information or suspicion is 'reasonable' or 'credible', the police is not accountable for the discretion of arresting or not arresting.[17]

In contrast, the Supreme Court in the landmark case of *Joginder Kumar v. the State of UP*[18] held that an arrest cannot be made just because it is lawful for the police officer to do so. The validation to exert power is not similar to the very existence of that power. Both arrest and

---

[12] Section 41 (1) (a) Code of Criminal Procedure, 1973.

[13] Section 41 (1) (b) and (ba), Code of Criminal Procedure, 1973.

[14] Emperor v. Vimlabai Deshpande, (1946) 47 CriLJ 831.

[15] M.C. Abraham v. State of Maharashtra (2003) 24 Orissa Criminal Reports (SC) 517.

[16] Gulab Chand Upadhyay v. State of UP, (2002) S.C.C. Online ALL 1221.

[17] *Id.* at 1226, para 9.

[18] (1994) 4 S.C.C. 260.

detention in police prison can result in mental trauma, loss of self-esteem and repute. Thus, a mere accusation about the commission of a crime is not enough to make an arrest. In the interest of protection of the Constitutional right of a citizen, it would be judicious for police personnel to ensure that no arrest is made without proper investigation with regards to the genuineness of a complaint. The police officer must be satisfied with the person's complicity to such an extent that it necessitates an arrest.

NOTICE OF APPEARANCE

As an alternative to the power of arrest, the Code[19] has incorporated a salutary provision that provides that where an arrest is not required, the investigating officer shall[20] issue a notice of appearance. Compliance with such notice will ensure that no arrests can be made unless, for reasons to be recorded, the police consider otherwise.

In light of the directions of the Supreme Court in *Arnesh Kumar v. the State of Bihar*[21], it may be stated that in cases where an offence is punishable for a term up to 7 years or which may extend to 7 years, a notice of appearance should generally be served on the accused within 2 weeks from the date of institution of the case, which may be extended by the Superintendent of Police of the District, based on reasons to be recorded. Thus, the arrest of the accused in such cases should not be a matter of routine; rather, the investigation officer must satisfy himself about the necessity of arrest in terms of Section 41 of the Code, 1973. Where however arrest is to be conducted, the investigation officer is vested with the responsibility to endow materials along with adequate reasons that compelled the arrest of the accused. The same should be forwarded to the Magistrate and the latter, only after recording his satisfaction, from the perusal of the report shall authorise detention. In *Sanmay Banerjee v. State of West Bengal*[22], where a freelance journalist

---

[19] Code of Criminal Procedure (Amendment) Act, 2008 (5 of 2009).

[20] The word 'may' was substituted by 'shall' vide Section 3(a) of Code of Criminal Procedure (Amendment) Act, 2010) (41 of 2010).

[21] (2014) 8 S.C.C. 273.

[22] (2019) S.C.C. Online Cal 3941.

and a whistle blower was arrested on frivolous grounds for his criticism of the ruling dispensation, without any prior notice, the High Court held that people have the right to criticize the dispensation running the administration of the country, and the Judiciary and Legislation are not exempt from fair criticism. Furthermore, Section 41A categorically provides that notice of appearance be 'served' to the accused; mere attempts to serve will not satisfy the meaning of the section[23]. But, where despite notice, the accused fails to cooperate with the investigation, as also issues threat to the victim/complainant, an arrest would be necessary and the police may proceed to take the accused into custody.[24]

MANNER OF ARREST

Section 60A of the Code, 1973 indicates that all arrests are to be made in compliance with the provisions of the Code. Thus, adherence to the legalities of arrest is important to uphold its validity. Sections 46–49 of the Code, 1973 enumerate how an arrest may be made. It may be summarized as below:

- While making an arrest, the police officer or any other person who makes the arrest should not touch or detain the body of the person to be arrested unless the person submits to the custody by word or action.
- The police officer or the other person may effectuate the arrest through all means in case the offender repels the attempts to arrest or evades arrest.
- While making an arrest the police officer shall not cause the death of the accused under any circumstances where he has not committed a crime punishable with death or life imprisonment.
- The police officer shall use proportional force and not subject the accused to more restraint than what is required to avert his escape.

In an actual sense, an arrest is a restraint of the liberty of a person. It can be executed only by contacting or touching the body of the person who

---

[23] See, Hema Mishra v. State of UP, (2014) 4 S.C.C. 453.

[24] Bhupinder Singh v. Gurmeet Singh, COCP no. 3079 of 2016 decided on 27 July 2017, https://indiankanoon.org/doc/25445389/

is to be arrested. An oral announcement of arrest without real contact or submission to custody will not amount to an arrest[25]. In certain circumstances, words may amount to arrest if the words indicate that the person is under compulsion to submit himself and subsequently he succumbs to such compulsion.[26] As explained by the Court *in State of Uttar Pradesh v. Deoman*[27],

> Section 46 CrPC does not contemplate any formality before a person can be said to be taken in custody. Submission to the custody by word of mouth or action by a person is sufficient. Again, when a person, who is not in custody, approaches the police officer and provides information, which leads to the discovery of a fact, which could be used against him, it would be deemed that he had surrendered to the authority of the investigating agency.[28]

Where, however, an accused, resists the arrest, the law authorises the police officer to use as much force as is necessary to bring him into submission. Such force may extend to the causing of death, provided the person is accused of an offence punishable with death or life imprisonment. 'Necessity' is the crux on which the justifiability of use of force must be considered. Where the exigencies of the situation demand, such as the private defence of the police, or due discharge of his duties to apprehend the accused, the police is legally entitled to use force. As held by the apex court,

> In a given case, if a dreaded criminal launches a murderous attack on the police to prevent them from doing their duty, the police may have to retaliate, and in that retaliation, such a criminal may get killed. That could be a case for a genuine encounter.[29]

Speaking in the context of encounters carried out by Police, it is a situation that is forced upon the policeman who is performing his/her duties of arresting a wanted criminal. When the criminal opens fires,

---

[25] Harmohanlal v. Emperor (1929) 30 CriLJ 128.

[26] State of Haryana v. Dinesh Kumar, (2008) 3 S.C.C. 222.

[27] (1961) 1 S.C.R. 14.

[28] State of Uttar Pradesh v Deoman, A.I.R. 1960 S.C. 1125, at para 12.

[29] Rohtash Kumar v. State of Haryana, (2013) 14 S.C.C. 290, at 298.

the situation gets precipitated and the police have no choice but to fire them back in due discharge of their duties. The Supreme Court has clarified that

If the version of the police with respect to the incident in question were true, there could have been no question of any interference by the Court. Nobody can say that the police should wait till they are shot at. It is for the force on the spot to decide when to act, how to act, and where to act. It is not for the Court to say how the terrorists should be fought. ...The courts may not be the appropriate forum to determine those questions.[30]

In moments of excitement or disturbed mental equilibrium, such as an encounter scenario, a person cannot be expected to weigh the proportionality of force in golden scales. A person must be left to decide as to what force he will use in circumstances where he is threatened. Nevertheless, the action of the police must be 'right, just and fair' in consonance with the constitutional guarantees.[31] Where the circumstances show that the use of force was unnecessary to apprehend the accused, an inquiry by an independent agency must be conducted and the police must be held liable for their actions.[32]

THE ARREST OF A WOMAN

A new clause has been added to Section 46 of the Code in 2005[33] prohibiting the arrest of a woman any time after sunset and before sunrise, except, where exceptional circumstances exist and arrest is important for investigation, the woman police officer must obtain prior permission from the Judicial Magistrate First Class after submitting a written report. Furthermore, arrests of women, so far as possible, are to be made by lady constables. Thus, in a case where the accused, a woman, was alleged to have committed the serious offence of murder,

---

[30] People's Union of Civil Liberties v. Union of India, (1997) 3 S.C.C. 433, at 438.

[31] D.K. Basu v. State of West Bengal, (1997) 1 S.C.C. 416.

[32] Rohtash Kumar v. State of Haryana, (2013) 14 S.C.C. 290.

[33] Act 25 of 2005.

and an order was made by the Magistrate authorizing her arrest after sunset, such arrest was held to be not violative of Section 46(4) of the Code[34]. In S. *Vijaylakshmi v. Director General of Police,*[35] the Madras High Court stated that the rights guaranteed under Article 21 of the Indian Constitution are equally applicable to all the citizens of the country and hence a convict cannot be denied this right. The same truth applies to an accused in custody who might be convicted after trial as well as a suspect who might be converted to an accused after investigation. It is an onus upon the State to guarantee that there is no violation of the indefeasible right of a citizen to life and liberty, which he cannot be deprived of without following the procedure established by law. In this case, the arrest of the petitioner at about 20.00 hours in pursuant to a crime was declared as illegal and in utter disregard of the provisions of Section 46(4) CrPC, 1973 as no written report was made to the Judicial Magistrate prior to the arrest[36].

In the case of women, it is also imperative that separate lock-ups be provided for them in police stations. Such lockups should be guarded by female constables with due regard to the safety of the women prisoners. Furthermore, the interrogation of women should be carried out only in the presence of female police officers/constables.[37]

CONSEQUENCES OF NON-COMPLIANCE WITH ARREST PROCEDURES

While the Code enunciates elaborate procedures with regard to arrest, the consequences of non-compliance have to be seen from two perspectives- those which are merely irregular and those in blatant contravention of the law or, in other words, illegal. From the point of view of trial, mere irregularity in arrest does not vitiate the proceedings. As emphasized by Kelkar, 'The question whether the police officer making the arrest was acting within or beyond his capacity in effecting the arrest, does not affect the question whether the accused person

---

[34] Ankita Harinath Mishra v. State of Maharashtra, (2019) S.C.C. Online Bom 1560.

[35] S. Vijaylakshmi v. Director General of Police, (2019) S.C.C. Online Mad 24482.

[36] Rajkumari v. SHO Noida, (2003) 11 S.C.C. 500.

[37] Sheela Barse v. State of Maharashtra A.I.R. 1983 S.C. 378.

was guilty or not guilty of the offence with which he is charged'.[38] In such cases of irregularity, the police officer may not be held liable since it may be viewed as a mere technical lapse in due discharge of duty. However, where the power exercised is manifestly illegal, Section 220 IPC, 1860, provides that a public servant who knowingly exercises authority and makes an arrest in contravention of the law can be prosecuted and punished for the same. Such illegal arrest is also punishable as wrongful confinement under Section 342 IPC, 1860.

From the point of view of the accused, illegal arrest equates itself with false imprisonment[39] for which a police officer can be held liable for damages in a civil action. The State can also be made vicariously liable. In *Nagendra Rao v. State of Andhra Pradesh*[40] the Supreme Court ruled that the State can be held liable for the wrongful acts of the police officers. The same has been reiterated by the Gujarat High Court[41] which emphasized that in the realm of the welfare state, the plea of sovereign immunity based on feudalistic notions does not exist; rather the state, like any other ordinary citizen, is liable for the wrongs of its servants.

RIGHTS OF AN ARRESTED PERSON

The police have been vested with numerous powers for making arrests. However, the powers are not absolute. This is to ensure that the interests of the persons to be arrested are adequately protected, along with the society at large. The rights of the arrested persons may be enumerated as under:

1. **Right to be informed of the grounds of arrest:** Section 50 provides that any person arrested without a warrant shall immediately be informed of the grounds of his arrest and if the arrest is

---

[38] K.N. Chandrasekharan Pillai, R.V. Kelkar's Criminal Procedure, Eastern Book Co. 6th Edn. Rep. 2012.

[39] See, John M. Manos, *Police Liability for False Arrest of Imprisonment* 16 CLEV.-MARSHALL L. REV. 415 (1967).

[40] A.I.R. 1994 S.C. 2663.

[41] Circulate the Judgment Amongst...v. State of Gujarat C/LPA/473/1996 Decided on 4 August 2017, https://indiankanoon.org/doc/174816823/

made in a bailable case, the person shall be informed of his right to be released on bail. A similar provision in case of arrest with a warrant is provided in Section 75.

The right to be informed of the grounds of arrest is a precious right of the arrested person[42] conferred under Article 22(1) of the Indian constitution. It is intended to afford the earliest opportunity to the arrested person to remove any mistake, misapprehension or misunderstanding in the minds of the arresting authorities and, also, to know exactly what the accusation against him is so that he can exercise the second right, namely of consulting a legal practitioner of his choice and to be defended by him[43].

The grounds of arrest should be communicated to the arrested person in the language understood by him. The words 'as soon as maybe' in Article 22(1) would mean as early as is reasonable in the circumstances of the case; however, the word 'forthwith' in Section 50(1) of the Code creates a stricter duty on the part of the police officer making the arrest and would mean 'immediately'[44].

2. **Right to information to family, friends:** Though capped in the language of 'duty', this right may be considered as a consequent right of the arrested person to inform his family, friends of his arrest. Section 41B as included in the Code, 1973 requires the police to wear accurate, visible and clear identification at the time of making arrests. Further, he must prepare a memo of arrest which has to be attested by at least one witness belonging to the family of the arrested person at the time of the arrest. Alternatively, information about the arrest has to be sent to relatives, friends of such arrested person. The Magistrate is under an obligation to satisfy himself about the compliance of the police in this regard.

This provision emerges from the Supreme Court decision in *Joginder Singh* and *Basu* cases, referring to a common practice amongst policemen to pick up persons and take them into custody or unknown destinations without due intimation to family. On occasions, the family is also deprived of the chance to see the person

---

[42] Udaybhan Shuki v. State of UP 1999 CrLJ 274 (All.)

[43] Madhu Limaye, *re*, (1969) 1 S.C.C. 292.

[44] K.N. Chandrasekharan Pillai, R.V. Kelkar's Criminal Procedure, Eastern Book Co. 6th Edn. Rep. 2012.

alive thereafter. Thus, the provision imposes an obligation on the police to provide due intimation and make an entry to that effect in the register.

3. **Right to be taken before Magistrate without delay:** In cases where the arrest is made without warrant by a police officer or under the warrant by any person, the person making the arrest must bring the arrested person before a judicial officer without unnecessary delay. An arrested person must be sent to the police station instantly after arrest. Sections 56 and 76 relate to the necessary rights in this regard. According to Section 56 of the Code, in case the police does not grant bail to the accused, he may be taken to the Magistrate who has jurisdiction to try the case.

4. **Right of not being detained for more than 24 hours without judicial scrutiny:** It is a mandate to bring the arrested person before the Magistrate within 24 hours of the arrest. Also, as enumerated in Section 57 of the Code of Criminal Procedure, a person arrested without a warrant shall be brought before Magistrate within 24 hours, except in cases where there is a special order of a Magistrate under Section 167, or in cases where the time of journey from the place of arrest to the Magistrate's court exceeds 24 hours. The intention is to i) preclude arrest and detention in order to extract a confession, or as a means of compelling people ii) to prevent police stations being used as prisons iii) to afford an early recourse to a judicial officer independent of the police on all questions of bail or discharge.[45] With the incorporation of Article 22(2) in the Constitution of India, these rights are further fortified.

The Supreme Court[46] has urged the State and police authorities to meticulously observe the legal requirement under Section 57 of the Code of Criminal Procedure and re-instated that a violation of the same will result in wrongful detention by police authorities.[47]

---

[45] Mohd. Suleman v. King Emperor (1925–26) 30 C.W.N. 985.

[46] Khatri v. State of Bihar, (1981) 1 S.C.C. 627; DG & IG of Police v. Prem Sagar, (1999) 5 S.C.C. 700; Vachhalabai v. State of Maharashtra, (2019) S.C.C. Online Bom 2937.

[47] Sharifbhai v. Abdul Razzak, A.I.R. 1961 Bom 42. See, CBI v. Kishore Singh, (2011) 6 S.C.C. 369.

5. **Right to consult a legal practitioner and free legal aid:**
Article 22(1) of the Constitution provides that no person who is arrested shall be denied the right to consult a legal practitioner of his choice. Section 303 of the Code, 1973 also provides that any person against whom proceedings are instituted under the code may of right be defended by a pleader of his choice. The right of an arrested person to consult his lawyer begins from the moment of his arrest and continues thereafter[48].

Section 304 places on a statutory footing the right of the accused without sufficient means to engage a lawyer to be defended at the expense of the state. The right to free legal aid is reasonable, fair, just and implicit in Article 21 of the Constitution. The accused must be informed of his right to avail of free legal aid at the cost of the State. The Magistrate or the Sessions Judge before whom the accused appears will inform him of this right in case he is unable to hire a lawyer due to poverty or otherwise.[49] Disregard this provision or failure to inform the accused of this right will vitiate the trial.

6. **Medical examination:**
Section 54 has been amended to give the accused the right to have himself medically examined to enable him to defend and protect himself. It is considered desirable and necessary

> that a person who is arrested should be given the right to have his body examined by a medical officer when he is produced before a magistrate or at any time when he is under custody, with a view to enabling him to establish that the offence with which he is charged was not committed by him or that he was subjected to physical injury.[50]

The accused person must be informed about his right to be medically examined by the Magistrate[51]. In case the examination takes place at the instance of the accused, a copy shall be given to him.

---

[48] Moti Bai v. State, (1954) 55 CrLJ 1591.

[49] Khatri v. State of Bihar, (1981) 1 S.C.C. 627; Hussainara Khatoon v. State of Bihar, (1980) 1 S.C.C. 98; Mohd. Ajmal Amir Kasab v. State of Maharashtra, (2012) 9 S.C.C. 1.

[50] Report of the Joint Committee of the Parliament (1972), p. 9.

[51] (1983) 2 S.C.C. 96, at 104.

In this regard, Section 55A imposes a further duty on the Police to ensure that reasonable care is provided for the health and safety of the accused in custody.

7. **Right not to be subjected to torture, abuse:**

Police powers of arrest and custody provide a fertile ground to subject the accused to various forms of ill-treatment, mainly to extract confessions. The right against torture can be read within the context of Article 21 of the Indian Constitution. It is an inbuilt guarantee against torture or assault by the State or its functionaries. Article 20(3) and 22 of the Constitution further manifest the constitutional protection and the guarantees held out for making life meaningful and not mere animal existence[52].

In this regard, Section 25 Indian Evidence Act, 1872 prohibits confession recorded by the police as inadmissible in evidence before the court. Even Section 316 CrPC, 1973 mentions that no influence by means of promise or threat shall be used on an accused person to induce him to disclose or withhold any matter within his knowledge. Torture in custody flouts the basic rights of the citizens and is an affront to human dignity. It is punishable under Sections 330 and 331 IPC, 1860, as also entitles the person to the right to compensation[53].

The Supreme court has specifically ruled that an accused in custody shall not be handcuffed or fettered routinely. Even in extreme situations where handcuffs have to be put, the escorting party shall record the reasons for doing so in writing and take the Court's permission.[54] Even any mental agony and humiliation meted out to the accused in custody is strictly prohibited within the confines of the four walls of the police station or lockup.[55]

---

[52] Shakila Abdul Gafar Khan v. Vasant Raghunath Dhoble, A.I.R. 2003 S.C. 4567.

[53] *Shakila Abdul Gafar Khan v. Vasant Raghunath Dhoble AIR 2003 SC 4567Id*; Munshi Singh Gautan v. State of Mp, (2005) 9 S.C.C. 631; P. Amaravathy v. Govt. of Tamil Nadu 1996 (2) C.T.C. 478.

[54] Prem Shankar Shukla v. Delhi Adm., A.I.R. 1980 S.C. 1535; Citizens for Democracy v. State of Assam, A.I.R. 1996 S.C. 2193.

[55] Dr. Mehmood Nayyar Azam v. State of Chattisgarh JT 2012 (7) S.C. 178.

MISUSE OF POWER AND INTERVENTIONS BY AUTHORITIES

The law has given wide powers to the police officers for the arrest of lawbreakers with a view to maintaining peace and order and controlling crime by bringing the offenders to justice. Yet we cannot say the law and order in the country are impartially and correctly maintained, and the criminal cases are promptly and properly investigated and the offenders are brought to justice. The National Human Rights Commission and the State Commissions are recipients of a huge number of complaints against police torture, death in custody, death in false encounters, wrongful arrests, etc.[56] Though a small percentage of them are exaggerated allegations, yet from the size of the complaints, it cannot be denied that the police establishment in the country needs overhauling.

According to the National Police Commission[57], 60 per cent of the total arrests are unnecessary and more than 42 per cent of the total funds allotted to jails are spent on the prisoners who should not have been arrested in the first place. The National Police Commission recommended some restrictions on the discretionary power of police officers to arrest during the investigation of a cognizable case. The Commission suggested that in one or other of the following circumstances arrest may be permitted: cases involving grave offences like murder, dacoity, robbery, rape, etc., and it is necessary to arrest the accused, or the accused is likely to abscond and evade the processes of law; the accused is violent in behaviour and is likely to commit further offences; or the accused is a habitual offender.

The Law Commission of India[58] also highlighted the conferment of vast, sometimes absolute, as well as unguided and arbitrary powers of arrest upon police officers.

---

[56] See, National Human Rights Commission, India, *Annual Report 2017–18* (2019), https://nhrc.nic.in/sites/default/files/NHRC_AR_EN_2017-2018.pdf

[57] National Police Commission, *Third Report*, Government of India (1979), https://police.py.gov.in/Police%20Commission%20reports/3rd%20Police%20Commission%20report.pdf

[58] Law Commission of India, Government of India, *One Hundred and Seventy Seventh Report on Law Relating to Arrest* (December 2001), https://lawcommissionofindia.nic.in/reports/177rptp1.pdf

A reading of the above provisions and in particular, of Sections 41 and 42 show the width of power of arrest vested in police officers.... The generality of language and the consequent wide discretion vesting in police officers is indeed enormous—and that has been the very source of abuse and misuse. The qualifying words 'reasonable', 'credible' and 'reasonably' in the section mean nothing in practice. They have become redundant; in effect.[59]

Again referring to the power under Section 151 of the Code, 1973, the Commission remarked that the section empowers a police officer to arrest any person, 'if it appears to such officer' that such person is designed to commit a cognizable offence. The use of these words indicates the enormity of the power. Though it is argued that the expression is not subjective, but objective, yet in India, it seldom remains objective. Among plenty of reasons for not remaining objective, some are i) motive for personal gain (extortion), ii) pressure of influential people to which the officer succumb, because he is vulnerable, iii) pressure of senior officer, iv) direction of the political bosses. This has been so rampant that, not to speak of illegal arrest, but even extrajudicial killings are committed on a nod from the ruling party bosses. The Commission made several recommendations for reforms of the arrest provisions. Similarly, the NHRC also issued extensive guidelines to contain the abuse of police powers, particularly those of arrest and detention[60] as evident in the inclusion of clauses (a), (b), and (ba) of Section 41, 41A to D, 55A as also Sections 60A of the Code[61].

CONSEQUENCES OF NON-COMPLIANCE

While the Code enunciates elaborate procedures with regard to arrest, the consequences of non-compliance have to be seen from two perspectives- those which are merely irregular and those in blatant

[59] Law Commission of India, Government of India, *Consultation Paper on Law Relating to Arrest*, Part I (December 2001) pp. 2–3, https://lawcommissionofindia. nic.in/reports/Annexure%20III%20of%20177th%20report.pdf

[60] National Human Rights Commission, India, *NHRC Guidelines Regarding Arrest, available at*: https://police.py.gov.in/NHRC%20Guidelines%20Regarding/ NHRC%20Guidelines%20Regarding%20arrest.PDF

[61] The recommendations were inclusive of the Supreme Court directions in D.K. Basu v. State of West Bengal, (1997) 1 S.C.C. 416 and Joginder Singh v. State of UP, (1994) 4 S.C.C. 260.

contravention of the law or, in other words, illegal. From the point of view of trial, mere irregularity in arrest does not vitiate the proceedings. As emphasized by Kelkar, 'The question whether the police officer making the arrest was acting within or beyond his capacity in effecting the arrest, does the affect the question whether the accused person was guilty or not guilty of the offence with which he is charged'.[62] In such cases of irregularity, the police officer may not be held liable since it may be viewed as a mere technical lapse in due discharge of duty. However, where the power exercised is manifestly illegal, Section 220 IPC, 1860, provides that a public servant who knowingly exercises authority and makes an arrest in contravention of the law may be prosecuted and punished for the same. Such illegal arrest is also punishable as wrongful confinement under Section 342 IPC, 1860.

From the point of view of the accused, illegal arrest equates itself with false imprisonment[63] for which a police officer can be held liable for damages in a civil action. The State can also be made vicariously liable. In *Nagendra Rao v. State of Andhra Pradesh*[64] the apex court ruled that the State can be held liable for the wrongful acts of the police officers. The same has been reiterated by the Gujrat High Court[65] which emphasized that in the realm of the welfare state, the plea of sovereign immunity based on feudalistic notions does not exist; rather the state, like any other ordinary citizen, is liable for the wrongs of its servants.

CONCLUSION

'The horizon of human rights is expanding. At the same time, the crime rate is also increasing. Of late, this court has been receiving complaints about violations of human rights because of indiscriminate arrests. How are we to strike a balance between the two?'[66] To put it rather more lucidly, it is a conflict between the protection of citizens and society from crimes and criminals on the one hand and on the other,

---

[62] Kelkar, 89.
[63] See, Manos, *supra* note 39.
[64] A.I.R. 1994 S.C. 2663.
[65] Circulate the Judgment Amongst…, *supra* note 41.
[66] Joginder Kumar v. State of U.P., (1994) 4 S.C.C. 260, at 263.

protection of an individual citizen's life and ensuring safety which is also the sacred duty of the state.

Articles 21 and 22 are the cornerstone of the protection of the individual life of citizens from unlawful arrest and detention. It is important that the powers conferred on the Police are exercised with due regard to the notions of liberty and dignity. Towards that end, several reforms have been introduced in the Code of Criminal Procedure, 1973. These have intended to provide clear guidelines as to when the powers may be exercised, and subject to what conditions, failing which they may be held to be violative of individual's rights. Yet, we cannot turn a blind eye to the realities presenting themselves in recent times. The arrest of noted journalists, activists, comedians and numerous such instances have once again posed big questions as to whether the police act according to law or some unknown dictates. It is necessary to once again rekindle the debate on the extent of police powers as well as reforms in the structure and organisation of police whereby a balanced system can emerge.

Chapter 4

Anatomy of Preventive Detention Laws in India
A Historical and Critical Perspective

Yogesh Pratap Singh

INTRODUCTION

Preventive detention is a state device by which a person can be detained before trial only on the suspicion and supposition that he may be detrimental to the larger interest of society[1] and fair investigation.[2] Preventive detention was practised ordinarily in dictatorial regimes. The Soviet Union used this device in cases where an alleged person

---

[1] The term 'Preventive Detention' lacks any precise and authoritative definition. In the Indian context, it ensued in the Legislative Lists of the Government of India Act, 1935 and later as Item 9 of List I and Item 3 of List III in the Seventh Schedule to the Constitution. The term probably originated in England when Law Lords while expounding the nature of detention under Regulation 14 (B) of the Defence of Realm Consolidation Act, 1914. The word 'preventive' was used in contradistinction to the word 'punitive' as Lord Finlay described in *Rex v. Halliday* [(1) [1917] A.C. 260, at 269], that 'it is not a punitive but a precautionary measure'. *See* opinion of Justice B.K. Mukherjee in A.K. Gopalan vs. State of Madras A.I.R. 1950 S.C. 27.

[2] See www.britannica.com/topic/preventive-detention

was perceived as a security threat. These countries voiced a very petite concern for individual liberty and therefore preventive detention was exclusively left at the mercy of the police.

However, countries that preached liberty as the essence of constitutional order practised preventive detention only during emergencies or wartime. England legislated preventive detention law during the two World Wars.[3] The Defence of Realm Act during the First World War and the Emergency Powers (Defence) Act during the Second World War endowed the state with the power to preventively detain any person in the name of public interest, safety and security. However, these Acts expired at the end of the respective wars. The Defence of India Act, 1915, created a similar mechanism for British India during the First World War. Though this Act expired at the end of the Second World War, two new regressive preventive detention legislations viz. Rowlatt Act[4] and the Bengal Criminal Law Amendment Ordinance were passed by the government.

The Rowlatt Act[5] stirred nationwide agitation. Several nationalist leaders including Gandhiji actively participated in this movement, which finally concluded with the Amritsar holocaust.[6]

This chapter proposes to sketch the Indian experience with preventive detention despite having a humanistic and justice-oriented constitution. It also examines the regressive role played by the Supreme Court of India with respect to preventive detention.[7]

---

[3] Derek P. Jinks, *The Anatomy of an Institutionalized Emergency: Preventive Detention and Personal Liberty in India* 22 MICH. J. INT'L L. 311 (2001), 324, https://repository.law.umich.edu/mjil/vol22/iss2/3

[4] This repressive law was passed pursuant to the recommendation of a committee under Mr Justice Rowlatt. See https://www.oxfordreference.com/view/10.1093/oi/authority.20110803100431140

[5] The Anarchical and Revolutionary Crimes Act of 1919, prevalently known as the Rowlatt Act.

[6] BISHAMBHAR N. PANDE, A CENTENARY HISTORY OF THE INDIAN NATIONAL CONGRESS: 1885–1985 (Vol. 2, Academic Foundation Academic Found 2012), https://archive.org/details/centenaryhistory02pand

[7] P. K. TRIPATHI, SPOTLIGHTS ON CONSTITUTIONAL INTERPRETATION, 188 (N.M. Tripathi Publications, 1972).

CONSTITUTION MAKING: VESTED GOVERNMENTAL INTEREST
VIS-À-VIS CONSTITUTIONAL SENTIMENT

The Government of India Act, 1935, distributed the legislative powers between the Federal government and the states identically as was later embraced in the Constitution of 1950. The Act empowered the States to legislate on 'preventive detention connected with the maintenance of public order; persons subjected to such detention'.[8] Pursuant to this, many Provinces passed public safety acts.

The Constituent Assembly which drafted the constitution was also working as a provisional government and this fact paradoxically justified the provision for preventive detention as a necessary evil during peacetime.[9] The vested and dominant governmental feeling prevailed over constitutional sentiments which reflected in the statement of Alladi Krishnaswami Ayer[10]:

Having guaranteed personal liberty, having guaranteed that a person should not be detained or arrested for more than 24 hours, the problem necessarily had to be faced as to detention, because detention has become a necessary evil under the existing conditions of India. Even the most enthusiastic advocate of liberty says there are people in this land at the present day who are determined to undermine the Constitution and the State, and if we are to flourish, and if liberty of person and property is to be secured, unless that particular evil is removed or the State is invested with sufficient power to guard against that evil there will be no guarantee even for that individual liberty of which we are all desirous.

Sardar Patel was more concerned about united India and hence wanted to control the sabotaging activities of communists, RSS and other such groups. The speeches of Sardar Patel indicates the situation[11]:

Why are these Communists creating trouble there (Hyderabad)? How did they grow? To the Communists, my appeal may be in vain, because

---

[8] Item I of List II, Seventh Schedule to the Government of India Act, 1935.

[9] Jinks, *supra* note 3.

[10] CAD IX, 1536.

[11] VALLABHBHAI PATEL, FOR A UNITED INDIA, SPEECHES OF SARDAR PATEL, 1947–1950 (Publications Division, MIB, Government of India 1967).

they do not listen. I told them immediately after my release from jail last time that I was prepared to take all the Communists into the Congress, to forget the past and keep the doors open provided they give up violence and cease to draw their inspiration from foreign countries.

We are not going to allow them to play with fire so that the house is not set on fire. It would be criminal to allow young men to indulge in acts of violence and destruction, to let the lessons that our neighbouring countries have learnt be wasted on us. Thus I have spoken to the RSS and to the Communists.[12]

Preventive Detention Act, 1950, was passed considering the unstable political climate due to partition. But successive governments used this as a weapon to control their opponents and curtail citizenry liberty even though preventive detention laws are ordinary piece time legislations.

LEGITIMIZATION OF PREVENTIVE DETENTION LAW OUTSIDE EMERGENCY CONTEXT

Founded on ancient Indian philosophy and influenced by the liberal philosophies of *Aristotle, John Locke and John Rawls*,[13] the Constituent-Assembly of independent India was very passionate about giving life to the idea of India in an inclusive manner based on basic human values and principles of justice. These values were the humane content of the legal system which created a legitimate expectation for the people that governmental power will be systematized, exercised and controlled in all spheres of human life. Following the American traditions, the Constitution of India decided to build an equitable society based on principles of justice, liberty and individual freedom.

However, the Constitution of India conferred on the Parliament exclusive legislative power to legislate with respect to 'Preventive detention[14] for reasons connected with Defence, Foreign Affairs or the

---

[12] *Id.*

[13] Waheed Hussain, *The Common Good*, in STANFORD ENCYCLOPAEDIA OF PHILOSOPHY (Zalta ed, Stanford University 2018), https://plato.stanford.edu/entries/common-good/

[14] India strongly defended the legality of preventive detention outside emergency conditions on international forums.

Security of India; persons subjected to such detention'. Concurrent legislative powers were also given to the State legislatures to make laws with respect to 'Preventive detention for reasons connected with the security of a State, the maintenance of Public-order, or the maintenance of supplies and services essential to the community; persons subjected to such detention'.[15] An individual is also deprived of the normal right of legal defence if he is detained under preventive detention. Instead, Article 22 (5) provides a despicable substitute.[16] The right to be informed about the grounds of detention was too restricted by the next clause which enables the detaining authority to refuse the communication of such facts which is considered to be against the public interest.[17]

The sweeping curtailment of the right of complete legal defence in preventive detention cases was not only the low-water mark of the civil liberties placed so high in the constitutional scheme but also signposts the serious vulnerability spot that may demolish the entire edifice of fundamental rights. Governments ordinarily tend to abuse the preventive detention power to control spiteful adversaries.[18]

All successive governments in India have frequently and routinely used this power and enacted laws authorizing preventive detention, a power that is meant for emergencies. The Parliament of India passed the first comprehensive preventive detention law in the year 1950, that is, The Preventive Detention Act, originally for 1 year but continued in force for a long time. Both the Act and its application by the judiciary were based on the experience of the period immediately before the constitution.

While introducing the Preventive Detention Bill, Sardar Patel echoed the viewpoint of the drafters.[19] Patel was clear on two issues: *one* preventive detention was necessary and therefore he wanted to equip and arm the government to deal with any kind of emergency

---

[15] Entry 9 of List 1 (Union List), and Entry 3 of List III (Concurrent List), respectively.

[16] Item I of List II, *supra* note 8, at 189.

[17] *Id.*

[18] *Id.* at 189–90.

[19] Jinks, *supra* note 3.

and *two*; these laws would contravene fundamental rights protections recognized in the constitution.

The political condition in the wake of partition was nonetheless extraordinary; therefore, the Preventive Detention Act (PDA), 1950 authorised the government to detain someone in the name of public safety merely on suspicion.[20] In *A. K. Gopalan v. State of Madras*,[21] the first case brought before the Indian Supreme Court, the Court upheld the constitutionality of the PDA. The Court, in particular, observed that Article 22 of the Constitution constitutes a complete code on the essential procedural safeguards for preventive detention.[22] The PD Act was, though, confronted on the grounds of violation of Articles 14, 19, and 21, the apex court upheld the constitutional validity saying that it satisfied the provisions of Article 22 (5).

The PD Act expired in 1969 but very soon another draconian preventive detention law entitled Maintenance of Internal Security Act (MISA) was enacted. MISA enabled the government once again to arrest and detain a person for up to 1 year without trial. MISA was misused as a political weapon during the mid-1970's national emergency and finally lapsed in 1978.

PREVENTIVE DETENTION REGIME HUMANIZED BUT NOT ENFORCED

The 1975–77 Emergency saw embattled amendments which undermined the spirit of constitutionalism. The new Parliament on 30th April 1979 exercised its constituent power under Article 368 of the Constitution and enacted Section 3 of the Constitution (Forty-fourth Amendment) Act, 1978. The vital features of the said section were:

1. Period of detention under any preventive detention act was reduced from 3 to 2 months;
2. Advisory Board must give its opinion for the extension of detention period beyond 2 months before the expiry of 2 months;

---

[20] See R.K. AGRAWAL, THE NATIONAL SECURITY ACT 5–9 (2nd ed. 1993).
[21] *Supra* note 1.
[22] *Id.* at 30–39.

3. The composition of the Advisory Board has been specified so as to ensure the rule of law for the detenue in actual practice so that justice is not only done but seen to be done in case of preventive detention. The Board consists of a service judge of the appropriate High Court as the Chairman and two retired or serving High Court judges as members.

However, the Central government was empowered by Section 1(2) to notify various provisions of the Forty-fourth Amendment Act on such dates as it may, by notification, in the official gazette decide. It was also given the discretion to fix different dates for notifying different provisions of this Act. Parliament conferred on the Union Government as to when it would bring the amendment in to force by notification but not with any discretion that it will bring the amendment into force at all, so as to defeat Parliament's will in enacting the amendment.

National Security Act Conceived

Indira Gandhi once again returned to power and enacted a new preventive detention law, that is, the National Security Act (NSA), 1980, which continues till present. The NSA empowers the central and state governments to exploit preventive detention[23] in certain cases.[24] The central and state governments, as well as district magistrates and police commissioners,[25] are authorised to 'detain any person in order to prevent him from acting in any manner prejudicial to' state interest including public order and national security.[26] Any detention under NSA is required to be referred to Advisory Board within 3 weeks of detention and[27] the board has to give its report within 7 weeks of detention.[28] Advisory Board consists of Judges of the High Court or persons qualified

---

[23] Jinks, *supra* note 3.

[24] NSA § 3.

[25] The authority to issue detention order may be delegated by the executive to local district magistrates or commissioners of police for specified time period which may go up to 3 months at a time. See NSA § 3(3).

[26] NSA § 3(l)(a).

[27] *Id.* § 10.

[28] *Id.* § 11.

to be appointed as the judge of a High Court. However, a person detained does not have the right to be legally represented.[29]

The design and application of NSA raised many baffling jurisprudential questions and as a result, it produced a very complex series of case laws construing virtually each and every phrase of the NSA.[30] The NSA was too far from the standards of international human rights.

The nature and justification of preventive detention laws in India have been the subject matter of court's scrutiny generally on four parameters: (1) the grounds upon which detention orders may be issued, (2) the subjective satisfaction[31] of the detaining authority (3) the quasi-judicial nature of the executive review process,[32] and (4) the procedural rights guaranteed to detainees.[33]

Indian legal regime allows detention even in absence of any alleged wrongdoing on the vague and broad grounds of 'public order' and 'national security'. Neither the constitution nor any Acts endeavoured to define the range of acts that may be considered against public order and national security or the range of acts that supports the inference that an individual is likely to indulge in such acts. This advances a fundamental challenge to the legality and legitimacy of preventive detention.

---

[29] *Id.* § 9(2).

[30] A person detained under NSA must be communicated the grounds of detention within 5 days which may be extended to 10 days in exceptional circumstances. The maximum permissible period of detention under NSA is 12 months.

[31] The courts as usual do not seem to be interested in lifting the veil of subjective satisfaction with a view to appreciate its objective sufficiently. [*See* Anil Dey v. State of West Bengal]. They have however, emphasized that the satisfaction should be 'honest and real, and not fanciful and imaginary'. The NSA was amended in order to limit the scope of non-application of mind and provided that the courts will consider the identified 'grounds' of detention as severable.

[32] The NSA sets the similar procedure for detention as provided for arrest under the Code of Criminal Procedure.

[33] This progressive procedural rights regime guaranteed by the Constitution under Article 21 and 22 is not applicable in preventive detention cases. These minimum guarantees fall short of established international human rights standards. The Court in A. K. Roy v. Union of India, A.I.R. 1982 S.C. 710, first acknowledged the significance of this progressive right but later expressed its feebleness due to destitute choice given under Article 22 (3) (b) read with Article 22 (1).

The absence of clear legislative policy shifts unnecessary and huge discretion on the courts to review whether the action of authorities threatens public order and national security. Unfortunately, the judicial trend has also failed to establish a clear and consistent jurisprudence on all the above-mentioned four crucial parameters.

The Supreme Court in *Licil Antony v State of Kerala* held that:

> There should be 'proximate and live link' between detention grounds and the purpose of detention. This test of proximity is not a mechanical or rigid test, but the court has to ensure in each case of a delay that such a link is not broken. If such delay is caused by the detenu to avoid detention, then such a link will not be considered to be broken. Further, the detention should be made on some valid grounds and not on some stale grounds.[34]

In *Ramesh Yadav v District Magistrate,* the Supreme Court held that:

> person cannot be detained merely on the ground that the detenu, being an under-trial prisoner, was likely to be released on bail.[35]

Broad sweeping powers in the hands of the executive and secret board proceedings predictably have led to the misuse of NSA. NCRB data suggests an upward rise: 697 NSA detainees in 2018 against 501 in 2017. By August 2020, the Yogi Adityanath Government in Uttar Pradesh has invoked this draconian law against 139 people. Out of these 76 cases for cow slaughter, 13 linked to anti-Citizenship Amendment Act protests in the state, six to crimes against women and children, and 37 to heinous crimes.

EVER-SCEPTICAL AND INCONSISTENT SUPREME COURT

With the dusk of emergency, the apex court opened its doors to reinstate its institutional legitimacy and also the content of fundamental rights. This prompted opinions such as *Maneka Gandhi*[36] which

---

[34] (2014) 11 S.C.C. 326.
[35] (1985) 4 S.C.C. 232.
[36] A.I.R. 1978 S.C. 597.

stretched the scope of Article 21 to include later many un-enumerated rights including the right to counsel, which was broader than Article 22(1) guarantee. While Article 22(1) guaranteed a right to counsel *of choice*, Article 21 included within it a *right to* counsel, thus prohibiting deprivation of life and personal liberty made in absence of legal aid.

This recognition of the significance of legal assistance with respect to personal liberty also discoursed in the sphere of preventive detention. Subsequent benches of the Court in *Gopalanachari v. State of Kerala*[37] and *Nand Lal Bajaj*[38] highlighted the significance of legal assistance, particularly in those cases where detention is made without a trial. The court observed that a detenu still had a right to *request* legal assistance which must be considered by the state. This thought was eventually subject to judicial review, providing some degree of oversight. Justice Krishna Iyer observed:

> Preventive sections privative of freedom, if incautiously proved by indolent judicial processes, may do deeper injury. They will have the effect of detention of one who has not been held guilty of a crime and carry with it the judicial imprimatur, to boot. To call a man dangerous is itself dangerous; to call a man desperate is to affix a desperate adjective to stigmatise a person as hazardous to the community is itself a judicial hazard unless compulsive testimony carrying credence is abundantly available.[39]

In *Nand Lal Bajaj* also the court expressed its anguish on the scheme of preventive detention and observed:

> It is incomprehensible that a person committing a crime should have under Art. 22(1) of the Constitution the right to consult and be defended by a legal practitioner of his choice, but a person under preventive detention, more often than not for his political beliefs, should be deprived of this valuable right.[40]

---

[37] A.I.R. 1981 S.C. 674.
[38] A.I.R. 1981 S.C. 2041.
[39] Gopalanachari, *supra* note 37.
[40] Nand Lal Bajaj, *supra* note 38.

The court further observed:

> It cannot be denied that preventive detention is an anachronism in a democratic society like ours. The detention of individuals without trial for any length of time, however short, is wholly inconsistent with the basic ideals of a parliamentary system of government. In the nature of things, under the law as it exists, a person under preventive detention is not entitled to legal assistance.[41]

Because this question was not a fact in the issue, the above-mentioned remarks would remain as *obiter dicta*.

In *Maneka Gandhi*, the Supreme Court muscularly echoed that Articles 14, 19, and 21 would offer a composite test for any legislation or executive action rather than examining it in silos. It also enthusiastically supplanted 'procedure established by law' in Article 21, with 'Due Process' despite the extensive debates in the Constituent Assembly pointing to the contrary. Yet, the attitude of the Supreme Court with respect to preventive detention law has not changed. In this context, the SC examined the constitutional validity of the National Security Act in *A.K. Roy v. Union of India*.[42] The court not only entirely upheld the validity of the NSA but also declined to ask the government to implement the amendments made in Article 22 (4) to (7) by the Constitution (Forty-fourth Amendment) Act. The Bench unanimously upheld the validity of Section 11(4) of the NSA which deprived detenues the right of legal representation before Advisory Boards. The Bench relied upon Article 22(3)(b) and held that the right to consult and be defended by a counsel of choice under Article 22(1) cannot be applicable in preventive detention cases. The Bench also opined that preventive detention laws will have to pass the test of Articles 14, 19 and 21 in addition to Article 22. The Court was not swayed by the argument that since Article 22(3) (b) only excluded Articles 22(1) and (2), the right to counsel under Article 21 will still be available. The majority branded it 'impossible' on the

---

[41] *Id.*

[42] A.I.R. 1982 S.C. 710.

ground that what one part of the Constitution had denied, another cannot provide:

> It would be stretching the language of Articles 19 and 21 a little too far to hold that what is regarded as reasonable by Article 22(3)(b) must be regarded as unreasonable within the meaning of those articles. For illustrating this point, we may take the example of law which provides that an enemy alien need not be produced before a magistrate within twenty-four hours of his arrest or detention in custody. If the right of production before the magistrate within 24 hours of the arrest is expressly denied to the enemy alien by Article 22(3)(a), it would be impossible to hold that the said right is nevertheless available to him by reason of the provisions contained in Article 21.[43]

The Bench further held that the original text of the Constitution was *per se* 'just, fair, and reasonable' and so could not fall foul of Article 19 or 21. It means, if the *original* text of the *constitution provided that* detenue do not get legal assistance, it would be highly unjustified to construe that a law not providing this right is unconstitutional because of violation of another right contained in Article 21. However, at the end of the verdict, the Bench tried to moderate the severity of this conclusion which it had reached 'regretfully'. The Bench observed that where the government engaged counsel, a detenu must also be provided a similar opportunity. In addition, detenu can seek help from a 'friend' in proceedings before the Advisory Board.

While dealing with Section 3 of the Constitutional (Forty-fourth Amendment) Act, 1978, the Constitution Bench in *A. K. Roy* trusted the wisdom of the Central Government to decide with respect to the implementation of various provisions of the 44th Amendment. However, it opined that the Parliament, in no circumstances, would have anticipated that the Government will use a veto over its constituent will by not notifying Amendment at all.[44]

In a similar issue where the Union Government failed to notify Section 30 of the Advocates Act, 1961, for 27 years, the Supreme Court

---

[43] *Id.*
[44] *Id.*

in *Aeltemesh Rein v. Union of India*[45] while accepting that it cannot issue a writ of mandamus to Central Government to bring a statute into force, decided to issue a writ in the nature of mandamus to consider whether the time for bringing Section 30 of the Advocates Act, 1961, into force has arrived or not, since the discretionary power vested in the executive to notify the amended Act had to be exercised in a just, fair and reasonable manner. The Supreme Court directed the Central Government to consider within a reasonable time the question of whether it should bring Section 30 of the Act into force.[46]

In *Common Cause v. Union of India*,[47] the inaction of the Union of India to the Delhi Rent Act, 1995,[48] was again subjected to judicial review by the apex court. But apex court once again abandoned its obligation and held that when the legislature itself has vested the power in the Central Government to notify the date of commencement of Act, then, the Government is well within its domain to take into consideration various facts while considering when the Act should be brought into force or not. No mandamus can be issued to the Central Government to issue the notification.[49]

The issue of subjecting to judicial review the exercise of discretion by the Union of India to bring into force a duly enacted amendment is an issue of the fundamental right to liberty under Article 21 because in this case Section 3 of the 44th Amendment concerned the preventive detention of persons. The reasonable, fair, and just procedure under Article 21 as mandated since the decision of *Maneka Gandhi* includes the bona fide application of mind by the executive in exercising the discretion conferred on it by Parliament to bring or not to bring an amendment in force. The Union of India has not applied its mind

---

[45] A.I.R. 1988 S.C. 1768.

[46] The apex court further used its decision in *Aeltemesh Rein* by specifically examining the reasons stated by Union of India on affidavit as to why for about 20 years it had not brought into force the Industrial Dispute Amendment Act, 1982.

[47] A.I.R. 2003 S.C. 4493.

[48] Section 1(3) of the Act delegated power to Central Government to implement the Act on such date as it may deem appropriate.

[49] See also Union of India vs. Shree Gajanan Maharaj Sansthan, (2002) 5 S.C.C. 44.

or not applied it in a bona fide manner to the exercise of its discretion to bring or not to bring Section 3 of the Constitution (Forty-fourth Amendment) Act, 1978, into force by a notification, since all other amendments of the various Acts under the same Constitution Amendment Act, 1978, have already been notified by the government. This is hostile discrimination as far as the personal liberty of a person detained under any preventive detention law is concerned.

INSTITUTIONALIZED DEROGATORY PREVENTIVE DETENTION REGIME: THE UNLAWFUL ACTIVITIES (PREVENTION) ACT

Pursuant to the acceptance of the recommendations of the Committee on National Integration and Regionalization appointed by the National Integration Council, the Constitution (Sixteenth Amendment) Act, 1963, was enacted. In furtherance of this, the Parliament enacted the Unlawful Activities (Prevention) Act, 1967, to provide effective prevention of certain unlawful activities of individuals, associations, terrorist activities, and matters connected therewith. The UAPA was amended in the years 2004, 2008, 2013 by the governments to make it more severe.

In 2016, 922 cases, in 2017, 901 cases and in 2018, 1,182 cases were registered under UAPA.[50] 92 per cent of these cases were registered in five states (Uttar Pradesh, Jammu and Kashmir, Assam, Jharkhand and Manipur).[51] Its rampant misuse can be illustrated by the example that the police invoked this draconian law to book several people for using social media via a VPN. UAPA faced severe criticism because it was used to curb dissent.[52]

The NCRB in addition to these offences announced a new category of offence, that is, 'violence by anti-national elements'. This was further classified into four categories: (a) north-east insurgents, (b) 'Jihadi'

---

[50] See NCRB Data.

[51] See Pooja Dantewadia & Vishnu Padmanabhan, *Sedition Cases in India: What Data Says?* MINT, https://www.livemint.com/news/india/sedition-cases-in-india-what-data-says-11582557299440.html

[52] *Id.*

terrorists (c) Naxalites and (d) other terrorists. Like UAPA, cases of sedition also increased in the present regime.[53]

UAPA initially applied specifically to what was termed 'unlawful activity'. But the Act was once again amended in August 2019 by the government to add certain provisions relating to various facets of terrorism. This term is defined[54] in terms of actions taken by associations which are intended to or which support 'the cession of a part of the territory of India or the secession of a part of the territory of India from the Union'; or which incite others to bring about cession or secession; or which disclaim, question, disrupt or are intended to disrupt the 'sovereignty and territorial integrity of India'. The term 'action' has been given broad amplitude, and extends to the commission of an act; words (either spoken or written); signs; and visible representation. It may be noted that the Act treated actions as unlawful only if they were committed by 'associations' defined in Clause (g), and not by individuals. The recent amendments in UAPA expanded its scope to include terrorist activities.

The UAPA Amendment Act, 2019

The result of the recent amendment is a statute that strongly resembles its predecessors TADA and POTA, which are in fact, severer than them. **Both TADA and POTA had sunset clauses for 3 and 2 years, respectively, but UAPA has taken the shape of anti-terrorism law without any sunset clause.** The problems in the law are manifolds such as the wide definition of terrorism, the presumption of guilt, period of police remand, denial of bail, and breach of privacy and liberty.

1. The amended Act expanded the definition of terrorist activities to individuals. Further, the definition of 'terrorism' in Section 15 is drafted in extremely wide terms. The component of the *mens rea* set out in Clause (1) concerns the intention or likelihood of striking terror among sections of the populace in India or abroad. But

---

[53] *Id.*
[54] UAPA, S. 2(f).

the terms such as 'terror,' intention or likelihood of threatening are not defined anywhere. 'Economic security' has been defined in Section 2(ea) to include 'financial, monetary and fiscal stability, security of means of production and distribution, food security, livelihood security, energy security, ecological and environmental security.' None of these terms have been defined, which makes it difficult to ascertain when these threats constitute acts of terrorism. Moreover, the presence of terms such as 'including' in Section 2(ea); and 'by any other means of whatever nature' and 'any other person' in Section 15 makes the definition of terrorism in the statute an inclusive and not an exhaustive one.

2. The amendment envisages two circumstances[55]: one; where arms, explosives, or other substances reasonably believed to be used for committing a terrorist act are recovered from the possession of the accused; and two; where fingerprints or other 'definitive evidence' suggesting the involvement of the accused is found. In either circumstance, the accused are presumed to have committed the crime, and the burden shifts to them to establish their innocence. The circumstances in which the burden of proof shifts are too broad and it can give rise to apprehensions of evidence being planted in order to reverse the presumption of innocence. Further, Section 43E is in certain aspects inclusive in character, as indicated by the use of terms such as 'other substances of a similar nature in Clause (a).

3. The amendment increases the period of police remand from 15 days to 30 days, thereby giving rise to apprehensions of custodial torture and ill-treatment. The period of judicial remand is increased to a blanket 90 days, regardless of the gravity of the offence.[56] More consequentially, the proviso to sub-clause (b) enhances the time limit of judicial custody to a maximum of 180 days. This means that for about 6 months the accused remains in custody without even a charge sheet being filed.

4. The UAPA excludes Section 438, CrPC 1973[57] from applying to terrorist acts.[58] Clause (e) stipulates that no person shall be released

---

[55] *Id*. Section 43E.
[56] *Id*. Section 43D (2).
[57] Direction for grant of bail to person apprehending arrest.
[58] UAPA, Section 43D (2) (e).

on bail or on his own bond unless the Public Prosecutor is heard. Clause (f) operates independently from Clause (e) and states that if the court is satisfied that the case diary or the investigating officer's report under 173, CrPC 1973 sustain a reasonable belief that the accusations against the person are *prima facie* true, then bail shall not be granted. These provisions make securing bail almost impossible; in fact, they transform bail into a narrow exception rather than the norm. Clause (e) makes no stipulations as to what the public prosecutor needs to establish; the stipulations of Clause (f) reduce to little more than the court's subjective satisfaction that a reasonable *prima facie* case exists.

5. The transfer of broad and increased powers of investigation has allowed searches, seizures and arrests based on 'personal knowledge' of the police officers with prior approval of only the Director-General of Police, which means without a written validation from a superior judicial authority. This interferes with the privacy[59] and liberty of individuals which is not only by a fundamental right but also against international standards.[60]

CONCLUSION

Preventive detention is a despicable evil that negates the essence of libertarian philosophy. Justice B.K. Mukherjee in *A. K. Gopalan v. State of Madras* expressed doubts on the wisdom and propriety of making express provisions relating to preventive detention in the constitution. However, considering the political climate of partition, it was justified to state that democracy needs protection at both ends. While it needs to be protected against uncontrolled executive power, equally it requires protection against any internal forces trying to sabotage the democratic constitution. It appeared realistic that time to make preventive detention constitutionally permitted but keeping all

---

[59] A Nine-judge bench of Supreme Court in Justice K.S. Puttaswamy v. Union of India, (2017) 10 S.C.C. 1, held that privacy is an attribute of human dignity.

[60] It is contrary to the provisions of the International Convention on Civil and Political Rights (ICCPR), which guarantees against any arbitrary and unlawful interference with a person's privacy.

through preventive detention as a routine practice raises serious doubts. Constitution provided certain restrictions on the exercise of this power and also provide safeguards which were further fortified in 1978 but failed to implement which again raises serious doubts on the intention and *modus operandi* of the executive.

The courts have also been suspicious of declaring detention orders invalid on account of the vagueness of the grounds communicated to the detenu.[61] As a result of this muddled jurisprudence, the courts have endorsed a very broad interpretation of 'acts prejudicial to the maintenance of public order'. For instance, courts have upheld detention orders on grounds that detenu had committed robbery,[62] associated with a notorious gang of dacoits,[63] brandished and fired a weapon in a public place,[64] hurled stones at the car of his political opponents,[65] set fire to a school building, threatened violence to coerce a contractor to provide him employment[66] and fired at police officers.[67]

So, preventive detention is one area where all the principal organs of the State have been betrayed. Preventive detention will remain in the constitutional scheme, however, a well-defined criterion specifying limited circumstances in which preventive detention powers may be exercised must be ensured. These standards must be designed to allow meaningful judicial review of the official's actions.

FUTURE COURSE OF ACTION

1. The first reform which is required is that the Government should bring Section 3 of the Forty-fourth Amendment Act, 1978, into effect, thereby reducing the permitted period of detention to 2 months.

---

[61] Dr. Ram Krishan Bharadwaj vs. The State of Delhi, A.I.R. 1953 S.C. 318.

[62] Gora v. State of West Bengal, A.I.R. 1975 S.C. 473.

[63] Rajendra Kumar v. Superintendent, District Jail Agra, 1985 Cr. L.J. 999, 1004.

[64] Kali Charan Mal v. State of West Bengal, A.I.R. 1975 S.C. 999.

[65] Somaresh Chandra Bose v. Dist. Magistrate, Burdwan, (1972) 2 S.C.C. 476.

[66] Yogendra Singh v. State of Bihar, 1984 B.B.C.J. 727 (Pat); Madhu v. Police Commissioner, Thana, 1985 Cr. L.J. 341, 344 (Bom.).

[67] Kanu Biswas v. State of West Bengal, A.I.R. 1972 S.C. 1656.

2. There seems to be too much secrecy in the operation of the preventive detention and proceedings of the advisory board. The public has an interest in knowing generally about the operation of law, grounds of detention, factual allegations against him, probable prejudicial acts sought to be prevented by means of detention; how do the advisory boards view the allegations, the grounds, the apprehensions, and the representations; in what kind of cases do these boards seek more information from the appropriate government; in what circumstances, if at all, do advisory boards report that there is no sufficient cause of detention. This requires lifting the blanket provision of secrecy from the proceedings and reports of the advisory boards and arranging for adequate publicity of all but specified cases, or, at least, of specified cases.

3. The possibility of providing legal assistance also needs attention. The appearance of a lawyer need not necessarily make the proceeding judicial process but it may help the detenu understand the ground communicated to him and may help him in preparing his defence. It may perhaps help to obviate the difficulties created by the vagueness of the grounds communicated to the detenu which is so normally predominant.

4. The current legal regime for preventive detention also needs severe surgery. The rising number of cases and abysmally low conviction rate under the current UAPA strikingly shows that it is not meant for conviction. The purpose of this law is only to detain people without any accountability on the part of the administration. The detention eventually might result in acquittal but who shall be responsible for the substantial time of one's life detained in jail. Considering the hard constitutional reality, the following amendments may be made to the existing regime to avoid excessive use of police power.

   a. The definition of terrorism needs to be revised and made more specific. The inclusive terms present in the definition need to be removed. An exhaustive and restrictive definition of terrorism will restrict the discretion of authorities.

   b. Section 43 E should be amended so that the reversal of the presumption of innocence is restricted to only exceptional situations. Specifically, mere possession should not be made a ground for reversal, so as to minimize the possibility of evidence being planted. Also, inclusive terms such as 'other substances of a similar nature should be removed from the provision.

c. The provision enhancing police remand should be removed. If at all extending judicial remand to 180 days is necessary, surely it is justified only in the most exceptional cases, and not as a matter of routine. Hence the requirement for extending judicial remand beyond 90 days should be made more stringent.

d. Bail should be made the rule and not the exception. Denial of bail must be made valid only on specific grounds, such as the possibility of tampering with evidence, or influencing witnesses, or committing further crimes, etc. Specific grounds for refusing bail should be incorporated into the statute.

e. Finally, there must be a provision for initiating mandatory legal action against errant officers who allegedly invoke the stringent provisions of NSA or UAPA wrongfully. Government must also be vicariously held responsible if the detention is proven wrong.

Chapter 5

Preventive Detentions in India
Constitutional 'Sanctions' and 'Safeguards'

P. Puneeth

INTRODUCTION

Preventive detention has a pre-constitutional history in India. It is a legacy of the British Empire.[1] It is, doubtlessly, one of the extraordinary measures as it envisages the detention of free individuals without criminal charge or trial or prospect thereof. Though it is incompatible with the constitutional guarantee of individual freedom, the Constitution of India accords explicit sanctions for preventive detention purportedly to enable the 'state' to prevent the possible abuse of those freedoms by anti-social and subversive elements, which might imperil the collective interest of the state/society. The Constitution lays down the basic framework by authorizing both the Parliament and State Legislatures to enact preventive detention laws for specific purposes. It permits preventive detentions both during wartime as well as peacetime if so authorized by a law enacted by the competent legislature. The powers of both the Parliament and the State Legislatures to enact preventive detention laws are, however, hedged with certain safeguards, which are guaranteed as fundamental rights in Part III of the Indian Constitution.

---

[1] GRANVILLE AUSTIN, THE INDIAN CONSTITUTION—CORNERSTONE OF A NATION (OUP 2003).

These safeguards are provided to mitigate the harshness of preventive detention laws and to balance the interests of the individuals, on the one hand, and that of the nation/society, on the other.

This chapter seeks to examine to what extent and for what purposes the Constitution sanctions preventive detentions and the efficacy of safeguards provided to prevent the possible abuse of power to enact preventive detention laws and detain individuals under such laws.

PREVENTIVE DETENTIONS IN INDIA BEFORE INDEPENDENCE

Preventive detention is distinct from both pre-trial and punitive detentions known under criminal law. Their purposes are entirely different. Whereas the pre-trial detentions are made prior to the commencement of or, in some cases, during the trial on criminal charges. Punitive detentions are made after a person is found guilty of having committed an offence. One of the basic purposes of pre-trial detention is to secure the attendance of the person, who has been accused of having committed an offence, at the trial and the purpose of punitive detention is to punish the person in case of conviction after the completion of the trial.

The objective of preventive detention is entirely different. As Lord Finlay stated, the word 'preventive' refers 'not to a punitive but precautionary measure'.[2] Whereas punitive detention comes after the illegal act is actually committed and its commission is proved in a court of law by following established procedure, preventive detention is based on reasonable apprehension of wrongdoing in the (immediate) future.[3] It is not even based on the accusation of having committed an offence, much less the proof thereof. The basis of preventive detention is the suspicion or subjective opinion of the detaining authority that there is a reasonable probability that a person would commit certain subversive or anti-social acts. The person subjected to preventive detention has no right to defend oneself in a court of law against any charge for any specific offence as there exists no such charge in the first place. In simple words, preventive detention is based on no accusations, no

---

[2] Rex v. Halliday, 1917 A.C. 260.
[3] Lokhinarayan v. Province of Bihar (1950) S.C.J. 32.

charges, and no trial but mere suspicion. The purpose of preventive detention is not to punish but to prevent the person, who is likely, in the opinion of the detaining authority, to indulge in subversive activities from doing so.[4] Such detentions are made not merely to prevent individuals from acting in a 'particular way' but also from achieving a 'particular objective'.[5]

Preventive Detention was introduced in India by the British. The East India Company Act, 1784 (well known as Pitt's India Act), was the earliest law that authorized preventive detention. Ever since then, in order to keep and reinforce preventive detention powers throughout their reign, the British enacted various preventive detention laws *viz.*, The Bengal State Prisoners' Regulation, 1818; the Defence of India Act, 1915; the Anarchical and Revolutionary Crimes Act, 1919 (Rowlatt Act), and the Defence of India Act, 1939. Preventive detention has, thus, had more than 150 years of history by the time the Constituent Assembly embarked upon the task of drafting the Constitution for the governance of free India.

CONSTITUTIONAL SANCTIONS FOR PREVENTIVE DETENTIONS

The Constitution of India is the fundamental law of governance. Respect for basic human rights is the central pillar of the governance structure envisaged in the Constitution. The framers of the Indian Constitution, have recognized certain basic human rights and these rights were accorded the sacrosanct status of fundamental rights in the Constitution. Though the resolve of the freedom fighters was to guarantee them 'in a manner which will not permit their withdrawal under any circumstances',[6] the framers of the Constitution did not (perhaps, could not) ensure that. In addition to the reasonable restrictions, they allowed the fundamental rights to be withdrawn or curtailed to a greater

---

[4] Chowdarapu Raghunandan v. State of Tamil Nadu, (2002) 3 S.C.C. 754.

[5] Rajesh Gulati v. Govt. of NCT of Delhi, (2002) 7 S.C.C. 129.

[6] The Nehru Committee appointed by the All Parties Conference has stated in its report submitted in 1928 that 'It is obvious that our first care should be to have our fundamental rights guaranteed in a manner which will not permit their withdrawal under any circumstances'.

extent by incorporating certain extraordinary provisions providing for the enactment of preventive detention and martial laws and also for the proclamation of emergency.

Circumstances prevailing at the time of enactment of the Constitution perhaps made the framers hedge the rights with many restrictions and also to provide for their withdrawal in some cases. The partition of the country and also the process of unification of states, in the aftermath of independence, have created such conditions, which warranted the need for writing into the Constitution certain extraordinary provisions.

The provisions for preventive detention, though considered to be apparently incompatible with the constitutional promises of individual freedoms, have been written into the Constitution purportedly to prevent the abuse of such freedom by anti-social and subversive elements to the detriment of national interest. The incompatibility of preventive detention with the fundamental rights was acknowledged by Patanjali Shastri, J. as early as in 1950 in *A.K. Gopalan* v. the *State of Madras*.[7] He, however, found and articulated the rationale for its inclusion notwithstanding the incompatibility. He observed thus[8]:

> This sinister-looking feature, so strangely out of place in a democratic Constitution, which invests personal Liberty with the sacrosanctity of a fundamental right, and so incompatible with the promises of its preamble, is doubtless designed to prevent the abuse of freedom by anti-social and subversive elements which might imperil the national welfare of the infant republic.

It may be of value to note that preventive detention is not unknown in other democratic countries. Countries like UK, USA and Australia permit it but mostly as a wartime or emergency measure. The Constitution of India authorizes both the Parliament and the State Legislatures to enact preventive detention laws that can be enforced if so permitted by such laws, both during wartime as well as peacetime. The need may have been felt to permit preventive detention even during

---

[7] 1950 S.C.R. 88.
[8] *Id.*, para 134.

peacetime owing to unstable law and order situations, etc. during the formative years of the country.

Whereas it is true that the Constitution of India authorizes both the Parliament and the State Legislatures to enact preventive detention laws, which can be enforced both during the war and peace, it confers powers on them to enact such laws 'only' on specific grounds. The powers of both the Parliament and State Legislatures to enact preventive detention laws can be located in Article 246 of the Constitution. It confers on them the power to legislate over different 'fields of legislation' allotted to them in different lists of the schedule-VII of the Constitution. Schedule VII contains three different lists *viz.*, union list, state list and concurrent list. The union list (Entry-9) and the concurrent list (Entry-3) contain specific entries relating to preventive detention and the state list does not contain any such entry. It is to be noted that by virtue of Article 246(1), the Parliament has the exclusive power to legislate on the fields of legislation enumerated in the union list and by virtue of Article 246(2), the Parliament and, subject to its power, the State legislatures too have the legislative competence to legislate on the fields of legislation enumerated in the concurrent list.

Both the aforementioned entries contain three grounds each. The Parliament, under Article 246(1) read with Entry 9 of the union list, has the exclusive power to enact preventive detention law(s) for reasons connected with: (a) defence, (b) foreign affairs or (c) security of India. Under Article 246(2) read with Entry-3 of the concurrent list, both the Parliament and the State Legislatures have legislative competence to enact preventive detention laws for reasons connected with: (a) security of a state, (b) maintenance of public order, or (c) maintenance of supplies and services essential to the community.

It is pertinent to note that the Constitution explicitly authorizes preventive detention only for reasons connected with the aforementioned six grounds. Further, it is amply clear from the above that the Parliament, compared to the State Legislatures, has wider legislative powers in the matter of preventive detention as it can enact laws providing for preventive detention for reasons connected with all the six grounds mentioned in both Entry-9 (union list) and Entry-3 (concurrent list) whereas the State Legislatures can enact such laws only for reasons connected with the three grounds mentioned in the latter entry. It is also to be noted that the power of the State Legislatures under Article 246(2) to enact laws on the subject matters in the concurrent list is inferior to the Power of the Parliament.[9]

Having regard to the well-established cardinal principle of interpretation of legislative entries in the Schedule-VII that 'they shall be given the widest scope of which their meaning is fairly capable',[10] it can reasonably be stated that the aforementioned six grounds are very broad and create wide space for enacting preventive detention laws in India. Further the identical phrase 'preventive detention for reasons connected with…' in both the entries also indicates that as long as the law in question is relatable to any of the grounds specified in those entries, no exception can be taken to such law. This can be inferred from the observations of the apex court made in *Attorney General for India* v. *Amratlal Prajivandas*.[11] While rejecting the arguments of the petitioners that the Conservation of Foreign Exchange and Prevention of Smuggling Activities Act, 1974 (COFEPOSA), which provide for preventive detention, is not relatable either to Entry 9 of the union list or to Entry 3 of the concurrent list, the court opined:[12]

COFEPOSA is clearly relatable to Entry 3 of List III inasmuch as it provides for preventive detention for reasons connected with the security of the State… 'Security of a State' is a much wider expression. A State with a weak and vulnerable economy cannot guard its security well. It will be an easy prey to economic colonisers. …In the modern world, the security of a State is ensured not so much by physical might but by economic strength… It is, therefore, idle to contend that COFEPOSA is unrelated to the security of the State.

It is, thus, clear that as long as there exists some (reasonable) connection between the law in question and any of the grounds specified in those entries, the same cannot be said to be beyond the legislative

---

[9] See, Article 254.

[10] Union of India v. Shah Goverdhan L. Kabra Teachers' College, (2002) 8 S.C.C. 228, Para 6.

[11] (1994) 5 S.C.C. 54.

[12] *Id.*, para 23.

competence. The position seems to be fairly well settled. The important question, however, is whether the aforesaid two entries exhaust the entire legislative area of the Parliament to enact preventive detentions law(s)? Or, in other words, can the Parliament enact preventive detention law for reasons not connected with any of the six grounds mentioned in those entries?

If the rule *expressio unius est exclusio alterius* is adopted to interpret the entries, the answer to the latter question would be in the negative. Given the extraordinary nature of the preventive detention and its incompatibility with the constitutional guarantee of individual freedoms, it would have been appropriate to adopt the said rule of interpretation and restrict the power of the Parliament to enact preventive detention laws only for reasons connected with the grounds enumerated in the aforesaid Entries 9 and 3 and also of the State Legislatures to the grounds enumerated only in the latter. But the apex court does not seem to hold this view. In *Attorney General*,[13] the nine-judge constitutional bench of the apex court, after holding that the COFEPOSA is relatable to 'security of the state' and it is idle to contend otherwise, went on to observe, in its unanimous judgment, that:[14]

> Be that as it may, it is not necessary to pursue this line of reasoning since we are in total agreement with the approach evolved in *Union of India* v. *H.S. Dhillon* [(1971) 2 S.C.C. 779]... The test evolved in the said decision is this in short: Where the legislative competence of Parliament to enact a particular statute is questioned, one must look at the several entries in List II to find out... whether the said statute is relatable to any of those entries. If the statute does not relate to any of the entries in List II, no further inquiry is necessary. It must be held that Parliament is competent to enact that statute whether by virtue of the entries in List I and List III or by virtue of Article 248 read with Entry 97 of List I. In this case, it is not even suggested that either of the two enactments in question are relatable to any of the entries in

---

[13] Attorney General for India, *supra* note 11.

[14] *Id.*, para 23. In this case, the court was examining the legislative competence of the Parliament to enact COFEPOSA and Smugglers and Foreign Exchange Manipulators (Forfeiture of Property) Act, 1976. For COFEPOSA, also see Manekben v. Union of India, I.L.R. 1975 Del. 820.

List II. If so, we need not go further and enquire to which entry or entries do these Acts relate. It should be held that Parliament did have the competence to enact them.

There is no gainsaying that the test relied upon by the bench is well established and consistently followed for determining the legislative competence of the Parliament. In view of the general scheme of distribution of legislative powers envisaged under the Constitution, only those fields of legislation earmarked and assigned to the states exclusively (i.e., subject matters in the state list) are prohibited for the Parliament to legislate (except in certain cases) but every other field is open to it. If a particular legislation enacted by the Parliament is not relatable in 'pith and substance' to any of the subject-matters enumerated in the state list, it is well within the competence of the Parliament.

The most pertinent question, however, is just because the Parliament has legislative competence to legislate on any field (except the ones in the state list), does that mean that it can enact preventive detention laws for reasons connected with any of the fields over which it has legislative competence? The Constitution bench answered this question in the affirmative that too in passing without thorough analysis. The bench said, as stated above, '[I]f the statute does not relate to any of the entries in List II (state list), no further inquiry is necessary'. The fact that the bench said so for upholding the legislative competence of the Parliament to enact COFEPOSA, which provides for preventive detention, clearly implies that the preventive detention law can be enacted by the Parliament for reasons connected with any of the subject matters in any of the entries in the Union list or concurrent list or even in the exercise of its residuary legislative power.

If that is so, then, by analogy, even the State Legislatures can also enact laws providing for preventive detention for reasons connected with any of the subject matter in any of the entries in the state list or concurrent list.

According to the apex court, the grounds mentioned in Entry 9 (union list) and Entry 3 (concurrent list) are not exhaustive of the entire legislative area of the Parliament or the State Legislature, as the case may be, to enact preventive detention law(s). Their power to enact preventive detention law is as wide as their general legislative powers. They can enact laws providing for preventive detentions for reasons connected with any of the subject matters over which they have legislative powers. This interpretation does not seem to be in accord with the intention of the framers of the Constitution. Had they intended to confer such wide powers on them to enact preventive detention laws for any reason, they would not have included two specific entries explicitly providing for it. Instead, they would have included, at the end of each list, entries identical with Entry 93 (union list) and Entry 64 (state list). Both entries read: 'Offences against laws with respect to any of the matters in this List'. Similarly, if the idea of the framers was to empower the Parliament and the State Legislatures to enact preventive detention laws with respect to any of the matters over which they have legislative competence, the framers would (or could) have added, at the end of each list, identical legislative entries stating: Preventive detention for reasons connected with any of the matters in this list. But that is not what the framers chose to do. It clearly indicates that the idea was to restrict preventive detention, which is an extraordinary measure, to only those grounds specified in the aforementioned Entries 9 and 3. Though the Constitution has sanctioned it for limited purposes, the constitution bench has dramatically, albeit unjustifiably, expanded the power to enact preventive detention laws.

If the interpretation accorded by the constitution bench of the apex court prevails, the Parliament and the State Legislatures can enact preventive detention laws for various purposes, which are then likely to be used by the executive authorities indiscriminately. There can be no greater danger for individual freedoms than the possible extensive (ab)use of preventive detention powers. Though the Parliament and the State Legislatures may be trusted not to abuse that power, the fact that there is such a possibility itself is a threat to individual freedoms protected under the Constitution.

Further, it must be noted that the Constitution, which empowered both the Parliament and State Legislatures to enact preventive detention laws, has made their powers subject to certain safeguards provided under clauses (4) to (7) of Articles 22 of the Constitution. Article 22 providing for 'protection against arrest and detention in certain cases' is a fundamental right. Clauses (4)–(7) particularly deal with protection against preventive detention and exceptions thereto. They are provided to mitigate the harshness of preventive detention laws by placing fetters on legislative powers. The following section explains and examines the efficacy of those safeguards.

CONSTITUTIONAL SAFEGUARDS AGAINST PREVENTIVE DETENTIONS

Article 22 of the Constitution, as stated above, provides certain protection against arrest and detention. A quick look at the drafting history of the Constitution reveals that Article 22 (Article 15A of the draft Constitution) was not part of the original draft Constitution and was inserted later[15] into the draft as a 'compensation' for what was lost by replacing 'due process' clause with 'procedure established by law' clause in Article 21 (Article 15 in the draft Constitution) in the Constituent Assembly.[16] It was meant to provide 'substance of the law of due processes'[17] in the matter of arrest and detention.

Article 22, Clauses (1) and (2) provide certain protections to every person, who is arrested and detained under any law. Article 22(3), however, denies those protections to (a) an enemy alien, and (b) a person arrested or detained under any law providing for preventive detention. The person detained under any of the preventive detention laws is entitled to certain other safeguards under Clauses (4)–(7) of Article 22. Laws providing for preventive detention shall be in conformity with these provisions.

After the infamous 1975 emergency, when preventive detention laws were used extensively, the Parliament amended these provisions to strengthen the safeguards as the ones envisaged under the original scheme proved to be inadequate and inefficacious. But unfortunately, Section 3 of the Constitution (Forty-fourth Amendment) Act, 1978, which amended Clauses (4) and (7) of Article 22 to strengthen the

---

[15] Article 15A was moved in the Constituent Assembly on 15 September 1949.

[16] Per B.R. AMBEDKAR, IX CONSTITUENT ASSEMBLY DEBATES 1499 (Lok Sabha Secretariat 2014).

[17] *Id.*

safeguards has not yet been brought into force for the reasons best known to the successive governments in power ever since then. What is astonishing to note is that though some of the prominent emergency detenues have been part of those governments, they have not ensured the implementation of Section 3 to date. Owing to its non-implementation, even today persons detained under any of the preventive detention laws are entitled to only those safeguards that were envisaged under the original Constitution.

Safeguards Envisaged Under the Original Constitutional Scheme

As per the provisions contained in Article 22, Clauses (4)–(7), which are still in force in the same form, persons detained under preventive detention laws are entitled to four safeguards.

The *first* safeguard is the right not to be detained beyond 3 months without confirmation by an Advisory Board (Board). Article 22(4)(a) of the Constitution of India mandates the consultation with the Board for detaining a person beyond the initial period of detention. It is one of the most important safeguards that restrict the power of the Parliament and State Legislatures. As per the provision, the preventive detention law enacted by either of them shall not authorize the detention of a person for a period longer than 3 months without the scrutiny of the Board constituted for the purpose. If the law contemplates detention beyond 3 months, such law shall mandatorily provide for the consultation with the Board consisting of either serving or retired judges of the high court or persons qualified to be appointed as such. Though the provision does not specify the minimum number of persons to be appointed to the Board, the words 'consisting of persons who are...' indicate that it was intended to be a multi-member Board.

According to Article 22(4)(a), detention can be continued beyond 3 months only if the Board certifies that 'there is in its opinion sufficient cause of such detention'. It is mandatory that such confirmation needs to be obtained within 3 months from the date of detention.[18] Detention beyond 3 months without obtaining confirmation within

---

[18] D.S. Roy v. State of W.B., A.I.R. 1972 S.C. 1924.

that period would be illegal.[19] Further, if the Board reports that there is no sufficient cause for detention, then the detaining authority is duty-bound to revoke the detention order.[20]

This requirement of seeking confirmation from the Board aims at checking the arbitrary exercise of the extraordinary power of preventive detention. The law cannot authorize the detaining authority, who has the power to detain any person on reasonable apprehension/ suspicion, to decide on his own even the period for which such person shall be detained. The detaining authority can decide how long beyond 3 months the person can be detained only after receiving the confirmation from the Board as to the sufficiency of the cause of detention.

It is important to briefly examine how efficacious this safeguard is in checking the possible abuse of preventive detention powers. It is clearly evident from the provision that the consultation with the Board is mandatory only in cases where the detention is required to be continued beyond the period of 3 months and not otherwise. The detaining authority may be permitted to detain a person for any period less than 3 months without the scrutiny and confirmation by the Board. Further, the Board is required to examine only the sufficiency of the cause of detention and not the period of detention.[21] It is for the detaining authority to decide, after obtaining confirmation from the Board, how much longer than 3 months the detenue shall be kept in detention. The Board can only examine the sufficiency of the cause and once it does so and expresses its satisfaction before the expiry of 3 months, its role ends. Then the detaining authority can determine the period of detention subject to the maximum period, if any, prescribed under the law.

Another important aspect to be noted is that the safeguard provided in the form of the Advisory Board is not indispensable. Article 22(7) (a) contains an exception. It authorizes the Parliament to specify the

---

[19] Abdul Latif v. B.K. Jha, A.I.R. 1987 S.C. 725.

[20] Shibban Lal Sakshena v. State of U.P., A.I.R. 1954 S.C. 179.

[21] Puranlal Lakhanpal v. Union of India, A.I.R. 1958 S.C. 163; S. Mukharjee v. State of W.B., A.I.R. 1972 S.C. 1356; A.K. Roy v. Union of India, A.I.R. 1982 S.C. 710.

'circumstances under which, and the class or classes of cases in which' this safeguard can be dispensed with. If the Parliament chose to do so, then the detaining authority is fully competent to take a unilateral decision, under such circumstances or cases, to detain a person for a longer period than 3 months. Here, it may be pertinent to note that though the Constitution authorizes both the Parliament and the State Legislatures to enact preventive detention laws, it authorizes only the Parliament, and not the State Legislatures, to dispense with the requirement of consulting the Board.

The power conferred on the Parliament to dispense with this safeguard renders it inefficacious. The Parliament by creating sweeping exceptions to the rule can neutralize the safeguard in a large number of cases.

The *second* important safeguard is the right not to be detained beyond the maximum period prescribed by law. Once the confirmation is obtained from the Advisory Board, a detenue may be detained beyond 3 months. As stated before, it is for the detaining authority to decide how much longer than 3 months a detenue must be kept under preventive detention. The detaining authority, however, cannot continue the detention beyond the maximum period prescribed by law. The proviso to Article 22(4)(a) guarantees this right. Further, Article 22(7)(b) has specifically empowered the Parliament to prescribe 'the maximum period for which any person may in any class or classes of cases be detained under any law providing for preventive detention'. The State Legislatures are not specifically empowered to do so. The words 'any law providing for preventive detention' indicate that the Parliament may prescribe the maximum period of detention even for those detained under any of the preventive detention laws enacted by any State Legislature. It is pertinent to note that the Parliament need not prescribe the maximum period in terms of years, months or days. It can prescribe the same in terms of the occurrence of any event or continuance of any state of affairs like an emergency. Even in cases where the consultation with the Board has been dispensed with, the detaining authority cannot detain a person beyond the maximum period of detention prescribed by the Parliament. What weakens this safeguard is that the Parliament is not bound to prescribe the maximum period of detention.[22] The words 'Parliament may by law prescribe' in Article 22(7) indicate that it is not mandatory.

The *third* safeguard is the right to be informed of the grounds of detention. Article 22(5) imposes an obligation on the detaining authority to communicate to the detenue the grounds on which the detention order has been made. By virtue of the said clause, the detaining authority is duty bound to communicate to the detenue all the basic facts and particulars which influenced his decision to pass the detention order.[23] 'Grounds' to be communicated should include not just the 'conclusions of fact' but also the 'basic facts' on the basis of which the conclusions were drawn.[24] The detaining authority is required to communicate all facts and materials relied upon by him[25] but not those facts and materials, though considered, not relied upon while formulating the grounds of detention.[26] The detenue is entitled to know even the source of the information.[27] Since the provision requires the communication to be made 'as soon as may be', failure to communicate the grounds within reasonable time vitiates the detention.[28] Non-communication of the grounds on the very same day on which the order of detention is served does not vitiate it.[29]

The efficacy of the right to be informed of the grounds, which includes all the basic facts, is diluted to some extent by the exception created under Article 22(6). It allows the detaining authority to withhold 'facts', the disclosure of which, in his opinion, is 'against the public interest'. It must be noted that even in such cases, he can only withhold the 'basic facts' and not the 'grounds'. He is required to

---

[22] Fagu Shas v. State of W.B., A.I.R. 1974 S.C. 613.

[23] Khudiram Das v. State of W.B., A.I.R. 1975 S.C. 550.

[24] Prakash Chandra Mehta v. Commissioner and Secretary, Government of Kerala, A.I.R. 1986 S.C. 687.

[25] Icchu Devi v. Union of India, A.I.R. 1980 S.C. 1983; Amir v. Hmingliana (1991) 3 S.C.J. 154.

[26] Farooq v. Union of India, (1990) J.T. 3 S.C. 102; Abdul Kadar v. Union of India, (1990) 1 S.C.C. 480.

[27] Har Jas v. State of Punjab, A.I.R. 1973 S.C. 1983.

[28] Pritam Nath Hoon v. Union of India, A.I.R. 1981 S.C. 92; Mangalbhai Motiram v. State of Maharashtra, A.I.R. 1981 S.C. 510.

[29] Union of India v. Dimple Happy Dhakad, (2019) 20 S.C.C. 609.

communicate the grounds, that is, conclusions drawn from the facts without disclosing the basic facts. But the problem with this exception is that non-disclosure of basic facts seriously impairs the right to seek redressal against the detention.

The *fourth* and the last safeguard provided against preventive detention is the right to make representation. Under Article 22(5), the detaining authority, in addition to the obligation to communicate grounds, also has an obligation to afford the detenue 'the earliest opportunity of making a representation against the order'. Consideration of representation made under this provision is independent of the requirement of reference to the Advisory Board.[30] It is a valuable constitutional right and not an empty formality.[31] It is axiomatic to state that the very object of communicating the grounds of detention to the detenue is to enable him to seek redressal by making a representation against the order of detention.[32] It is in order to enable the detenue to make an effective representation, the apex court insists that the grounds shall be communicated to him in a language, which he understands[33] and in unambiguous terms. Communication of grounds in vague terms amounts to infringement of the right to make representation and, thus, renders the order of detention void *ab initio*.[34] The order is considered to be vague if it cannot be intelligently understood.[35]

It is abundantly clear that the safeguards provided under Article 22 (4)–(7) against preventive detention are neither adequate nor efficacious. They are not inviolable even during peacetime. The Constitution either creates an exception or permits dilution of each of the safeguards. Owing to these, Article 22 (4)–(7) can hardly be considered to be a bulwark against the possible abuse of extraordinary power of preventive detention.

Further, it should also be noted that Article 22 is not a non-derogable provision. All the protections provided against arrest and detention,

---

[30] Ankit Ashok Jalan v. Union of India, (2020) 16 S.C.C. 127.
[31] Abdul Karim v. State of West Bengal, A.I.R. 1969 S.C. 1028.
[32] Shibban Lal, *supra* note 20.
[33] Ankit Ashok Jalan, *supra* note 31.
[34] State of Bombay v. Atmaram, (1951) S.C.R. 167; Puranlal, *supra* note 21.
[35] Lawrence D' souza v. State of Bombay, A.I.R. 1965 S.C. 531.

including preventive detention, can be withdrawn during the national emergency proclaimed under Article 352 of the Constitution. Once such a proclamation is issued, the President of India, under Article 359, has the power to suspend the enforcement of, *inter alia*, all or any of the protections provided under Article 22 of the Constitution. When Article 22 remains suspended, authorities would have unbridled power of arrest and detention during the period of such suspension. This has led to massive abuse of preventive detention powers during the infamous 1975 emergency in India.

The Forty-fourth Amendment: Half-hearted Attempt to Strengthen the Safeguards

The 1975 emergency exposed, *inter alia*, the weaknesses in the constitutional protection accorded to individual liberties. In order to strengthen the constitutional framework, in particular the protection accorded to individual liberties, the Constitution was amended by the successive governments that came to power after the emergency. The Constitution (Forty-fourth Amendment) Act, 1978, *vide* Section 40, amended Article 359 and made fundamental rights guaranteed under Articles 20 and 21 non-derogable even during the emergency. For reasons not entirely convincing, Article 22, which was originally inserted to the Constitution with a view to provide 'substance of the law of due processes',[36] was not elevated to the status of non-derogable rights. Attempts were only made to strengthen the safeguards provided thereunder by amending clauses (4) and (7) of Article 22. Amendment introduced three major changes: (a) It reduced the initial period of detention, before confirmation by the Advisory Board, from three to 2 months. (b) It altered the composition of the Advisory Board to make it more independent. As per the original scheme, the Board was to consist of 'persons who are, or have been, or are qualified to be appointed as, Judges of a High Court'. There was no express stipulation of the minimum number of members to be included in the Board. As per the amended provision, the Board shall consist of 'a Chairman and not less than two other members, and the Chairman shall be a serving Judge

---

[36] AMBEDKAR, *supra* note 17.

of the appropriate High Court and the other members shall be serving or retired Judges of any High Court'. Further, it shall be constituted in accordance with the recommendations of the Chief Justice of the appropriate High Court. The amendment, thus, restricted the possibility of handpicking those who toe the official line. (c) It took away the power of the Parliament to dispense with the requirement of obtaining confirmation from the Board. The amendment made the scrutiny and confirmation by the Board mandatory in all cases for continuing the detention beyond 2 months.

All these changes introduced by Section 3 of the Forty-fourth Amendment Act still remain only on paper. Though the other provisions of the amendment Act were brought into force as early as 1979 itself, Section 3 has not yet been brought into force. As a result, detenues detained under various preventive detention laws are entitled to only those safeguards envisaged under the original constitutional scheme and they are, as pointed out earlier, weak and inefficacious.

Availability of Procedural Rights Flowing from Article 21

Preventive detention, like any other detention, results in the physical detention of a person in a cell. It is trite that a detenue cannot exercise various freedoms guaranteed under the Constitution. What makes preventive detention exceedingly detrimental to individual freedoms is that it is based on no accusation, no charge and no trial. It is detention based on suspicion. That is precisely the reason why it is considered to be an arch enemy of personal liberties guaranteed, particularly, under Articles 19(1) and 21 of the Constitution.

Having regard to the harsh consequences of preventive detention on personal liberties, it is pertinent to ask whether the law providing for preventive detention shall, in addition to providing safeguards envisaged under Article 22 (4)–(7), also meet the requirements of Articles 19 and 21 of the Constitution.

When the said question first arose for consideration in *A. K. Gopalan*,[37] the apex court, by a majority, answered it in the negative. The majority

---

[37] Gopalan, *supra* note 7.

adopted an exclusionary approach and treated each of the fundamental rights as silos. In its opinion, preventive detention laws can only be tested against Article 22 (4)–(7) and not against Article 19 or Article 21.

The correctness of the exclusionary approach of treating each fundamental right as self-contained code came to be doubted by the apex court and gradually given up in the later years. The court recognized, developed and strengthened the idea of the interrelationship between fundamental rights in several cases.[38] This approach came to be firmly established in *Maneka Gandhi* v. *Union of India*,[39] where it was categorically stated that fundamental rights are not mutually exclusive. Krishna Iyer, J., in his characteristic style observed:

[n]o article in Part III is an island but part of a continent, and the conspectus of the whole part gives the direction and correction needed for interpretation of these basic provisions. Man is not dissectible into separate limbs and, likewise, cardinal rights in an organic constitution, which make man *human* have a synthesis.[40]

The adoption of the new approach allowed the apex court to assert that, in view of the adverse consequences of preventive detention on personal liberties, the laws providing for it must also meet the requirements of articles 19 and 21 as well.[41] As a result, a person detained under preventive detention laws can claim, in addition to the specific safeguards provided under Article 22 (4)–(7), the procedural rights that flow from Article 21.[42]

It is, however, pertinent to state here, albeit briefly, that the expansive interpretation of article 21 by the apex court in the later years to include many procedural and substantive fairness principles associated with the due process clause within its ambit does not render article 22 redundant or superfluous. The provision is still significant in as much

---

[38] See R. C. Cooper v. Union of India, A.I.R. 1970 S.C. 564; Shambu Nath Sarkar v. State of West Bengal, A.I.R. 1973 S.C. 1425; Hardhan Shah v. State of West Bengal, A.I.R. 1974 S.C. 2154; Khudiram Das, *supra* note 23.

[39] (1978) 1 S.C.C. 248. Also see, Justice K. S. Puttaswamy v. Union of India, (2017) 10 S.C.C. 1.

[40] *Id.*, para 96.

[41] Roy, *supra* note 21.

[42] Francis v. Administrator, A.I.R. 1981 S.C. 946.

as it ensures that the specific safeguards enumerated thereunder are not subject to vicissitudes of the judiciary. Further, the judicial decisions which expanded the scope of article 21 do not support the view that even if article 22 is omitted from the Constitution, persons detained under any preventive detention law can claim all those safeguards, without exception, by relying on article 21 itself. Procedural rights flowing from article 21 only supplement the safeguards specifically enumerated under Article 22.

CONCLUSION

In order to harmonize, at least to some extent, preventive detention with individual freedoms, which are apparently incompatible, the constitutional framework needs to be revisited. The first and foremost aspect that needs to be considered is the necessity of providing for preventive detention during peacetime. It was sought to be justified in the formative years on the ground that the same was necessary to protect the infant republic. India is no longer an 'infant republic'. It is now a mature and vibrant democracy. It has a fully developed legal system and law enforcement and adjudicative machinery. There appear to be no compelling and adequate reasons, except administrative expediency, to permit recourse to preventive detention during peacetime. Recourse to it shall be permitted only during officially proclaimed emergencies. Second, the decision of the apex court in the *Attorney General*[43] shall be reconsidered. It gave the Parliament and, by analogy, also the State Legislatures *carte blanche* to enact preventive detention laws for reasons connected with any of the subject-matters over which they have legislative competence. The interpretation accorded by the court does not seem to be in accord with the intention of the framers of the Constitution. Third, Section 3 of the Forty-fourth Amendment Act which has strengthened the safeguards against preventive detention shall be brought into force, and Article 22 shall be elevated to the status of non-derogable fundamental rights. Harmonious balance can, thus, be struck between the interests of the individuals, on the one hand, and that of the state and society on the other.

---

[43] Attorney General for India, *supra* note 11.

PART II

Legislative Perspectives on Arrest and Detention

Chapter 6

Role of Remand Proceedings
A Step Away from the Mechanical Approach

R. S. Cheema and Tarannum Cheema

INTRODUCTION

Remand though not defined in the Code of Criminal Procedure, 1973, (hereinafter referred to as CrPC or the code) finds its prominence in Chapter V dealing with *Arrests of Persons* and Chapter XII covering the aspects related to *Information to the Police and Their Powers to Investigate*. The concept of 'remand' also finds its genesis in Article 22 of the Constitution titled *Protection against arrest and detention in certain cases*. The juxtaposition that the Constitution requires centres around the proposition that any detention curtailing personal liberty must be made under the due process of law and what must flow should be a reasoned approach. A combined reading of Sections 56 and 57 of CrPC indicates that when a person is arrested without a warrant, he must be produced before a Magistrate, and if such detention is to continue for more than 24 hours, then the period has to be extended by a special order of a Magistrate, as envisioned under Section 167 of the code.

The power of remand, which in plain language would constitute sending the accused into custody, is contained in Section 167(2) of the code. The Section necessitates that the Magistrate has the discretion to warrant detention of an accused in custody for a term not exceeding

15 days and further beyond the said period, 'if he is satisfied that adequate grounds exist for doing so',[1] as is incorporated in the language of the Section itself. The Section further contemplates the time periods for up to which the custody can be extended and the circumstances under which the Magistrate can exercise the power. The time periods stipulated under the Section which grant the maximum time for incarceration during the pendency of investigation is 90 days where the offence is punishable with death, imprisonment for life or an imprisonment for a term of not less than 10 years and 60 days where the investigation relates to any other offences.[2] On expiry of the time periods set out in section, the accused person shall be released on bail if the investigation has not resulted in filing of the charge sheet. This is conveniently called default bail. It is only in the event of the non-availability of a Judicial Magistrate that an Executive Magistrate, upon whom powers of a Judicial Magistrate or Metropolitan Magistrate have been conferred, can exercise limited jurisdiction in the matter of dealing with a prayer for passing an order of remand.

The Constitutional safeguard in relation to curtailing of personal liberty emerges from the provisions of Article 22, whereby the person detained is entitled to be informed of the ground of their arrest and his right to be defended by a legal practitioner of their choice.[3] The Article entails that the person so detained must be produced before a Magistrate within a period of 24 hours and any further detention cannot continue without the authority of a Magistrate.

Interestingly, the International Covenant on Civil and Political Rights in Article 9 also contains the underlined parameters to be observed when a person is being detained and recognizes the concept that that anyone arrested or detained must be informed of any charges against him and shall be promptly brought before a judge. The law further envisions that a person so arrested is entitled to a trial within a reasonable time or to release.[4]

---

[1] Section 167 (2)(a) of CrPC.
[2] Section 167 (2)(a)(i)(ii) of CrPC.
[3] Article 22 Constitution of India.
[4] Article 9 International Covenant on Civil and Political Rights.

LEGISLATIVE HISTORY OF REMAND

Before discussing the implications that the grant of remand has on the rights of an accused, it would be appropriate to examine the legislative history of the provisions dealing with remand. This historical perspective would inform our understanding of how the grant of remand operates in practice today and whether current practice is consistent with the intent underlying the legislative changes.

The history of the exercise of remand under the CrPC is a history of an increasing judicial control of investigation. The treatment of remand under the Original Code of 1898 and its existing treatment are vastly different. Under the Original Code, the power of remand was conferred upon both Executive Magistrate and Judicial Magistrates except for some states where the power was conferred only upon Judicial Magistrates. The 37th Law Commission Report recommended that the power of remand should vest only with the Judicial Magistrate.[5] This was in consonance with the Bombay model where power of remand stands exclusively with the Judicial Magistrate as opposed to the Punjab Model. This rationale suggested in the Report was significant as it recognized that the power of remand is essentially a judicial function and not merely an executive function, hence the application of mind being the underlying intent. In recommending conferring of the power to grant remand with Judicial Magistrates, the 37th Law Commission was cognizant that these judicial authorities, by virtue of training, evaluate the material and weigh the evidence carefully. In bringing about this change, the gamut of what is included in remand expanded from being an order merely to maintain law and order to an order taking into account the liberty of the accused.

Another check on the investigation recommended by the 37th Law Commission was to statutorily provide that the accused shall be physically present before the Magistrate at the time when the police apply for remand, and the grounds on which they ask for remand should also be made known to the accused. It is evident that inclusion of such a provision was to enable the accused to controvert the allegations of the

---

[5] Law Commission 37th Report, p. 138, para 482.

investigating agency and prevent them from placing material on record obtained behind the back of the accused. This invites the accused to test the material found during the course of investigation and further endows him/her with a positive role at the stage of remand itself. Thus, it should be noticed how the grant of remand was considered as having a serious impact on the rights of the accused requiring the physical presence of the accused.

Judicial check on the investigation was further intensified under the Amendment Act, 1978,[6] whereby certain consequences followed in case the investigation was not completed within certain time limits. These time limits operate as a limitation against protracted investigations without justifiable cause. Section 167 (5) provides that if the investigation is not concluded within a period of 6 months from the date of arrest of the accused, in a case where the offence is not punishable with imprisonment for more than 2 years, the investigation may be stopped, or the accused may be discharged.

With these changes, the role which the remanding authority was tasked to perform perceptibly changed under the code. What was once considered a ministerial act became a judicial function. The rights of the accused have been brought to the forefront and are to be protected by the Judicial Magistrate from the very initiation of the process. What exactly is the role of the Magistrate at this stage will be discussed in the course of this chapter; it suffices to note that legislative history undoubtedly demonstrates that the power to remand was increasingly treated as a matter of serious concern. One possible explanation for this, which arises from the deliberations of various Law Commissions dealing with the matter, is that the investigating authorities tend to make a charade of the rights of the accused by prolonging investigation without justification.

It is not only the rights of the accused which were increasingly protected by subsequent amendments. The time limits to investigate were also extended. Originally, under the code, remand could not have been ordered for more than 15 days in the whole. However, this led to an

---

[6] The evolution of the changes brought in by the Amendment Act, 1978, has been traced in Satyanarayana v State of A.P., A.I.R. 1986 S.C. 2130.

anomalous situation where the police would file a half-baked charge sheet and resort to Section 344 which was intended to be invoked only after cognizance of the offence had been taken by the Magistrate. The result was that the charge sheet filed would not be in the prescribed form. A solution was offered by the 14th Law Commission where a decision was taken to extend the time period of investigation from 15 days to 60 days.[7] However, this was not accepted by the 37th Report as it was apprehended that the 60-day period would be resorted to in a routine manner by the investigating agencies.[8] As the law today stands, the outer limit is a period of 90 days for an offence punishable with death, imprisonment for life or imprisonment for a term not less than 10 years and 60 days where the investigation relates to any other offence.

IMPORTANCE OF REMAND PROCESS

The first instance of the journey that the investigation into an offence is purporting to take emerges at the stage of remand where the investigating agency has invoked its right to arrest. In a practical situation, where the accused under arrest may not know the nature of the allegations against him, the application for remand preferred by the investigating agency would shed light on the nature of investigation being undertaken and goes a long way forward for the accused to address his immediate defence strategy. While in many cases the entire process is sadly followed in a mechanical manner and all the ammunition is reserved until the stage of bail, the initial case set up by the investigating agency would emerge at the stage of remand and, in most cases, becomes an aid while arguing the bail.

> The grant of order for police remand should be an exception and not as a rule and for that the investigating agency is required to make out a strong case and must satisfy the learned Magistrate that without the police custody it would be impossible for the police authorities to undertake further investigation and only in that event police custody would be justified as the authorities specially at the magisterial level

---

[7] 14th Law Commission Report, Vol. 2, p. 758.

[8] *Supra* note 1, para 478.

would do well to remind themselves that detention in police custody is generally disfavoured by law. The scheme of Section 167 of the Criminal Procedure Code, 1973 is unambiguous in this regard and is indented to protect the accused from the methods which may be adopted by some overzealous and unscrupulous police officers which at times may be at the instance of an interested party also. But it is also equally true that the police custody although is not the be-all and end-all of the whole investigation, yet it is one of its primary requisites particularly in the investigation of serious and heinous crimes. The legislature also noticed this and, has therefore, permitted limited police custody.[9]

The law makes its obligatory that police remand is to be allowed by the Magistrate in specific circumstances and for specific reasons, depending upon the intricacies of the case.

The investigating agency has the responsibility to showcase at the first instance regarding whether within the scope of their investigation, the detention of the person arrested is required to be prolonged in each case. The steps undertaken during the investigation must be clearly spelt out along with the reasons for detention to continue, when the request for police remand is made before the Magistrate. The notion of due process must manifest from the application made by the investigating agency. At the same time, it must be borne in mind that the investigating agency cannot be given a free hand to sew up a case where none existed at the time of asking for remand. Remand proceedings cannot be used by the investigating agencies as a tool to create evidence and harass the person detained. 'Remand applications are to be filed by the Investigating Agency' to satisfy the Court that there are justifiable grounds to detain an accused already arrested, in police or judicial custody. By such applications, the investigating agency is required to bring to the notice of the court the materials collected against an arrested accused to persuade the Court to remand him to custody for the purpose of further investigation.[10]

---

[9] Satyajit Ballubhai Desai v. State of Gujarat, (2014) 14 S.C.C. 434, at pp. 439–49, para 9.

[10] State of Maharashtra v. Ramesh Taurani, (1998) 1 S.C.C. 41, at p. 43, para 4

REMAND ORDER MUST REFLECT APPLICATION OF MIND

The plain reading of the section reveals that the balance which is required to be targeted is the need of an effective investigation into a cognizable offence on the one hand and the protection of civil liberties guaranteed to the citizens of the country on the other hand. The powers granted to the Magistrates under Section 167 are based upon the existence of 'adequate grounds', which must necessarily reflect application of mind. The guidelines enumerated in the various high court rules showcase that application of mind lies at the essence of remand proceedings.

As per the Delhi High Court Rules on the subject, a Magistrate authorizing the detention of an accused must record his reasons for doing so, and if he is not a District Magistrate or a Sub-Divisional Magistrate, he must forward a copy of his order and reasons to the Magistrate to whom he is immediately subordinate. The Magistrate shall sign and date every page of the case diaries or copies thereof in token of his having seen them.[11] The judicial pronouncements on the subject of due application of mind are conscious of the twofold requirement of perusal of record before passing the order and reasons to flow from the reading of the order. A police remand ought only to be granted in cases of real necessity and when it is shown in the application that there is good reason to believe that the accused can point out properly or otherwise assist the police in elucidating the case.[12]

However, a trend has emerged where the investigating agencies tend to believe that remand to police custody must be given for asking. Perhaps this perception has been guided by the mechanical nature of the process, which though discouraged by judicial precedent, seems to be the norm followed by the Magistrates while conducting these proceedings. The remand is not a mere mechanical process but demands application of judicial mind on the part of the Magistrate. It is for this reason that strict safeguards are insisted upon in the matter of remand,

---

[11] Section 10, Part A, Procedure of Magistrate granting remand, Delhi High Court Rules, Chapter 11.

[12] Section 4, Part B, Remand to be granted in cases of real necessity, Delhi High Court Rules, Chapter 11.

and it is the sacred and solemn responsibility, as also the legal obligation, of the Magistrates to see that the provisions of the Criminal Procedure Code and the directions contained in the High Court Rules and Orders are not abused.[13] Before making an order of remand to police custody under Section 167 of CrPC, the Magistrate should satisfy himself that (a) there are grounds for believing that the accusation against the person sent up by the police is well founded; (c) there are good and sufficient reasons for remanding the accused to police custody instead of detaining him in magisterial custody. To form an opinion as to the necessity or otherwise of the remand applied for by the police, the Magistrate should examine the copies of the diaries submitted under Section 167 and ascertain what previous orders (if any) have been made in the case, and the longer the accused person has been in custody, the stronger should be the grounds required for a further remand to police custody. The accused person must always be produced before the Magistrate when a remand is asked for.[14]

It is incumbent upon the Magistrate before whom the application for seeking remand is being made to satisfy himself, based on the material placed by the investigating agency, that grant of remand is necessitated in the given situation, the essential corollary being that an order sans reason cannot withstand the test of judicial scrutiny. While laying down the tests considered to fall within the gambit of reasonableness, various courts have laid down that the scrutiny of materials must be explicit and the order must exhibit application of mind. The concept of what is termed to be 'Reasonable cause for remand' would essentially cover a case where there is sufficient evidence on record pointing towards the complicity of an accused and more evidence can be obtained by remand. 'The guidelines clearly contained in the statue but the discretion being judicial is required to be exercised on general principles guided by rules of reason and justice on the facts of each case and not in any arbitrary or fanciful manner'.[15]

---

[13] Madan Lal v. Superintendent Tihar Jail, (1967) S.C.C. OnLine Del 85, para 11.

[14] Section 7, Part B, Accused must be produced before the Magistrate who should satisfy himself about necessity for remand, Delhi High Court Rules, Chapter 11.

[15] A. Lakshmanarao v. Judicial Magistrate, (1970) 3 S.C.C. 501, at p. 506, para 8.

The powers encompassed in the Section are vast and enjoin the Magistrate to delve into the purpose for which remand is being sought and also provides him with an opportunity to arrive at a reasoned order by even asking questions from an accused. This reminds us of a recent famous case where the accused was a former Cabinet Minister and a coveted senior advocate himself. At the stage of remand, he sought permission to address the court on his questioning during custody; however, this prayer was vehemently opposed by a senior counsel representing the government. The very opposition was in stark contrast with the law on remand, as enunciated in various decisions of the Apex Court. The decision as to whether a further remand is necessitated in a given case ought to be made by the Magistrate by taking note of all the relevant circumstances when the detainee is produced before him. 'As the magistrate has to apply his judicial mind, he himself can take note of all relevant circumstances when the person detained is produced before him and decide whether further remand is necessary'.[16]

TRANSIT REMAND

The question of jurisdiction is inherent in the section dealing with remand, and on first principles, the section contemplates a situation where the powers engraved in the section are exercisable sans the question of jurisdiction at the very outset. The underlying theme of the remand proceedings is that when a person is detained, he has to be produced before the nearest Magistrate as mandated by law, and the period of any further detention can be extended by the order of the Magistrate. However, what is essential in an order of Magistrate, even when dealing with a case for remand not falling under his jurisdiction, is the application of mind to give a reasoned order based on the materials placed before him by the investigating agency. The order would carry reasons that mandated the police officials from another jurisdiction to detain the person arrested.

Even in a case where the jurisdictional question about the production of the person arrested arises in a remand proceeding, given the

---

[16] Raj Narain v. Superintendent, Central Jail, New Delhi, (1970) 2 S.C.C. 750, at p. 760, para 38.

mandatory requirement of production before a Judicial Magistrate within 24 h in terms of Article 22 (2) of the Constitution and Section 57, CrPC, the transit remand application must be filed accompanied with the copies of entries made in the case diary that ought to be produced before the concerned Magistrate in compliance of Section 167 (1), CrPC. In exercising the powers available to him, such nearest Judicial Magistrate is obliged to determine that an offence has been committed and that the police officer seeking a remand is properly authorized. He is further required to apply his mind to ensure that there exists material in the form of entries in the case diary that justifies the prayer for transit remand.[17]

REMAND SOUGHT BY INVESTIGATORS UNDER SPECIAL STATUES

There has been a trend in the recent past to enact special statues covering varied offences and empower the investigators falling under such statutes with special powers, which may be in direct contravention of the protections so fittingly catered for in the code. Remarkably, while those entrusted with powers under these Special Acts tend to exercise the controls available to police officers under the code, at the same time, the safeguards against use of such powers are often shunned. The power to remand an accused to any custody must be bestowed by law and would be traceable to some provision of the statue.[18] In examining the cases falling under the Narcotic Drugs and Psychotropic Substances Act (NDPS), 1985, and the contours of Section 167, CrPC, the Hon'ble Supreme Court concluded that there is a clear mention of Section 167, CrPC, in the Act for the exercise of the power of remand. The legislative intent of not excluding the applicability of the provision to Sub-section (2) of Section 167, CrPC, in case of arrest made for commission of offences under NDPS is quite evident and was duly noted by the Hon'ble Supreme Court in *Union of India v. Thamisharasi.*

Courts are often vexed with the question, in cases dealing with special statues, on the applicability of Chapter XII of CrPC to the officers under the special statues. When the powers akin to those entrusted to the police officers are exercised, the officers under the special statues

---

[17] Gautam Navlakha v. State (NCT of Delhi) (2018) 253 D.L.T. 392 (DB).

[18] Union of India v. Thamisharasi, (1995) 4 S.C.C. 190, at p. 199, para 16.

often take the defence of the narrow scope of their applicability to special statues. One such issue arose regarding the applicability of Section 167, CrPC, and the troublesome question as to the extent of its applicability. While the applicability of Section 167, CrPC, to officers of the Directorate of Enforcement stood to be decided on the question of the time period of detention, there emerged varying views of the high courts. The situation becomes complicated in as much as to say that the powers of remand, as envisaged under Section 167, CrPC, can be exercised by a Magistrate in a case of Directorate of Enforcement; however, the time periods of detention as laid down in the section are not applicable to the Directorate of Enforcement. The Supreme Court held that the section in its entirety must be applicable. It was held that 'Sub-section (1) and (2) of Section 167 are squarely applicable with regard to the production and detention of a person arrested under the provisions of Sections 35 of FERA and Sections 104 of Customs Act'.[19] In cases emanating under the Prevention of Money Laundering Act, 2002 (PMLA), provisions of Section 167(2), CrPC, were found to be applicable by the Hon'ble Supreme Court.[20]

On the question whether chapter XII CrPC is applicable to officers of Directorate of Enforcement, the Delhi High Court held that the powers under PMLA for offences under the Act would be governed by CrPC, if not otherwise by PMLA, and this is mandated by Articles 21 and 22 of the Constitution of India.[21] The case now stands transferred to the Hon'ble Supreme Court and is tagged with a bunch of cases, almost close to 132, to finally decide the issue.[22]

HABEAS CORPUS AGAINST WRONGFUL REMAND

CrPC is not merely an enactment of procedural law. It is a procedural code regulating constitutional rights. Several provisions in the code trace its existence to Constitutionally protected freedoms. Section 161

---

[19] Directorate of Enforcement v. Deepak Mahajan, (1994) 3 S.C.C. 440, at p. 480, para 136.

[20] Ashok Munilal Jain & Anr. v. Assistant Director, Directorate of Enforcement, (2017) S.C.C. Online S.C. 1573.

[21] Rajbhushan Omprakash Dixit v. Union of India 2018 (168) D.R.J. 292.

[22] Vijay Madanlal Chaudhary & Ors. v. Union of India S.L.P. (Crl. 4634/2014).

was held to embody a facet of the right against self-incrimination.[23] It is, therefore, necessary to inquire and reflect upon the constitutional underpinnings of procedural provisions in criminal law.

Any violation of Section 167 will necessarily give rise to constitutional consequences. It has already been stated earlier that procedure of remand has its origins in the Constitution. The question though is one of remedy. An indefinite incarceration deprives the individual of the right to life. A mechanical and routine order of remand is an affront to a prisoner's right to liberty. Therefore, writ petitions under Article 32 and 226 must necessarily be maintainable in the form of a habeas corpus petition. The potential for abuse of Section 167 by the police, prison and the Magistracy is not unknown. In *Mantoo Majumdar v State of Bihar*[24], the Hon'ble Supreme Court converted letters by two prisoners into a habeas corpus petition upon finding that they were incarcerated for 7 years without any investigation having taken place, which was affirmed by the Magistrates who mechanically authorized repeated detentions 'unconscious of the provisions which obligated them to monitor the proceedings'. In the face of these facts, Justice Krishna Iyer elevated Section 167(2) to a constitutional plane in the following words:

> Section 167(2) which we have extracted above, empowers the Magistrate to authorise the detention of an accused in such custody as he thinks fit for a term not exceeding 15 days in the whole. More importantly, there is a precious interdict protective of personal freedom which states that no Magistrate shall authorise the detention of the accused person exceeding 90 days in grave cases and 60 days in lesser cases.

With these words, the doubt as to whether a habeas corpus petition was maintainable against remand orders should have been laid to rest. However, the Hon'ble Supreme Court today has repeatedly expressed the view that no habeas corpus petition can be sought against an order of remand and the only recourse available is to seek bail.[25] Unfortunately,

---

[23] R. Dineshkumar v. State, (2015) 7 S.C.C. 497.

[24] (1980) 2 S.C.C. 406.

[25] State of Maharashtra v. Tasneem Rizwan Siddiquee, (2018) 9 S.C.C. 745; Saurabh Kumar v. Jailor, Koneila Jail, (2014) 13 S.C.C. 436; Manubhai Ratilal Patel v. State of Gujarat, (2013) 1 S.C.C. 314.

in none of these decisions is the decision in *Mantoo Majumder* noticed, and thus, the constitutional importance of Section 167(2) was lost on the Court. In none of the cases of the Hon'ble Supreme Court holding that a habeas corpus petition is not maintainable against an order of remand is the intersection between the Constitution and criminal procedure discussed. The only possible inference is that the Court finds no intersection. Therefore, it becomes necessary to probe deeply into the foundations of procedural provisions lest we sacrifice rights of individuals at the altar of investigative agencies whose conduct today makes the proceedings of infamous Star Chamber appear sympathetic.

THE LARGER PERSPECTIVE: A CASE FOR ADDITIONAL SAFEGUARDS

The law regulating the grant or refusal of further detention in police custody directly and indirectly impacts the fairness and the intrinsic quality of investigation. The indiscreet refusal of police custody at a critical juncture may shut out vital or even clinching incriminating evidence, thereby leading to unwarranted acquittal. On the other hand, the indiscriminate use of power of remand in favour of the investigating agency, which is quite rampant despite the red flags being repeatedly raised by the higher judiciary, leads to gross abuse of power by the investigating agencies. Unwarranted remand, particularly for unduly long spells, results in custodial torture, extortion and fabrication of false evidence. At a belated stage, it becomes extremely difficult to see through the manipulations of an unscrupulous investigator and to disengage the truth from falsehood as the die is already cast. Any system governed by rule of law demands that adequate safeguards be incorporated in the statute in the first place and effectively implemented in practice. The Hon'ble Supreme Court of India has been very sensitive to the phenomena of unnecessary arrests and the consequential injustice. The rights of detainees/accused, during detention, have also attracted close attention from the Apex Court. The judgements of the Apex Court have resulted in statutory amendments aimed at eliminating the abuse of power connected with arrest, detention and further police custody.[26] However, it is necessary to explore as

---

[26] Joginder Kumar v. State of UP and Others, (1994) 4 S.C.C. 260; DK Basu v. State of W.B., (1997) 1 S.C.C. 416 and Arnesh Kumar v. State of Bihar and Another, (2014) 8 S.C.C. 273.

to whether any additional safeguards regulating the exercise of power for grant of remand are specifically called for.

Almost all the high courts in India have framed specific directions/ rules and orders governing the exercise of power of remand. These instructions largely emanate from the statutory law and the observations made by the higher courts from time to time. The instructions issued by various high courts lay emphasis on the presence of the accused at the time of consideration of prayer for remand, the production and perusal of case diaries, the need for care and caution in exercising the power for grant of remand and the freedom to engage a lawyer. It is indeed high time that a comprehensive set of rules and orders were adopted by the high courts in the country incorporating all the essential safeguards. We deem it extremely important that a lawyer representing the detainee must be given liberty of hearing at the stage of grant of remand to avoid delays. It may become imperative to ensure the presence of legal aid counsels with reasonable standing to aid and assist the Courts on the choice of the accused in instances where he is unable to engage a lawyer himself. We further deem it desirable that in these rules, a specific guideline requires to be inserted to the effect that there is sufficient evidence with the investigating agency that leads to a suspicion that the arrested accused has committed the offence and there is likelihood of surfacing of further evidence. How a judicious exercise of power of granting remand goes a long way to promote justice is best illustrated in the judgement of the Supreme Court in *State of Uttar Pradesh v. Ram Sagar Yadav and others*.[27] It was a case of custodial death which the guilty police officers had tried their best to cover up. A prayer for remand was made for further investigation of victim Brijlal. The concerned Magistrate acted strictly in accordance with the letter and spirit of the law and went out of court room to personally examine the said person and unearthed the truth, ultimately leading to the conviction of guilty persons. The following observations of the Supreme Court are relevant in this regard:

> ...It is notorious that remand orders are often passed mechanically without a proper application of mind. Perhaps, the Magistrates are

---

[27] (1985) 1 S.C.C. 552.

not to blame because, heaps of such applications are required to be disposed of by them before the regular work of the day begins. Shri Nigam has to be complimented for the sense of duty and humanity which he showed in leaving his seat and going to the verandah to see an humble villager like Brijlal. It is obvious that he was led into passing an order of remand on the basis of the usual statement that the offence of which the accused was charged was still under investigation. What is important is that Brijlal had not committed any offence at all for which he could be remanded and, far from being an accused, he was in the position of a complainant. Respondent I was the architect of his remand and the motive for obtaining the remand order was to keep Brijlal in custody so as to prevent him from disclosing to his people who beat him and where....

In another case decided by the Supreme Court, *Surinder Kumar v. State of Punjab*,[28] the accused stood convicted by the trial court and his appeal before the high court had been dismissed. The primary evidence relied upon by the prosecution was an extrajudicial confession statedly made by the accused. The defence contended that the said piece of evidence was not reliable because as per the claim of the prosecution, the accused was arrested based on the contents of the extrajudicial confession and thereafter produced in the Court. The defence contended that since the evidence against him was the extrajudicial confession allegedly made by him, the same must find mention in the remand application filed after his arrest, as the said confession constituted the only material against the accused. The Supreme Court overruled the view taken by the high court and discarded the confession on account of the omission, aforementioned.

We also find that the rules are not uniform regarding the requirement of the concerned Magistrate forwarding the orders of remand to a senior judicial officer. It is desirable to incorporate a direction to that effect. The rules issues by the Madras High Court require the filing of an accompanying affidavit by the investigating officer, not below the rank of Sub-inspector of police setting out necessary averments. Such requirement shall certainly introduce accountability into the process. The rule requiring that further police custody should be granted for

---

[28] A.I.R. 1999 S.C. 215.

as short as possible is followed in breach than in observance. Once the remand period is over, the matter practically loses all importance and much relevance. This encourages the exercise of powers in a summary manner. The necessary inference being that the accused be allowed to challenge their remand after the period of remand is over and pray that the said order be set aside in addition to other consequential reliefs. One effective guideline to introduce accountability into the process is to entail the specific mention of what the investigation has attained during the previous remand period. Even where the investigating agency presses for a remand to judicial custody after a spell of police custody, it must be specifically mentioned as to what evidence was collected during the detention of the accused in the custody of the police. The gist of evidence connecting the accused with the crime ought to be mentioned briefly to justify the arrest.

An objective analysis of the reality on the ground demonstrates that notwithstanding the legislative changes grafting safeguards and accountability and the strong and meaningful observations made by the Apex Court and the various high courts, the question of remanding an accused to police custody continues to be dealt with in a very casual manner. The accused is brought to the court at the last moment projecting an emergency situation and the Magistrate is obliged to deal with the issue without any material or opportunity to verify or question the fact situation as claimed by the investigating officer. The balance easily tilts against the liberty of the accused, and more often than not, remand is granted for the asking. It is essential to highlight that in cases of controversial nature, the investigating agency manages to leak selective one-sided information to the media to sensationalize the alleged crime. The media pressure again generates an atmosphere where the liberty of the individual loses priority. The only course available to maintain the required balance between the need for effective investigation on the one hand and the liberty of the citizen on the other hand, is sensitization of the Magistracy.

Chapter 7

Apprehension and Bail of Children in Conflict with Law
Procedure and Practice

Kumar Askand Pandey

INTRODUCTION

Persons under the age of 18 years, colloquially called children, constitute around 41 per cent of India's population[1] and are governed by a
different set of laws and procedures in all matters concerning them.[2]
The care and protection regime envisaged under these laws, the most
basic and essential being the Juvenile Justice (Care and Protection
of Children) Act, 2015 (hereinafter the JJ Act, 2015), not only takes
under its wings Children in Need of Care and Protection (CNCP) but
also Children in Conflict with Law (CICL).[3] The JJ Act, 2015, shall
apply'...to all matters concerning children in need of care and protection and children in conflict with law, including—(i) apprehension,
detention, prosecution, penalty or imprisonment, rehabilitation and

---

[1] https://censusindia.gov.in/census_and_you/age_structure_and_marital_status.
aspx#:~:text=The%20total%20number%20of%20children,in%20NCT%20
Delhi%20(97.5%25) (last visited 28 December 2020).

[2] See, Jitendra Singh v. State of U.P., 2013 (3) Crimes 319 (SC).

[3] See, JJ Act, 2015 Sections 2 (14) and 2 (13) of JJ Act, 2015, respectively.

social re-integration of children in conflict with law; …'.[4] Even the earlier law operating in the field, the Juvenile Justice (Care and Protection of Children) Act, 2000 (hereinafter the JJ Act, 2000), contained a similar provision that was added in the year 2006, giving it primacy in all matters of apprehension, detention and bail of children. However, even after two decades of enactment of these laws and rules framed thereunder, clarity on crucial questions of apprehension and bail eludes, primarily because the underlying objectives of the Act are not properly understood by the key functionaries of the juvenile justice system who often double as key functionaries of adult criminal justice system as well. It is, thus, difficult for them to keep the baggage of prior understanding of adult criminal jurisprudence out when entering the realm of juvenile justice system. Additionally, from the victim's point of view, it does not make a difference that the offence was committed by a child or an adult. The sense of victimization, the intensity of pain and trauma and the feeling of betrayal remain the same.

NATURE OF OFFENCES UNDER THE JUVENILE JUSTICE (CARE AND PROTECTION OF CHILDREN) ACT AND APPREHENSION OF CHILDREN

The JJ Act, 2015, classifies all offences into three categories: 'petty offence', 'serious offence' and 'heinous offence'. This classification is based on the quantum of prison term prescribed for the offence in question under any existing penal legislation, including the Indian Penal Code, 1860 (IPC). A petty offence is one where the maximum possible term of imprisonment does not exceed 3 years upon conviction. For an offence to be identified as a serious offence, the outer limit of possible prison term must be up to 7 years. A typical petty offence or serious offence will not ordinarily have a lower limit.[5] The third category is that of heinous offences where the minimum mandatory sentence should be 7 years imprisonment. Offences concerning rape and murder are obvious examples of heinous offences.

---

[4] Section 1(4), JJ Act 2015.
[5] Section 354, IPC carries a minimum prison term of 1 year and a maximum of 3 years. It is, by definition, a petty offence. Similarly, Section 370A (1) of IPC carries a minimum prison term of 5 years and a maximum of 7 years imprisonment.

However, the classification envisaged by the JJ Act, 2015, fails to place several offences in any of the three categories; for example, the offence of culpable homicide not amounting to murder is punishable with a minimum punishment of fine, life imprisonment being the outer limit of the punishment.[6] By definition, the offence is neither a serious offence nor a heinous offence. For almost 4 years of coming into force of the JJ Act, 2015, the statutory anomaly remained and the Juvenile Justice Boards (JJB) across the country arbitrarily placed all the offences where the maximum punishment is imprisonment for more than 7 years in the category of heinous offences.[7] This categorization, without any statutory basis, was antithetical to the principle of best interest of child. In *Shilpa Mittal v. State (NCT of Delhi)*,[8] the Supreme Court was called upon to clarify the mist surrounding the issue. In a unanimous opinion, the Supreme Court said that there is no ambiguity in the statutory definition, and even if an offence carries a punishment of imprisonment in excess of 7 years imprisonment, if the minimum punishment under the law is not imprisonment for 7 years, the offence in question is only a 'serious offence'.

It seems that the National Crime Record Bureau's (NCRB) data on crimes by children, which has consistently portrayed older children committing more crimes and also crimes such as rape and murder, provided the justification for classifying such offences as 'heinous'. The JJ Act, 2015, provides that a child in the age group of 16–18 years and accused of heinous offence may be tried as an adult.[9]

LOOKING AT CICL THROUGH THE LENS OF NCRB[10]

Crime statistics often present some peculiar facts that help the researchers to gain some not-too-obvious insights into the topic covered in the data. The objective of this part of the chapter is to find out, through official

---

[6] See, Section 304, IPC.

[7] KUMAR ASKAND PANDEY, JUVENILE JUSTICE—A COMMENTARY (Eastern Book Company, 1st ed. 2019/reprint 2020).

[8] (2020) 2 S.C.C. 787.

[9] See, Section 18 (3) of the JJ Act, 2015.

[10] See, https://ncrb.gov.in/en/crime-india (last visited 20 January 2021).

Table 7.1 *Crime Scenario: Adults Vis-à-Vis Children*

Year	Total Number of Crimes in India Reported to the Police	Number of Crimes by Children Reported to the Police	Overall Crime Rate	Percentage Share of Crime by Children	Crime Rate Among Children
2017	5,007,044	33,606	388.6	0.67	7.5
2018	5,074,635	31,591	383.5	0.62	7.1
2019	5,156,172	32,235	385.5	0.62	7.2

Source: Crime in India Reports, 2017–2019, National Crime Records Bureau, Govt. of India.

statistics on crimes committed by children, the factual position of number of apprehensions and release on bail. The Crime in India Reports for the years 2017, 2018 and 2019 have been used for relevant data and statistics.

From Table 7.1, it is evident that the percentage share of crime by children in overall crime statistics in India has been hovering between 0.62 per cent and 0.67 per cent in the past 3 years, for which the data are available. The crime rate, that is, number of crimes per 1 lakh population, is also only 7.1–7.5 for the children in the same period, whereas the overall crime rate is around 50 times higher.

The crime data for the same period reveal that more than one CICL is apprehended in around 21 per cent of cases registered against children. Around three-fourth of CICL apprehended by the police were in the age group of 16–18 years. The police regularly apprehend children under the age of 16 years for cognizable offences.

The number of CICL released on bail is not reported by NCRB in its reports as these only include the data on final disposal of cases.[11] On its homepage, NCRB claims that 'The report contains statistical information on cognizable crimes as reported in police stations during the reference year.'[12] It has been around 20 years that India

[11] See, Crime in India 2019, Bureau of Police Research and Development, Ministry of Home Affairs, Government of India, New Delhi.

[12] https://ncrb.gov.in/en/crime-india (last visited 20 December 2020).

Table 7.2 *Number of Apprehended CICL*

Year	Number of Crimes by CICL Reported to the Police and Converted into FIR	Total Number of Apprehended CICL	Number of Apprehended CICL Under the Age of 16 Years (Percentage Share)	Number of Apprehended CICL Between the Age of 16 Years and 18 Years (Percentage Share)
2017	33,606	40,420	11,226 (27.8)	29,194 (72.2)
2018	31,591	38,256	9,389 (24.5)	28,867 (75.5)
2019	32,235	38,685	9,601 (24.8)	29,084 (75.2)

Source: Crime in India Reports, 2017–2019, National Crime Records Bureau, Govt. of India.

had its UNCRC[13]-compliant juvenile justice regime; the classification of offences as 'cognizable' and 'non-cognizable' has no relevance to the JJ Act, 2015, but NCRB still collects, collates and presents data using the same parameters that is used for adult criminals.

In Chapter VA of the Crime in India Reports titled 'Juveniles in Conflict with Law (States & UTs)', among the crime heads of IPC offences, only a handful are those offences that have been classified as 'heinous' in the JJ Act, 2015. The prime examples would be the offences concerning murder, rape and waging war against the Government of India. The same is the case with the offences under Special and Local Laws (SLL offences) where barring a few, inter alia, under the Protection of Children from Sexual Offences Act, 2012, the Unlawful Activities Prevention Act, 1967, and the Explosive Substances Act, 1908, most of the offences are either 'petty' or 'serious'. Interestingly, theft constitutes almost 25 per cent of all the crimes reported against children, and the offences of hurt and grievous hurt account for around 18 per cent of crimes reported against children. These three offences constitute around 43 per cent of all the offences reported to the police and none of these are heinous.

---

[13] United Nations Convention on Rights of the Child was adopted and opened for signature, ratification and accession by General Assembly resolution 44/25 of 20 November 1989 and entered into force on 2 September 1990. Indian ratified the UNCRC in 1992.

FIRST INFORMATION REPORT AGAINST CHILDREN IN CONFLICT WITH LAW

Of the various principles governing the juvenile justice, an important principle is the principle of diversion. The principle of diversion enshrined in Section 3 (xv) of the JJ Act, 2015, says that 'Measures for dealing with children in conflict in law without resorting to judicial proceedings shall be promoted unless it is in the best interest of the child or the society as a whole'. Diversion of CICL from judicial proceedings cannot be made unless diversion from adult police system is made in the first place. Registration of a First Information Report (FIR) upon receipt of information about commission of a cognizable offence is a peculiar feature of adult criminal justice system.[14] As already mentioned, registration of FIR leads to arrest in most cases irrespective of whether the accused is an adult or a child. Indian police is especially notorious for arresting accused persons upon registration of FIR without substantial reasons.[15] Things have only worsened as may be gauged from the figures of the under-trial detainees in Indian prisons, which account for around 70 per cent of total prison population.[16]

Notably, the JJ Act, 2015, does not recognize and follow the Code of Criminal Procedure (CrPC) classification of offences. The seriousness of an offence reflected in the quantum of punishment has little to do with the law relating to apprehension of CICL.

Section 8 of the JJ Act, 2015, on the question of apprehension of CICL, unequivocally stipulates that 'there shall be no FIR against a child accused of a petty or a serious offence'; FIR may be registered only where the alleged offence is 'heinous' or such offence has been

---

[14] See, Lalita Kumari v. Government of Uttar Pradesh, (2014) 2 S.C.C. 1.

[15] Consultation Paper on Law Relating to Arrest, *177th Report of the Law Commission of India*, at 9, https://lawcommissionofindia.nic.in/reports/177rptp2.pdf (last visited 13 January 2021).

[16] Prison Statistics India 2019, National Crime Records Bureau, Ministry of Home Affairs, Government of India, https://ncrb.gov.in/en/prison-statistics-india-2019 (last visited 18 December 2020).

allegedly committed by CICL in association with an adult.[17] In all other cases, the JJ Act, 2015, provides that the police, upon receiving information of commission of an offence by a child, shall make a General Diary entry and proceed according to the provisions of the JJ Act, 2015, and not in accordance with CrPC. Rule 8 of the Juvenile Justice (Care and Protection of Children) Model Rules, 2016 (hereinafter the JJ Rules, 2016), details the procedure to be followed where a child is alleged to have committed an offence. Rule 9 of the JJ Rules, 2016 elaborately lays down the mechanism for producing CICL before JJB.

The figures shown in Table 7.2 portray a grim picture of implementation of the JJ Act, 2015. FIRs are being registered by the police even in cases of petty and serious offences and CICL are being apprehended by the police and sent to the observation homes (See Table 7.3). In a 'rapid assessment' conducted by the author in the observation homes in the state of Uttar Pradesh (UP), it was found that all the observation homes have inmate CICL beyond their capacities as the JJ Act, 2015, is not being followed by the key functionaries of the juvenile justice system.[18]

Table 7.3 *Children Apprehended in Petty and Serious Offences*

Year	Theft	Kidnapping and Abduction	Hurt and Grievous Hurt	Outraging Modesty of a Woman
2017	8,406	919	6,092	1,456
2018	8,332	893	5,640	1,408
2019	8,697	963	6,055	1,220

Source: Crime in India Reports, 2017–2019, National Crime Records Bureau, Govt. of India.

---

[17] However, empirically, even if the offence is the one designated as 'petty offence' but is classified as 'cognizable' by CrPC, FIR would be registered if a child was involved in its commission with an adult. Such FIR would necessarily include the child as a co-accused.

[18] The rapid assessment was conducted by Dr Ram Manohar Lohiya (RML) National Law University, Lucknow under the directions of Department of Women and Child Development, Government of Uttar Pradesh (DWCD) in the month of May 2016. The rapid assessment report of government-run observation homes was submitted to DWCD on 21 May 2016.

As on 3 April 2020, the date on which the Supreme Court in a *suo motu* writ petition[19] passed an order for release of children in institutional care, including CICL, UP with 24 functional observation homes, had a sanctioned capacity of 1,295 children. Thus, against the average capacity of 54 CICL, for each of the 24 observation homes, there were 2,044 children lodged therein. That amounts to a whopping 157 per cent occupancy rate,[20] worse than correctional institutions.[21] The Supreme Court passed a slew of directions for addressing the unprecedented pandemic in Child Care Institutions having both CICL and CNCP in mind. At around the same time, the Committee on the Rights of Child (CRC) on 8 April 2020, issued several guidelines[22] for mitigating the impact of the pandemic on children, especially those children who are apprehended and placed in detention. It said that

> …Authorities should evaluate all child detainees in the justice system for possible release, giving priority to children under the age of 16; children detained pre-trial; those detained for low-level or nonviolent offenses; those held for probation violations or failure to appear in court; those with medical conditions that may make them at particular risk of serious illness or death from COVID-19 infection, or that the institution would likely be unable to address appropriately given increased attention to COVID-19 cases; pregnant girls and those who are primary caregivers for their own or other children; and those nearing the end of their sentences.

CRC also asked the state parties to UNCRC to refrain from arresting or detaining children for violating directives relating to COVID-19 and ensure that any child who was arrested or detained is immediately returned to his or her family.

---

[19] In re COVID-19 Contagion in Child Protection Homes, 2020 S.C.C. OnLine S.C. 354.

[20] Ministry of Women and Child Development, Government of India, *The Report of the Committee for Analysing Data of Mapping and Review Exercise of Child Care Institutions Under the Juvenile Justice (Care &Protection of Children) Act, 2015 and Other Homes*, Vol. I, https://wcd.nic.in/sites/default/files/CIF%20Report%20 1_0_0.pdf (last visited 14 January 2021).

[21] See, Executive Summary, *The Prison Statistics India-2019*, https://ncrb.gov. in/sites/default/files/Executive-Summary-2019.pdf (last visited 21 January 2021).

[22] https://tbinternet.ohchr.org/Treaties/CRC/Shared%20Documents/1_ Global/INT_CRC_STA_9095_F.docx (last visited 10 June 2021).

Table 7.4 *CICL in Observation Homes in Uttar Pradesh as on 4 April 2020*[23]

Nature of Offence	Number of Children	Age Between 16 Years and 18 Years	Age Between 10 Years and 15 Years	Age Below 10 Years
Petty	22	10	11	01
Serious	91	53	36	02
Heinous	1,931	1,278	639	14

Source: The author.

All these children were kept in the observation homes pursuant to FIRs registered by the police. Even children as young as 10 years or below are kept at observation homes after being apprehended by the police (See Table 7.4). The Supreme Court directed that 'JJB shall consider taking steps to release all children on bail, unless there are clear and valid reasons for the application of the proviso to Section 12, JJ Act, 2015'. This was an important direction not only because many of CCIs in India lack basic facilities to address routine health and hygiene concerns, but also because most of the observation homes have children beyond their capacities, thereby putting the children to greater risk of the contagion.

In compliance with the order of the Supreme Court, in UP, 456 CICL were released on 'interim bail'[24] as on 17 May 2020. Of these, 159 were allegedly involved in petty offences, 268 in serious offences and 29 in heinous offences. In the same period, 7 CICL allegedly involved in serious offences, 2 in petty offences and 28 in heinous offences were also released on bail. It is submitted that this decongestion exercise was conducted as the Supreme Court had kept its watchful

---

[23] The data, not available in public domain, were compiled through the Divisional Technical Resource Persons, appointed by Dr RML National Law University, Lucknow for strengthening the child protection system in Uttar Pradesh, as part of a UNICEF-supported project of which the author is the project director.

[24] Interestingly, the JJ Act, 2015, does not use the term 'interim bail' in the only bail-related provision, that is, Section 12. Bail, whether interim or regular, must be granted or denied within the four corners of this provision.

eyes upon the developments in CCIs across the country, and there was no systemic understanding that detention and apprehension in most cases was unwarranted in the first place. Sadly, during the same period, even a greater number of children were being apprehended and sent to the observation homes for violation of lock-down rules, thus making the whole exercise a worthless formality.[25] It is also noteworthy that the number of CICL in observation homes in UP that stood at 656[26] rose by more than 300 per cent in the year 2020. In this period, no new observation homes were opened in the state.

Importantly, barely 2 months before this order was passed by the Supreme Court, it had passed another order in the ongoing petition highlighting abuse of children in institutional care. Upon the amicus curiae drawing the attention of the Court to certain instances of children being detained in police custody and tortured in UP and Delhi, the Court ordered that all JJBs in the country must follow the letter and spirit of the provisions of the JJ Act, 2015. The Supreme Court added that

> the JJBs are not meant to be silent spectators and pass orders only when a matter comes before them. They can take note of the factual situation if it comes to the knowledge of the JJBs that a child has been detailed in prison or police lock up: It is the duty of the JJBs to ensure that the child is immediately granted bail or sent to an observation home or a place of safety. The Act cannot be flouted by anybody, least of all the police.[27]

THE BAIL CONUNDRUM

The law on bail of CICL is simpler in form and substance but in its actual implementation has thrown complex challenges due to the preconceived notions and failure of the police, JJB and the courts to appreciate its true connotation.

---

[25] Although many states have framed their own state rules under the JJ Act, 2015, the basic framework and major provisions, inter alia, on apprehension and bail of children are common in all. Some states, such as Uttar Pradesh, have adopted the JJ Rules, 2016, in totality without any changes or modifications.

[26] *Supra* note 24.

[27] Re Exploitation of Children in Orphanages in the State of Tamil Nadu v. Union of India, MANU/SC/0339/2020.

The only provision in the JJ Act, 2015, that deals with bail is to be found in Section 12. The provision uses the phrase 'apparently a child', thereby implying that bail shall be granted to a person when the person's physical appearance suggests that the person is a child, even if no documentary proof of age is available at the time. Granting bail is mandatory irrespective of the fact whether the alleged offence is bailable or non-bailable. A closer look into the provision of bail in the JJ Act, 2015, brings out the following key features of the bail jurisprudence:

1. Bail is the rule and detention in observation home an exception.
2. Nature of offence, that is to say, the offence being bailable or non-bailable has no bearing on the decision of bail.
3. Even the police is empowered to release a child on bail, irrespective of the nature of the offence.
4. Release on bail may be without surety; alternatively, CICL shall be placed under the supervision of a probation officer or under the care of a fit person, including the child's parents or guardians.
5. A child not released on bail can be kept only in an observation home or place of safety.
6. The period of such detention in observation home or place of safety, pending inquiry, shall be as specified in the order.
7. Bail order is liable to modification if the conditions of bail are so onerous that they cannot be fulfilled by CICL within 7 days from its issuance.

Denial of bail is justified only on the following three grounds:

1. Bring the child in association with a known criminal;
2. expose him or her to social, moral and psychological danger; or
3. against the interest of justice.

Section 12 of the JJ Act, 2015, is a complete Code, and bail of a child is governed exclusively by this provision and no other.[28] A Division Bench of Chhattisgarh High Court has held that the general provisions of bail under CrPC, 1973, have no application to the bail of

---

[28] Karamdeep Kaur v. State of Punjab, 1995 (3) R.C.R. (Criminal) 5.

CICL and the same shall be governed exclusively by Section 12.[29] Denial of bail to a child should, therefore, be justified in terms of any of the circumstance envisaged under the proviso to Section 12, JJ Act, 2015.

Apparently, in order to prove 'association' with a 'known criminal', there must be evidence on record to show that the persons in association with each other share a common purpose and also that there exists a mental connection between their ideas. Therefore, where a person had joined a criminal or criminals in a single isolated case, such joining shall not be sufficient to infer that his or her release on bail shall bring the person in association with any known criminal. Similarly, a person cannot be said to be a known criminal unless he has been habitually committing offences and has a crime record (history sheet) with the police, whether ever convicted or not.

Exposure to moral, physical and psychological dangers can also be a ground for denial of bail; for example, in cases where the child is homeless and without any parental care or where the members of the family of the child have criminal antecedents, releasing the child on bail shall be barred on the aforementioned ground. Where the father of CICL gave an affidavit to the effect that he would take all measures to ensure that his remains afar from any criminal or bad elements in society and he shall be taken care of, physically, morally and psychologically, the Delhi High Court released the child on bail.[30]

It is important to note that the decision to release or not to release the child on bail should be taken on the basis of the Social Investigation Report[31] (SIR) and Social Background Report[32] (SBR). As SBR is prepared by Child Welfare Police Officer (CWPO), ideally, it should be prepared within 24 h of apprehending a child. SIR, a more detailed report about the child's circumstances and prepared by the Probation Officer or Child Welfare Officer or a social worker, must be submitted to JJB without waiting for an order for its submission and without

---

[29] Tejram Nagrachi v. State of Chhattisgarh, 2019 Cri LJ 4017. See also, CCL 'A' v. State (NCT of Delhi), 2021 Cri LJ 1251.

[30] Niku Chaubey v. State, 2006 (3) R.C.R. (Criminal) 372.

[31] See, Form 6 of the JJ Rules, 2016.

[32] See, Form 1 of the JJ Rules, 2016

any delay.[33] What SBR and SIR envisage is presentation of qualitative data to enable JJB or Court to take a decision in accordance with the letter and spirit of law. In *Rajesh Lakra v. State of Chhattisgarh*,[34] the Chhattisgarh High Court relied on SBR wherein the Probation Officer had opined that not releasing the child on bail and keeping him in the observation home shall have detrimental impact on his moral, physical and psychological development. Similarly, in *Shashi Kumar Saini v. State*,[35] the Delhi High Court noted that SIR reported the child to be of 'normal religious feeling' who had 'no delinquency regarding members of family' and the 'parents have normal affection and strong cohesive feeling'. Perusing SIR in totality, it was held that the child is entitled to bail. Unfortunately, in majority of cases, SBRs and SIRs are not being prepared or prepared in a mechanical manner, thereby leading to denial of bail in many genuine cases.[36]

In a significant observation, the Allahabad High Court in *Kanchan Sonkar v. State of U.P.*,[37] recently said that in a case where there is very little or no prima facie evidence against the child, testing his or her case on the touchstone of the proviso to Section 12 of the JJ Act, 2015, shall be violative of right to equality enshrined in Article 14 of the Constitution. If an adult person would have obtained bail on the ground that there is no prima facie case against the accused, in absence of any material connecting the child to the offence, bail cannot be denied to a child taking refuge under the proviso of Section 12, JJ Act, 2015.[38]

Intriguingly, there is no uniformity in the approach of the courts as to when can it be said that releasing a child on bail shall 'defeat the ends of justice'. Often, the courts have refused bail on the ground that the offence complained of is very grave in nature and therefore, releasing CICL on bail shall 'defeat the ends of justice'.[39]

---

[33] See, Rule 64 of JJ Rules, 2016.

[34] 2014 (5) M.P.H.T. 58 (CG).

[35] 2005 (3) R.C.R. (Criminal) 913.

[36] Afsal Ibrahim v. State of Kerala, 2013 Cri L.J. 4945.

[37] MANU/UP/2078/2020.

[38] See also, Dharmendra (Juvenile) v. State of U.P., 2018 (7) A.D.J. 864.

[39] See, Sonu v. State of U.P., MANU/UP/1512/2020, where the Allahabad High Court denied bail to a child aged between 16–17 and accused of an offence under Section 6 of Protection of Children from Sexual Offences Act, 2012. See also, Mangesh Rajbhar v. State of U.P., 2018 (2) A.C.R. 1941.

In *Aaraf Khan v. State of M.P.*[40] the single bench of Madhya Pradesh High Court sought guidance from Section 18 of the JJ Act, 2015, on the question of bail of CICL who was accused of committing aggravated penetrative sexual assault on a 14-year-old survivor. The Court while denying bail to the accused said that

> Thus, it is no ultimate rule that a juvenile below the age of 16 years has to be granted bail and can be denied the privilege only on the first two of the grounds mentioned in the proviso... It can be equally refused on the ground that releasing a juvenile that includes a juvenile below 16 years would "defeat the ends of justice.

Interpreting the phrase 'defeat the ends of justice' used in the proviso to Section 12 of the JJ Act, 2015, and calling it a disentitling legislative edict, the Court said that nature and gravity of offence is, inter alia, one of the relevant considerations for invoking this part of the proviso. However, it is to be noted that in many earlier decisions, the Allahabad High Court has exhibited a contrary pattern consistently holding that gravity of the offence allegedly committed by a child is no ground to refuse bail.[41] 'Since gravity of the offence is not incorporated as one of the reasons for refusal of bail, this ground cannot be taken into consideration for rejection of request for bail.'[42] The Orissa High Court has also expressed similar views.[43] In *Niku Chaubey v. State (NCT of Delhi)*,[44] the Delhi High Court held that the nature of offence is not germane to the grant or refusal of bail to a child. While holding that SIR must be read and relied on carefully, the Court deprecated the approach of the courts below in invoking the 'defeat the ends of justice' clause for denying bail in a mechanical manner.[45]

---

[40] MANU/MP/1409/2020.

[41] See, Shiv Kumar alias Sadhu v. State of U.P., 2010 (68) A.C.C. 616(LB); Abdullah @ Abdul Hassan v. State of U.P., 2015 (90) A.C.C. 204; Maroof v. State of U.P., 2015 (6) A.D.J. 203; Amit Kumar v. State of U.P., 2010 (71) A.C.C. 209.

[42] Neha v. State of Punjab, 2018 (2) R.C.R. (Criminal) 226; Sahil v. State of Haryana, MANU/PH/0431/2020.

[43] A. Juvenile v. State of Orissa 2009 Cri L.J. 2002.

[44] 129 (2006) D.L.T. 577.

[45] Sandeep v. State (NCT of Delhi), 2008 (1) R.C.R. (Criminal) 146.

It is submitted that the interpretation proffered by the Madhya Pradesh High Court and, of late, the Allahabad High Court is not in line with observations made by various other high courts; even the other benches of the same High Court, in as much as the phrase 'defeat the ends of justice' shall mean 'defeat the ends of justice as envisaged under the juvenile justice laws'.[46] Evidently, the idea of justice under the JJ Act, 2015, is sans any element of retribution and vengeance.

ANTICIPATORY BAIL TO CHILDREN IN CONFLICT WITH LAW

Invocation and application of anticipatory bail provision in the scheme of CrPC has been the most contentious and greyest area vis-à-vis the JJ Act, 2015. Needless to mention that the anticipatory bail provision was engrafted in the criminal jurisprudence to protect an individual from unnecessary restraint on personal liberty.[47] However, maintainability of an anticipatory bail application of a child is far from settled and different high courts have shown different approaches. The Rajasthan High Court, in *Sachin v. State of Rajasthan*,[48] observed that the concession of anticipatory bail can be denied to persons, including a child, accused of grave offences.

In arriving at the conclusion that Section 438 has no application to a child, a Division Bench of Madras High Court in *K. Vignesh v. State*[49] preferred a hyper technical interpretation of the word 'apprehend' as used in the different provisions of the JJ Act, 2015, holding that as the legislature has used the expression 'apprehended' in Section 10 of the JJ Act, 2015, it did not intend to empower the 'arrest' of CICL, and therefore, an application for anticipatory bail to the High Court or a Sessions Court is not maintainable.[50]

Recently, the Allahabad High Court, in *Shahaab Ali v. State of U.P,*[51] said that once FIR is registered against a child or information otherwise

---

[46] See, Mohd. Adnan Aftab v. State (NCT of Delhi), (2007) S.C.C. OnLine Del 844; Paplu v. State of U.P., (2015) 2 All L.J. 92.

[47] Siddharam Satlingappa Mhetre v. State of Maharashtra, (2011) 1 S.C.C. (Cri) 514.

[48] 2002 (3) R.C.R. (Criminal) 221.

[49] MANU/TN/1491/2017.

[50] See also, Lakshmanan v. State, MANU/TN/0086/2016.

[51] 2020 (2) A.D.J. 130.

is recorded against a child for his or her complicity in an offence, Section 438 of CrPC stands excluded and the provisions of Sections 10 and 12 of the JJ Act, 2015, shall apply. The Court further said that the provision of anticipatory bail as contained in Section 438 of CrPC shall have an application only in the case of a child against whom, though no FIR has been registered, apprehension or likelihood of arrest remains.[52]

It is submitted that the judicial approach of keeping Section 438, CrPC, completely at bay on the question of anticipatory bail is problematic, as even assuming that the JJ Act, 2015, and the JJ Rules, 2016, provide for a complete Code for dealing with children, Section 12 of the JJ Act, 2015, is in no way in conflict with Section 438 of CrPC. Importantly, Section 8 of the JJ Act, 2015, mandates that the powers of JJB may also be exercised by the high courts and the Children's Court when the proceedings come before them'…in appeal, revision or otherwise'.[53] As has been held by the Kerala High Court in *Mr. X S/O Baby V.M. v. State of Kerala*,[54] recognizing and maintaining a difference between 'arrest' and 'apprehend' would be an unnecessary technicality as 'the expression "apprehend" would include and necessarily involve the arrest of a person and consequently it cannot be held that an application for anticipatory bail could not be maintained by the child'. [55] It seems that the Allahabad High Court's decision of excluding Section 438 of CrPC stems from its opinion that the CrPC provision is fraught with the danger of imposing onerous conditions of bail, whereas Section 12 is a truly 'child friendly' provision.

In a significant decision, while replying to a reference made to it in view of conflicting decisions of coordinate benches, the Chhattisgarh High Court observed that

The application for grant of anticipatory bail under Section 438 of the Code of Criminal Procedure, 1973 at the behest of CICL before the

---

[52] See also, Preetam Pathak v. State of Chhattisgarh 2015 (3) Crimes 638(Chhatt.); Kapil Durgawani v. State of M.P., 2010 (IV) M.P.J.R. 155; Sandeep Singh Tomar v. State of M.P., 2014(IV) M.P.J.R. 49.

[53] Gopa Kumar v. State of Kerala, 2013 Cri L.J. 851.

[54] Bail Application No. 3320 of 2018 decided on 5 June 2018 (Crime No. 349 of 2018).

[55] See also, Sudhir Sharma v. State of Chhattisgarh, 2017 (3) C.G. L.J. 405; Birbal Munda v. State of Chhattisgarh, MANU/JH/1400/2019.

High Court or the Court of Sessions is maintainable under the law and the said remedy is not excluded by operation of Section 12 of the Act of 2000 or … Act of 2015.[56]

It is submitted that the view expressed by the Court that petition for anticipatory bail is maintainable in case of CICL is in keeping with the fundamental principle of best interest of child. It is further submitted that the JJ Act, 2015, shall exclude the application of any law in matters of children only when the latter is repugnant to the former. There is no repugnancy between Section 438 of CrPC and Section 12 of the JJ Act, 2015, except that the conditions of bail may be modified by JJB or the Court under the latter, if the same is too onerous for the child, whereas mellowing the conditions of bail is not possible under the former.

In *Tara Chand v. State of Rajasthan*,[57] while emphasizing on the word 'appears' in Section 12 of the JJ Act, 2015, the Court aptly said that the idea of anticipatory bail is inbuilt in the provision itself; where CICL has moved an application for being released on anticipatory bail, such case would be covered by the language 'appears … before the Board' and the application under Section 438 of CrPC shall be maintainable. There is no gainsaying that a person shall not 'appear' before JJB or the Court unless he or she has a reasonable apprehension of arrest.

CONCLUSION AND SUGGESTIONS

The crime data annually published by the NCRB portray a very grim picture of the implementation of the JJ Act, 2015. This is so even when the JJ Act, 2000, also contained elaborate provisions similar to the ones in the present Act, seeking to establish a justice system for CICL with the salutary objective of reformation, rehabilitation and reintegration of children in the mainstream of the society. The JJ Act, 2015, even bars use of stigmatizing semantics against children and lays down that the words generally used in the adult criminal justice system, namely arrest, trial, sentencing, punishment, etc. shall not be used in cases of CICL. Throughout the JJ Act, 2015, non-stigmatizing semantics are

---

[56] Sudhir Sharma v. State of Chhattisgarh, 2017 (3) C.G. L.J. 405.
[57] 2007 Cri L.J. 3047.

used: apprehension for arrest, inquiry for trial and dispositional order for punishment and sentence. However, in spite of the clear legislative edict, children are still being treated the same way their adult counterparts are treated. The state governments should organize orientation programmes for the key functionaries of the juvenile justice system at regular intervals to inculcate the value system envisaged under the JJ Act, 2015.

It is also important that Special Juvenile Police Unit (SJPU) is strengthened in the true spirit of the JJ Act, 2015, and CWPOs are chosen from an exclusive cadre of police officers with aptitude and understanding of child rights jurisprudence. The Principal Magistrates of JJB should also be oriented to the juvenile justice system and should exclusively sit in JJBs.

The divergent views expressed by different high courts and sometimes even by the coordinate benches of the same high court on critical issues of bail, including pre-apprehension bail, have only led to further mess in the juvenile justice system. It must be reiterated that the JJ Act, 2015, does not take away or abridge any of the rights recognized under other procedural laws. It shall override any other law only in case there is inconsistency between them.

It is hoped that the Supreme Court shall take stock of the sorry state of affairs in the ongoing writ petition[58] and issue appropriate directions to all the key functionaries of the juvenile justice system to follow the statutory provisions in letter and spirit.

---

[58] Re Exploitation of Children in Orphanages in the State of Tamil Nadu v. Union of India, MANU/SC/0339/2020.

Chapter 8

Inter-state Arrest
Safeguards and Remedies

Kavita Singh

INTRODUCTION

Inter-state investigation, effecting arrests in India, has historically called for scrutiny owing to bureaucratic and jurisdictional lapses that occurred due to lack of specific rules involving an arrest in another territory. In reality, all resolved concepts and problems were typically addressed by the principles followed in operation by the respective states or state administration framework. Under Section 48 of the Code of Criminal Procedure (CrPC), 1973, it has been allowed to pursue criminals in other jurisdictions. A police officer, for the purpose of arresting without a warrant whom he is allowed to arrest, may pursue an individual anywhere in India.[1]

However, compliance and regulation-wise, states have introduced activities not in accordance with the above law. Precedents have

---

[1] See, Tasleema v. State (NCT of Delhi) (2009) I.L.R. 6 Del 486, this Court noted 'with consternation that police officials from Gujarat were able to arrest and takeaway a juvenile from Delhi without informing the Delhi Police. Such practice is obviously contrary to the police manuals and if such actions go unchecked, it will amount to condoning lawlessness by the police force. In a country governed by the rule of law, this is simply unacceptable'.

historically demonstrated that a state's police are not empowered to undertake an arrest or detention in another State until the local police are informed.[2] Practices also cast a responsibility or requirement on the regulatory structure to bring prosecution and detention processes to the attention of the municipal police who only exercise authority and powers to influence indictment and related prosecutions. Here, Territorial Authority Boundaries are operative and effectively render the local police rights to make an arrest. The Investigating Officer (IO) (police) will actually seek assistance from the other State's local police and, the latter on intimation will move on to apprehend the perpetrator and deliver them within the specified timeframe of 24 hrs before a judge who will issue a transit remand. The accused is then handed over to the State's police custody where the offence was committed, in other words, where the case was registered. This is a common protocol in India among State police forces. Even, local police must be told of the inquiries and searches carried out in their state. It was found that maximum of local police incidents are typically involved with the other State's local police, owing to their position and area expertise.[3]

LAW, PROCEDURE AND SAFEGUARDS TO ARREST PERSONS FROM ANOTHER STATE

Chapter 5 of CrPC, 1973, lists down the procedure for the arrest of a person. Section 41 of the Code empowers a police officer to arrest a person without a warrant on the receipt of information regarding the commission of a cognizable offence. Section 48 of the Code gives a police officer the power to pursue any person in the territory in order to arrest them without a warrant, provided they are authorized to do so. If a warrant has to be executed out of the jurisdiction of a Court, that Court can forward that warrant to the Executive Magistrate (EM), Deputy Superintendent of Police (DSP) or Commissioner of Police (CP) of the jurisdiction where it needs to be executed.[4] Similarly, the Court may direct a warrant to a police officer to execute it outside the jurisdiction

---

[2] Section 166(3) CrPC, 1973.

[3] UNODC, *Handbook on Police Accountability, Oversight and Integrity*, https://www.unodc.org/documents/justice-and-prison reform/crimeprevention/PoliceAccountability_Oversight_and_Integrity_10-57991_Ebook.pdf

[4] The Code of Criminal Procedure, 1973, §78.

of the court.[5] In this case, the police officer will also have to get such a warrant endorsed by EM or a police officer not below the rank of Station House Officer (SHO) where the warrant has to be executed. However, if such a police officer has reason to believe that the obtainment of such endorsement would cause delay in the execution of the warrant, he can execute it outside the jurisdiction without such endorsement.[6] The arrested person should be presented before the local EM, DSP or CP for permission to be taken out of the State/UT, also known as transit remand.[7]

The word 'transit remand' is neither mentioned nor defined in CrPC and is rather a term that has evolved through its usage in common parlance. To put it simply, transit remand can be said to be the remand of the accused, sought by the police, for taking the accused from one place to another in their own custody, usually for the purpose of producing him before the concerned Magistrate who has jurisdiction to try/commit the case (Jurisdictional Magistrate). The primary purpose of such a remand is to enable the police to shift the person in custody from the place of arrest to the place where the matter can be investigated and tried. The concept of transit remand is implicit in Section 167, CrPC, 1973, and it can also be said to be a special type or a subspecies of police custody remand which is given for the particular purpose of the transit of the accused. Needless to say, when the police present the accused before the Jurisdictional Magistrate, they have to move a fresh application if they want police custody remand since the purpose of the transit remand stands extinguished/discharged.

Taking the example of the case of Vikas Dubey, the crime was said to have been committed in Kanpur, and as such the courts in Kanpur would ultimately have jurisdiction in the matter. As such, when the accused was arrested in Ujjain, it would have been necessary for the Uttar Pradesh (UP) Police to take the accused to Kanpur for further investigation and trial. Now in order for the police to have kept the accused in their own custody beyond 24 h and themselves produce him before the Jurisdictional Magistrate at Kanpur, the police would have had to seek the permission of the court at Ujjain for transit remand.

---

[5] *Id.*, §79.

[6] *Id.*, § 79(3).

[7] *Id.*, §80.

Another instance when a transit remand is sought is when the accused person is in jail (either during the investigation, during the trial or after conviction), and he is also an accused in another case which must be investigated and tried in a different district. In such a case, a request maybe made by the police authorities to the concerned court, which may grant such permission, if it deems fit, to transfer the accused person and produce him before the court where he has to be tried for the other case. In such a case, the accused would be formally arrested by the police, and such an order would be carried out in terms of Section 167(2), CrPC.

Although, in practice, the most commonly sought transit remand is the one as contemplated in Section 167, CrPC, being a generic word, the same is also used in other situations; for instance, transit remand may also be sought under Section 80, CrPC, 1973. The main difference in both the situations is that Section 80 is applicable only where the accused is arrested under a warrant issued by a court in a district which is different from the district where the accused is arrested. However, in cases like Dubey's, where the police officer arrests without a warrant, the transit remand which must be sought is the one contemplated under Section 167, CrPC.

Sections 78 and 79, CrPC, specifically talk about the procedure to be followed while initiating an arrest outside the jurisdiction. This section does not specify the extent of its applicability, but considering the applicability of the provisions such as 41, 42 and 46 CrPC, it is evident that the jurisdiction mentioned within the provisions does not restrict itself from pan-India applicability. Hence, Sections 78[8]

---

[8] Section 78 of CrPC—warrant forwarded for execution outside jurisdiction.

(1) When a warrant is to be executed outside the local jurisdiction of the Court issuing it, such Court may, instead of directing the warrant to a police officer within its jurisdiction, forward it by post or otherwise to any EM or DSP or CM within the local limits of whose jurisdiction it is to be executed, and EM or District Superintendent or Commissioner shall endorse his name thereon, and if practicable, cause it to be executed in the manner hereinbefore provided.

(2) The Court issuing a warrant under Sub-section (1) shall forward, along with the warrant, the substance of the information against the person to be arrested together with such documents, if any, as may be sufficient to enable the Court acting under Section 81 to decide whether bail should or should not be granted to the person.

and 79,[9] CrPC, would be applicable in instances where the arrest is to take place, that is, in another State or within the jurisdiction of another high court.

According to Sections 78 and 79, CrPC, the warrant must be served to SHO of the police station that has jurisdiction or EM of the court with the jurisdiction over the territory where such arrest is to be made. However, the procedure, the law and the safeguards remain the same as those for the arrest taking place within the jurisdiction. Therefore, no person shall be subject to brutality inducted by the police if the person so arrested submits to the custody; neither such person should be subject to any physical restraint like handcuffs or tied with a rope[10]. Furthermore, notwithstanding the nature of the arrest, due orders from the Magistrate are required to tie or handcuff a person. Similarly, as held by the Supreme Court in *Deoman Upadhya v. State,*[11] if a person approaches or proceeds towards the police station on the order of the police officer, then the person would be held to have submitted to the custody of the police officer.[12] However, if the conduct of the police officer making the arrest is not in compliance of Section 46, CrPC, such arrest is deemed to be liable to be void.[13]

---

[9] Section 79 of CrPC—warrant directed to police officer for execution outside jurisdiction.

(1) When a warrant directed to a police officer is to be executed beyond the local jurisdiction of the Court issuing the same, he shall ordinarily take it for endorsement either to EM or to a police officer not below the rank of an officer in charge of a police station, within the local limits of whose jurisdiction the warrant is to be executed.

(2) Such Magistrate or police officer shall endorse his name thereon and such endorsement shall be sufficient authority to the police officer to whom the warrant is directed to execute the same, and the local police shall, if so required, assist such officer in executing such warrant.

(3) Whenever there is reason to believe that the delay occasioned by obtaining the endorsement of the Magistrate or police officer within whose local jurisdiction the warrant is to be executed will prevent such execution, the police officer to whom it is directed may execute the same without such endorsement in any place beyond the local jurisdiction of the Court which issued it.

[10] Section 49 of CrPC, 1973.

[11] Birendra K. Rai v. Union of India, 1992 Cr L.J. 3866 (All).

[12] Deoman Upadhya v. State, A.I.R. 1960 S.C. 1131.

[13] Roshan Beevi v. Joint Secretary to Govt. of Kerala, 1984 Cr L.J. 134 (Mad) (F.B.).

However, there has been rampant misuse of these provisions by the police. There have been several instances where police officers of a lower rank did not seek permission from their senior officers and went to another jurisdiction to arrest someone. In many cases, police officers in civilian clothing effected such arrests without producing any warrant or providing the arrested person any reasonable cause for their arrest.[14] Arrests have also been made by producing fake police identity cards (IDs) and taking the arrested to undisclosed locations and torturing them.[15]

In one case, a married couple were arrested from their hostel in Jawaharlal Nehru University by officers of the UP Police, dressed in civilian clothing, based on a complaint filed by the woman's father. The man was taken to a jail in Ghaziabad, UP and was tortured for 3 days without being produced in front of a Magistrate. The Delhi High Court, while issuing a writ of habeas corpus, noted that the 'lawlessness' of the police compromised the safety and liberty of citizens and was a flagrant violation of due process.[16] The Court also directed the UP to give a compensation of ₹100,000 to the couple.

Recently, activist Disha A. Ravi was arrested by the Delhi Police in civilian clothes from her Bengaluru residence, apparently without informing her family or her lawyer. The Bengaluru Police stated that they were not aware of her arrest until she was on the flight to Delhi. A senior Karnataka police officer told *The Quint*[17] that though a judicial officer was present, local police officials were not involved. There are several speculations over whether the local police were informed and

---

[14] Press Trust of India, *Revisit Inter-State Arrest Procedure: HC*, THE HINDU, 28 August 2018, https://www.thehindu.com/news/cities/Delhi/revisit-inter-state-arrest-procedure-hc/Articleicle24796023.ece

[15] *Id.*

[16] Sandeep Kumar v. The State, W.P. (Crl.) No.2189/2018 Decided on 12 December 2019 (Delhi High Court), https://www.barandbench.com/news/litigation/cannot-condone-lawlessness-by-police-delhi-hc-orders-execution-of-guidelines-on-inter-state-investigation-and-arrest-read-guidelines

[17] https://www.thequint.com/news/law/disha-ravi-arrest-delhi-police-transit-remand-legal-representation-media-narrative-high-court-orders (last visited 21 March 2021).

involved in the arrest of Ravi, as contradictory claims are reported. A transit remand by production before the 'nearest magistrate' within 24 h was also disregarded, and she was directly produced before the duty Magistrate in the Patiala House Court. She was only formally arrested in Delhi, not Bengaluru, and the transit remand's compliance went entirely unchecked.[18]

GUIDELINES LAID DOWN BY COURTS

The courts have played an active part in ensuring that due respect is paid to human rights while arresting persons and taking them into custody. The Supreme Court has placed safeguards upon the wide discretionary powers of the police by laying down various guidelines. The Supreme Court in *Nandini Satpathy v. PL Dani*[19] sought to differentiate between the police's power to arrest and the justification to do so. It noted that a person cannot be arrested based on mere allegations made in a complaint. Any arrest should be made based upon the police officer's 'reasonable satisfaction', which should be endeavoured to be recorded in writing. The Supreme Court further laid down comprehensive and exhaustive guidelines in *DK Basu v. State of West Bengal*.[20] Apart from reiterating the guidelines in *Nandini Satpathy*, the Court suggested many preventive measures to ensure transparency in the process of arrest.

The Delhi High Court also formed a Commission, comprising of retired Justice S. P. Garg and former Director General of Police (Investigation) Kanwaljit Deol, to suggest guidelines on inter-state arrests. Following were the guidelines suggested by them in their report[21]:

1. The Police Officer, to whom a case is assigned and has to go out of the State/UT to carry out investigation in this regard, will first have to seek the sanction of their higher/superior officer in writing.

---

[18] https://thewire.in/rights/disha-ravi-arrest-police-disregard-safeguards-law (last visited 21 March 2021).

[19] 1978 A.I.R. 1025.

[20] (1997) 1 S.C.C. 416.

[21] MANU/DE/4326/2019.

2. A police officer has to record the facts of the case, reason and necessity of arrest in writing before effecting the arrest of any person. At first, the police officer should approach the Judicial Magistrate for issuing a warrant under Sections 78 and 79 of CrPC. Where there is an exigency and dearth of time, and the arrest has to be made immediately, the police officer may not approach the Magistrate for the above-mentioned warrant. However, here too, the police officer must record in writing the 'compelling reasons' to not obtain such a warrant and proceeding to another State/UT.

3. The police officer must make a comprehensive departure entry in the daily diary of his police station. It should contain names of the police officials and private individuals accompanying him, registration number of the vehicle to be used, purpose of visit, specific place(s) to be visited and time and date of departure. Only official vehicle should be used for transportation purposes, the use of which should be recorded in a logbook.

4. In case a female person is to be arrested, at least one lady police officer should be a part of the team making the arrest. The police officers should have their IDS with them on all times. They should be dressed in their official uniforms with badges clearly stating their name and designation. The information provided on these name badges should be accurate.

5. The police officer must contact and inform the local police station under whose jurisdiction they want to effect the arrest. The complaint/FIR should be translated into the local language of the State/UT which the police officer is visiting and copies of the same should be provided to the local police station.

6. The local police station should be approached first to seek legal assistance and cooperation and SHO of the said police station should provide such assistance. Entry to this effect must be made at the said police station.

7. Investigation should be done in compliance with the procedure laid down u/s 100 of CrPC and in presence of public witnesses. Arrests, if any, should be made in compliance with the procedure laid down under Sections 41A, 41B, 50 and 51, CrPC. The team should also make sure that the guidelines laid down by the Supreme

Court in the case of *DK Basu v. State of West Bengal*[22] should be complied with strictly.

8. The arrestee must be informed of the grounds of arrest and shall be allowed to contact their lawyer before they are taken out of the State/UT, in compliance with Article 22 (1) of the Constitution.

9. Before leaving the concerned State/UT, the police officer should make an entry in the daily diary of the local police station. This entry should specify the name and address of the arrested person(s) and a list of all the articles recovered. The entry should also mention the name of the complainant/victim.

10. The police officer should obtain the transit remand required under Section 80, CrPC, from the nearest Magistrate. However, if the police officer fails to do so due to any exigency, the arrestee should be presented before the Magistrate having jurisdiction of the case within 24 h from the time such arrest is made in accordance with Section 57, CrPC.

11. The Magistrate should grant transit remand only after proper application of mind to the facts at hand. The written entries made by the police officer should be thoroughly scrutinized in this regard. The act of directing the remand of the person arrested is a judicial decision.

12. Names and addresses of the persons arrested and designation of the police officers who made the arrest must be displayed. Control Room at state level must collect details of the persons so arrested.

13. The arrestee may be permitted to be accompanied by a family member/acquaintance till the time they are presented in front of the Magistrate.

14. On arriving back to the police station with jurisdiction, the police officer must make an arrival entry recording the details of the investigation carried out by them, the name of the arrestee and the articles recovered. The senior officers should be informed immediately.

15. The police officer should be made liable for departmental inquiry and contempt of Court for failure to follow these guidelines. Such police officer may also be directed to pay monetary compensation to the persons arrested under public law and tort law of strict liability.

---

[22] (1997) 1 S.C.C. 416.

In the case of *Sandeep Kumar v. State (NCT of Delhi)*,[23] guidelines were explicitly set for CrPC Sections 48,77,[24]79 and 80 as follows:

1. Police officers must alert senior-level officers after assignment of certain cases and request authorization to go out of State/UT for investigation.
2. Police officers shall report the compelling reasons for arrest of the accused.
3. Officers shall contact a Jurisdictional Magistrate Court to secure an arrest warrant and shall also mention grounds for not obtaining a warrant in emergency situations.
4. Departure and appearance entry shall be recorded in police station's kept diary.
5. Until entering other state jurisdiction, officers can preferably call the local authority police station and locate an inquiry node. Additionally, he must carry copy of the FIR or complaint.
6. Upon entry, the nearest police station involved shall be informed to request help for arrest of the offender. The police arrest procedure must comply with the guidance provided in D. K. Basu case and CrPC provisions.
7. The accused shall have the right to contact a counsel before being removed from the jurisdiction.
8. The police shall procure a transit warrant/remand after the detention before the nearest Magistrate.

However, these guidelines have only been issued by the Delhi High Court and have not been affirmed by the Supreme Court yet. These have not been notified, either by the Central or State Government, National Police Commission (NCP) or National Human Rights Commission (NHRC). It remains to be seen how the implementation of these guidelines pans out.

---

[23] W.P. (Crl.) No. 2189/2018.
[24] Section 77 CrPC—*this Section is essential for the purposes of carrying out arrests through state borders as it states that a warrant of arrest is executable at any location in India.*

HUMAN RIGHTS ISSUES WHILE EFFECTING ARREST

Many human rights are said to be infringed while effecting an arrest. While some of them may be unjustified and denial of basic human rights, some human rights can be lawfully curtailed by the operation of law.[25] In some cases, such denial of rights is made while trying to balance the interest of the society as well as the arrested person. The arrested person is, after all, a normal human being having a right to enjoy all his rights. However, in cases where the arrested person has committed a grave offence and the interest of the society is prejudiced, some rights of the arrested person may be curtailed. Looking at the entire process of arrest of the accused person, the following human rights issues arise:

Before arrest—in cases of cognizable offences where the police may arrest without a warrant,[26] the police can arrest a person only on grounds of some information or a reasonable suspicion. If the arrest is challenged in court, the police officer has the burden of proving that he had reasonable grounds to suspect the arrested person. CrPC provides a safeguard against arbitrary and unjustified arrests.

Arrest made—when a person is arrested, the first human right that is said to have been infringed is his personal liberty and freedom of movement. If the arrest is made unlawfully and without a warrant (in case of a cognizable offence), then such arrest would be invalid under the law and the arrested person's right under Article 21 would be said to have been violated.[27] Article 21 right cannot be denied to arrested persons and prisoners, except through procedure established by law. Special care must be taken when the arrested person is a female, where only a female officer can arrest. However, if the female officer is not present, the male officer shall not touch the arrested woman, while following the time restrictions laid down in the Code. If at any time, the accused person forcibly resists the

---

[25] Nilabati Bhera v. State of Orissa and Ors., (1993) 2 S.C.C. 746.
[26] Under Section 41 of CrPC, 1973.
[27] Maneka Gandhi v. Union of India, A.I.R. 1978 S.C. 597.

arrest or attempts to evade the arrest, then the police can use all means necessary to effect the arrest. Once the arrest is made, the accused person has the right to know the grounds on which he has been arrested and his right to bail.

Post-arrest detention—the law permits the detention of arrested persons. However, such period cannot be longer than 24 h during which time he must be produced before a Magistrate. If the arrested person is not produced within 24 h, this would be a violation of Article 22 (2). In *Khatri vs State of Bihar*,[28] the Supreme Court held that the legal requirement of producing the arrested person within 24 h must be scrupulously observed. If the arrest is made for a non-cognizable and bailable offence, then the arrested person can furnish a bond and be released on bail under Section 50 (2). There must not be any shortcoming in the duties of the police officer while effectuating an arrest because it is the personal liberty and basic human rights of an individual that is hampered. Legal aid must also be provided to those arrested persons who can afford the services of a lawyer. This ensures that both sides are heard, and the principles of natural justice are upheld.

A lot of times, when the police arrest a person, the person is subjected to different modes of torture to extract confession. For this, the accused person has a right to ask for a medical examination, under Section 54, by a medical officer. This would show whether or not the police have tortured the arrested person after arrest.

NCP too has noted that the judicial and legislative guidelines are breached more than they are followed. It noted the power of arrest as one of the chief sources of corruption in police.[29] It observed that there have been several instances of flagrant violation of human rights of the arrested persons—manifesting in vexatious arrests, obstruction of legal counsel, custodial torture, indefinite detentions, etc. An arrest is a restriction on the person's freedom and liberty, and it can also impact their reputation in the society.[30] Hence, it is imperative that utmost care is taken to effect an arrest and all due procedure is followed. The Law

---

[28] A.I.R. 1983 S.C. 378.

[29] National Police Commission, Third Report, p. 31.

[30] Joginder Kumar v. State of UP, (1994) 4 S.C.C. 260.

Commission of India noted this and requested NHRC to frame guidelines for enforcement of human rights during the procedure of arrest.[31] NHRC issued the Guidelines on Arrest, 1999, listing various safeguards to be followed in the pre-arrest, arrest and post-arrest phases[32].

CHALLENGES IN THE INDIAN SYSTEM

Proper documentation is required by the officer of one police station while effecting arrest in another State regarding identification of person to be apprehended who either fled to another State or lives in another State. A Station House Diary should be kept with proper records and required to be produced, if questioned in this regard. The person concerned required to be arrested, prosecuted and placed to a court of jurisdiction is responsibility of the investigation officer. The intimation of such arrest is required to be made to the local police station of the jurisdiction from where the arrest is to be effected. It is a settled procedure of law that the local SHO must be provided the details about the accused to be apprehended by way of arrest in their jurisdiction. The police diary must be revised at frequent intervals by entries whenever there are correspondences. Similarly, with a message obtained from another jurisdiction, steps should be taken to check and access the documents involved. The reply should be submitted dependent on inquiries. Respective States are expected to follow the procedure laid down in the law while effecting an inter-state arrest. However, it is seldom followed.

> The conflict gets reflected either in displaying disrespect to the executive authority of the one State by another or in refraining to extend the support needed for maintaining the harmony between the States. The rift between the Governments of Bihar and Maharashtra, on the matter of investigation of the death of the Sushant Singh Rajput, is a testimony of such conflicts and presents a reason to examine the States' statuses in the constitutional scheme. The inquiry becomes relevant

---

[31] The Law Commission of India, *Law Relating to Arrest*, Report No. 177 (December 2001).

[32] https://police.py.gov.in/NHRC%20Guidelines%20Regarding/NHRC%20 Guidelines%20Regarding%20arrest.PDF (last visited 2 January 2021).

due to the State's co-equal status on the matter of legislative and executive powers under the constitutional framework. The constitutional enquiry will facilitate in ironing out the differences and streamline the functioning of the States' agencies. The work explains the idea of co-equality of States and the relevance under the Indian Constitution. Further, it also looks into possible ways to resolve the issue of conflict between the States.[33]

Nowadays, the rules often allow for communications with other States that essentially involve direct correspondence between officers of various states on a daily and non-controversial basis to promote day-to-day administration more efficiently and legitimately. Correspondence with police officers of corresponding grades in other states, with certain limitations, allow for significant information exchange regarding illegal movements, individuals' arrests, crime details, etc. To satisfy the specified message type, wireless contact should be embraced. The main challenges before the investigation agencies are as follows:

1. **Non-submissiveness to inter-state arrest and prosecutions**
   Methodology is developed by the country's procedural rules, but the absence of successful enforcement has culminated in procedures that are not cooperative. The authoritative territorial jurisdictions have also established protocols under which state and political interference are inevitable. In *K.V. Rajendran v. Superintendent of Police, CBCID, Chennai*,[34] the conflict between the two State governments on, who among the two is competent to investigate the case, was apparent. The three-judge bench held that transfer of investigation must be conducted in rare and exceptional cases in order to do complete justice between the parties and to instil straight confidence in the public mind[35]. While the steps taken by the Mumbai police in the limited inquiry under Section 174, CrPC, may not be faulted on the material available before the Court, considering the apprehension voiced by the stakeholders of unfair investigation, the Court must strive to ensure that search for the truth is undertaken by

---

[33] Uday Shankar, Co-Equal Status of The States: Constitutional Perspective, 2020 S.C.C. Online Blog Oped 149.

[34] (2013) 12 S.C.C. 480.

[35] *Id*, at p. 485, para. 13.

an independent agency, not controlled by either of the two state governments. Most importantly, the credibility of the investigation and the investigating authority must be protected

> as because both states are making acrimonious allegations of political interference against each other, the legitimacy of the investigation has come under a cloud. Accusing fingers are being pointed and people have taken the liberty to put out their own conjectures and theories. Such comments, responsible or otherwise, have led to speculative public discourse which have hogged media limelight. These developments unfortunately have the propensity to delay and misdirect the investigation. In such situation, there is reasonable apprehension of truth being a casualty and justice becoming a victim.[36]

2. **Inter-state police cooperation**

   It has also been found that inter-state police cooperation is poor and serves as an impediment to the proceeding itself. Control is seldom extracted from procedural rules, and it is undermined in execution where coordination between two states is necessary. Rightly so, inter-state detention frequently contributes to a control tussle between two state police agencies.

3. **Complex state of affairs**

   It is evident that the state of affairs in a given state inevitably influences the implementation of laws owing to opposing opinions. This takes a toll on the police's collective cohesion and potentially hamper the reasonable and proper examination to be undertaken in order to enforce justice. Complex state of affairs has traditionally been culminated in administrative lapses, while current structures do not resort to Section 48 in a literal context. States should respond to another State's advance request for help and should support and collaborate with each other by sharing offender details and records. States should collaborate in establishing and enforcing peace and protection initiatives.

CONCLUSION AND SUGGESTIONS

In inter-state arrests, it is evidently clear that the law and provisions on inter-state arrest derive from general procedures implemented by the respective State police forces and are subject to the same limitations and

---

[36] Rhea Chakraborty v State of Bihar, 2020 S.C.C. OnLine S.C. 654, para 39.

restrictions. However, the subject is writ with problems as States have repeatedly violated established rules of (inter-state) arrest. The absence of clear regulations on cooperation and collaboration hold that the police forces are forced to create ties at their own peril; the State machinery itself does not provide for it as the laws are silent on the matter. Increasing inter-state crimes and declining coordination between State governments and State agencies have culminated in a system where conflicts and complaints have heightened, with no proper redressal of these issues.

Recently, police officers and agencies have conducted outreach campaigns focused on police regulations to standardize inter-state detentions and prosecutions or inquiries conducted outside a State's municipal jurisdiction. Through its numerous decisions, the Court has also endeavoured to resolve the situation on arrest law and the procedural lapses resulting from inter-state operations. The following may be suggested to overcome the hurdles:

1. While effecting the arrest, the police officer **cannot take shelter under another person's belief or judgment.** He must effect **arrest at his own risk and responsibility** as the effect of illegal arrest could result in wrongful confinement, punishable under Section 342 IPC. Burden lies on the Investigating Officer to satisfy the Court about his bona-fide.
2. No arrest can be made because it is lawful for the police officer to do so. The provision where arrest has been sanctioned based on mere suspicion should be revoked, since the police department should be satisfied on prima facie facts and evidence that the person so arrested was involved or has committed offence. This provision will reduce promotes in the procedure and consequent oppression by police authorities.
3. Upholding due process by cooperation between two States' police in effecting arrest is a sine qua non for healthy working of a democratic country. Increasing interaction can only be sought if proper mechanism is devised for investigation and arrest.
4. The logbook of the vehicle used for transportation must be maintained and signed, and IO should indicate whether the vehicle was official or private including the name of the driver and how and by whom it was arranged.

5. Custody records must be maintained to increase transparency.
6. Proper transit remand must be obtained to transport an arrested person to another State jurisdiction.
7. Proper periodical training and sensitization of IOs relating to inter-state arrests and protection of human rights must be conducted.
8. Delinquent Police officer must be held liable in cases of human right violations.

Lastly, it is concluded that the impressions of arrest on the life and psychology of an innocent person is long lasting. Arrest has diminishing and demoralizing effects on his personality. Therefore, it is necessary to assure a balance between the societal interests and individual rights. Hence, it is the right time to change our archaic laws into the modern legal system to cope with the evolving society and modernized crimes and criminal tendencies.

Chapter 9

Arrest and Seizure under Narcotics Drugs Law

Nirmal Kanti Chakrabarti and
Surja Kanta Baladhikari

INTRODUCTION

Arrest, as a part of an investigation, ordinarily means detention or apprehension of a person by legal authority resulting in deprivation of liberty. In the administration of criminal justice, the police are authorized to arrest any person, either under orders of the court or without such order. It is the most effective method of securing the attendance of the accused of violating any criminal legislation. Besides securing the attendance of the accused at the time of trial, arrest becomes necessary as a preventive measure, or in respect of persons committing a cognizable offence, or a habitual offender, as in the case of Narcotic Drugs and Psychotropic Substances (NDPS) Act, 1985, etc. The NDPS Act, 1985 is a special statute to address the problems of abuse of narcotic drugs and psychotropic substances and the illicit traffic therein, where ordinarily the provisions of Code of Criminal Procedure (CrPC), 1973, would prevail otherwise than when some powers and functions are specially mentioned in the NDPS Act, 1985.

This paper is an attempt to look into the procedural aspects which investigating officers must keep in mind during arrest, search, seizure, drawing of samples as procedures for completion of an investigation in a case under NDPS Act, 1985. The authors also take into consideration the various judicial decisions concerning the role of investigating officers under the NDPS Act, 1985.

JUSTIFICATION FOR ARREST

The Royal Commission Report in Criminal Procedure[1] recommended restrictions on the power of arrest on the basis of the principle of 'necessity'. Sir Cyril Philips stated the following where one or more is to be considered before arrest:

1. The unwillingness of a person to be identified for the purpose of serving the summons.
2. The urgency to prevent an ongoing offence or stop its repetition.
3. The need to protect the person who is arrested or others or any property.
4. The need for obtaining evidence by questioning the person who may have committed the offence.
5. The urgency of production of the person in the court of law to answer any charge made against him.

The Fourth Law Amendment of the United States refers to arrest as the paradigmatic state seizure and the need for balance between the interest of the State, law enforcement agency and the arrestee. The arrest of a person based upon probable cause is the proper justification that the cause' is lawful and thereafter would not require any further justification.[2]

The three components[3] of a reasonable arrest are:

1. The police must be backed by the law before going ahead with arrest, search or seizure.
2. The go-ahead must be based on a reasonable process.
3. The process carried out must be in a reasonable manner.

---

[1] Royal Commission on Criminal Procedure (Philips Commission): Records 46 (1978–1981).

[2] Agnello v. United States, 269 U.S. 20, 30 (1925).

[3] Rachel A. Harmon, *Why Arrest?* 115 MICH. L. REV. 307 322 (2016).

The Indian law has incorporated the concept of 'notice of appearance' in Section 41A, CrPC, 1973 which allows the power of arrest to be exercised on the basis of necessity. It could be now seen as a sort of 'interview', convenient for both the accused and investigating officer. It also balances the principle of criminal law that an innocent man must be set free; similarly, a person's liberty and freedom guaranteed under the Constitution should not be curtailed by making an arrest which later may turn illegal or unnecessary.

Arrest or detention of a person in a police lockup also causes irreparable harm to one's reputation and self-esteem. The police officer making an arrest must understand that he just cannot arrest someone because it is lawful to do so. The officer must be able to justify the need for arrest which is very different from his power to arrest a person. Thus, the police officer must not arrest as a routine exercise but only after reasonable satisfaction.[4]

THE PROBLEM OF DRUG ABUSE AND NATURE OF CASES

Drug trafficking is a global illicit trade involving the cultivation, manufacture, distribution and sale of substances that are subject to drug prohibition laws. Estimated to be a 13-billion-dollar industry, it has affected the world at large with huge demands for opioids, cannabis, cocaine and other banned substances. The United Nations has pledged to eliminate the problem and achieve a drug-free society. Towards that end, it has passed three Conventions in 1961, 1971 and 1988. The first one sought to eliminate the illicit production and non-medical use of narcotics, whereas the 1971 convention extended the scope to psychotropic medications or synthetic drugs; the third Convention against illicit trafficking was targeted at the suppression of the illegal global market, and the restriction was extended to precursor chemicals. Based on these Conventions, the United Nations assists the Member States to develop national legislation on drugs.[5] As a signatory to the

---

[4] See, *Third Report National Police Commission* (27 July 2020, 10:04 AM), https://police.py.gov.in/Police%20Commission%20reports/3rd%20Police%20 Commission%20report.pdf

[5] UNODC and the Response to Drugs, https://www.unodc.org/lpo-brazil/ en/drogas/index.html

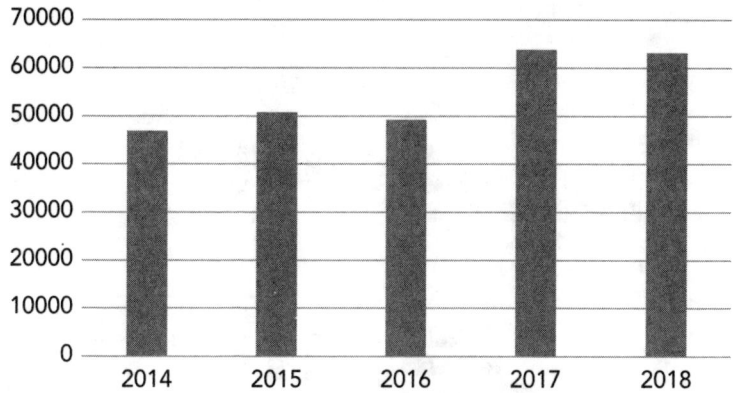

Figure 9.1 *No. of Cases Booked under NDPS Act, 1985*

Source: Crime in India Report, 2014–2018, National Crime Records Bureau, Govt. of India.

Convention, India established an Expert Committee to look into the issue of drug and alcohol abuse in India. The Committee's report was submitted in 1977 and the Drug De-addiction Programme was rolled out. During the same time, India enacted the Narcotic Drugs and Psychotropic Substances Act, 1985 'to prevent and combat drug abuse and illicit trafficking', an apparent emphasis on supply reduction.[6] The Act establishes authorities for the prevention, control and regulation of drugs as well as creates offences for contravention of the provisions. It also prescribes the procedure whereby such offences have to be investigated, in addition to the procedures laid down under the general law.

Facts and figures indicate a rising trend in case of offences under the Act. As reported by Crimes in India,[7] the number of cases booked under the NDPS Act for possession of drugs for personal use and trafficking has increased by over 25 per cent in 2017 and 2018 as compared to the earlier 3 years (see Figure 9.1). Maharashtra and Punjab reported more than 10,000 cases in 2018 (see Figure 9.2).

---

[6] Ajit Avasthi and Abhishek Ghosh, *Drug Misuse in India: Where Do We Stand and Where to Go from Here?* 149(6) INDIAN J. MED. RES. 689–92 (June 2019).

[7] Crime in India, 2014–2018, National Crimes Records Bureau, MHA, Govt. of India.

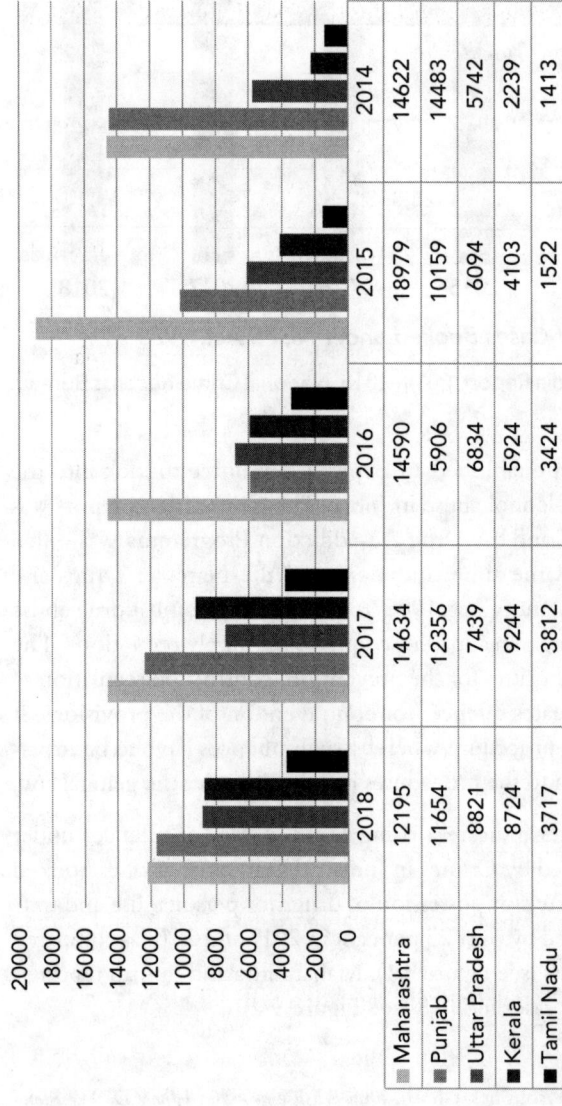

	2018	2017	2016	2015	2014
Maharashtra	12195	14634	14590	18979	14622
Punjab	11654	12356	5906	10159	14483
Uttar Pradesh	8821	7439	6834	6094	5742
Kerala	8724	9244	5924	4103	2239
Tamil Nadu	3717	3812	3424	1522	1413

Figure 9.2 *Incidence of Crime under NDPS Act in Five (Highest) States*

Source: Crime in India Report, 2014–2018, National Crime Records Bureau, Govt. of India.

Table 9.1 *Conviction under NDPS Act 1985*

	Total Cases for Trial	Cases Convicted	Conviction Rate	Total Cases
2014	157,375	19,414	74.3	46,923
2015	181,601	26,554	77.2	50,796
2016	199,412	25,782	72.4	49,256
2017	208,941	23,929	86.7	63,800
2018	234,897	28,333	74.4	63,137

Source: Crime in India Report, 2014–2018, National Crime Records Bureau, Govt. of India.

Conviction rates in NDPS Act, 1985 have also remained satisfactory during the entire period, above 70 per cent (Table 9.1), though many cases fail due to procedural irregularities.

NDPS is special legislation where arrests should only be made to justify a crime. The purpose of arrest is to secure the conviction of the arrestee, with an objective to either punish the carrier of the illegal substance, or the accomplice. In most cases under NDPS Act, 1985, arrests are closely associated with the search of the accused. In other words, where a person is searched by the officer and prohibited substances are recovered from his possession, the officer may proceed to seize the substances as well as arrest the person for any of the offences under the Act. As cases suggest, most of the searches and seizures are made, either on information received, or on spot searches based on suspicions, and thereupon the case proceeds for investigation and trial. Thus, an arrest is integrally linked with the recovery of illegal substances from the possession of a person. It is incumbent in these cases, those proper procedures are followed to uphold the legalities of the action taken by the authorities.

THE PROCEDURE UNDER NDPS ACT, 1985

A Magistrate of first class or Metropolitan Magistrate or any Magistrate of the second class, empowered by the Government can issue a warrant[8] for the purpose of carrying out an arrest as per the NDPS Act, 1985.

---

[8] Section 41 of NDPS Act, 1985.

They are also qualified to order for search irrespective of day or night, in any building, conveyance or place where the officer has reason to believe any substance amounting to an offence is kept. This would also include any document or article which may furnish evidence about the commission of the offence under the NDPS Act, 1985. Property which are obtained illegally and used for the purpose of committing any offence under this Act can also come under the purview of search or seizure.

Gazetted Officers[9] of central excise, narcotics, customs, revenue intelligence or any other officer of the Central Government or State Government, paramilitary forces or armed forces have the power to direct arrest or search. If the officers, upon receiving information from any person in writing or from personal knowledge, believe an offence under NDPS Act, 1985 has been committed or any document or article may be furnished as evidence to reveal commission of the offence under NDPS Act, 1985, can authorize any officer subordinate to them but above the rank of peon, sepoy or constable to arrest such person or search a building, conveyance or place, either in day or night or can also himself go ahead for completing the arrest or search.

Empowered Officer

The term 'investigation' is found in Section 2 (xxix) of the NDPS Act, 1985, associated with Section 2(h) of CrPC, 1973, would mean all the proceedings under the CrPC, 1973 for the purpose of collection of evidence collected by a police officer or any other person who is authorized by a Magistrate.[10]

The investigating officer is also referred to as the 'empowered officer'. Under Section 53 of the NDPS Act, 1985 the Central Government, in consultation with State Government, may invest any officer of the department of central excise, narcotics, customs, revenue intelligence or any other department with the powers of an

---

[9] Government of Jammu Kashmir Home Department, Circular no. 02 of 2017 dated 25 September 2017.

[10] H.N. Rishud and another v. State of Delhi, A.I.R. 1955 S.C. 195; State of Madhya Pradesh v. Mubarak Ali, A.I.R. 1959 S.C. 707.

officer-in-charge of a police station for the investigation of the offences under this Act. The State Government may also invest any officer of drugs control, revenue or excise or such other Department with the powers of the officer in charge.

This means the officer to whom the warrant is designated under Section 41(1) of NDPS Act, 1985 to perform arrest or search is said to be the empowered officer within the meaning of Section 42 of NDPS Act, 1985.

On the question of whether officers under the NDPS Act, 1985 can be referred to as 'police officers', the Court in *Tofan Singh v. State of Tamil Nadu*[11] has held that the officers invested with powers under Section 53 of the NDPS Act 1985 are 'police officers' within the meaning of Section 25 of the Evidence Act, 1872 and any confessional statement recorded under Section 67 of the Act, 1985 is barred under the said provisions and cannot be taken into account to convict an accused under the Act.[12]

Power of Search and Arrest

Under Sections 42, the following powers to enter, search, seizure and arrest has been given:

1. Enter a place and search such building, conveyance or place.
2. Break open any door or remove obstacles at the entry when faced with any kind of resistance.
3. Seize drug or substance along with all other materials used for the purpose of manufacture or any other things which is supposedly used for commission of the offence and could be a tool for furnishing evidence.
4. Detain, search and arrest, if necessary, after having reasons to believe that the person has committed an offence punishable under this Act. The provision also enables the officer, in exemplary situations, when it is difficult to obtain search warrants or authorization,

---

[11] (2013) 16 S.C.C. 31.
[12] Mohd. Fasrin v. State, (2019) 8 S.C.C. 811.

between sunset and sunrise, to enter and search any building and arrest ant person, after recording the grounds of his belief that an offence is committed under NDPS Act, 1985.

Where an officer records his belief in writing, he is required to send a copy of the same to his immediate superior. Section 43 specifically speaks of search and arrest in 'public places'. The word has been taken to include any public conveyance, hotel, shop or other place intended for use by, or accessible to the public. It has been held that in *Deep Chand*,[13] that where the search took place on a street, the provisions of Section 42(2) do not apply and the SHO is not required to send a copy of the source information forthwith to the immediate superior. In these cases, that is search in public places, the officer is authorised to arrest the person having in his possession any narcotic drug or psychotropic substance if he believes that to be unlawful.

Where, however, the officer conducting search, seizure or arrest under Sections 42, 43 or 44, conducts the proceedings without reasonable ground of suspicion or vexatiously and unnecessarily, the officer is liable for punishment.[14] Any malicious exercise of powers of arrest is also punishable. Therefore, arrest, search and seizure under the Act, 1985 must be based on 'satisfactory' grounds, either from information received or own belief, and the burden will be on the officer to establish the same.

Legalities of Procedure

Compliance of Section 50 NDPS Act, 1985 demands an obligation to inform the person to be searched about his right as mandated under the NDPS Act, 1985. Thus, where an officer is about to search a person on the belief that the person has committed an offence punishable under the Act, 1985, he must ensure the following:

1. The empowered officer must approach the nearest Gazetted Officer[15] or nearest Magistrate, if such person to be searched so requires.

---

[13] Deep Chand v. State of Rajasthan 1996 Cr L.J. 54 (Raj.).
[14] Section 58(1).
[15] Section 50, NDPS Act, 1985.

2. In case requisition is made, the officer performing search or arrest can detain the person until he can be brought before the Gazetted Officer or Magistrate. The Gazetted Officer or the Magistrate has the power to deny such search upon finding no reasonable ground or let the search be continued.

3. A female can only be searched by a female, though the provision does not mention the need of a female 'officer'.

4. In case the officer about to search has a reason to believe that a offence has been committed under the NDPS Act, 1985 and it is not possible to produce the person before the Magistrate or Gazetted Officer, without parting with the contraband substance, he can himself proceed to search the person in accordance with the provisions of Section 100 CrPC 1973.[16]

5. After the search, the officer needs to issue the seizure list, record the details of an independent witness, other witnesses including their addresses.[17]

In *M.S. Ahalwat v. the State of Harayana*,[18] contraband brown sugar packets were recovered during the search of the accused person but the accused could not be convicted because the accused person was not informed that he had a right to be searched in presence of a Magistrate of a Gazetted Officer. In *Joseph Fernandez v. the State of Goa*,[19] the suspect was asked before being searched that 'if you wish you may be searched in the presence of a Gazetted Officer or a Magistrate'. The Supreme Court held that this is 'substantial compliance' with Section 50 of the NDPS Act, 1985. The court[20] also clarified the situation that offering the accused the right of being searched in the presence of a Magistrate or a Gazetted Officer would only be applicable when the substance is found from 'the person' and if the contraband is found in a bag which belongs to the accused and not from him directly, it is not necessary to offer the accused of being searched in presence of a Magistrate or Gazetted Officer.[21] In the case of *Himachal Pradesh v.*

---

[16] *Id.*

[17] NICFS, A Forensic Guide for Crime Investigators.

[18] 1999 (4) Crimes 297 S.C.

[19] (2001) 1 S.C.C. 707.

[20] Kalema Tumba v. State of Maharashtra 1999 (4) Crimes.

[21] Madan Lal v. Himachal Pradesh, A.I.R. 2003 S.C. 3642.

Pawan Kumar,[22] the word 'person' as expressed in Section 50 of NDPS Act, 1985 was held that to mean a human being with appropriate coverings and clothing and also footwear and would not apply to bags, briefcase or container, etc. carried by the person/suspect.

In *Gurbax Singh v. the State of Harayana,*[23] while checking was done by the staff of a second-class compartment in the train, the appellant in the case panicked and left the train with a gunny bag on his left shoulder. The Sub-Inspector of Police who was present on the platform for checking smuggling and other antisocial elements, on having suspicion, nabbed the accused and found him carrying poppy straw of 7 kgs. The Court affirmed that in this situation the police officer could not have the information, nor knowledge or any reason that offence under NDPS is committed which makes compliance of Section 50 not applicable. Thus, while exercising the powers in compliance with Section 42, it is necessary to ascertain the source of information about the contraband substance, whether it is from personal knowledge or information received. Where there is no reason to believe, nor any information, the police would not be expected to follow the procedure laid down in the Section. The court clarified that the police in such circumstances had only the option to 'suspect', but not have 'reason to believe' that any contraband item would be found.[24]

In case the empowered officer or authorized officer had prior information, the search of the person must be carried before a Gazetted Officer or Magistrate. This is said to be the right of the person to be searched, a failure would be noncompliance with Section 50. However, the compliance of Section 50 would not be applicable when sudden recoveries or searches are made or during the usual investigation.

In the case of *State of Punjab v. Labh Singh*[25] it was held that each case must be seen and considered based upon the facts and circumstances

---

[22] (2005) 4 S.C.C. 350.

[23] (2001) 3 S.C.C. 28.

[24] State of Himachal Pradesh v. Sunil Kumar, A.I.R. 2014 S.C. 2564.

[25] (1996) 5 S.C.C. 520.

about the contraband seized and the following needs to be considered before arriving at any decision:

1. the time of the search
2. place of search
3. opportunity with the police of having prior information
4. the article being in transport or at lockdown place
5. the opportunity of police to ensure the presence of the gazetted officer
6. delay in securing the presence of the gazette officer which would result in the escape of the accused or contraband article be destroyed.

The following was again reaffirmed by the Court in *Baldev Singh*[26]:

1. When the opportunity was there about prior information, the duty to inform about the right under Section 50 to the person being searched who is later referred to as the accused cannot be denied.
2. Information need not be in writing.
3. Failing to take the person to the magistrate or gazetted officer when he demands so as a right would make the recovery or seizure in question and conviction liable to be set aside.
4. Evidence collected without extending the right under Section 50 would render a trial unfair.

Informant/Complainant and Investigating Officer

The importance of a fair trial can hardly be overemphasized. It demands that the trial is free from any bias, which may be read as one of the cannons of criminal jurisprudence as implicit in Articles 20 and 21 of the Constitution. Thus, an officer who registers a complaint should not, generally be the person to conduct the investigation. There may be implications of bias or conflict of interest which may be a strike at the very basis of fairness. Right from *Bhagwan Singh*[27] till the recent judgment in the case of *Varinder Kumar*,[28] the Court has been of the

---

[26] State of Punjab v. Baldev Singh, A.I.R. 1999 S.C. 2378.
[27] (1976) 1 S.C.C. 15.
[28] (2019) S.C.C. Online S.C. 170.

opinion that the complainant/informant and the investigator must not generally be the same person. The same is in consonance with the age-old principle of natural justice which emphasizes that 'justice should not only be done but appear to have been done.' And justice can never be said to be done if a man acts as a judge in his own cause or is himself interested in its outcome.[29] It is the touchstone on which all actions are to be weighed in order to uphold free, fair and unbiased investigation and adjudication across legal systems.

In *Mohan Lal v. the State of Punjab*[30] the three-judge bench of *Ranjan Gogoi, R. Banumathi and Navin Sinha,* JJ. dealt with the question as to whether in a criminal prosecution, it will be in consonance with the principles of justice, fair play and a fair investigation, if the inform-ant and the investigating officer were to be the same person. The case arose out of the NDPS Act, 1985 where the FIR was lodged by the Sub Inspector of a police station, which mentioned that while on patrol duty, on suspicion, he searched the appellant leading to the recovery of opium in a bag carried by him. Subsequently, the investigation was carried out by the same Sub-Inspector and the appellant was put on trial and convicted. In an appeal before the Supreme Court, it was argued that the NDPS, 1985 being a stringent law carrying a reverse burden of proof, required strict adherence to the law and procedures. It is imperative that the investigation in such cases must not only be fair and judicious but must appear to have been so; the investigation being carried out by the same police official leaves a genuine apprehension in the mind of the accused that it was not fair and bona fide. The apex court while taking note of the serious discrepancies in the case, stated that, a fair trial to an accused, a constitutional guarantee under Article 21 of the Indian Constitution, would be a hollow promise if the inves-tigation into an NDPS, 1985 case were not to be fair or raise doubts about its fairness apparent on the face of the investigation. However, in a subsequent case,[31] the Five judges Constitutional bench overruled the judgement in *Mohan Lal v State of Punjab.*[32] In the case, the apex court

[29] J. Mohapatra and Co. v. State of Orissa, A.I.R. 1984 S.C. 1572.
[30] (2018) 17 S.C.C. 627.
[31] Mukesh Singh v. State (Narcotic Branch of Delhi), Manu/SC/0660/2020.
[32] Mohapatra, *supra* note 29.

took the view that when the Investigating Officer and the informant are the same person, the trial is not automatically vitiated. The court did not find any reason to doubt the investigation merely on the ground that the informant had investigated the case and therefore, acquit the accused. The court held that the question of prejudice along with the question of bias has to be decided on the facts of each case. Hence, the decision in cases like *Mohan Lal* is not good law and overruled the same.

Post-arrest and Seizure Procedure

Once an accused has been arrested under Sections 41, 42, 43 or 44 of the NDPS Act, 1985, she/he must be informed of the grounds of arrest. The words used in the section are 'as soon as may be' and therefore, may be construed as, at the earliest opportunity, though not 'forth-with', as required under Section 50 CrPC, 1973. The seized article and every arrested person must be forwarded without unnecessary delay to the magistrate who had issued the warrant. In other cases, the person arrested must be forwarded to the officer-in-charge of the police station or the officer empowered under Section 53 of NDPS Act, 1985. Information about such arrest and seizure must be made through a full report which includes all particulars about the search and arrest within forty-eight hours to the superior officer in pursuance of Section 57 of NDPS Act, 1985.

In *State of Himachal Pradesh v. Sudarshan Kumar,*[33] it was observed that the provisions in Sections 52(1) and 57 are mandatory in character. The right to be informed about the grounds of arrest contained in Section 52(1) and the requirement of Section 57 that any person making an arrest or seizure shall make a full report to his superior officer within 48 hours confer a valuable right on the accused. When informed about the grounds of arrest at the earliest opportunity, the accused becomes aware of, at the very outset, what he has to meet in the long run. Failure to do so would certainly prejudice his defence. Similarly, the provision requiring the person to make a full report to his immediate superior officer within 48 hours, brings into existence a document that can be

---

[33] 1989 Cr L.J. 1412.

used for purposes of cross-examination in defence. The making of such a report within 48 hours will also bring to an end the possibility of improving the prosecution version after that time. If these provisions are not strictly complied with, the prosecution must fail.[34]

DEALING WITH ARRESTED PERSONS AND ARTICLES SEIZED

It is incumbent on the investigating officer to follow certain procedures after arrest and seizure:

1. The investigating officer after apprehending the accused must approach the nearest Magistrate for custody. It must be ensured that no person is unnecessarily kept in custody without due orders. The accused is required to be produced without undue delay.
2. The intercepting officer must not continue the investigation as the investigating officer to maintain transparency.
3. The investigating officer must deposit the seal by which the substance was seized in the court. The officer must seal the substance, reseal it again, and then deposit it in the police *malkhana*.
4. Substances seized must be sent to forensic laboratories within 72 hours.
5. Following the procedure under 52A of the NDPS Act.

The officer in charge of the police station is the custodian of the seized articles and must keep them in safe custody.[35] He has the power to draw samples from it and affix his seal to such articles or samples. Proper custody of the contraband articles must be adhered to till such time the case is disposed of or there is time for appeal or revision. Any lapse on the part of the investigating agency is fatal for the prosecution.[36]

Section 52A further enunciates that the officer in charge must prepare an inventory of the narcotics etc. seized along with the quality,

---

[34] Smt. Zubeda Khatoon v. Assistant Collector of Customs, Legal Bangalore 1991 Cr L.J. 1392.
[35] Section 55 NDPS Act 1985.
[36] Sohan Lal v. State of Punjab, 1997 Drugs Cases 460 (P&H) (DB).

quantity, mode of packing and other particulars. He shall make an application to a Magistrate for the purpose of certifying the correctness of the inventory so prepared, as well as taking photographs of such drugs or substances or allowing to draw the present samples of such drugs or substances.

In *Mobin Fathu Bhai Mulani v. NCB*[37] the property of the case was tied with help of a string and it was showcased in the court that contraband item which was preserved in the cardboard box could have been taken out from the box without touching the attached paper slip and seals affixed. The Delhi High Court observed that it cannot be concluded that the item examined by the FSL unit is the one that was recovered from the accused person, which would result in giving benefit to the accused person. Again, in *Nathiya v. State*[38] around thirty-one packets of samples were taken by the SHO from seized items found in the possession of the accused. Thereafter, an official of the Border Customs Department obtained some more samples from the sealed packets of the same seized item which was kept in the *malkhana* of the police station. It was found that there was no order from the Magistrate about obtaining samples on the second occasion when the packets were reopened. The Rajasthan High Court was of the opinion that there were serious doubts in the prosecution case.

Along with the above norms, departmental manuals like police manuals of States enumerate certain procedures which must also be followed which would help the prosecution[39] to prove that the items seized were kept in safe custody.

In *Suresh Kumar Sahu v. the State of Orissa*[40] it was held by the Orissa High Court that in absence of any proper evidence about sealing and proper custody, it may be difficult to conclude that the seized items

---

[37] 90 (2001) D.L.T. 117.

[38] 1992 Cr L. J. 2342.

[39] It casts a duty upon the prosecution to lead evidence and explain about the location of the custody of the seized items to draw the link that the items which were seized were the articles which was examined and now are used as evidence. Similarly, if the same items are lying for a long time in the police station a statement to effect that the parcels were not tampered must be given.

[40] 1997 Cr L. J. 462.

were recovered from the possession of the accused person. The absence of the same would entitle the accused to express doubts about the seizure, custody and sealing of the articles, which, in turn, would entitle him for an acquittal.[41]

GRANT OF BAIL TO ACCUSED

Section 37 of the NDPS Act 1985 states that offences under the Act are cognizable and non-bailable. With regard to bail, in addition to the conditions laid down in the CrPC 1973, the Act states that no accused shall be released on bail unless the Public Prosecutor is given an opportunity to oppose the application and the Court is satisfied that there are reasonable grounds for believing that he is not guilty of such offence and is not likely to commit any offence while on bail. Thus, the conditions for grant of bail are two-fold: one, not guilty of the offence as alleged, and second, he will not commit any further offence.

In *Union of India v. Ram Samujh*[42] the Court cautioned that while a murderer commits the murder of one or two persons, one dealing with narcotics causes the death of a number of innocent young victims. They are a hazard to society and are likely to repeat the crime in all probability if released on bail. The scheme of Section 37 reveals that the exercise of power to grant bail is not only subject to the limitations under Section 439 CrPC but also subject to twin conditions in Section 37. If either of these two conditions is not satisfied, the ban for granting bail operates. The Court held that the expression 'reasonable grounds' means more than mere prima facie grounds. It contemplates substantial probable causes for believing that the accused is not guilty of the alleged offence. The reasonable belief contemplated in the provision requires the existence of such facts and circumstances as are sufficient in themselves to justify satisfaction that the accused is not guilty of the alleged offence.[43]

---

[41] Valsala v. State of Kerala 1993 Cr L. J. 333(S.C.) 1993.

[42] (1999) 9 S.C.C. 429.

[43] State of Kerala v. Rajesh, (2020) 12 S.C.C. 122.

Where huge quantities of acetic anhydride were recovered from company premises and it was alleged that the accused were members of an international drug syndicate, the Supreme Court set aside the order of bail granted by the High Court on the ground that there was no application of judicial mind in the case. Section 37 of the NDPS Act, 1985 provides the applicable legal norms in determining the question of bail. The seriousness of the offence has not been considered by the court below, rather the educational qualification of the accused was considered which ought not to have been weighed.[44]

In *Fabian Helmchen v. the State of Goa*[45] where the contraband was 'charas' allegedly of commercial quality seized from the apartment of a woman, and the accused was her mere acquaintance, the Court, while granting bail to the accused, held that the possession under NDPS, 1985 has to be conscious and exclusive. The person possessing the contraband must have knowledge and control of the same. In the instant case, the Court found that the information to the Police did not indicate the involvement of a male person and also, the woman, the principal accused, was out on bail. Similarly, in another case, where substantial quantities of ganja were recovered in the car and the police seized the items and arrested the accused, the Andhra Pradesh High Court granted bail to the accused who were languishing in custody for 5 months.[46]

With regard to anticipatory bail, the NDPS Act,1985 makes no mention of the same, as distinguished from Section 36A (3), which refers to powers of the High court under Section 439 CrPC, 1973. It has been held[47] that the non-mention does not mean that the powers of the Sessions Court or High Court to grant bail under Section 438 CrPC stand excluded when an offence under the Act is involved. No such limitation can be imported into or read into the provisions of the Act. However, what is important is that the powers of anticipatory bail

---

[44] Union of India v. Prateek Shukla, (2021) S.C.C. Online S.C. 214.

[45] (2021) S.C.C. Online Bom 311.

[46] Guddu Kumar v. State of AP, (2021) S.C.C. Online AP 601.

[47] Baljit Singh v. State of Assam (2003) 3 G.L.R. 130; See, Narcotics Control Bureau v. Kishan Lal, A.I.R. 1991 S.C. 558; Balchand Jain v. State of MP, A.I.R. 1977 S.C. 366.

must be exercised in light of the limitations imposed under Section 37 of the NDPS Act, 1985. In *Amit Ranjan v. NCB*,[48] the Delhi High Court opined that

> [A]nticipatory bail may be granted when there is material on record to show that prosecution was inherently doubtful or where there is material on record to show that there is a possibility of false implication. However, when the element of criminality is involved; the custodial interrogation is required and/or the other aspects and facts are required to be unfolded in the investigation, the applicant is not entitled to anticipatory bail.[49]

In the instant case, the Court was of the opinion that custodial interrogation of the accused was required to unearth the wires of conspiracy with regard to narcotics being sent to foreign countries by the accused and hence rejected the plea of anticipatory bail.

FAILURE OF CASES UNDER NDPS ACT, 1985

The success of NDPS cases depends on a number of factors, ranging from investigation, prosecution and trial. Over the years, some of the common reasons for the failure of cases under NDPS Act, 1985 have been identified as procedural lapses in the investigation, such as both investigating officer and complainant being the same person, samples not drawn properly, search not conducted before Gazetted officer or Magistrate, delay in receiving FSL reports, mismatch with the weight of the contraband item seized from the spot from the seizure list, test identification parades not conducted, etc.; lapses during prosecution and trial include Gazetted officers not examined as witnesses, independent witnesses involved in the preparation of arrest memo or seizure list not examined, police officers in charge of *malkhana* not examined, witnesses turning hostile, cases entirely based on confessions, a property associated with the case not produced before court, etc.[50] NDPS is a special

---

[48] (2019) S.C.C. Online Del 9104.

[49] *Id.*, at para 30.

[50] Government of Jammu Kashmir Home Department, Circular no. 02 of 2017 dated 25 September 2017.

legislation that intends to create deterrence in terms of the production, distribution, consumption of contraband substances. Hence it lays down offences and prescribes severe punishment for the same. It is important that the procedure prescribed for the purpose of conducting search, seizure and consequent apprehension of the offenders is done in strict compliance with the procedures in order to maintain the conviction at a later stage. If there are any drawbacks with regard to the officers in due discharge of their functions, the benefit accrues to the accused.

CONCLUSION

The problem of drug abuse and trafficking is a global issue. Especially amongst the children, youth and other marginalized segments of society, the problem is rampant. The object of the NDPS Act, 1985 is to ensure that prevention and protection from illicit traffic and abuse of drugs can be achieved in society. However, there are problems encountered in NDPS cases due to lapses on the part of officers in charge including non-compliance with the conditionalities of the Act, non-application of forensic techniques or not adequately securing evidence. Proper training and awareness of the officers dealing with these narcotics cases, as also Judicial Officers, is important in order to attain success in courts of law. Every search, seizure, arrest must be done methodically with due regard to the processes ingrained in the Act. Proper implementation of NDPS Act, 1985 also needs infrastructural development, in terms of increased manpower, technological advancements, the strength of FSLs in the country which will facilitate prompt and effective justice.

Chapter 10

Arrest and Detention under Armed Forces Act
A Test Case of Human Rights Violation

Bhabani Sonowal

INTRODUCTION

Following the adoption of the United Nations Declaration on Human Rights in 1948, the human rights issue became a prominent theme in the international legal domain. Human rights are universally enjoyed by every human being devoid of their caste, culture, religion, sex or geographical location, and these rights should be free from any state arbitrariness. The State, as a sovereign entity, is obliged to maintain law and order and protect its subjects from any external aggression or internal threat, so as to ensure the rule of law. For this purpose, it may enact any law conferring necessary powers. However, at the same time, the State must ensure the protection of the human rights of all citizens from any arbitrary action.

Yet, over the last 60 years, there has been a paradox to this basic principle of rule of law in India's North-East. There have been instances of gross violations and human rights abuses in the region committed by the state forces in the name of maintaining security by virtue of the immunity provided by the Armed Forces (Special Powers) Act, 1958

(AFSPA). Today, a vast majority of the population who have borne the brunt of brutalities stand defeated and crushed under the mighty power of the State which has belied their minimum expectations of life and well-being. Though their battle for justice is still ongoing, their voices are least heard by the mainstream media and the administration. This chapter highlights the ramifications of arbitrary arrest under the regime of AFSPA, 1958 by relying upon the narratives of those whose rights have been violated by the action of the State.

BRIEF HISTORY

India's North-East has been the theatre of the earliest and longest-lasting insurgency in the country.[1] Since the inception of the Indian Republic, the North-Eastern region has been gripped by insurgencies and political unrest, which are directed in similar measures against different ethnic groups and the authorities.[2] In an attempt to contain the situation, the Armed Forces (Assam and Manipur) Special Powers Ordinance was proclaimed by the erstwhile President of India, on 22 May 1958. Subsequently, the Bill received the President's assent,[3] conferring additional power to the security forces to act arbitrarily and engage in extrajudicial murders of a race of people, who tried to integrate with the Indian mainstream as 'distinct people' of NSGT (Non-Self-Governing Territories).[4]

Initially, the AFSPA 1958 was applicable only to 'disturbed areas' of Assam and the Union Territory of Manipur but, later on in 1972, the Act was amended to include the states of Assam, Manipur, Meghalaya, Nagaland and Tripura and the Union Territory of Arunachal Pradesh.

---

[1] SAMIR KUMAR DAS, CONFLICT AND PEACE IN INDIA'S NORTH-EAST: THE ROLE OF CIVIL SOCIETY. Policy Studies 42 (East-West Centre, 2007).

[2] Sanjay Barbora, *Rethinking India's Counter Insurgency Campaign in North-East* 41(35) ECON. POLIT. WKLY. 3805–12 (2006).

[3] U.C. Jha, *Terrorism and Human Rights Laws: A Comment* 44(37) ECON. POLIT. WKLY. 70–71 (2009).

[4] Dr. Naorem Sanjaoba, *AFSPA, 1958—A Law Review—The Reich State*, http://www.epao.net/epSubPageExtractor.asp?src=education.AFSPAA_Law_Review.AFSPA A_Law_Review_4 (last visited 12 January 2021).

Subsequently, it was lifted from Tripura[5] and Meghalaya and partially revoked in Arunachal Pradesh.[6] At present AFSPA, 1958 is effective in the whole of Nagaland, Manipur (except Imphal Municipal areas), Assam, and some parts of Arunachal Pradesh.[7]

CONTOURS OF ARMED FORCES (SPECIAL POWERS) ACT, 1958

The AFSPA 1958, with only six sections, operates in the 'disturbed areas' of the North Eastern Regions of India. The Preamble to the Act reads as follows:

> An Act to enable certain special powers to be conferred upon members of the Armed Forces in disturbed areas....

'Section 4 of the Act confers upon a commissioned officer..., the power to shoot, arrest without warrant, any person he suspects; as well as enter and search or destroy any premises he believes are sheltering the rebels'.[8] Section 4(a) of the Act provides,

> if he is of the opinion that it is necessary so to do for the maintenance of public order, after giving such due warning as he may consider necessary, fire upon or otherwise use force, even to the causing of death, against any person who is acting in contravention of any law or order for the time being in force in the disturbed area....[9]

---

[5] Syed Sajjad Ali, *Tripura Withdraws AFSPA, Says Insurgency on the Wane*, THE HINDU, 28 May 2015, http://www.thehindu.com/todays-paper/tp-national/tripura-withdraws-afspa-says-insurgency-on-the-wane/article7253121 (last visited 15 February 2021).

[6] Rahul Tripathi, *AFSPA Revoked from Meghalaya, Eight Police Stations in Arunachal Pradesh*, THE INDIAN EXPRESS, 24 April 2018, https://indianexpress.com/article/india/afspa-removed-from-meghalaya-eight-police-stations-in-arunachal-pradesh-5148386/ (last visited 5 February 2021).

[7] Vijaita Singh, *AFSPA Revoked in Meghalaya, Parts of Arunachal Pradesh*, THE HINDU, 23 April 2018, https://www.thehindu.com/news/national/afspa-removed-from-meghalaya-parts-of-arunachal/article23647009 (last visited 6 February 2021).

[8] Armed Forces (Special Powers), 1958 (Act 28 of 1958), Section 4.

[9] *Id.*, Section 4 (a).

The two aspects of the exercise of power are: a) his opinion and b) due warning.

Under sub-section (c).[10] the armed forces have the power of arrest, without a warrant, any person who has

- committed or about to commit a cognizable offense;
- against whom a reasonable suspicion exists that he has committed a cognizable offence;
- may use necessary force to effect the arrest.

Such powers also extend to enter and search without warrant any premises to make any such arrest as aforesaid, and may for that purpose use such force as may be necessary under subsection 4 (d).

Section 5 of the Act stipulates that any person who is arrested should be handed over to the nearest police station with the least possible delay along with the report of his arrest.[11] Finally, Section 6 provides immunity to the armed forces operating in disturbed areas.[12] It denotes that 'a prior sanction has to be obtained from Central Government before the institution of prosecution or legal proceedings'.[13]

ARREST UNDER AFSPA AND PROCEDURAL LEGITIMACY

An arrest is a deprivation of life and personal liberty. It should be effected only by following the procedure established by law and any deviation from the established procedure in making of arrest can be declared as illegal.[14] As stated in Article 21, 'No person shall be deprived of his life or personal liberty except according to 'the procedure established by law'.[15] The procedure prescribed must conform to the norms of justice and fair

---

[10] *Id.*, Section 4 (c).

[11] *Id.*, Section 5.

[12] *Id.*, Section 6.

[13] General Officer Commanding v. Central Bureau of Investigation, A.I.R. 2012 S.C. 1890.

[14] Kavita Manikikar v. CBI, (2018) S.C.C. Online Bom 1095.

[15] The Constitution of India, Article 21.

play.[16] 'Procedure which is unjust or unfair in the circumstances of a case, attracts the vice of unreasonableness, thereby vitiating the law which prescribes that procedure and, consequently, the action taken under it'.[17]

Under AFSPA 1958, however, the procedural legalities have not been clearly enumerated. The 'opinion' of the officer is sufficient for the purpose of arrest without a warrant if there exists reasonable suspicion against any person. They may use any amount of force necessary to make the arrest[18]; no limitations as to the exercise of 'minimum' force have been mandated. Further, the powers conferred under this provision read with Section 5[19] provide that after the arrest, the person must be handed over to the nearest police station with the 'least possible delay', within 24 hours of the arrest.[20] In *Horendi Gogoi*,[21] the court observed that where a person is arrested, the arrestee must be handed over to the officer-in-charge of the nearest police station without the least possible delay. The said action has to be exercised in conformity with Section 57 Code of Criminal Procedure (CrPC), 1973 and Article 22 Clauses (1) and (2) of the Constitution of India. However, Section 6 of the Act provides a sort of blanket immunity to the armed forces from any action,[22] even though arbitrary or illegal.

The Apex Court while strengthening the constitutional validity of the AFSPA, 1958 in *Naga Peoples Movement of Human Rights, etc. v. Union of India*[23] declared that the powers conferred on the officers, including non-commissioned officers, are subject to the following limitations[24]:

1. While exercising the powers conferred under Section 4(a) of the Act, an officer in the Armed Forces shall use minimal force required

---

[16] Olga Tellis v. Bombay Municipal Corp., (1985) 3 S.C.C. 545.

[17] *Id.* at 578.

[18] Armed Forces (Special Powers), 1958 (Act 28 of 1958), Section 4 (c).

[19] *Id.*, Section 5.

[20] Bacha Bora v. State of Assam, (1991) 2 G.L.R. 119.

[21] Horendi Gogoi v. Union of India, (1991) Gau C.R. 3081.

[22] General Officer Commanding v. Central Bureau of Investigation, A.I.R. 2012 S.C. 1890.

[23] (1998) 2 S.C.C. 109.

[24] *Id.*, at 156–58.

for effective action against the person/persons acting in contravention of the prohibited order.[25]

2. The person who is arrested by an officer must be handed over to the officer in charge of the nearest police station, together with a report mentioning the circumstance of the arrest, with the least possible delay and to be produced before the nearest magistrate within 24 hours of such arrest.[26]

3. The property including arms, ammunition, etc., seized during the course of a search must be handed over to the officer in charge of the nearest police station, together with a report of the circumstances occasioning such search and seizure.[27]

4. Section 6 of the Central Act, insofar as it confers a discretion on the Central Government to grant or refuse sanction for instituting prosecution or suit or proceeding against any person does not suffer from the vice of arbitrariness. Since the order of the Central Government is subject to judicial review, the Central Government shall pass an order giving reasons.[28]

5. While exercising the power conferred under Clauses (a) to (d) of Section 4, the officers of the Armed Forces shall strictly adhere to the instructions listed in 'Dos and Don'ts' issued by the Army authorities, which are binding and any disregard would entail suitable action under the Army Act, 1950.[29]

6. To assure an effective check against misuse of powers by the members of the Armed Forces, the court directed that for thorough inquiry on any complaint containing an allegation about misuse or abuse of the powers, if on inquiry the allegations are found to be correct, the victim should be suitably compensated, and the necessary sanction should be granted by the Central Act for the institution of prosecution or suit or other proceedings.[30]

The Constitution Bench directed the instructions placed by the learned Attorney General in the form of a list of 'Dos and Don'ts' that are issued

---

[25] *Id.*, at 156, para 74.

[26] *Id.*

[27] *Id.*

[28] *Id.*, at 157, para 74.

[29] *Id.*

[30] *Id.*

by the Army Headquarters, which must be followed while acting under Armed Forces (Special Powers) Act, 1958.[31]

List of Dos[32]

1. **Action before Operation.**
   a) Act only in the area declared 'Disturbed Area' under Section 3 of the Act.
   b) Power to open fire using force or arrest is to be exercised under this Act only by an officer/JCO/WO and NCO.
   c) Before launching any raid/search, definite information about the activity has to be obtained from the local civil authorities.
   d) As far as possible co-opt representative of local civil administration during the raid.

2. **Action during Operation.**
   a) In case of necessity of opening fire and using any force against the suspect or any person acting in contravention to law and order, ascertain first that it is essential for the maintenance of public order. Open fire only after due warning.
   b) Arrest only those who have committed the cognizable offence or who are about to commit the cognizable offence or against whom a reasonable ground exists to prove that they have committed or are about to commit cognizable offence.
   c) Ensure that troops under command do not harass innocent people destroy the property of the public or unnecessarily enter into the house/dwelling of people not connected with any unlawful activities.
   d) Ensure that women are not searched/arrested without the presence of female police. In fact, women should be searched by female police only.

3. **Action after Operation.**
   a) After arrest prepare a list of the persons so arrested.

---

[31] Id.

[32] Id., See, Amnesty International, *India: Briefing on the Ares Forces Special Powers Act, 1958* (2005), pp. 29–32, https://www.refworld.org/pdfid/45c1c2b62.pdf (last visited 5 February 2021).

b) Handover the arrested persons to the nearest Police Station with the least possible delay.

c) While handing over to the police, a report should accompany detailed circumstances occasioning the arrest.

d) Every delay in handing over the suspects to the police must be justified and should be reasonable depending upon the place, time of arrest and the terrain in which such person has been arrested. The least possible delay maybe 2–3 hours extendable to 24 hours or so depending upon a particular case.

e) After the raid make out a list of all arms, ammunition or any other incriminating material/document taken into possession.

f) All such arms, ammunition, stores, etc. should be handed over to the police station along with the seizure memo.

g) Obtain receipt of persons and arms/ammunition, stores, etc. so handed over to the police.

h) Make a record of the area where the operation is launched having the date and time and the persons participating in such raid.

i) Make a record of the commander and other officers/JCOs/NCOs forming part of such force.

j) Ensure medical relief to any person injured during the encounter, if any person dies in the encounter his dead body be handed over immediately to the police along with the details leading to such death.

List of Don'ts[33]

1. Do not keep a person under custody for any period longer than the bare necessity for handing over to the nearest Police Station.

2. Do not use any force after having arrested a person except when he is trying to escape.

3. Do not use third-degree methods to extract information or to extract a confession or other involvement in unlawful activities.

4. After the arrest of a person by the member of the Armed forces, he shall not be interrogated by the member of the Armed forces.

[33] *Id.*

5. Do not release the person directly after apprehending on your own. If any person is to be released, he must be released through civil authorities.
6. Do not tamper with official records.
7. The Armed Forces shall not take back a person after he is handed over to civil police.

The Supreme Court's guidelines pertaining to the procedures to be followed by the security forces while in operation, assured the conduct of the security forces in accordance with the procedures provided under CrPC 1973. The court also affirmed that 'special law doesn't prevail over general law unless provided by statute and the deployment of armed forces in disturbed areas doesn't nullify the civil powers and other procedural mandates'. Though the validity of the Act was upheld by the higher judiciary, it also recognized the excessive use of powers by the security forces.

ALLEGED ILLEGALITIES UNDER AFSPA

'The spirit of any law should necessarily be the concern for the right to life and security of every individual. And every law is an expression of that part of human nature, which privileges the security over unrestrained freedom'.[34] AFSPA, 1958 has been condemned in the Northeast for the last six decades due to the violence inflicted by the armed forces upon innocent civilians by excessive use or misuse of powers.[35] The unprecedented powers to shoot, arrest on the frivolous ground, search without warrant and destruction, in the pretext of insurgency, without the appropriate Constitutional and procedural fairness have led to widespread violations affecting the common citizens of the region.[36] Fake

---

[34] B. Jagannatham & G. Haragopal, *Terrorism and Human Rights: Indian Experience with Repressive Laws* 44(28) ECON. POLIT. WKLY. 76–85 (2009).

[35] Parvaiz Bukhari, *AFSPA Repeal: An Ominous Refusal* 6(IV) EAST. QUART. 156–63 (2010).

[36] Human Rights Watch, *Getting Away with Murder - 50 Years of the Armed Forces (Special Powers) Act, 1958* (August 2008), https://www.hrw.org/legacy/backgrounder/2008/india0808/india0808web.pdf (last visited 8 February 2021).

encounters, massacres, torture, harassment,[37] 'illegal detention', 'forced disappearance', 'killing as a result of mistaken identity',[38] rape and destruction of property have been widespread.[39] The 'Malom Massacre' in Manipur on 2nd November 2000 bears evidence as to how civilians have become victims in the hands of the security forces in Manipur. The Act, which also reinforces other oppressive legislation such as Unlawful Activities Prevention Act 1967, National Security Act 1980, Prevention of Terrorist Activities Act 2002, Prevention of Seditious Meetings Act 1911 converted Manipur into a permanent state of siege,[40] that is, 'State of Exception' according to Giorgio Agamben for a similar situation.[41] The Act being applied for half a century with expanding scope has only confirmed the rife between what is and what is not India.

THE EXPERIENCE OF VICTIMS

They kept on pouring water into my nostrils until the water came out in my ears; I felt warm inside my ears. Then they stamped on both my thighs while two persons held my feet while another man sat on my head... They touched the wires' ends to my chest and gave me shocks three times. Each time I felt as if my whole body had contracted... I keep remembering how they used to beat me and see everything that happened to me vividly.

> —14-year-old child tortured by Indian soldiers
> in the North-Eastern State of Manipur[42]

---

[37] *Army Terror unleashed again in Kacha*, People's Democratic Movement (1 May 1991), Imphal.

[38] Guarding the Guards. (1990). *Economic and Political Weekly, 25*(23), 1228–1228. http://www.jstor.org/stable/4396363

[39] Udayon Mishra, *Review: Human Rights Violations in North East* 19 (51) Econ. Polit. Wkly. 2157, 2159–60 (1984).

[40] Malem Ningthouja, *Violence as AFSPA 1958 and People's Movement Against It* 6(IV) Eastern Quarterly 145–55 (2010).

[41] Giorgio Agamben, State of Exception 11–22 (University of Chicago Press 2004).

[42] Human Rights Watch, *Witness Statement of Arrest and Torture in Manipur*, August 2008, https://www.hrw.org/legacy/backgrounder/2008/india0808/india0808web.pdf (last visited 10 April 2021).

In an attempt to reveal the nature of the atrocities that have happened under the shadow of the AFSPA, 1958 the author had a close interaction with the victims and the families to document the stories of the affected people and how it impacted their lives. Among the seven North- Eastern States, the researcher limited the study to Assam and Manipur, owing to reasons of accessibility and personal safety. An initial survey, with the help of local NGOs and human rights organizations, was done of 150 victim-survivors; among them, only 50 victims and/ or families agreed to participate and speak about the incidents and their sufferings. The interview was unstructured, as the experience of the victims and families were very heart-breaking. It was a daunting task on the part of the researcher to convince them to speak out. Special efforts were taken while talking to them with due respect to their emotions and sentiments. In few cases, especially that of sexual assaults, the victims and family members refused to recount the trauma undergone. Rather, they directed the researcher to a friend or advocate who was well versed with the occurrence and the legal process, if any. The researcher has thereafter conducted in-depth interviews with the appointed person.

Some of the narrations (in brief) of the experiences are produced below:

Incident 1: On the day of the incident, November 4, 2008, at around 3:30 pm, Meena received a call from her husband stating that he was apprehended by personnel of the Manipur Police Commandos and asked her to contact the SP, Imphal East District so as to secure his release. Immediately after some time when she tried to call her husband's number, there was no response. That was the last time when she could contact her husband.

She waited for her husband to return home. At around 9 pm, the news came in ISTV, a local news channel in Manipur that two dreaded militants were killed in an encounter and the dead bodies were lying in the mortuary of RIMS Hospital in Manipur. Santosh was declared as a member of the underground militant outfit, and to prove the statement made by the police, a Chinese hand grenade and three empty casings (9mm) were kept beside his dead body. Later, a judicial inquiry established that it was a fake encounter and an amount of ₹500,000 was paid.

Incident 2: In another incident, on April 6, 2007, Mikhel left home for the market to buy a film roll for his camera, to celebrate the first birthday of their son. He was on his Honda Activa. On the way, Brojen and Bobi also joined him. They were asked to stop at the Kwakeithal checkpoint by a team of six RAPFs. Mikhel panicked and sped off on his Activa. The police team gave chase and shot him down Mikhel while killing the other two youths as well.

It all happened in broad daylight in front of all the residents of that place. As Renu (his wife) recounted:

> I was waiting for my husband to come back. Instead of him, people came with the news of his death. After I received the news, I reacted as if nothing had happened because the death of my husband was unacceptable to me. I did all the household work, took care of my child and stayed in that state for almost three days.

She continued, 'Life has not been easy for me after the incident; I had to struggle a lot for survival.... With the little money I earn by doing beautician work and by selling clothes, I have to look after my kid'.

Incident 3: Khunsa, Anao, Tumba and Bomcha were liquor traders in their late twenties at the time of death. On August 16, 2010, following their daily routine, they started from home at early hours in the morning towards the Myanmar border to provide liquor to their distributors. That was the last time that they were last seen alive by their families. They were shot dead by the Army on their way back home. On September 5, 2010, a complaint was filed in the nearby Police Station, but no action was taken. Eventually, an ex-gratia amount of ₹50,000 was paid to each of the victim's families. Their families, in abject poverty, stated that 'Where our survival has become impossible, we cannot think of any other thing. At this moment we need financial assistance from the government to rehabilitate our lives'.

Incident 4: Girin, thirty-eight at the time of his death, was married and the father of three children. He was employed as a fourth-grade staff in a school. During those days, they were constructing their new house. On February 12, 2009, Girin was on his way to market to get some materials for construction, when he was picked up from the market by the Police Commandos. The next day morning the family got the news that Girin was picked up by the Manipur Police Commando and shot dead in an unknown place. Girin's wife recounts:

> My husband was the sole bread earner of the family, after his demise, the entire sky fell upon us; my kids had to drop out from the school, and I have to work in others houses and what else remains for us. I have to lose my husband and become a widow at an early age; my kids have to compromise with their childhood and take the responsibility of the family.

She claimed her husband to be innocent, but the truth was never made known to her. She expects justice to be in such a way that it gives the victims their rights and the perpetrators accountable under the law.

Incident 5: Emina, married to Bijou and mother of three children, lives in Imphal West in a small house close to the western wall of the Assam Rifles camp. On the evening of October 6, 2001, a soldier in civil dress and armed with weapons broke into the house asking for women. Immediately, he attacked Bijou and tried to drag Emina; when her sister-in-law tried to resist, the soldier hit her with the rifle. Eventually, the soldier dragged Emina outside the house and sexually assaulted her behind the bushes. Hearing Emina's frantic call for help, her neighbours immediately rushed to the spot and caught hold of the soldier. Later, the perpetrator was tried and convicted with 7 years of imprisonment. Emina received a compensation amount of ₹200,000.

Incident 6: Agamani, a 59-year-old married woman, was raped by two soldiers of the Indian Army at her home. The incident happened in the presence of her husband and two sons. The incident was so brutal that she was admitted to the hospital for 3 days, followed by the removal of her womb.

The perpetrators were court-martialled publicly on the demand of the people and dismissed from their service. Agamani received a compensation amount of ₹100,000 from the Indian Army. Further, in the year 2003 Agamani filed a writ petition before the Gauhati High Court, Imphal Bench, claiming a compensation amount of ₹1 million. In 2008, the High Court ordered compensation of

₹200,000 to Agamani. The incident however changed her life completely. The victim had to leave her house for security reasons and take shelter in the community hall. She along with her family then shifted to another place. Her marital relation was affected, her husband lost faith in her and started torturing her. She had to work as a domestic help as her husband did not look after her. Later, she engaged herself with the women activist group to fight for women victims like her.

Incident 7: Suresh, twenty-eight at the time of his death, lived with his family. On February 18, 2011, at around 11:50 pm he was abducted from his residence by the Indian State Agents in military uniforms. On the following day, when his family did not receive any information regarding his whereabouts, they filed a missing complaint in the Wangoi Police Station. The Manipur Police Department, as well as the Army, denied the arrest of Suresh and thus the investigation remained inconclusive. Later, on February 28, a habeas corpus petition was filed by the family, before the Gauhati High Court, Imphal Branch. However, the case remained unheard of and is pending to date. The whereabouts of Suresh are not known to the family. In the words of the family members, 'We still live in the hope that he will return one day and we will be able to see him again, and those responsible for the abduction will be punished and made accountable'.

Incident 8: Mustafa, a 20-year-old daily wage worker at the time of his death went out for work early in the morning on February 5, 2009. When he reached the Keishampat Junction, the Police Commandos arrested him (as witnessed by other people) and took him to Police Station. The family members were informed by some people in the market that Mustafa had been picked by the Police Commandos. Later, the next day they got the news that Mustafa was killed in custody.

Mustafa's brother visited the Police station to file an FIR for the said custodial killing, but his complaint was denied on the ground that Mustafa, a dreaded militant, was killed in an encounter with the 39 Assam Rifles and Manipur Police Commandos and an FIR was already registered by the Manipur Police Commando alleging the same.

GRAPHICAL ANALYSIS OF FINDINGS

Nature of Offences

The respondents (victims) were categorized into four types of offences in the study, that is, extrajudicial killings, custodial death, sexual offences, and enforced disappearances. The majority of the respondents are from the category of extra-judicial killings followed by custodial death. In terms of percentage, 63 per cent of respondents fall under the category of extrajudicial killings, 18 per cent under custodial deaths, whereas 15 per cent are victims of sexual offence, and another 4 per cent of enforced disappearances (See Figure 10.1).

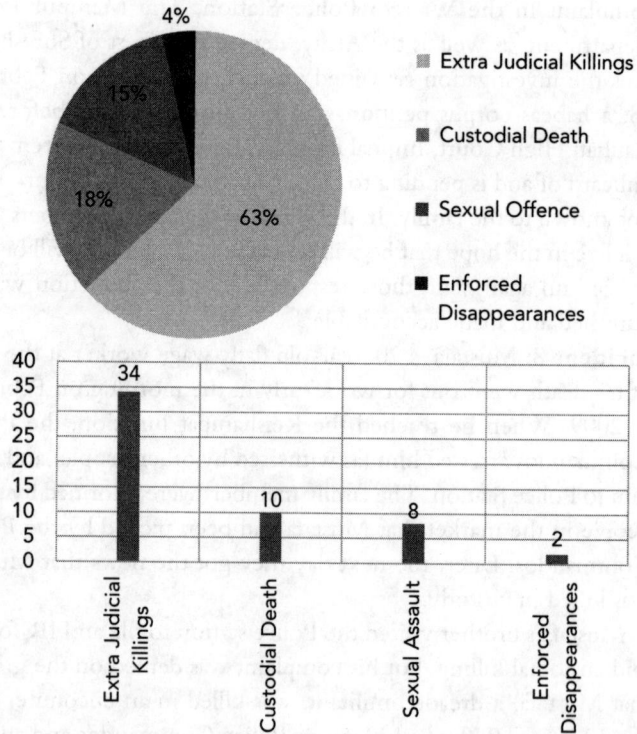

Figure 10.1 *Nature of Offences*

Source: The author.

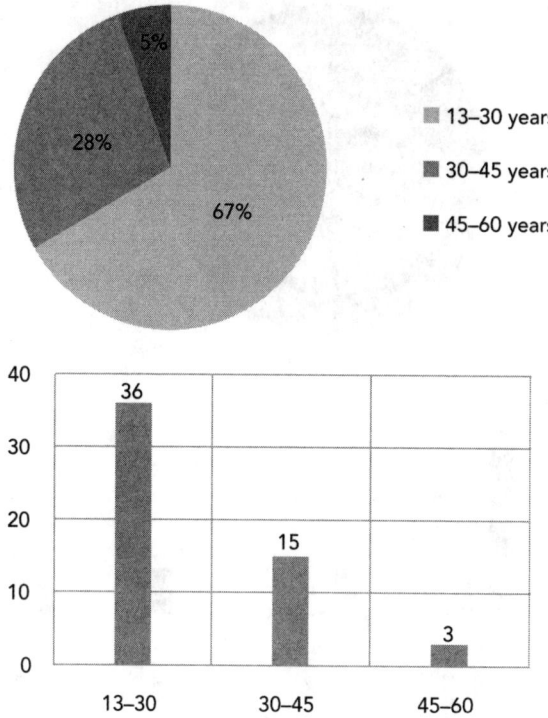

Figure 10.2 *Age Distribution*

Source: The author.

Age Distribution

The victims are between the age group of 13–60 years. Sixty-seven per cent were in the category of 13–30 years. Another small portion of 5 per cent is within the age group of 45–60 years and the rest 28 per cent of them are from 30–45 years (See Figure 10.2).

Gender Composition of the Victims

The findings reveal that male victims constitute a higher number (approx. 80%) whereas 20 per cent are female victims. The number of female victims is mostly in the category of sexual offences (See Figure 10.3).

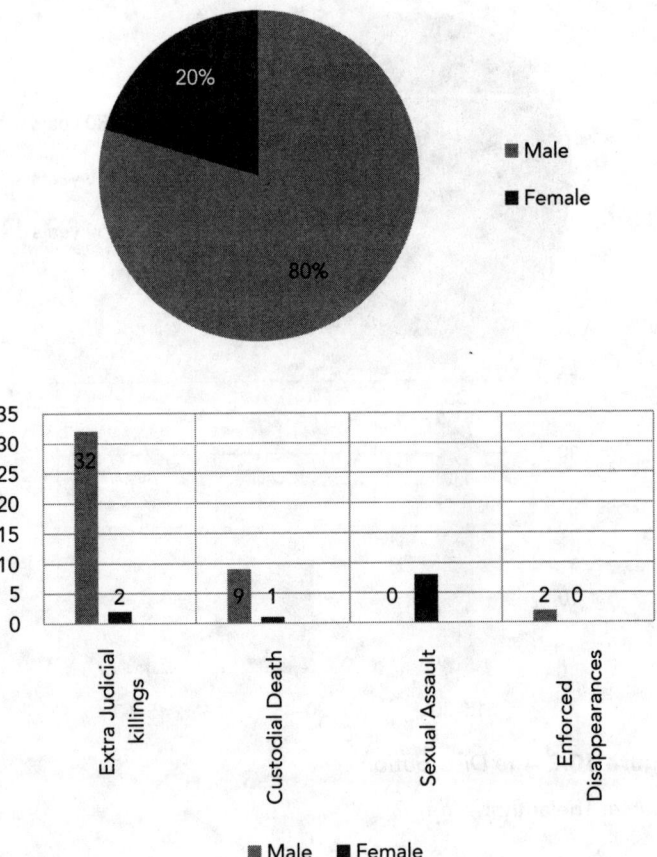

Figure 10.3 *Gender Composition*

Source: The author.

Victims Profile

The victims are divided into three sections: sole earners, students and dependents. Fifty-six per cent of the victims were sole earners of the family; 11 per cent of the respondent comprised of school and college-going students, while another 33 per cent are mainly dependents, other than students (See Figure 10.4).

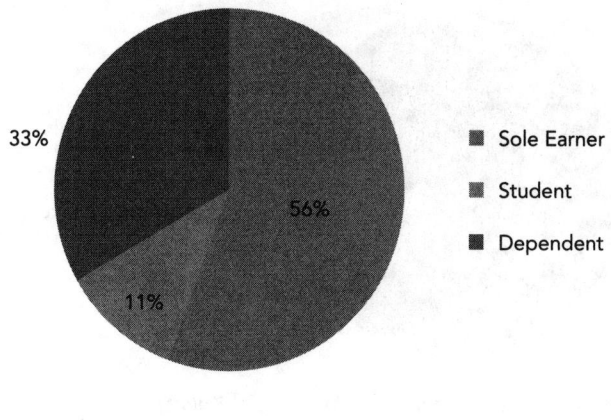

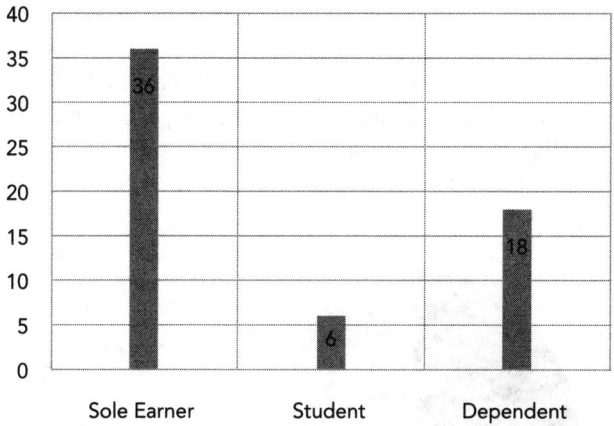

Figure 10.4 *Victim Profile*

Source: The author.

Extra-Judicial Killings

The findings reveal that extrajudicial killings constitute the maximum number of respondents, in the present field study. However, the action taken is unsatisfactory, 21 per cent of the surveyed respondents proceeded with written complaints to the higher authority; whereas, in another 79 per cent, no action was taken (See Figure 10.5).

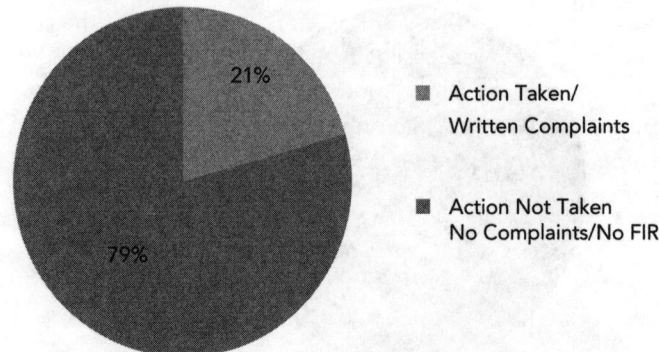

Figure 10.5 *Action Taken: Extra-Judicial Killings*
Source: The author.

As regards institutional interventions, approximately 56 per cent were inquired into by the judicial committees, 6 per cent were inquired by the NHRC and near about 9 per cent were inquired by CBI. However, another 29 per cent never had any institutional intervention (See Figure 10.6).

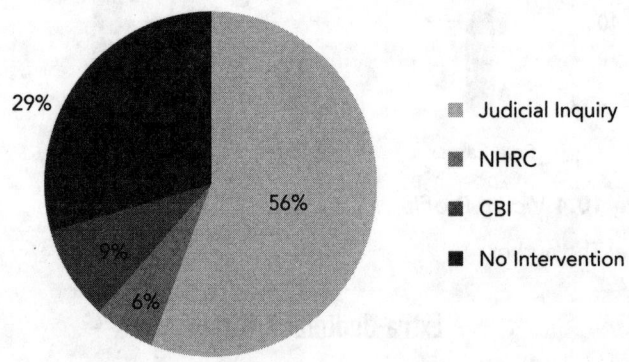

Figure 10.6 *Institutional Intervention*
Source: The author.

When asked about the assistance, the respondents were found to have received assistance in the nature of compensation, ex-gratia and government jobs (See Figure 10.7). 56 per cent of the surveyed respondents were awarded compensation ranging from ₹300,000 to ₹700,000 (See Figure 10.8). Another 29 per cent received an ex-gratia amount of ₹50,000 each and only 3 per cent, that is, one respondent received Govt. job, whereas 12 per cent were left out without any kind of assistance.

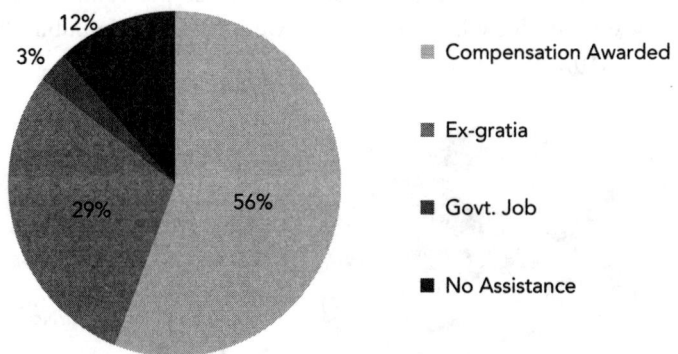

Figure 10.7 *Nature of Assistance*

Source: The author.

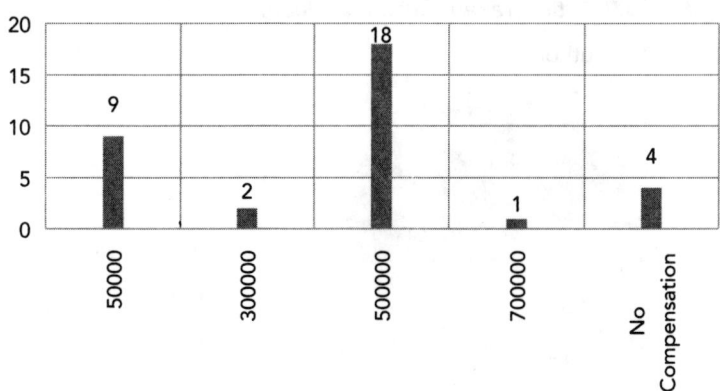

Figure 10.8 *Compensation Awarded*

Source: The author.

Custodial Death

When it comes to the question of custodial death, the data exhibits almost the same percentage for both action taken and institutional intervention. Only in 11 per cent of the cases, FIRs were filed, whereas the cases where no action was taken constitutes the majority (approximately 89%) (See Figure 10.9). Similarly, in the majority of cases (80%), there was no institutional intervention and only in 20 per cent, a judicial inquiry was conducted, which reports were never made public (See Figure 10.10).

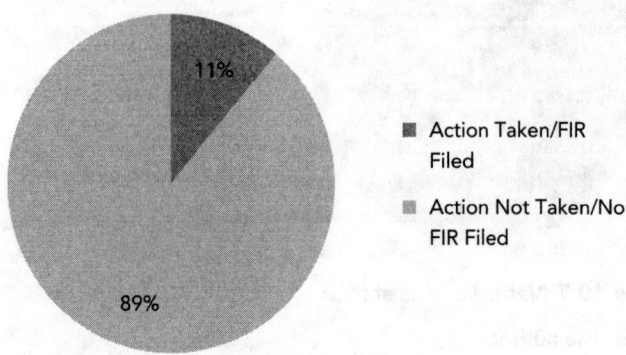

Figure 10.9 *Action Taken: Custodial Death*
Source: The author.

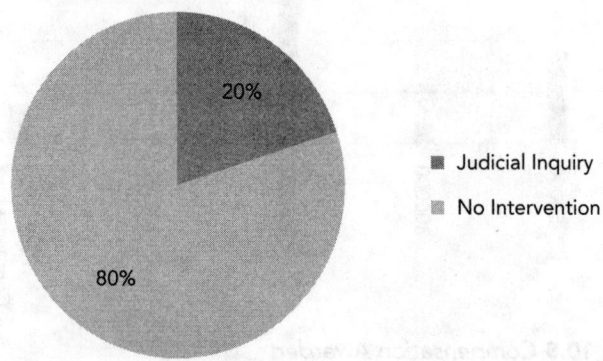

Figure 10.10 *Institutional Intervention*
Source: The author.

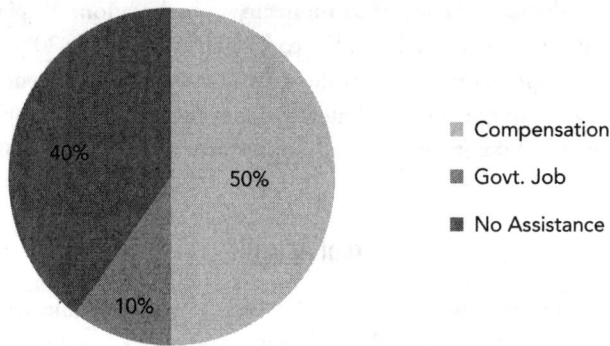

Figure 10.11 *Nature of Assistance*

Source: The author.

When asked about assistance, the respondents in cases of custodial death replied that majority of the assistance was provided by means of monetary compensation, that is, 50 per cent of them received compensation ranging from ₹200,000 to ₹700,000. A minority of 10 per cent were assisted with government jobs. However, a significant number of 40 per cent were left out without any assistance (See Figure 10.11).

Figure 10.12 shows the responses of the participants as to what was the scale of compensation awarded to them. It is an extension of

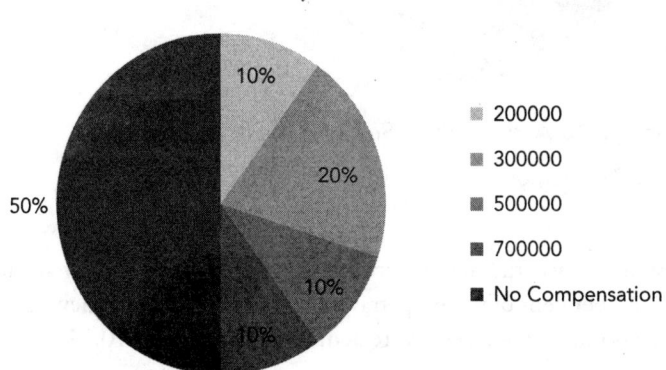

Figure 10.12 *Compensation Awarded*

Source: The author.

the above discussion relating to monetary compensation. 10 per cent were paid on the scale of ₹200,000 to ₹700,000. Another 20 per cent received compensation on the scale of ₹300,000 and 50 per cent never received any compensation. Generally seen, there are huge disparities in the award of compensation and no uniform scale was maintained.

Sexual Assault

A different feature has been observed in cases of sexual assaults wherein, in the majority of the cases, the action was taken by the authority, primarily due to public protest and outrage, according to the respondents. In more than 62 cases, FIRs were filed, but in 38 per cent there was no action taken (See Figure 10.13).

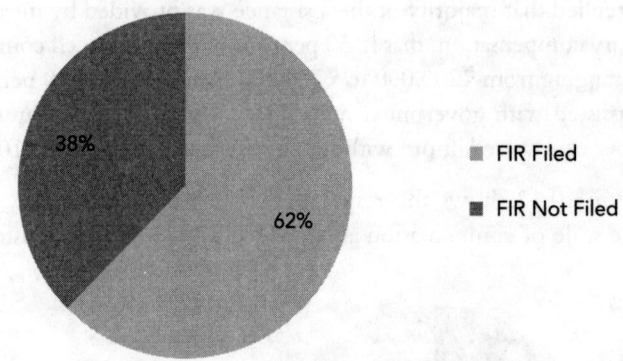

Figure 10.13 *Action Taken: Sexual Assault*
Source: The author.

As there was the active participation of the civil society in filing FIRs, 63 per cent of the perpetrators were held liable for their actions, while another 37 per cent were acquitted (See Figure 10.14).

On asking the respondents about institutional interventions, if any, they revealed that in few cases, that is, in only 25 per cent of cases, there were judicial inquiries, whereas, for the rest 75 per cent, no inquiries

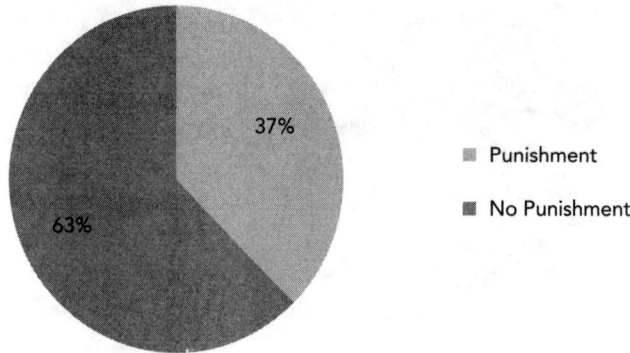

Figure 10.14 *Imposition of Punishment*
Source: The author.

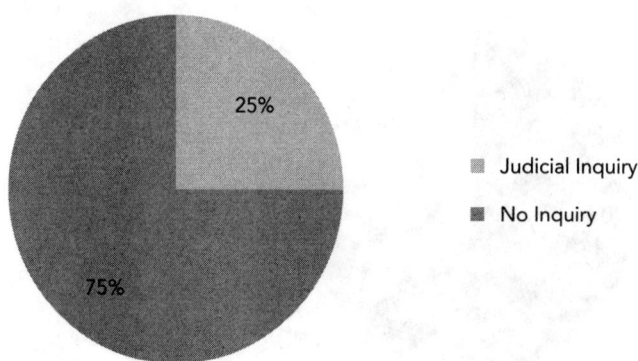

Figure 10.15 *Institutional Intervention*
Source: The author.

were conducted, specifically because police actions had been initiated with the registration of first information report (See Figure 10.15).

When asked about the means of assistance they received, the respondents replied that monetary compensation was the only means of assistance provided; 50 per cent received compensation while for another 50 per cent, no compensation was awarded (See Figure 10.16). Hence, in cases of sexual offences also, no other means of reparation were provided to the respondents.

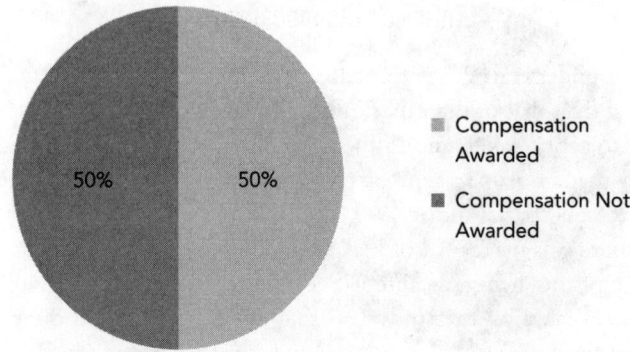

Figure 10.16 *Nature of Assistance*
Source: The author.

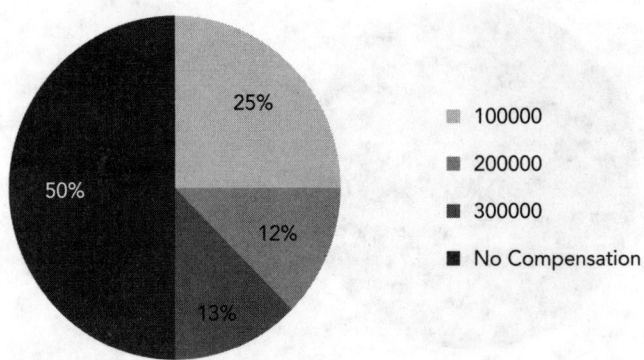

Figure 10.17 *Compensation Awarded*
Source: The author.

Figure 10.17 is the extension of the above Figure 10.16. As compensation was awarded to 50 per cent of the respondents, this figure attempts to indicate the range of such compensation. 12 per cent of the respondent were awarded compensation on the scale of ₹200,000, while 25 per cent were awarded ₹100,000 and another 13 per cent received payment of ₹300,000.

Enforced Disappearances

The respondents in the enforced disappearances were comparatively minimal than that of the other offences. When queries were put with regard to action taken and institutional intervention, the respondents replied that in 50 per cent of cases, there were written complaints made to the civil authority, whereas in another half, that is, 50 per cent, there was no record of FIR being filed, nor any record of written complaints being accepted (See Figure 10.18). Another unique feature revealed by the study was that after the enforced disappearances of the person, neither State police nor the Central armed forces took the responsibility for the act, which again is a great hurdle for the respondents to trace the disappeared person.

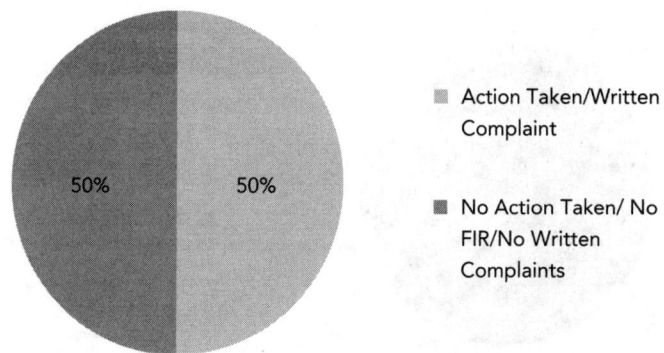

Figure 10.18 *Action Taken: Enforced Disappearance*
Source: The author.

It also remains a cause of concern that in cases of enforced disappearances, no role was played by the institutional authorities to provide any sort of assistance to the families (See Figure 10.19). As there was no action taken, no institutional intervention, so the question of assistance doesn't ever come into the picture. For 100 per cent of respondents, no assistance was provided (See Figure 10.20).

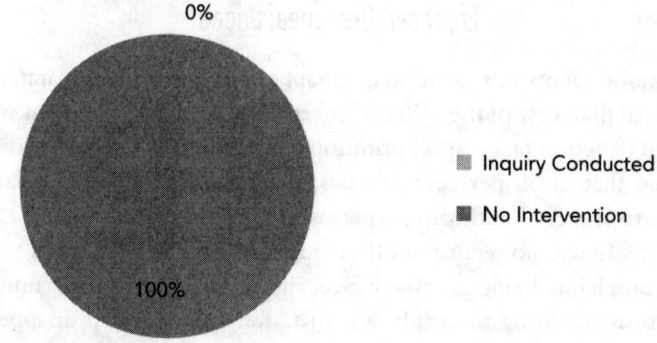

Figure 10.19 *Institutional Intervention*
Source: The author.

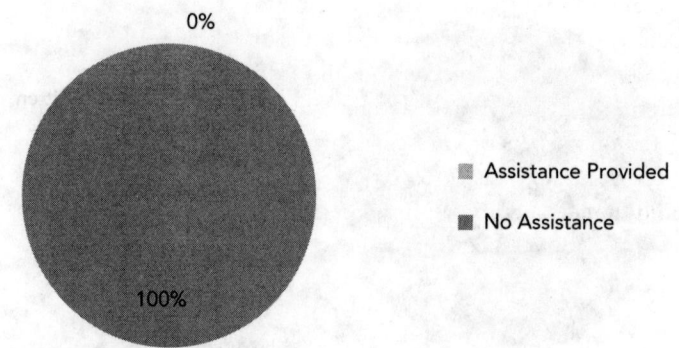

Figure 10.20 *Assistance Provided*
Source: The author.

CONCLUSION

It is evident from the above discussion that indiscriminate violence is a stark reality in the lives of common people in the North-East under the AFSPA. In the name of arrest and search, powers are exercised arbitrarily without proper application of rule of law. Due to the lack of adequate procedure mentioned within the provisions of the Act, the very essence of the fundamental rights of the people is violated.

The most unfortunate of all is the denial of state action for the harms inflicted upon the people by the arbitrary action of the Armed forces. Neither the wrongful act of the armed personnel's under the regime of the Act are recognized, nor the plight of the victims recognized under the penal law. Living in constant fear of their lives and security, the victims are denied basic access to justice. Cases are never accepted nor alleged violations investigated by the State machinery. Taking recourse to judicial bodies, some victims have secured respite through ex-Gratia payments or compensation which is too meagre before the insurmountable losses incurred by them. What is important is to revisit the law operating in the region and the extent of powers conferred thereunder. It is important that the Armed forces as well as civil police operating in the region are subject to strict conditionalities in the exercise of their powers of arrest, search, and use of force. Any violation by the authorities should be subject to mandatory inquiry and penalised, on proof of guilt and the immunity granted under the Act should be used, but sparingly. To redress the plight of the victims, upholding the dignity and respect of the rights of victims, and acknowledging the violations inflicted upon them are also fundamental requirements.[43] The time is ripe for the State to act proactively to end the crisis in the region and uphold the life and liberty of the people.

---

[43] Researcher's personal interview with the victims.

PART III

Arrest and Detention: A Global Perspective

Chapter 11

Arrest, Detention and Human Rights
International Standards

Dipa Dube

INTRODUCTION

Liberty is the most cherished of human rights. It stands for the right of a person not to be subjected to arbitrary arrest or detention, unless provided by law. In a civilized nation governed by the rule of law, it is imperative that no one should be deprived of his liberty, except where justified or necessary. Furthermore, even where there are grounds for deprivation of liberty, it must be ensured that torture and ill-treatment are not inflicted on the detainees by their captors nor are they confined in inhuman conditions. Right to liberty encompasses a plethora of protections, which overall, seeks to prevent the arbitrary use of detention powers by putting in place safeguards to eradicate ill-treatments.[1]

Liberty in the modern sense did not exist in ancient societies. However, the concept was not unknown. 'There did exist so-called

---

[1] Maryan Isaku Gwangndi & Abubakar Garba, *The Right to Liberty Under International Human Rights Law: An Analysis* 27 J. LAW POLICY GLOB. 213–18 (2015).

'free men' as opposed to slaves and underprivileged classes'.[2] With the emergence of the Renaissance and Reformation in Europe and the scientific and industrial revolution, a new sense dawned whereupon people became conscious of their rights. The Magna Carta (1215), the Petition of Rights (1628) and the English Bill of Rights (1689) in England marked the emergence of a new era. They testified to the fact that there were certain basic eternal and inalienable rights conferred on every human being that could never be renounced. Article 39 of the Magna Carta states[3]:

> No free man shall be taken or imprisoned, or be disseised of his free-hold, or liberties or free customs, or be outlawed, or exiled or any otherwise destroyed; nor will we not pass upon him nor condemn him, but by lawful judgement of his peers, or by the law of the land.

The protection of Article 39 did not extend to all citizens, but only to sections of the feudal class. Nevertheless, the Charter imposed a restriction on the regal powers and represented the first significant step towards acknowledgement of the right to freedom from arbitrary arrest and detention.[4]

The works of different philosophers, including Montesquieu, Rousseau, Locke, further exerted a profound influence and 'sought to discover and act upon universally valid principles governing nature, humanity and society, including the inalienable "rights of Man"'.[5] The French Declaration of the Rights of Man and the Citizen of 1789 decreed several 'natural and imprescriptible rights of man,' including the freedom from arrest and detention. Consequently, the two world wars renewed interest in the value of human life and the establishment of the United Nations signalled the real beginning of the 'momentous

---

[2] B. P. Srivastava, *Right Against Arbitrary Arrest and Detention Under Article 9 of the Covenant as Recognized and Protected Under the Indian Law* 11(1) J. IND. L. INSTT. 29–56 (Jan–March 1969), at pp. 29–30.

[3] Laurent Jr Marcoux, *Protection from Arbitrary Arrest and Detention Under International Law* 5 B. C. INT'L & COMP. L. REV. 345–76 (1982).

[4] *Id.*

[5] Burns H. Weston, *Human Rights*, Encyclopedia Britannica, Mar. 5, 2020, *available at*: https://www.britannica.com/topic/human-rights/Natural-law-transformed-into-natural-rights#ref219323

international journey' towards upholding the human rights universally protected by the rule of law.[6]

THE BEGINNING

The basic protection of the rights against arbitrary arrest and detention may be read in the Universal Declaration of Human Rights (UDHR) and the International Covenant on Civil and Political Rights (ICCPR). These instruments were adopted to promote the dignity of all human beings, including those accused of crime.[7]

The UDHR, a milestone in the history of human rights, was proclaimed by the UN General Assembly in Paris on Dec 10, 1948, as a common standard of achievements for all peoples and nations. Article 1 of the UDHR proclaims the inherent dignity, freedom and equal status of all humans, while Article 3 guarantees the right to life, liberty and security of all persons. Article 9 UDHR specifically delves into arbitrary arrest and detention and prohibits imposition of restrictions on personal liberty within a state. The words 'arrest' and 'detention' in this context have been given their primary functional meanings[8]:

Arrest means the act of taking a person into custody under the authority of the law or by compulsion of another kind and includes the period from the moment he is placed under restraint up to the time he is brought before an authority competent to order his continued custody or to release him.

Detention applies to the act of confining a person to a certain place, whether or not in the continuation of arrest, and under restraints which prevents him from living with his family or carrying on his normal occupational or social activities.

---

[6] MASHOOD A. BADERIN & MANISULI SSENYONJO, INTERNATIONAL HUMAN RIGHTS LAW - SIX DECADES AFTER THE UDHR AND BEYOND (Routledge 2010).

[7] United Nations, *Human Rights and Pre-trial Detention, A Handbook of International Standards Relating to Pre-trial Detention*, 1994, http://hrlibrary.umn.edu/Human%20Rights%20and%20Pre-trial%20Detention.pdf (last visited on Feb. 14, 2021).

[8] United Nations, *Study on the Right of Everyone to be Free from Arbitrary Arrest, Detention and Exile*, Dept. of Economic and Social Affairs, 1964, p. 5. https://undocs.org/pdf?symbol=en/E/CN.4/826/Rev.1

The prohibition in Article 9 extends to 'arbitrary' arrest and detention. In this context, the relevant provisions in the ICCPR may also be noted.[9] The first paragraph of Article 9 ICCPR lays down that[10]:

> Everyone has the right to liberty and security of person. No one shall be subjected to arbitrary arrest or detention. No one shall be deprived of his liberty except on the grounds and in accordance with such procedure as are established by law.

There are three aspects in this Article[11]:

1. A right accorded to personal liberty and security;
2. A prohibition on arbitrary arrest and detention;
3. A requirement that the deprivation of liberty be in consonance with procedures established by law;

CONCEPTUAL NOTIONS

Srivastava maintains that it is difficult to provide a comprehensive definition of liberty.[12] Encyclopaedia Britannica explains it as 'a state of freedom, especially as opposed to political subjection, imprisonment or slavery'.[13] It has been defined as a right 'not to be subjected to imprisonment, arrest or other physical coercion in any manner that does not admit legal justification'.[14] The United States Supreme Court[15] has given the word a wide meaning comprising all the

---

[9] Adopted by General Assembly resolution 2200A (XXI) of 16 December 1966. https://www.ohchr.org/en/professionalinterest/pages/ccpr.aspx

[10] *Id.*

[11] Claire Macken, *Preventive Detention and the Right of Personal Liberty and Security Under the International Covenant on Civil and Political Rights, 1966* 26 ADEL. L. REV. 1–28 (2005).

[12] Srivastava, *supra* note 2, at 31.

[13] Britannica, The Editors of Encyclopaedia, *Liberty*. Encyclopaedia Britannica, Feb. 16, 2018, https://www.britannica.com/topic/liberty-human-rights (last visited Mar. 4, 2021).

[14] A. V. DICEY & E. C. S. WADE, CONSTITUTIONAL LAW, 207–208 (9th ed. 1939).

[15] Belling v. Sharpe, U.S. 497 (1954), at 499.

freedoms and including all conducts which an individual is free to pursue subject to the protection of social interest by states through various means such as the power of the police, taxation, and eminent domain. The Indian Supreme Court[16] has regarded liberty as the right of an individual to be free from restrictions or encroachments. Srivastava asserts that such wide meanings cannot be attributed to the word as used in Article 9, but rather confined to its normal meaning as freedom from physical restraint and coercion.[17] The Human Rights Committee expressed the view that liberty guarantees the freedom from the confinement of the body, not general freedom of action, while the notion of 'security' concerns the freedom from injury to the body and the mind and the bodily and mental integrity.[18] Police custody, remand, imprisonment after conviction, house arrest, administrative detention, etc., are some examples of deprivation of liberty; while, personal security is violated for instance in case of unjustifiable infliction of bodily injury by State officials.[19]

The meaning of the word 'arbitrary' posed to be a tricky one and the question arose whether the word would be taken as akin to unlawful or illegal. In the discussion on the provision that ensued, it was emphasized that the term 'arbitrary' would mean 'illegal' or 'unjust' or 'both illegal and unjust'.[20] This, however, did not find favour and the Third Committee of the General Assembly held the view that an arbitrary arrest or detention would entail an act done 'without any legal grounds' or 'contrary to law' or in observance of a law which was in itself 'unjust' or 'incompatible with the dignity of the human person' or 'incompatible with the respect for the right to liberty and security of person'. The substance of the word was said to mean[21]

---

[16] Kharak Singh v. State of UP, A.I.R. 1963 S.C. 1295, at 1302 and 1306.

[17] Srivastava, *supra* note 2, at 31.

[18] Human Rights Committee, General Comment No. 35, UN Doc CCPR/C/GC/35, p. 1, *available at*: https://www.nichibenren.or.jp/library/ja/kokusai/humanrights_library/treaty/data/HRC_GC_35e.pdf

[19] *Id.*, at 2.

[20] United Nations, *supra* note 8, at 6.

[21] Srivastava, *supra* note 2, at 32.

Any act which violated justice, reason or legislation, or was done according to someone's whim or discretion, or which was capricious, despotic, imperious, tyrannical or uncontrolled.[22]

The Committee examined the reports of the United Nations seminars in the Philippines and Chile on the protection of human rights in criminal law and procedure. The word 'arbitrary arrest' was defined at the Philippines seminar as

an arrest authorized by a law which fails adequately to protect human rights because either a) the legal right to arrest has been too widely defined or be the means, circumstances or physical force attendant on the arrest exceed the reasonable requirements of effecting an arrest.[23]

At the seminar in Chile, three different connotations of the term arbitrary were put forward[24]:

1. action under a positive law which does not duly protect human rights;
2. improper application of the law; and
3. arbitrary in the sense of illegal, although it implied something that was done capriciously or that depended on the wheel alone.

The Committee came to the opinion that 'arbitrary' calls for a wider interpretation and is not synonymous with illegal.[25] Rather, the word is capable of a far broader meaning, wherein the laws of governments should comply with international standards while ensuring the widest amplitude to the right to personal liberty.[26] The Committee confirmed the following definition[27]:

---

[22] See, United Nations, *Human Rights in the Administration of Justice: A Manual on Human Rights for Judges, Prosecutors and Lawyers, available at*: https://www.ohchr.org/documents/publications/training9chapter5en.pdf

[23] United Nations, *supra* note 8, at 7–8.

[24] *Id.*, at 7; *Report of the Seminar on the Protection of Human Rights in Criminal Law and Procedure*, Santiago, Chile, May 19–30, 1958 (ST/TAA/HR/3), para. 70.

[25] Marcoux, *supra* note 3.

[26] *Id.*; cf. General Assembly, *Third Session, Summary Record of the 176th Meeting*, 3 U.N. GAOR C.3, pt. I, at 864, U.N. Doc. A/C.3/SR.176 (1948).

[27] United Nations, *supra* note 8, at 7.

An arrest or detention is arbitrary if it is

a) on grounds or in accordance with procedure other than those established by law, or

b) under the provisions of law the purpose of which is incompatible with respect for the right to liberty and security of person.

In support of its definition, the Committee quoted Article 29 (2) of the UDHR 1948 which subjected these rights 'only to such limitations as a determined by law' and which are in accordance with 'morality, public order and the general welfare in a democratic society'.[28]

STANDARDS ON PRE-TRIAL DETENTION

The basic protections of the rights of detained persons as found in the UDHR and ICCPR, while promoting the dignity of all human beings, provides special protection to persons accused of crimes including the rights to a fair trial, to the presumption of innocence, equal protection of the law and retrospective penal operation.[29]

Article 9 of ICCPR (The International Covenant on Civil and Political Rights) specifically enunciates that an arrested person has to be informed of his grounds of arrest as well as charges drawn against him. He should be promptly produced before a Judge to decide on the lawfulness of the arrest and should be released subject to guarantees to appear for trial.

Thus the legality of detention must be adjudged on legal grounds and procedures and court control over the detention. Prolonged pre-trial detention without bail should be discouraged as it is incompatible with Article 9 and call for specific justifications, as also periodic review. Besides being a violation of Article 9 of ICCPR, such indefinite detention violates other provisions of the Covenant; for example, Article 14, which guarantees s prompt trial before competent judicial authority

---

[28] *Srivastava, supra* note 2, at 33.

[29] See, Articles 10 and 11 of UDHR, 1948; Articles 14 and 15 OCCPR, 1966, *available at*: https://www.un.org/en/universal-declaration-human-rights/ and https://www.ohchr.org/en/professionalinterest/pages/ccpr.aspx

or Article 7, which prohibits torture and inhuman or degrading treatment or punishment, as also Article 10, which provides for humane treatment during detention. The notion of indefinite detention is also indicative of inhuman treatment and that in certain circumstances it may even constitute a form of torture.[30] Thus, wherein a case a person was held in detention for about 16 months to coerce him to reveal the whereabouts of his brother, though there were no charges against him, the Committee was of the firm opinion that it was a case of 'arbitrary arrest and detention' contrary to Article 9.[31]

Resolution 17 on pre-trial detention adopted by the Eighth United Nations Congress on the Prevention of Crime and Treatment of Offenders reiterates certain basic principles. They may be indicated as below[32]:

(a) Person suspected of having committed offences and deprived of their liberty should be brought promptly before a judge or other officer authorized by law to exercise judicial functions who should hear them and make a decision concerning pre-trial detention without delay;

(b) the pre-trial detention may be ordered only if there are reasonable grounds to believe that the person concerned has been involved in the commission of the alleged offences and there is a danger of their absconding or committing further serious offences or a danger that the course of justice will be seriously interfered if they are left free;

(c) In considering whether pre-trial detention should be ordered, account should be taken of the circumstances of the individual case, in particular the nature and seriousness of the alleged offence, the strength of the evidence, the penalty likely to be incurred, and the conduct and personal and social circumstances of the person concerned, including his or her community ties;

---

[30] Alfred de Zayas, *Human Rights and Indefinite Detention* 87(857) Int. Rev. Red Cross 15–38 (Mar. 2005).

[31] United Nations, *supra* note 22, at 166; cf. Communication No. 16/1977, D. Monguya Mbenge et al. v. Zaire (Views adopted on Mar. 25 1983), in UN doc. GAOR, A/38/40, p. 140, paras. 20–21.

[32] United Nations, *supra* note 7, at 1.

(d) Pre-trial detention should not be ordered if the deprivation of liberty would be disproportionate in relation to the alleged offence and the expected sentence;

(e) wherever possible, the use of pre-trial detention should be avoided by imposing alternative measures, such as release on bail or personal recognitions;

(f) if the use of pre-trial detention for juveniles cannot be avoided, they should receive care protection and all the necessary individual assistance that they may require in view of their age;

(g) Persons from for whom pre-trial detention is ordered should be informed of their rights, in particular:

    i) the right to be assisted promptly by legal counsel;

    ii) the right to request legal aid;

    iii) the right to have the validity of the detention determined by way of *habeas corpus, amparo* or other means, and to be released if the detention is not lawful; iv) the right to be visited or correspond with members of their families subject to reasonable conditions and restrictions as specified by law or lawful regulations;

(h) Pre-trial detention should be subject to judicial review at reasonably short intervals and should not be continued beyond that which is required in the light of the above-listed principles;

(i) all proceedings concerning persons in custody should be conducted as expeditiously as possible so as to reduce the period of pre-trial detention to the minimum;

(j) in the determination of the sentence, the period spent in pre-trial detention should either be deducted from the length of the sentence or be considered with a view to reducing the length of the sentence.[33]

The United Nations Standard Minimum Rules for Non-Custodial Measures, the so-called 'Tokyo Rules', in Rule 6.1, also enunciate 'pre-trial detention shall be used as a means of last resort in criminal

---

[33] UN Secretariat, *Report on 8th UN Congress on the Prevention of Crime and the Treatment of Offenders*, Havana Aug. 27–Sept. 7, 1990, New York, 1991, *available at*: https://digitallibrary.un.org/record/142947?ln=en; Peter Michael Muller, *Report of the 8th UN Congress on the Prevention of Crime and the Treatment of Offenders* 16(2) INT'L L. PRAC. 50–54 (1991).

proceedings, with due regard for the investigation of the alleged offence and the protection of society and the victim'.[34]

BODY OF PRINCIPLES, 1988

The General Assembly promulgated a body of Principles for the Protection of All Persons under any Form of Detention or Imprisonment in 1988 which is an important source of guidance in applying the general principles of UDHR and ICCPR.[35] The term 'arrest' has been defined herein to mean 'the act of apprehending a person for the alleged commission of an offence or by the action of an authority independently of criminal proceedings'.[36] The use of the words 'action by an authority' may be taken to refer to the apprehension of a person outside the criminal proceedings as well and is thus inclusive of 'arbitrary arrest'.[37] The detained person indicates the deprivation of personal liberty of any person except as a result of a conviction for an offence, and detention refers to the condition of the detained person.[38]

The Body of Principles, comprising of 39 formulations, lays down general and specific stipulations with regard to the arrest and detention of persons. Principle 1 enunciates the pivotal rule that all persons under any form of detention shall be treated in a humane manner, with due regard to the dignity of the person.[39] Arrest and detention must be carried out strictly in accordance with law and subject to effective control of the judicial authority.[40]

---

[34] United Nations, *supra* note 22, at 173.

[35] United Nations Office of the High Commissioner, *Body of Principles for the Protection of All Persons Under Any Form of Detention or Imprisonment*, Adopted by General Assembly resolution 43/173 of 9 December 1988, *available at*: https://www.ohchr.org/EN/ProfessionalInterest/Pages/DetentionOrImprisonment.aspx

[36] *Id.*

[37] Tullio Treves, *The UN Body of Principles for the Protection of Detained or Imprisoned Persons* 84(2) AM. J. INT. LAW 578–86 (Apr. 1990).

[38] United Nations Office of the High Commissioner, *supra* note 35.

[39] *Id.*, Principle 1.

[40] *Id.*, Principles 2 and 4.

The legalities of arrest have also been dealt with under the principles which require the reasons of the arrest to be promptly informed to the person, an effective opportunity of being heard, being defended by a counsel of choice and a judicial authority to review the detention.[41] It mandates the authority to identify himself during arrest and record reasons for arrest, including time, place and other particulars.[42] The issue of incommunicado detention has been addressed in Principle 16 which states that 'promptly after arrest and after each transfer from one place of detention or imprisonment to another', the detained or imprisoned person is allowed to inform members of his family or other appropriate persons. Principle 18 further clarifies that subject to certain exceptions, a person is entitled to maintain communication with his legal counsel and be visited by him without delay or censorship and in full confidentiality.

Principle 6 specifically prohibits the use of torture or cruel, inhuman or degrading treatment to arrested or detained persons, under any circumstances whatsoever, taking 'undue advantage of the situation of a detained or imprisoned person'.[43] Thus compelling a person to confess or giving an incriminating statement or testifying against any other person, as also, being subject to violence, intimidation, coercion or methods of interrogation which seriously impair his capacity of judgment are prohibited. The duration of interrogations, along with the intervals between them, as also the identity of the person who conducted it is to be recorded and necessary access to such records has to be given to the detained person as well as his counsel.[44]

Treves mentions that the effect of the Body of Principles seems to be twofold: one, to serve as a guideline for the shaping of national legislation, and two, to serves as a statement of basic international legal and humanitarian concept to which everyone can refer.[45] It has, in fact, shaped the development of rules in different jurisdictions, as well as identify abuses by states in the treatment of persons in detention.

---

[41] *Id.*, Principles 10 and 11.
[42] *Id.*, Principles 12.
[43] *Id.*, Principle 21.
[44] *Id.*, Principe 24.
[45] Treves, *supra* note 37, at 585.

STANDARDS ON TORTURE AND ILL-TREATMENT

Persons detained are many times subjected to torture and ill-treatment in order to compel them to confess to crimes or divulge information or to simply create fear and submit to the wishes of the torturer. Some common forms of physical and psychological torture include isolation, *falanga* (hitting on soles of feet), electric shocks, waterboarding, mutilation, sexual torture, mock execution, etc.[46] In 1975, the Declaration on the Protection of All Persons From Being Subjected To Torture And Other Cruel, Inhuman Or Degrading Treatment Or Punishment (DPT) was adopted by the UN General Assembly.[47] Subsequently, these provisions were given the force of international law under the Convention Against Torture And Other Cruel, Inhuman or Degrading Treatment or Punishment (CAT), 1984, and the prohibition of torture and ill-treatment is now a norm of customary international law.[48]

As laid down in the Convention, torture is strictly prohibited under all circumstances whatsoever, and countries are obliged to adopt necessary legal and other measures to prevent the practice. According to the definition, only an act that causes 'severe' pain or suffering and is 'intentionally' inflicted for obtaining information, or confession, etc. comes within the definition of torture.[49] It does not include 'pain or suffering arising only from, inherent in or incidental to lawful sanctions'. According to the US Department of State,[50] this distinction reflects the belief by the drafters of CAT that while the former must be 'severe' to come within the notion of torture, regular 'rough treatment'

---

[46] O. P. AGARWAL, INTERNATIONAL LAW AND HUMAN RIGHTS, 827 (Central Law Publications, 20th ed. 2014).

[47] *Declaration on the Protection of All Persons from Being Subjected to Torture and Other Cruel, Inhuman or Degrading Treatment or Punishment*, Adopted by General Assembly resolution 3452 (XXX) of 9 December 1975, *available at*: https://www.un.org/ruleoflaw/files/TH002.PDF

[48] United Nations, *supra* note 32, at 2.

[49] Article 1, *Convention Against Torture and Other Cruel, Inhuman or Degrading Treatment or Punishment*, General Assembly resolution 39/46 of 10 December 1984, *available at*: https://www.ohchr.org/en/professionalinterest/pages/cat.aspx

[50] LESLIE ALAN HORVITZ & CHRISTOPHER CATHERWOOD, ENCYCLOPEDIA OF WAR CRIMES AND GENOCIDE 106–7 (Viva Books 2010).

as is inflicted by police, though deplorable, cannot amount to 'torture' for the purposes of the Convention. As per the definition, torture has few elements; a 'specific intent' to cause severe pain and suffering as opposed to an act that results in 'unanticipated and unintended severity of pain and suffering'.[51] However, in this regard Article 16 may be invoked which obliges the State to prevent other acts of cruel, inhuman or degrading treatment which do not amount to torture within their jurisdiction. Therefore, acts that are not strictly 'torture' within the meaning of Article 1 of CAT, would still be included within the scope of the Convention.

> The Committee has clarified that the substantive provisions of the convention are 'likewise obligatory as applied to both torture and ill-treatment. This is because the conditions that give rise to ill-treatment frequently facilitate torture. Therefore the measures that are required to prevent torture must also be applied to prevent ill-treatment.[52]

The Convention specifies that an act of torture must be inflicted by a public official or other person acting in an official capacity. In its General Comment No. 2, the Committee has emphasized that a State which fails to recognize the acts of torture or ill-treatment by its officials and take appropriate action must be taken to adopt a permissive approach towards such behaviour. The Committee clarified that where the state officials display gross negligence and oversee acts of torture or ill-treatment thereby failing to prevent, investigate, prosecute and punish, the State must bear the responsibility and its officials must be held liable for their actions.[53]

The CAT obligates States to take necessary action to prevent acts of torture and ensure that such acts are punished as offences under the respective criminal laws, including[54]:

---

[51] *Id.*

[52] Redress, *The Convention Against Torture and Other Cruel, Inhuman or Degrading Treatment or Punishment*, A Guide to Reporting to the Committee Against Torture, Sept. 2018, p. 11. https://redress.org/wp-content/uploads/2018/10/REDRESS-Guide-to-UNCAT-2018.pdf

[53] *Id.*, at 9.

[54] Article 1, *supra* note 49, Articles 2 and 4.

1. A systematic review of interrogation roles, instructions, methods and practices as well as arrangements for the custody and treatment of persons under any form of arrest, detention or imprisonment[55];
2. Exclude any statement made as a result of torture from evidence in any proceedings, except in proceedings against an alleged torturer[56];
3. Prompt and impartial investigation where there is a reasonable ground to believe that an act of torture has been committed[57];
4. Victims right to complain to competent authorities and to have their cases promptly and impartially examined[58]; and
5. Victim's right to obtain redress and to compensation, including the right to full rehabilitation.[59]

An Optional Protocol to the Torture Convention was adopted by the General Assembly on 18 December 2002 which entered into force on 22 January 2006.[60] It established a system of regular visits by international and national bodies to places of detention in order to prevent torture and other ill-treatment. It also requires the setting up of a sub-committee to undertake such visits and support State parties and national institutions to perform in accordance with the obligations under the Convention.[61]

STANDARDS FOR LAW ENFORCEMENT

Whereas the international instruments discussed above have outlined the minimum standards to ensure the protection and promotion of human rights of the detained persons, it is worthwhile to note the

---

[55] *Id.*, Article 11.
[56] *Id.*, Article 15.
[57] *Id.*, Article 12.
[58] *Id.*, Article 13.
[59] *Id.*, Article 14.
[60] *Optional Protocol to the Convention Against Torture and Other Cruel, Inhuman or Degrading Treatment or Punishment*, Adopted on Dec. 18, 2002, General Assembly Resolution A/RES/57/199, *available at*: https://www.ohchr.org/EN/ProfessionalInterest/Pages/OPCAT.aspx
[61] Declaration on the Protection of All Persons, *supra* note 47.

conduct of law enforcement officials that have been enumerated in consonance with the standards set.

Law enforcement officers operate—with great power—in an area of the greatest sensitivity to the citizenry. Should not they, above all, be bound by a universal code delimiting their duties and powers? The ingredients of such code has long been recognized, in the UDHR, the ICCPR, the CAT and other international human rights' instruments that touch upon law enforcement.[62]

The UN Code of Conduct for Law Enforcement (UNCCLE), a small document of eight Articles, is a resolution of the United Nations General Assembly that was adopted on December 17, 1979.[63] It is not a binding document; the UNCCLE is a guideline which the General Assembly encourages its member states to abide by as well as incorporate in their national laws. Law enforcement officials primarily refer to the officers of the law who are entrusted with the powers of conducting arrest and detention under the national legislation. They may be the military or police or special officers in respective jurisdictions. They are required to fulfil the duties imposed upon them by law, by serving the community and protecting all persons against illegal acts, consistent with the high degree of responsibility required by the profession.[64] The fundamental duty of the police is to prevent and control crime and to protect and safeguard the lives and property of the people. They are required to help the weak and the marginalized in society. In the performance of their functions, they are expected to be governed by law and law alone and uphold the values of liberty, equality and justice. They should be responsive and accountable to the community in the performance of their functions. The words 'service to the community', in this regard is intended to include particularly the rendition

---

[62] Gerhard O. W. Mueller, *The United Nations Draft Code of Conduct for Law Enforcement Officials* 1(2) INT'L REV. POLICE DEVELOPMENT 17, 17–21 (June, 1978).

[63] *Code of Conduct for Law Enforcement Officials*, Adopted by General Assembly Resolution 34/169 of 17 December 1979, *available at*: https://www.ohchr.org/en/professionalinterest/pages/lawenforcementofficials.aspx

[64] *Id.*, Article 1.

of services of assistance to those members of the community who by reasons of personal, economic, social or other emergencies are in need of immediate aid.[65]

Article 2 of the UNCCLE provides that law enforcement officials shall respect and protect human dignity and maintain and uphold the human rights of all persons. Since 1948, the UN has drawn up a significant list of instruments emphasizing the right, dignity and worth of human beings. The enforcement of the law must be in furtherance of those rights and not in derogation thereof. The Code further entails that the use of force is justified only when strictly necessary and to the extent required for the performance of duties.[66]

In the exercise of the use of force by law enforcement, there are three key components that may be noted: necessity, proportionality and precaution.[67] The first two, necessity and proportionality, provide the threshold on the use of force, that is, how and when force may be used lawfully during policing actions. 'In contrast, the principle of precaution applies upstream; it requires states to ensure that law enforcement operations are planned and conducted so as to minimize the risk of injury'.[68]

Article 3 of the UN code stipulates that law enforcement officials may use force 'only when strictly necessary'. The commentary to the article emphasizes that the use of force should be 'exceptional'. Thereby it means that, in most instances, a force which is not legally permissible and non-violent measures should be adopted to ensure compliance.[69] Such means include persuasion, negotiation, and mediation backed by

---

[65] Commentary, Article 1, United Nations, *General Assembly Resolution on the Code of Conduct for Law Enforcement Officials* 19(2) INT'L LEG. MATER. 526–32 (March 1980).

[66] Mueller, *supra* note 62, Article 3.

[67] STUART CASEY-MASLEN & SEAN CONNOLLY, POLICE USE OF FORCE UNDER INTERNATIONAL LAW (Cambridge University Press 2017).

[68] Geneva Academy, *Use of force in Law Enforcement and the Right to Life: The Role of Human Rights Council*, Nov. 2016, p. 6, *available at*: https://www.geneva-academy.ch/joomlatools-files/docman-files/in-brief6_WEB.pdf

[69] Principle 5, *Basic Principles on the Use of Force and Firearms by Law Enforcement Officials* (United Nations 1990).

the inherent authority of the State.[70] It is further clarified in Article 3 that enforcement officials may use such force as is 'reasonably' necessary under the circumstances to prevent crime, or effecting arrest of offenders etc. Such force should not be used maliciously, or as a form of extrajudicial punishment. Discriminatory practices as regards the use of force should be discouraged. A third critical element of the principle is that no more than 'minimum' force that is necessary for the circumstances is to be used. Thus where an offender can be arrested, the police must not go ahead and shoot the person, instead of arresting him.[71] Basic Principle 5 elucidates the norm of proportionality, a correlation between the force used and the object to be achieved.[72] The use of force in apprehending a dreaded armed terrorist who attempts to break loose may be justified, whereas the use of force against an unarmed thief may be wholly unjustified. In this regard, the commentary to the Article mentions that[73]

In general, firearms should not be used except when a suspected offender offers resistance or otherwise jeopardises the lives of others and less extreme measures are not sufficient to restrain or apprehend the suspected offender. In every instance in which a firearm is discharged, a report should be made promptly to the competent authorities.

Article 5 of the UNCCLE further provides that law enforcement officials should not inflict, instigate or tolerate any act of torture or cruel, inhuman or degrading treatment or punishment. This article draws its inspiration from the DPT, as well as CAT which prohibits State parties from inflicting pain or suffering on any person to obtain information or confession or other stated purposes. Such torture is not justified even in exceptional situations like war, internal political instability, public emergency, etc. As stated by the Human Rights Committee,[74] States are required to ensure that all necessary and reasonable measures are

---

[70] CASEY-MASLEN & CONNOLLY, *supra* note 67, at 7.

[71] *Id.*

[72] Principle 5, *supra* note 69.

[73] Mueller, *supra* note 62, Commentary to Article 4.

[74] See, Human Rights Committee, General Comment N. 20, Article 7, para. 2, *available at*: https://www.refworld.org/docid/453883fb0.html

adopted to prevent the use of torture or inhuman treatment of persons within their jurisdiction, whether inflicted by people acting in their official capacity, outside their official capacity or in a private capacity. Necessary information to that end must be provided to the citizens, as also to the law enforcement officials, whereby they refrain from inflicting such acts. It may be noted here that

> the use of force that results in severe pain and suffering which, in the particular circumstances of the case, is considered excessive, unjustifiable or disproportionate, would amount to a form of ill-treatment. Thus, the use of force by law enforcement officers, both when the subject is under direct control (arrest, detention) and in cases of incident control (during riot control) may amount to torture…, or cruel, inhuman and degrading treatment.[75]

The Code of Conduct entails the obligation of law enforcement officials to refrain from corrupt activities, as is incompatible with their professional responsibilities; and ensure compliance of the law, to the best of their capabilities.[76] They should refrain from any activity which violates the present Code of Conduct.

CONCLUSION

As a member of the world community, we have come a long way in the promotion, protection and fulfilment of human rights. States, today, are bound by the international human rights standards etched out by the treaty documents vis-à-vis individuals within their jurisdiction. These obligations have also set the stage for imbibing good criminal justice practices across nations and encouraging legality and accountability in functions of law enforcement.

---

[75] UNODC, *Resource Book on the Use of Force and Firearms in Law Enforcement*, Criminal Justice Handbook Series, 2017, p. 12, *available at*: https://www.unodc.org/documents/justice-and-prison-reform/17-03483_ebook.pdf

[76] Code of Conduct for Law Enforcement Officials, *supra* note 63, Articles 7 and 8.

Arrest and Detention impinge on the very core of life and liberty of human beings. They are fundamental to the existence of humanity and must be protected and respected at all times; not restricted, either through derogations or limitations. Law enforcement officials must exhibit the highest strength of character and integrity in the discharge of their functions in strict compliance with the law. Corruption, discrimination, arbitrariness must not inform their actions; rather, due regard to the supreme values of liberty, equality, and justice must be the guiding principles.

Chapter 12

Constitutional Rights on Arrest and Detention
A Canadian Perspective

Sébastien Lafrance

A fundamental legal instrument was adopted in 1982 in Canada: the *Canadian Charter of Rights and Freedoms* (hereinafter *Charter*).[1] Even if it 'did not bring to life the existence in Canada of human rights and fundamental freedoms in the courts',[2] the rights and freedoms 'provided by the *Charter* have been given a "large and liberal interpretation"'.[3] The Supreme

---

This work was prepared separately from this author's employment responsibilities at the Public Prosecution Service of Canada. The views, opinions and conclusions expressed here in are personal to this author and should not be construed as those of the Public Prosecution Service of Canada or the Canadian federal Crown.

[1] *Canadian Charter of Rights and Freedoms*, Part I of the Constitution Act, 1982, being Schedule B to the Canada Act, 1982 (U.K.), 1982 c.1 (hereinafter *Charter*).

[2] Shruti Bedi & Sébastien Lafrance, *The Justice in Judicial Activism: Jurisprudence of Rights and Freedoms in India and Canada*, in THE SUPREME COURT AND THE CONSTITUTION – AN INDIAN DISCOURSE 74 (KHURSHID, MALIK & SINGH eds. Wolters Kluwer 2020).

[3] Sébastien Lafrance, *A Brief Overview of Quebec Civil Law and Constitutional Interpretation in Canada* (2020), see online: https://www.amicusinstitute.org/scholarship-series; R. v. Jacques, [1996] 3 S.C.R. 312, [20]: 'Contextual analysis of *Charter* rights and freedoms is well established'.

R. v. Big M Drug Mart Ltd., [1985] 1 S.C.R. 295, at 344; Hunter et al. v. Southam Inc., [1984] 2 S.C.R. 145.

Court of Canada (hereinafter 'Court') stated in *Grant*, 'Where questions of interpretation arise, a generous, purposive and contextual approach should be applied'.[4] Such a generous approach to the interpretation of fundamental rights is also reflected in the Indian judiciary's stance to the constitutionally protected right to counsel. Indeed, the Supreme Court of India wrote in *Sukur Ali vs State of Assam* that the 'provision [providing for the right to counsel] must be given the *widest* construction'.[5]

The *Charter* had from the very beginning of its existence,[6] and still has presently, an immense impact on the scope of the rights granted to Canadian citizens in their interactions with the State, that is, more specifically here, with law enforcement agencies[7]: 'The *Charter* is meant to protect individuals from the excessive exercise of state power'.[8] With respect to law enforcement agencies, let us note that '[p]olice powers and police duties are not necessarily correlative, [police] are not empowered to undertake any and all action in the exercise of that duty. Individual liberty interests are fundamental to the Canadian constitutional order'.[9]

In this chapter, we will closely examine the rights of Canadian citizens both at the time of an arrest and detention, with a particular focus on the right to not be arbitrarily detained and also on the right to be informed of the reasons for a detention or an arrest as well as on the right to counsel, bearing in mind that Section 10 of the *Charter* as a whole also applies to 'a great variety of detentions'.[10] All these rights will be studied through the most prominent and relevant Canadian judicial decisions, mostly decisions rendered by the Supreme Court of Canada.

---

[4] R. v. Grant, [2009] 2 S.C.R. 353, [15].

[5] *Sukur Ali v. State of Assam*, (2011) 4 S.C.C. 729.

[6] James Stribopoulos, *The Limits of Judicially Created Police Powers: Investigative Detention After Mann* 52 CRIM. L. Q. 299 (2013), 299: 'It was obvious from the start that the *Canadian Charter of Rights and Freedoms* was going to have a considerable effect on the criminal investigative process. A number of its provisions speak directly to the regulation of police authority'.

[7] Regarding the (non-)application of *Charter* rights for non-Canadian citizens who are located on the Canadian soil, see, for example, R. v. Delghani v. Canada (Minister of Employment and Immigration), [1993] 1 S.C.R. 1053.

[8] Steve Coughlan, *Great Strides in Section 9 Jurisprudence* 66(6) CR 75 (2009). https://works.bepress.com/stephen-coughlan/24/

[9] R. v. Mann, [2004] 3 S.C.R. 59, [35].

[10] R. v. Thomsen, [1988] 1 S.C.R. 640, [12].

The author truly hopes that this chapter will shed light on some areas of uncertainties for those who are not familiar with Canadian criminal law regarding arrest and detention, and that it may also assist the researchers interested in learning on this topic from a Canadian perspective,[11] while bearing in mind that 'one of the interests in comparative criminal law for the researchers is to allow a better knowledge of their own penal system'.[12]

DEFINING ARREST AND DETENTION
Arrest

In India, which has much in common with Canada,[13] '[a]n arrest is a deprivation of movement of a person for the purpose of answering any criminal charge potentially capable for conviction' and where '[a]rrest is not defined under the Code of Criminal Procedure',[14] in Canada, the Court in *Asante-Mensah*[15] took care of specifying not only what an arrest is, but also what it is *not*: 'Arrest consists of the actual seizure or touching of a person's body with a view to his detention. The mere pronouncing of words of arrest is not an arrest, unless the person sought to be arrested submits to the process and goes with the arresting officer'.[16] In *Niranjan Singh v. Prabhakar*, the Supreme Court of India also observed that the word 'arrest' is of 'elastic semantics but its core meaning is that the law

---

[11] See, for example, Sébastien Lafrance, *Should Canadian Law Matter to Indian Jurists? Advocating for More Substantial Legal Discussion Between the 'Long Lost Siblings'* CONTEMP. L. FORUM (2020), see online: https://tclf.in/2020/07/08/should-canadian-law-matter-to-indian-jurists-advocating-for-more-substantial-legal-discussion-between-the-long-lost-siblings/

[12] Khagesh Gautam and Sébastien Lafrance, *A Comparative Survey of the Law of Bail in India and Canada*, in TAKING BAIL SERIOUSLY – THE STATE OF BAIL JURISPRUDENCE IN INDIA, 126 (KHURSHID, LUTHRA, MALIK & BEDI eds. LexisNexis 2020).

[13] See, for example, Lafrance, *supra* note 11.

[14] Shyam Balakrishnan vs State of Kerala, Kerala High Court, 18 August 2010, [5].

[15] Asante-Mensah, [2003] 2 S.C.R. 3, para. 42; the court also noted, 'This definition was accepted as correct by a unanimous court in R. v. Latimer', [1997] 1 S.C.R. 217, [24].

[16] R. v. Whitfield, [1970] S.C.R. 46, 48.

has taken control of the person'.[17] In Canada, the Court also clarified in *Evans* that what counts is 'the substance of what the accused can reasonably be supposed to have understood, rather than the formalism of the precise words used ... The question is ... what the accused was told, viewed reasonably in all the circumstances of the case'.[18]

Detention

Generally speaking, 'there are two forms of detention: physical and psychological detention'.[19] When it comes to detention, 'it is not always easy to determine ... whether and when it legally occurs',[20] which may be explained by the fact that detention 'has been held to cover, in Canada, a broad range of encounters between police officers and members of the public'.[21] According to Coughlan, the Court 'has articulated a *reasonably clear* definition of the term "detention"'[22]; for instance, it was defined in *Grant* as 'a suspension of the individual's liberty interest by a significant physical or psychological restraint',[23] reaffirming its definition previously given in *Therens*.[24,25] The definition itself and the scope of

---

[17] A.I.R. 1980 S.C. 785, cited in BELLARY UMA DEVI, ARREST, DETENTION, AND CRIMINAL JUSTICE SYSTEM: A STUDY IN THE CONTEXT OF THE CONSTITUTION OF INDIA 42 (Oxford University Press 2012).

[18] R. v. Evans, [1991] 1 S.C.R. 869, 888.

[19] R. v. Reid, 2019 O.N.C.A. 32, [19].

[20] R. v. Schmautz, [1990] 1 S.C.R. 398, 415; see also NIHAL JAYAWICKRAMA, THE JUDICIAL APPLICATION OF HUMAN RIGHTS – NATIONAL, REGIONAL AND INTERNATIONAL JURISPRUDENCE 378 (Cambridge University Press 2017): '[i]n a case where there is no physical restraint or legal obligation, it may not be clear whether a person has been detailed'.

[21] Mann, *supra* note 9, [19]; see also R. v. Suberu, [2009] 2 S.C.R. 460, [23].

[22] Steve Coughlan, *Arbitrary Detention: Whither – or Wither? Section 9*, in SUPREME COURT LAW REVIEW: Osgoode's Annual Constitutional Cases Conference 40 (2008), 165 (italics added).

[23] Grant, *supra* note 4, [44(1)]; this definition applies to both s. 9 and s. 10 of the *Charter*.

[24] R. v. Therens, [1985] 1 S.C.R. 613, 644, defined 'detention' as a person who 'submits or acquiesces in the deprivation of liberty and reasonably believes that the choice to do otherwise does not exist'.

[25] Steven Penney & James Stribopoulos, *'Detention' Under the Charter After R. v. Grant and R. v. Suberu* 51 SUPREME COURT LAW REV. 439, 445 (2010).

application of 'detention' was also impacted greatly by the *Charter*. The Court in *Therens* had previously 'reasoned that detention under the Charter should be read *more broadly*'.[26] In that last decision, the Court also 'articulated three types of detention: (i) physical detention, where a person is actually subject to physical constraint, (ii) detention by lawful compulsion, where there are legal consequences for the failure to comply with a police officer's demand … and (iii) psychological detention, where although in fact the police have no authority to detain a person that person reasonably feels compelled to remain'.[27] The term 'detained' has the same meaning either it applies under Section 9 or Section 10 of the Charter.[28]

POLICE POWERS TO ARREST AND DETAIN
Police Arresting Powers

Historically, '[a]rrest powers have a long and unfortunate history being misused. In fact, at common law, it was the prevalence of complaints about false arrest and imprisonment that provided the forum for the evolution of arrest law',[29] but today '[t]here are no longer any common law … arrest powers in Canada … arrest powers are found exclusively in statutes. Arrest powers for criminal offences are found in the *Criminal Code*'.[30] Arrests may be with a warrant or warrantless, but this angle, that is, reasons supporting a warrant or warrantless arrest, will not be

---

[26] *Id.*, 442 (italics added); Therens, *supra* note 24, at 48; Steven Coughlan & Robert J. Currie, *Sections 9, 10 and 11 of the Canadian Charter*, in CANADIAN CHARTER OF RIGHTS AND FREEDOMS (MENDES & BEAULAC eds. 5th ed. LexisNexis 2013): 'Although with the benefit of today's perspective it seems obvious that a person who is flagged down by the police and would face criminal charges for refusing to comply is "detained", that was not the pre*Charter* position. In *Chromiak* the Court had settled a *Bill of Rights* challenge on those same facts by concluding that there had been no detention' see Chromiak v. The Queen, [1980] 1 S.C.R. 471.

[27] Coughlan & Currie, *Id.*

[28] R. v. Hufsky, [1988] 1 S.C.R. 621, [12]; Therens, *supra* note 24; R. v. Thomsen, *supra* note 10.

[29] James Stribopoulos, *Unchecked Power: The Constitutional Regulation of Arrest Reconsidered* 48 MCGILL L. J. 225, 235 (2003).

[30] *Id.*, at 236.

discussed here specifically, as it is beyond the scope of this chapter.[31] Let us just mention that '[i]n the case of an arrest made without a warrant', the Court stated in the seminal decision in *Storrey* that 'it is even more important for the police to demonstrate that they have ... reasonable and probable grounds upon which they base [an] arrest'.[32]

Stribopoulos commented, 'The *most important arrest power* is contained in paragraph 495(1)(a) [of the *Criminal Code*]. Under its terms, a police officer may arrest without warrant a person whom, "on reasonable grounds, he believes has committed or is about to commit an indictable offence." This provision is essential to the police, who must usually form their grounds for arrest based on information supplied to them by the public'.[33] As Coughlan and Luther wisely argued about this specific Subsection of the *Criminal Code*, '[o]n a literal reading, a power to arrest anyone who *has committed* an indictable offence would be extraordinarily too broad',[34] which 'broad reading could not be justified'[35]; 'the words "has committed" should [then] be understood, in essence, to mean "has *just* committed"'.[36]

In *R. v. Shinkewski*,[37] the Saskatchewan[38] Court of Appeal aptly summarized the judicial interpretation of the legal standard for 'reasonable

---

[31] For example, '[t]he *Criminal Code* contains numerous provisions that allow a judge to issue a warrant for the arrest of an accused person' (*R. v. Sheppard*, 2020 CanLII 43917 (NL PC), [22]), and this fact alone raises, and would then require a discussion of, an array of different issues other than the ones that are addressed in this book chapter.

[32] R. v. Storrey, [1990] 1 S.C.R. 241.

[33] Stribopoulos, *supra* note 29, at 237 (italics added).

[34] STEVE COUGHLAN & GLEN LUTHER, DETENTION AND ARREST 283 (Irwin Law Inc. 2nd ed. 2017), 264 (italics added).

[35] *Id.*, at 264 (italics added); see also R. v. Klimchuk, 1991 CanLII 3958 (BC CA).

[36] *Id.* (italics added).

[37] R. v. Shinkewski, 2012 SKCA 63, [13] (italics added).

[38] As a side note, Saskatchewan is one of the 10 Canadian provinces. In 1867, the British North America Act of 1867 created the Dominion of Canada. It united Upper Canada (Ontario), Lower Canada (Quebec), Nova Scotia and New Brunswick. The Canadian federation expanded with the addition of the provinces of Manitoba (1870), British Columbia (1871), Prince Edward Island (1873), Saskatchewan and Alberta (1905) and Newfoundland (1949). Canada is also comprised of three territories, namely Nunavut (created out of the Northwest Territories in 1999), the Northwest Territories and Yukon.

grounds to believe', which is key to be examined when assessing the validity of an arrest, which also developed over time:

1. an arresting officer must *subjectively* hold reasonable grounds to arrest and those grounds must be justifiable from an *objective* point of view....[39];

2. an arresting officer is not required to establish the commission of an indictable offence on a balance of probabilities[40] or a *prima facie* case for conviction[41] before making the arrest; but *an arresting officer must act on something more than a "reasonable suspicion" or a hunch.*[42]

3. *an arresting officer must consider all incriminating and exonerating information* which the circumstances reasonably permit, but may disregard information which the officer has reason to believe may be unreliable.[43] [...]

Keeping this legal standard in mind, Stribopoulos noted that '[p]olice officers are very much on their own in making arrest decisions',[44] even though they still must justify on a principled basis the exercise of such powers.[45] However, according to this author, '[i]n the field, the objective component of the reasonable and probable grounds is devoid of actual meaning'.[46]

Investigative Detention

The Court did not 'recognize a general power of detention for investigative purposes'.[47] However, it acknowledged that the common law

---

[39] R. v. Storrey, *supra* note 32.

[40] Mugesera v. Canada (Minister of Citizenship and Immigration), [2005] 2 S.C.R. 100.

[41] R. v. Storrey, *supra* note 32.

[42] R. v. Morelli, [2010] 1 S.C.R. 253.

[43] R. v. Storrey, *supra* note 32.

[44] Stribopoulos, *supra* note 29, at 243; see also Sébastien Lafrance, *Women in the Context of Canadian Criminal Offences* 36 VNU J. LEGAL SCI.: LEGAL STUD. 4, 44 (2020).

[45] R. v. Storrey, *supra* note 32, at 250.

[46] Stribopoulos, *supra* note 29, at 243.

[47] Mann, *supra* note 9, [17].

allows police officers to detain someone for investigative purposes, taking into account objectively the totality of the circumstances when 'there is a clear nexus between the individual to be detained and a recent or on-going criminal offence'.[48] However, it 'does not mean that every interaction with the police will amount to a detention for the purposes of the *Charter*, even when a person is under investigation for criminal activity, is asked questions, or is physically delayed by contact with the police'.[49] In addition, the Court took care to clarify that '[t]he investigative detention and protection search power are to be distinguished from an arrest and the incidental power to search on arrest'.[50] Also, '[t]he power to detain [for investigative purposes] cannot be exercised on the basis of a hunch, nor can it become a *de facto* arrest'.[51]

In *MacKenzie*, the Court clarified importantly the distinction that is to be drawn between the standard that is to be met either for a detention or an arrest: '*In the context of detention*, "reasonable grounds" means reasonable grounds *to suspect* that an individual is involved in particular criminal activity, which is synonymous with *reasonable suspicion*. However, *in other contexts, such as an arrest*, "reasonable grounds" means reasonable grounds *to believe* that an individual is or has been involved in a particular offence, which is synonymous with reasonable and probable grounds. *The former concept is a matter of possibilities, while the latter is one of probabilities*'.[52] In *Kang-Brown*, the Court explained that '"[s]uspicion" is an expectation that *the targeted individual* is *possibly* engaged in some criminal activity. A "reasonable" suspicion means something more than a *mere* suspicion and something *less* than a belief based upon reasonable and probable grounds'.[53] As noted by Coughlan and Luther, '[t]he type of evidence need to justify reasonable suspicion ... does not differ in kind from that needed for reasonable grounds: *all that differs is the amount*'.[54]

---

[48] *Id.*, [34].

[49] Suberu, *supra* note 21, [23], [28].

[50] Mann, *supra* note 9, [45] *in fine*.

[51] *Id.*, [35].

[52] R. v. MacKenzie, [2013] 3 S.C.R. 250, [38] (italics in the original and also added; emphasis added).

[53] R. v. Kang-Brown, [2008] 1 S.C.R. 456, [75] (italics and emphasis added).

[54] Coughlan & Luther, *supra* note 34, at 114 (italics added).

Psychological Detention

In India, the Allahabad High Court went as far as stating that '[t]he word coercion [by police] in modern times cannot be construed in a narrow sense. It includes psychological restraints, psychological restraints *are much deterrent* than physical restraints. They include all fear complexes of external origin which can be described infringements of personal liberty'.[55] Also, the Supreme Court of India interestingly stated, but in a different context than 'psychological detention', that is, regarding the right to privacy, in the seminal and oft-cited decision in *Puttaswamy* that '[i]n an uncivilized society where there are no inhibitions, only physical restraints may detract from personal liberty, but as civilization advances the psychological restraints *are more effective* than physical ones'.[56] Thus, this shows the importance of the role played not only by the physical actions taken by police officers in their dealings with the citizens but also by the words, among other things, they use in their interactions with them.

Generally, Jayawickrama defined 'psychological detention' as being 'established either where the individual has a legal obligation to comply with a restrictive request or demand or where a reasonable person would conclude by reason of the state conduct that he or she had no choice but to comply'.[57] Coincidentally or not, this last definition reflects, in slightly different words, how the Court in Canada first approached the concept of detention in 1985 in *Therens*.[58] and also, several years later, in 2019, when 'the Court returned to the issue [of psychological detention] to offer *a more complete definition*',[59] and, on that occasion, set out the legal test for psychological detention, several years later in 2009, in *Grant*[60]:

---

[55] Ooros Fatima Alias Nisha And Anr. v. Senior Superintendent of Police, Allahabad High Court (June 29, 1992), [13] (italics added).

[56] Justice K.S. Puttaswamy v. Union of India, A.I.R. 2017 S.C. 4161, citing the dissent of Subba Rao J. (as he then was) from Kharak Singh v. The State of U.P. & Others, 1963 A.I.R. 1295 (italics added).

[57] Jayawickrama, *supra* note 20, at 377–78.

[58] Therens, *supra* note 24, [57].

[59] Coughlan & Currie, *supra* note 26 (italics added).

[60] Grant, *supra* note 4, [30], [44]; as noted by the Ontario Court of Appeal in R. v. N.B., 2018 ONCA 556, [113]: '*Grant* remains the leading authority on assessing psychological detention', see also, more recently, R. v. Le, (2019) S.C.C. 34, [25].

To determine whether the reasonable person in the individual's circumstances would conclude that he or she had been deprived by the state of the liberty of choice, the court may consider, *inter alia*, the following factors:

(a) The circumstances giving rise to the encounter as they would reasonably be perceived by the individual: whether the police were providing general assistance, maintaining general order, making general inquiries regarding a particular occurrence or singling out the individual for focussed investigation.

(b) The nature of the police conduct, including the language used, the use of physical contact, the place where the interaction occurred, the presence of others and the duration of the encounter.

(c) The particular characteristics or circumstances of the individual where relevant, including age, physical stature, minority status and level of sophistication.

This test must be applied objectively, having regard to all the circumstances of the particular situation, but the individual's specific circumstances must also be taken into account.[61] Coughlan and Currie summarized that

[i]n practical terms, the question of whether someone is psychologically detained tends to arise in one of two circumstances. First, on occasion a person attends at a police station and is questioned: whether they did so by consent or because they felt compelled to is not always easy to determine. Second, the police sometimes engage a person on the street in conversation, which can lead to more intrusive things: whether that person feels an obligation to remain is often unclear'.[62]

More specifically, with respect to the words 'you're free to go at any time' that are often said by police officers, they 'might seem', according to the Court in *Kang-Brown*, 'a bit disingenuous'[63], but, according to Coughlan and Currie, 'it can [also] be a *significant* factor'[64] to be considered in the context of the *Grant* test (detailed above) to determine if there is psychological detention.

---

[61] See, for example, *Id.*, [116], [117].

[62] *Id.*

[63] R. v. Kang-Brown, *supra* note 53, [85].

[64] Coughlan & Currie, *supra* note 26 (italics added).

Penney and Stribopoulos praised the fact that the '*Grant*'s multi-factor approach' is 'flexible and nuanced'; however, '[i]t fails', according to them, 'to give police sufficient guidance on the scope of their authority'.[65] One should note that according to Hill, '[s]tandards of belief ... have generally been accepted by the [Canadian] courts as incapable of precise definition'.[66]

Paciocco observed that

> [t]he concept of 'detention' is a trigger for two kinds of *Charter* rights. Section 9, the right to be free from arbitrary detention ... Section 10 spells out the *Charter* rights that persons who have been taken control of by the state are entitled to enjoy.[67]

'Detention' has the same meaning for both Section 9 and Section 10.[68]

ARBITRARY DETENTION

Section 9 of the *Charter* provides that '[e]veryone has the right not to be arbitrarily detained or imprisoned'. As somewhat recently recalled by the Court in *Le*,[69] citing its seminal decision in *Grant*,

> [t]he purpose of s. 9, broadly put, is to protect individual liberty from unjustified state interference. Such interference extends not only to 'unjustified state intrusions upon physical liberty but also against incursions on mental liberty by prohibiting the coercive pressures of detention ... from being applied to people without appropriate justification.[70]

---

[65] Penney & Stribopoulos, *supra* note 25, at 439.

[66] Casey Hill, *Investigative Detention: A Search/Seizure by Any Other Name?* SUPREME COURT LAW REV.: Osgoode's Annual Constitutional Cases Conference 40, 185 (2008).

[67] David M. Paciocco, *What to Mention About Detention: How to Use Purpose to Understand and Apply Detention-based Charter Rights* 89(1) CAN. BAR REV. 65, 67 (2011). The author of this paper is now a judge at the Ontario Court of Appeal.

[68] Hufksy, *supra* note 28, [12].

[69] R. v. Le, (2019) S.C.C. 34, [152].

[70] Grant, *supra* note 4, [20].

In the same last decision, the Court made clear that '[a] lawful detention is not arbitrary within the meaning of s. 9, unless the law authorizing the detention is itself arbitrary. Conversely, a detention not authorized by law is arbitrary and violates s. 9'.[71]

Stribopoulos argued in 2008 that

> [a]lthough the Court has supplied *some* guidance on when a law authorizing detention or imprisonment will run afoul of section 9, it has steered clear of explaining the larger purpose of the section or addressing in any meaningful way the far more common question: when should an individual police officer's decision to detain or arrest be characterized as having been made 'arbitrarily'?[72]

In the same spirit, Coughlan also criticized the same year the fact, at least then, that 'we still have no section 9 jurisprudence. It is not that there have been no decisions at all concerning the right not to be arbitrarily detained, of course, but taken in total they do not come anywhere near *setting out an analytical framework*'.[73]

A year later, in 2009, the Court rendered the decision in *Grant* where it 'created an analytical structure to be used in deciding section 9 cases'.[74]

In practice, '*Charter* claims under section 9 [may] arise [for example] where incriminating evidence (usually a confession) is obtained following an unlawful arrest'.[75] What also comes from the practice is that, as noted by Coughlan, 'an alleged violation of section 9 is unlikely to arise *in isolation*'[76] and is often paired, in an accused's claim, with Section 8[77] or 10(*b*) of the *Charter*. Because section 9 rights

---

[71] *Id.*, [54].

[72] James Stribopoulos, *The Forgotten Right: Section 9 of the Charter, Its Purpose and Meaning* 40 SUPREME COURT LAW REV. 2(d) 211, 212 (2008) (italics added).

[73] Coughlan, *supra* note 22, at 147 (italics added).

[74] Coughlan, *supra* note 8.

[75] Stribopoulos, *supra* note 29, at 228.

[76] Coughlan, *supra* note 22, at 148 (italics added).

[77] This section of the *Charter* relates to search and seizure.

often comes along with other rights on which there is more focus, section 9 jurisprudence evolved more slowly in comparison with the development of section 10 (b), and also section 8,[78] jurisprudence that expanded a lot, and evolved greatly since the enactment of the Charter in 1982.

RIGHT TO BE INFORMED OF REASONS FOR DETENTION OR ARREST

Historically, '[s]ince the enactment of the *Charter*, pretextual arrests have been held to be a violation'[79] of Section 10(*a*) of the *Charter*, which generally requires the police to inform *promptly* an individual who is arrested or detained of the reasons for such arrest or detention. In India, with respect to the same right,[80] '[t]he words "as soon as may be" have been held to mean *as early as is reasonable in the circumstances of the case*, though it has been said that *no definite period of time* can be laid down as reasonable in all cases'.[81] As the Department of Justice (Canada) puts it[82]:

> *Section 10(a) is founded on a double rationale.* First, there is the notion that one is not obliged to submit to an arrest without knowing the reasons for the arrest. A person needs to know the reasons for an

---

[78] Section 8 *Charter* is not relevant for what is examined in this chapter, but it had to be mentioned in that context.

[79] Stribopoulos, *supra* note 29, at 246. However, 'well-trained police officers would know that they cannot, as a general rule, conduct *pretext* traffic stops', for example: R. v. Tran Huu, 2019 ONSC 2516, [59] (italics added).

[80] Section 22(1) of the Indian Constitution.

[81] B. P. Srivastava, *Right Against Arbitrary Arrest and Detention Under Article 9 of the Covenant as Recognized and Protected Under the Indian Law* 11 J. IND. L. INSTT. 1, 39 (1969) (italics added); see Tarapada De v. State of West Bengal, A.I.R. 1951 S.C. 174, cited with approval, but for different reasons, in a more recent decision Sharafat Sheikh vs Union of India (Uoi) And Ors., Delhi High Court (15 January 2005), [8].

[82] Department of Justice, Government of Canada, *Section 10(a) – Right to be Informed of Reasons for Detention or Arrest*, see online: https://www.justice.gc.ca/eng/csj-sjc/rfc-dlc/ccrf-ccdl/check/art10a.html (italics added); Evans, *supra* note 18; R. v. Borden, [1994] 3 S.C.R. 145.

arrest in order to decide whether to submit to it. Second, this right recognizes that an individual must fully understand the reasons for his or her arrest or detention....

This obligation to inform, and that an individual fully understand the reasons for his or her arrest or detention, applies to 'each offence for which [a person] is being detained or arrested'[83]; for example, breaches of Section 10(a) may happen when, for example, the police officer does not tell the 'real' reason of the arrest or of the detention.[84] This means that the individual detained or arrested must be given 'sufficient information to allow [him or her] making an informed and appropriate decision as to whether to speak to a lawyer or not'[85]; however, this does not mean that this individual needs to be 'aware of the precise charge faced or of all the factual details of the case'.[86] What matters in the assessment of whether the police complies with the obligations provided by Section 10(a) of the *Charter* is, as previously stated (but in a different context), '[t]he substance of what the accused can reasonably be supposed to have understood, rather than the formalism of the precise words used, which must govern'.[87]

Similar to Canada, this right, from an Indian perspective, provides for 'sufficient particulars [that] must be furnished in a language understood by the person so that the arrested person may understand why he has been arrested'.[88]

Sections 10(a) and 10(b) of the *Charter* are intertwined since the former entails the application of the latter for an arrested or detained

---

[83] Borden, *Id.*, 166.

[84] See, for example, R. v. Caines, 2012 CanLII 4 (NL PC), [53].

[85] R. v. Smith, [1991] 1 S.C.R. 714, 728; see also R. v. Sinclair, [2010] 2 S.C.R. 310; R. v. Black, [1989] 2 S.C.R. 138.

[86] Smith, *Id.*

[87] Evans, *supra* note 18, at 888.

[88] Srivastava, *supra* note 81; see also, more recently, see, for example, Gekonde Boston Yophes, *Custodial Atrocities and the status of Human Rights: An Analytical Study with Reference to Women in the State of Gujarat*, PhD Thesis, Saurashtra University, 2005, 172: 'sufficient particulars must be furnished to enable the arrested person to understand why he has been arrested'.

individual,[89] that is, someone who is arrested or detained needs to know the reasons supporting it in order to exercise his or her right to counsel.

RIGHT TO COUNSEL

'[T]he right to counsel was recognized in Canadian law well before the advent of the *Charter*',[90] but the *Charter* made it a constitutional right.[91] Penney observed that 'Section 10(b) is one of the *most important*—and *most frequently litigated*—legal rights in the *Canadian Charter of Rights and Freedoms*. Its language is *deceptively* simple: [e]veryone has the right on arrest or detention ... to retain and instruct counsel *without delay* and to be *informed* of that right'.[92] This is more than the 'one phone call' of legend, and police are obliged to facilitate the accused's efforts[93], which includes 'the duty to offer the [detainee] the use of [a] telephone'[94], but 'in light of privacy and safety issues, the police are under no legal duty to provide *their own cell phone* to a detained individual'.[95]

The duty to inform a detained person of their right to counsel arises 'immediately' upon arrest or detention.[96] Once the detainee has access to a phone, he or she must also be able to consult counsel in private.[97] Nonetheless, 'specific circumstances may justify some delay

---

[89] Evans, *supra* note 18; Smith, *supra* note 85.

[90] R. v. Manninen, [1987] 1 S.C.R. 1233, [21].

[91] Bedi & Lafrance, *supra* note 2, at 75: even if the existence of the *Canadian Bill of Rights* precede that of the *Charter*, and that it includes a right to counsel—pursuant to its section 2(*c*)(ii)—'one of the distinctions between the Charter and the *Canadian Bill of Rights* is that the first is a constitutional document, and the latter is not' (emphasis added).

[92] Steven Penney, *Triggering the Right to Counsel: 'Detention' and Section 10 of the Charter* 40 SUPREME COURT LAW REV.: Osgoode's Annual Constitutional Cases Conference 271 (2008) (italics added).

[93] Coughlan & Currie, *supra* note 26 (italics added).

[94] Manninen, *supra* note 90, [22].

[95] R. v. Taylor, [2004] 2 S.C.R. 495, [27] (italics added).

[96] Taylor, *Id.*, [24]; Suberu, *supra* note 21, [38], [42]; R. v. Bartle, [1994] 3 S.C.R. 173, at 19192.

[97] Sean Ellacott, *s. 10(b) and the Right to Consult with Counsel in Private*, in 28th Annual Criminal Law Conference 12 (2016); R. v. Ogbaldet, 2010 ONCJ 477, [61]:

in providing a detainee access to counsel. Those circumstances often relate to police safety, public safety, or the preservation of evidence'.[98] That being said, 'concerns of a general or non-specific nature ... cannot justify delaying access to counsel'.[99]

In *Sinclair*, the Court summarized the obligations stemming from Section 10(*b*) that are triggered immediately upon an individual's arrest or detention[100],[101]:

> Section 10(*b*) fulfills its purpose in two ways. First, it requires that the detainee be advised of his right-to counsel. This is called the informational component. Second, it requires that the detainee be given an opportunity to exercise his right to consult counsel. This is called the implementational component. Failure to comply with either of these components frustrates the purpose of s. 10(*b*) and results in a breach of the detainee's rights ... Implied in the second component is a duty on the police to hold off questioning until the detainee has had a reasonable opportunity to consult counsel.

In addition, the Court 'engrafted two requirements upon the informational component: first, information about access to counsel free of charge provided by provincial Legal Aid where an accused meets financial criteria with respect to need, and second, information about access to duty counsel, who provide immediate and temporary legal advice to all accused, irrespective of financial need'.[102] The informational component of the right to counsel should not be conflated with the right to be informed of the reasons of an arrest or detention, previously discussed.

'The nature of the right to counsel and privacy is well established. Privacy is inherent in the right to retain and instruct counsel'.

[98] R. v. Rover, 2018 ONCA 745, [26].

[99] *Id.*, [27].

[100] Because 'the concerns about selfincrimination and the interference with liberty that s. 10(*b*) seeks to address are present as soon as a detention is effected': Suberu, *supra* note 21, [41].

[101] Sinclair, *supra* note 85, [27] (italics added); R. v. Willier, [2010] 2 S.C.R. 429, [29]; Bartle, *supra* note 96; Manninen, *supra* note 90, [23].

[102] Latimer, *supra* note 15, [33]; R. v. Brydges, [1990] S.C.R. 190.

CONCLUSION

This chapter gave us the occasion to summarize, examine and explain some complex issues and legal concepts of Canadian criminal law, which, in turn, only represent the tip of the iceberg of this fascinating topic, that is, the constitutional rights on arrest and detention in Canada. Sharing a similar criminal law tradition, Canada and India clearly have similarities with respect to constitutional rights on arrest and detention, not only regarding the content and the scope of those rights, for example, the definition of an arrest, psychological detention, etc., but also with the way these rights are to be interpreted by courts, that is, widely, for India, and generously, for Canada. The peculiarities of the Canadian legal rules and jurisprudence regarding those rights might be beneficial for the development of the same in India.

Chapter 13

Pretrial Hearing in Arrest and Detention
The Indonesian Experience

Amira Paripurna

INTRODUCTION

When enforcing the law, the state apparatus has the authority to limit a person's freedom of movement through arrest, detention or various other actions. In Indonesian procedural law, this authority is referred to as *upaya paksa* (coercive action).[1] There are several kinds of coercive action, including arrest, detention, confiscation and searches by investigators and public prosecutors. In general, each coercive action represents a reduction and restriction of the suspect's independence and human rights. Therefore, coercive actions should be conducted under the applicable legal provisions (due process of law) because they relate to a person's freedom, and by extension, their human rights.

The Indonesian Code of Procedural Law (Kitab Undang-Undang Hukum Acara Pidana abbreviated as KUHAP) and Special Laws stipulate the limits and procedures for arrest and detention. However, their

---

[1] Indonesian Code of Procedural Law, 1981, Article 1, Sections 16, 17, 20, 21.

implementation is often contrary to expectations.[2] O. C. Kaligis, in his article 'Criminal Procedure Law in Law Enforcement and Human Rights', stated that detention very often lasts for months, on the justification that it is made necessary by the investigation. In reality, the examination only lasted 7 days, with 40 questions recorded in the police investigation dossier (*Berita Acara Pemeriksaan*). The suspect was detained because the police feared that he would damage or destroy physical evidence. This is always used as a formal reason for detention, even when the investigator has obtained all required evidence.[3] In principle, all forms of action or coercion that deprive or restrict freedom are prohibited. However, the state can limit a person's freedom under certain conditions. Therefore, the emphasis should be on how the arrest was carried out, ensuring that it is in line with the applicable law, not exceeding the state's authority, and not conducted arbitrarily. In the context of law enforcement, coercion must be 'for the sake of examination' and absolutely 'indispensable'.[4]

According to the law, when carrying out arrests and detention, the police and public prosecutors should observe certain formal and material requirements. In the application of subjective material requirements, it is difficult to apply the standard. This creates a grey area that can be misused by the police or public prosecutors.[5] There are some criticisms to be made of the detention rules in Indonesia's criminal procedural law. Law enforcement and legal instruments support the abuse of authority for personal gain. The current detention rules enable law enforcement officials to interpret the permissibility of detaining a suspected criminal subjectively. In other words, the investigator's authority to carry out detention is not entirely dependent on juridical criteria but is largely subjective.

---

[2] Berlian Simamarta, *Pengawasan terhadap Pelaksanaan Penahanan menurut KUHAP dan Konsep RUU KUHAP* 23 MIMBAR HUKUM 1 (2011), at 193.

[3] O. C. Kaligis, *Hukum Acara Pidana dalam Pelaksanaan Peradilan di Indonesia (Tinjauan Empiris terhadap Keseimbangan Penegakan Hukum dan Perlindungan Hak Asasi Manusia)* 37 JURNAL HUKUM DAN PEMBANGUNAN 2 (2007), at 249–50.

[4] M. YAHYA HARAHAP, PEMBAHASAN PERMASALAHAN DAN PENERAPAN KUHAP PENYIDIKAN DAN PENUNTUTAN (Sinar Grafika 2006), at 157–58.

[5] KOMISI HUKUM NASIONAL, PENYALAHGUNAAN WEWENANG DALAM PENYIDIKAN OLEH POLISI DAN PENUNTUTAN OLEH JAKSA DALAM PROSES PERADILAN PIDANA, EXECUTIVE SUMMARY PENELITIAN (Komisi Hukum Nasional 2007), at 6.

In terms of arrest and detention, the discretion of the investigator is very wide.[6] Article 18, paragraph 1, states that a copy of the arrest warrant must be given to the suspect's family immediately after the arrest. In practice, the word 'immediately' is defined according to field conditions; there is no maximum time limit. 'Immediately' can be interpreted as meaning 12 hours or several days.[7] Another concern relates to the provisions of Article 21, paragraph (1) of the Code of Criminal Procedure (CrPC). The article reads '(1) A warrant of detention or warrant of further detention shall be served on a suspect or an accused who is strongly presumed to have committed an offence based on sufficient evidence, in cases where there are circumstances which give rise to concern that the suspect or the accused will escape, damage or destroy physical evidence and/or repeat the offence'. Its implementation is entirely based on the subjective views of the officers. According to the National Law Commission and the Criminal Justice Reform Institute, investigators and prosecutors using their powers of detention depend on their feelings regarding a suspect's condition.[8] However, the enactment of the CrPC in 1981 was a major effort by the state to accommodate the principles of protecting human rights, especially those of suspects. Before the CrPC, criminal procedural law used the *Herziene Inlandsch Reglement* (HIR), one of the legacies of the Dutch colonial government.[9] The legislators of the CrPC considered that HIR lacks human rights protection. Josua Sitompul stated that the replacement of HIR aimed for two things. First is to incorporate the human rights

---

[6] Gita Putri Damayana, *Mengapa Kita Perlu Melakukan Revisi KUHAP Dan Mengapa Sebaiknya Tidak Dilakukan Sekarang*, https://www.jentera.ac.id/publikasi/mengapa-kita-perlu-melakukan-revisi-kuhap-dan-mengapa-sebaiknya-tidak-dilakukan-sekarang/ (last visited 15 December 2020).

[7] Just after 2013, based on Constitutional Court Decision Number 3/PUU-XI/2013, the phrase 'immediately' had been defined clearly. The Court decided that the phrase 'immediately' must be interpreted as immediate and not more than 7 days.

[8] ANGGARA (ed.), PRAPERADILAN DI INDONESIA: TEORI, SEJARAH DAN PRAKTIKNYA (Institute of Criminal Justice Reform 2014), at 90.

[9] ROMLI ATMASASMITA, SISTEM PERADILAN PIDANA KONTEMPORER (Prenada Media Group 2010), at 35; ANDI HAMZAH, HUKUM ACARA PIDANA INDONESIA (Sapta Artha Jaya 1996), at 51–55; Heleen Gall, *An Introduction to Indonesian Legal History* 1 J. S. AFR. LAW 116 (1996).

aspect in the rights and obligations of parties in the national criminal justice system. Second is to preserve the codification and unification or the law according to the Constitution of Indonesia and *Pancasila*.[10]

The main concern is whether the CrPC provisions protect the rights of suspects from potential abuse by law enforcement officials. This study uses an exploratory descriptive approach and consists of three parts. The first part examines the legal guarantee of preventing unlawful and arbitrary deprivation of liberty. The second part discusses how criminal proceedings under the CrPC accord with international human rights standards, especially the 'Body of Principles for the Protection of All Persons under Any Form of Detention and Imprisonment'. The Body of Principles is the main standard for assessing the CrPC's compatibility with international human rights standards. The third part discusses the function of pretrial hearing procedures (*Praperadilan*) as a control mechanism over the use of coercive force by law enforcers. It analyses the extent to which the pretrial hearing mechanism (*Praperadilan*) can protect suspects and defendants from arbitrary arrest and detention.

LAWS ON ARREST AND DETENTION IN INDONESIA

Every arrest and detention contravenes a person's freedom according to restrictions laid down in statutory regulations. These restrictions take the form of conditions, mechanisms or procedures for a person's arrest and detention. The CrPC is the main reference for the authority of investigators in detaining suspects. However, after the enactment of the CrPC in 1981, numerous laws have been passed which stipulate criminal procedures that extend or even diverge from the CrPC in particular circumstances; for example, some laws, such as the Juvenile Justice System Law,[11] the Human Rights Court Law,[12] the Anti-Narcotics Law[13] and the Terrorism Eradication Law,[14] expand the powers of investigators

---

[10] Josua Sitompul, *Improving the Role of Experts Under Indonesian Criminal Procedure Law: Lessons Learned from the Dutch Legal System* 8 INDONES. LAW REV. 1 (2018), at 112.

[11] Act 11 of 2012.

[12] Act 20 of 2000.

[13] Act 35 of 2009.

[14] Act 5 of 2018.

and authorities. However, this chapter only discusses arrest and detention in the context of the rules of the CrPC.

According to Article 17 of the CrPC, law enforcers must have an arrest warrant and sufficient preliminary evidence, and must avoid arbitrary arrests. Article 21, paragraphs (1) and (4) of the CrPC regulates conditions of detention. A suspect or defendant's detention is not mandatory and can only be conducted when it meets certain criteria and conditions. According to Article 1, point 20 of the CrPC, an arrest is an act of temporarily restricting a suspect's freedom. Article 21 of the CrPC regulates the limits and conditions of how detention may be conducted. For instance, the detained person should be strongly suspected, on the strength of sufficient preliminary evidence, to have committed a criminal act. The criminal acts committed should be subject to a criminal sanction of five years imprisonment or greater. Furthermore, detention may be carried out when the suspect has committed certain criminal acts, including sexual crimes, procuring, assault, fraud, embezzlement, and crimes against navigation and aviation.

According to Articles 17 and 21 of the CrPC, to carry out a legal arrest and detention, formal and material conditions should be fulfilled. 'Formal conditions' are based on objective judgement through having a clear benchmark. 'Material conditions' may mean conditions of implementation derived from the subjective judgements of law enforcers. An arrest as a material condition requires sufficient initial evidence.[15] In practice, the 'sufficient initial evidence' required by Article 17 of the CrPC should be interpreted as the 'minimal evidence' referred to in the rule of evidence regulated by Article 184, paragraph (1) of the CrPC.[16] This guarantees that investigators cannot be forced to stop investigating someone suspected of committing a crime. Furthermore, an arrest order cannot be exercised carelessly but should be addressed to those strongly suspected of committing a criminal act. The formal requirements include an arrest warrant and a copy thereof.[17]

---

[15] Chandra M. Hamzah, Penjelasan Hukum tentang Bukti Permulaan yang Cukup (Pusat Studi Hukum dan Kebijakan Indonesia 2014), at 6, 17.

[16] The evidence includes: the testimony of a witness; the testimony of an expert; a document; an indication; the testimony of the accused.

[17] The Criminal Procedure Code, 1981, art. 18, para. 1.

The formal requirements of the rules of detention include committing an act which carries a penalty of 5 years or more, or certain crimes listed in the CrPC. In addition, detainees may include those likely to escape, damage or destroy physical evidence and/or repeat the offence. This second requirement is subjective because the assessment that a suspect may 'escape', 'damage or destroy physical evidence' or 'repeat the offence' is based on the subjective judgement of each law enforcer. Moreover, the detained person should be given a detention warrant, and a copy of it should be handed over to their family. One of the methods for controlling arrest and detention is the requirement for an arrest and detention warrant. The warrant letter provides legal certainty to people arrested and detained. It should set out the basis for their arrest and detention and identify the party that arrested or detained them. Furthermore, legal certainty should also be given to detainees' families, through the requirement that the person arrested or detained deliver a copy of the letter to them. As well as providing legal certainty, arrest and detention warrants (and their copies) support the suspect's right to prepare their own defence.

According to Article 19, paragraph 1, the period of arrest cannot be more than 1 day. This means that if, within 24 hours of examination, suspects do not meet the requirements to be classed as detainees, they must be released by law. The CrPC also places restrictions on the period of detention. At the investigation stage, detention may only be carried out for 20 days and may be extended for another 40 days.[18] Detention at this stage is carried out by the police, while the public prosecutor carries out the extension. The public prosecutor is also authorized to impose detention for 20 days, with a possible extension of 30 days.[19] Further extensions of the detention period can be carried out for two more 30-day periods, provided that the case being investigated is punishable by imprisonment of 9 years or more. Such further extensions are also possible when the suspect or defendant is suffering from serious physical or mental disorders, as indicated by a doctor's certificate.[20] Detention authority also exists at the trial examination stage, from court level one

---

[18] *Id.*, art. 24, para.1–2.

[19] *Id.*, 1981, art. 25, para. 1–2.

[20] *Id.*, art. 29, para. 2.

to cassation. However, this chapter will only focus on the detention authority by the police and public prosecutors.[21]

COMPATIBILITY OF THE CRIMINAL PROCEDURE CODE WITH INTERNATIONAL HUMAN RIGHTS STANDARDS

The 1948 Universal Declaration of Human Rights (UDHR), especially Article 9, states that 'No one may be arrested, detained or disposed of arbitrarily'. This guarantee is regulated in detail by Article 9 of the International Covenant on Civil and Political Rights (ICCPR).[22] ICCPR stipulates that each person arrested should (a) be informed of the reasons and (b) be immediately notified of the allegations, and that (c) anyone arrested or detained (i) should be brought immediately before a judge or other official authorized to exercise judicial powers and (ii) be tried within a reasonable time or acquitted.[23] Apart from the two main instruments above, in 1988, the United Nations General Assembly also announced a set of the *Body of Principles for the Protection of All Persons under Any Form of Detention or Imprisonment*, which serve as guidelines for UDHR and ICCPR implementation related to pretrial detention. This document describes the measures needed to protect the human rights of detainees.[24]

The CrPC was passed in compliance with and respect for human rights. However, it is questionable whether the CrPC is compatible with international human rights standards. The CrPC regulates the use of coercive actions. However, the procedures for use of force are still limited to administrative matters. Substantively, there are no rules that prohibit the use of violence in coercive actions. Meanwhile, Rule No. 2 in the Body of Principles states that 'Arrest, detention or imprisonment shall only be carried out strictly based on the provisions of the law and

---

[21] *Id.*, art. 26–28, para. 1–2.

[22] STEVEN SEMERARO, TWO THEORIES OF HABEAS CORPUS, Research Paper Series on Public Law and Legal Theory (Thomas Jefferson School of Law 2005).

[23] Indonesia ratified the ICCPR through Law no. 12 of 2005.

[24] UN General Assembly, *Body of Principles for The Protection of All Person Under Any Form of Detention or Imprisonment*, GA Res 43/173, GAOR, UN Doc/A/Res/43/173 (Dec. 9, 1988).

by competent officials or persons authorised for that purpose'. Under other administrative provisions of the CrPC, the use of brute force is difficult to prove but is categorized as illegal coercive action.[25]

Rule No. 11 in the Body of Principles confirms that every person detained has the right to be heard or defended before a judicial or other authorized institution prior to detention. The CrPC provides for a pretrial hearing facility that can determine whether or not a person's detention violates the law. However, there are differences of emphasis between the principles set out in the Body of Principles and the pretrial system. In the Body of Principles, before people are detained, they have the right to file a defence before the judicial institution. Hence, such people are not detained, and the judicial institution determines objectively whether they should be detained or not. Under the CrPC, however, a person who files for a pretrial hearing should already have been detained by an authorized investigator.

The Chief of Police Regulation No. 8 of 2009 on the Implementation of Human Rights Principles requires police officers to respect human rights while executing their duties, though they are limited to normative only. Torture by law enforcement officials has not yet been identified as a specific criminal offence in Indonesia. Even, the CrPC does not specifically prohibit the use of torture during direct arrest and detention. Rule No. 6 in the Body of Principles declares that it is forbidden to use torture and powers that exceed the limits of authority of the party arresting or detaining. According to the Rule No. 24 in the Body of Principles, a suspect or defendant has a right to receive medical care. In contrast to Rule No. 24 in the Body of Principles, the CrPC does not require that medical care be offered unless it is requested. Furthermore, the CrPC stipulates that each detention can only be conducted by judicial institutions, including investigators, public prosecutors and judges. However, there is no corrective mechanism requiring these institutions to examine the urgency of detention.

From the above discussion, it can be seen that the CrPC has not fully complied with international human rights standards. In the light

---

[25] The Criminal Procedure Code, *supra* note 17, Articles 16–31.

of this, it is not surprising that between 2006 and 2018, at least 49 cases had been presented in the Constitutional Court that represented 87 attempts to contest the coherency and constitutionality of the provisions of the CrPC.[26] At present, efforts to adapt the CrPC to meet international standards of respect for human rights principles are ongoing. The government has recognized the need to renew the current CrPC, including improving the legal protection of suspects, defendants, witnesses and victims.[27] The draft amendment to the CrPC has reformulated the arrest rules, though the rules are still inadequate by international human rights standards. The fundamental changes proposed by the draft amendment only revolve around the duration of arrest and the period of notification of arrest. The rest does not differ greatly from the current CrPC.[28]

THE EFFECTIVENESS OF PRETRIAL HEARING (*PRAPERADILAN*) AS A REVIEW MECHANISM FOR ARBITRARY ARREST AND DETENTION

In the Constitutional Court's decision regarding the judicial review of the CrPC, the pretrial hearing (*Praperadilan*) represents a break-through for the Indonesian criminal justice system. Pretrial hearing is intended for monitoring and evaluating the legitimacy of coercive actions by investigators and public prosecutors. This mechanism is seen as a means of monitoring the rights of suspects and defendants during preliminary examination. From the point of view of judicial structure, pretrial hearing is not an independent court, but rather part of the court of first instance. Pretrial hearing decisions cannot be proposed for appeal or cassation. The emergence of the pretrial concept arises from the historical need for strict judicial scrutiny of all acts involving deprivation of civil liberties. Pretrial hearing is a form of respect for human dignity in regard to coercive actions. The Constitutional Court has also emphasized that every coercive action,

---

[26] Sitompul, *supra* note 10, at 114.

[27] SUPRIYADI W. EDDYONO, ASPEK-ASPEK PERLINDUNGAN SAKSI DAN KORBAN DALAM RUU KUHAP (Institute of Criminal Justice Reform 2014).

[28] SUPRIYADI W. EDDYONO, KOMENTAR ATAS PENGATURAN PENANGKAPAN DALAM RANCANGAN KUHAP (Institute of Criminal Justice Reform 2013).

such as arrests, searches, confiscation, detention and prosecution, that violates statutory regulations is a form of deprivation of human rights. The existence of pretrial hearing is intended to strengthen the protection of suspects' human rights.

Under the CrPC, pretrial hearing has three kinds of authority. At the first level, the court has authority to examine the legality of an arrest and detention, with an examination carried out at the request of the suspect, family or a representative party. Second, the court has authority to examine the legality of terminating an investigation or prosecution for the sake of upholding law and justice. Third, the court has authority to examine requests for compensation or rehabilitation in respect of coercive actions by investigators and public prosecutors. Such requests are submitted by the suspects, their family or their representatives. The examination hearing in the pretrial process is unrelated and does not aim to prove a criminal act. Conversely, the pretrial hearing verdict may serve as a basis for releasing the suspect from illegal arrest or detention. It may also help with any claim for compensation arising from illegal coercive action.[29]

In its implementation, pretrial hearing does not function in accordance with its aims; for example, the Institute of Criminal Justice Reform (ICJR) and the National Legal Reform Agency (BPHN) reported that pretrial hearing was only considered a procedural, administrative control over investigators and prosecutors' detention actions.[30] Responding to these criticisms, the Constitutional Court ruled that under Article 77 of the CrPC, as the legal basis of pretrial, the pretrial hearing should assess not only the formal or administrative aspects of detention but also whether or not the detention is required.[31] In addition, the authority of the pretrial hearing was strengthened by the decision of the Constitutional Court.[32] In essence, the decision expanded the pretrial hearing examination mechanism by adding further objects for pretrial hearing examination, especially those related to searches and

---

[29] The Criminal Procedure Code, *supra* note 17, Article 1, para. 10.

[30] ANGGARA, *supra* note 8, at 85.

[31] Constitutional Court Case No. 018/PUU-IV/2006.

[32] Constitutional Court Case No. 21/PUU-XII/2014.

confiscation. However, in 2016, the Indonesian Supreme Court issued Supreme Court Regulation (PERMA) No. 4.[33] According to Article 2, paragraph (2) and (4) of this regulation, the pretrial hearing examination of requests regarding the validity of suspect detention should only assess formal questions, including the presence or absence of valid evidence, not entering the case material and presided by a single judge. This is because the examination is brief in nature and concerned only with formal matters. For these reasons, the subject to be examined by the pretrial hearing is in practice limited to the conditions of detention, which are administrative considerations. Judges should pay more attention to the fulfilment of formal conditions arising from an arrest or detention, such as the presence or absence of an arrest or detention warrant, and should not test or assess the material requirement. These material or subjective requirements determine whether a person may be subject to coercive actions through arrest or detention by an investigator or public prosecutor.

Pretrial hearing emerged from the need to include the concept of *habeas corpus* in the criminal procedural law system.[34] The Habeas Corpus Act in the United States provides the right to petition a court to release someone from wrongful detention.[35] The lawsuit determines whether the detention conforms to the law and is in line with the applicable legal provisions. Even if they do not apply the concept of *habeas corpus*, countries that adhere to the civil law system or the legal system of continental Europe also place importance on judicial supervision of deprivation of civil liberties (strict judicial scrutiny); for instance, in France, there is a juge d'instruction (judge of inquiry) who orders and leads the criminal investigation process,[36] while the Netherlands introduced the

---

[33] Article 2 paragraph (1) states that the pretrial objects are: a. whether the arrest, detention, termination of investigation or prosecution, determination of suspect, confiscation and search is legal or not; b. compensation and or rehabilitation for someone whose criminal case is terminated at the level of investigation or prosecution.

[34] ANGGARA, *supra* note 8, at 4–5.

[35] James Landman, *You Should Have the Body: Understanding Habeas Corpus* 72 SOC. EDUC. 2 (2008).

[36] Jacqueline Hodgson, *The Police, The Prosecutor and The Juge D'Instruction: Judicial Supervision in France, Theory and Practise* 41 BR. J. CRIMINOL. 2 (2001).

Rechter-Commissaris (supervisory judge) who has a supervisory function.[37] The form of legal mechanism and pretrial hearing authority is not commensurate with the original concept of *habeas corpus*. In the pretrial hearing examination, the judge only checks administrative procedures, such as the availability of an arrest warrant.

In the use of their authority, judges at pretrial hearing are passive. Their powers are only used upon request and cannot be used without a request from the suspect for legal action against the police or public prosecutors. The pretrial hearing judge should not act proactively or take his own initiative to assess an alleged violation on the part of the investigator or public prosecutor towards a suspect or defendant. Under such a closely regulated pretrial mechanism, the protection of suspects' rights remains weak. The material requirements determine whether a person can be subjected to coercive action. However, in the pretrial hearing, the judge does not examine the investigator's or prosecutor's material requirements. Pretrial hearing judges rarely question the presence of sufficient preliminary evidence.[38] The study of *Komisi Hukum Nasional* shows that abuse of authority often happens in violation of the CrPC provisions regarding 'sufficient preliminary evidence'. This is because the CrPC has never adequately explained the meaning and limits of 'sufficient preliminary evidence', which is ultimately interpreted by the discretion of law enforcement officials.[39] This leads to legal uncertainty and the tendency of law enforcers to arrest first and ascertain probable cause afterwards.[40]

---

[37] J.H. CRIJNS, B.J.G. LEEUW & H.T. WERMINK, PRE-TRIAL DETENTION IN THE NETHERLANDS: LEGAL PRINCIPLES VERSUS PRACTICAL REALITY (Eleven 2016), at 12.

[38] SYPRIANUS ARISTEUS, HUKUM TENTANG PERBANDINGAN ANTARA PENYELESAIAN PUTUSAN PRAPERADILAN DENGAN KEHADIRAN HAKIM KOMISARIS DALAM PERADILAN PIDANA (Badan Pembinaan Hukum Nasional 2007), at 113.

[39] After more than three decades since the enactment of the Criminal Procedure Code in 1981, the phrase 'sufficient preliminary evidence' received interpretation from the Constitutional Court decision in 2014 under the decision of Constitutional Court No. 21/PUU-XII/2014. The Constitutional Court specifically at least two evidence in Article 184 of Law No. 8 of 1981 concerning Criminal Procedure Law.

[40] KOMISI HUKUM NASIONAL, PENYALAHGUNAAN WEWENANG DALAM PENYIDIKAN OLEH POLISI DAN PENUNTUTUTAN OLEH JAKSA DALAM PROSES PERADILAN PIDANA (Komisi Hukum Nasional 2007), at 81–82.

The 2014 Constitutional Court decision provided more legal clarity on the meaning of 'sufficient preliminary evidence'. In its ruling, the Constitutional Court stated that

> as an effort to reduce the excessive authority use by investigators or public prosecutors in carrying out detentions ... detention by an investigator or public prosecutor should be based on sufficiently rational considerations and not carry out detention based on the subjective interest of the investigator or public prosecutor...; The existence of Article 21 paragraph (1) of the Criminal Procedure Code cannot be separated from Article 77. Based on the Article 21 paragraph (1) of the Criminal Procedure Code, the aspect of sufficient evidence aims to reconcile two interests, including the public interest to uphold order and individuals' interests whose human rights should be protected. This article is further strengthened by the existence of pretrial hearing under Article 77 of the Criminal Procedure Code....

The pretrial hearing mechanism should require an investigator to provide details about a person 'strongly suspected of committing a criminal act based on sufficient evidence' sufficient to meet the '*prima facie* evidence' requirement. This has become a question for investigators and prosecuting authorities to interpret. At pretrial hearing, subjective conditions related to detention need to be assessed. It is not appropriate for pretrial hearing judges to only examine formal evidence and disregard the facts (material). The judge may take a different view from the objectives of the criminal court process, which seek material truth. It is very difficult to establish material truth in the pre-adjudication stage if the judge only checks the formal evidence considered in the pretrial hearing.[41] One of the material requirements for detention is concern that the suspect may escape, damage or destroy evidence, or commit further crime. This condition depends on the subjective judgement of the police and public prosecutors. However, in the pretrial hearing process, the judge does not examine whether there exist real, concrete reasons for such concern. Pretrial hearing judges accept that this is solely

---

[41] Komisi Hukum Nasional, Kajian terhadap Rancangan Undang-Undang Kitab Undang-Undang Hukum Acara Pidana (RUU KUHAP) (Komisi Hukum Nasional 2009).

a matter for the subjective assessment of the investigator or prosecutor.[42] In other words, the judge leaves it entirely to the discretion of the investigator or public prosecutor.

Provisions regarding pretrial hearing, especially on the procedural law, are laid down in a limited manner in Articles 77–83 of the CrPC. However, the existing regulation is too brief and does not provide clarity about the procedural law to be used. Due to the unclear regulation and its form as a petition, many judges use principles from civil procedural law. A rule on burden of proof is also lacking in the CrPC.[43] There are material requirements for carrying out detention, such as 'a concern from law enforcers that the suspect may escape'. Due to the unclear burden of proof, the principles of civil procedural law are used to prove 'concern' in the pretrial hearing. The principle is 'whoever argues must prove'. In this context, when suspects, as pretrial petitioners, argue that detention does not meet material requirements, they must prove that the 'concern' of law enforcers is not justified. In this context, it would certainly be fairer to expect that the party required to prove the element of 'concern' should be the law enforcer. A more precise procedural law would reduce uncertainty as to whether criminal or civil procedural law applies in the pretrial hearing. Although the pretrial hearing procedure falls within the realm of criminal procedural law, in practice, it uses the principles of civil procedural law. This leaves it unclear as to which party is required to provide proof at the pretrial hearing.

Many aspects of pretrial hearing have proved to be ineffective because pretrial hearing does not guarantee legal certainty or access to justice. In response, the Draft Amendment to the Criminal Procedure Code (R-KUHAP) proposes the creation of a Preliminary Examiner Judge (HPP). HPP would replace the pretrial hearing function because its authority would be broader than that of the pretrial hearing. HPP would play a supervisory role and exercise control over coercive action

---

[42] SUPRIYADI WIDODO EDDYONO, ERASMUS NAPITUPULU, PROSPEK HAKIM PEMERIKSA PENDAHULUAN DALAM PENGAWASAN PENAHANAN DALAM RANCANGAN KUHAP (Institute Criminal Justice Reform 2014), at 4.

[43] ANGGARA, *supra* note 8, at 7, 127.

by the police and public prosecutors. In contrast to passive pretrial hearing judges, HPP would be active. Without waiting for a request from the suspect, it could exercise active control over all pre-adjudication processes under its authority. HPP's active authority would give it a large responsibility in the preliminary examination of criminal cases. HPP would have the authority to conduct unannounced inspections of the investigator and public prosecutors. This would help in checking whether there was any abuse of authority violating the pre-adjudication provisions. On the one hand, activists and scholars complain that HPP would not fully correct the loopholes in the pretrial hearing procedure.[44] On the other hand, both the police and the prosecutor's office have rejected the HPP proposal on the grounds that its terms of reference and authority are too broad.[45]

CONCLUSION

The CrPC contains human rights principles protecting the rights of suspects. However, this protection is not fully in line with international human rights standards. This is evident when comparing the Code with the 'Body of Principles for the Protection of All Persons under Any Form of Detention and Imprisonment' guidelines for implementing UDHR and ICCPR related to pretrial detention. The criminal procedural system in Indonesia provides mechanisms for controlling arrest and detention through pretrial hearing (*Praperadilan*). These are intended to serve as a complaint mechanism against the arbitrary deprivation of a person's civil liberties by law enforcement officials. However, the pretrial hearing mechanism does not provide effective supervision and remedy for suspects whose rights have been violated.

The pretrial hearing (*Praperadilan*) is not held before coercive action has taken place. The examination of arrest and detention is limited to administrative tests. In practice, pretrial hearing only examines formal administrative conditions of detention. The judge pays more attention to fulfilment of the arrest warrant or detention warrant than to questions

---

[44] Luhut M.P., Pangaribuan, *Hakim Pemeriksa Pendahuluan (HPP) dalam Rancangan Sistem Peradilan Pidana di Indonesia* TEROPONG 1 (2014).

[45] *Id.*

of probable cause and reasonableness. Pretrial hearing judges are passive and only exercise their authority upon request. The judge waits for a petition from suspects who feel their rights have been violated by the coercive actions of investigators or public prosecutors. To guarantee everyone's right to freedom and personal security, reform of the pretrial hearing (*Praperadilan*) system is needed.

SUGGESTED READINGS

A. Wisnubroto & G. Widiartana, Pembaharuan Hukum Acara Pidana (Citra Aditya Bakti 2005).

Act 11 of 2012.

Act 20 of 2000.

Act 35 of 2009.

Act 5 of 2018.

CNN Indonesia, *Kontras Temukan 643 Kasus Kekerasan oleh Polisi*, July 1, 2019, *available at*: <https://www.cnnindonesia.com/nasional/20190701183351-20-408051/kontras-temukan-643-kasus-kekerasan-oleh-polisi>

Constitutional Court Case 65/PUU-IX/2011.

Constitutional Court Case No. 018/PUU-IV/2006.

Constitutional Court Case No. 21/PUU-XII/2014.

Eddy O. S. Hiariej, *Criminal Justice System in Indonesia: Between Theory and Reality* 2 Asia Law Rev. 2 (2005).

M. Nowak, UN Covenant on Civil and Political Rights CCPR Commentary (2nd revised ed, NP Engel Publisher 2005).

Setyo Puji, *Jadi Korban Salah Tangkap Polisi Pria ini Dianiaya hingga Babak Belur, Dilepas karena Tidak Terbukti* Kompas, June 19, 2020, *available at*: <https://regional.kompas.com/read/2020/06/19/05350051/jadi-korban-salah-tangkap-polisi-pria-ini-dianiaya-hingga-babak-belur>

Supriyadi W. Eddyono, Pretrial Hearing in Indonesia: History, Theory and Practice (Institute for Criminal Justice Reform 2014).

The Criminal Procedure Code, 1981.

UN Human Rights Committee, CCPR General Comment No. 35: Article 9, Liberty and Security of Persons, CCPR/C/GC/35 (16 December 2014).

Chapter 14

Arrest and Torture
Law and Its Implementation in Nepal

Balram Prasad Raut*

INTRODUCTION

The criminal justice system of Nepal, comprising police, prosecutor and the court, plays a vital role in the administration of criminal justice system. However, there are other actors as well, such as, chief district officer (CDO)[1], district forest officer, custom officer, special police department and others. Upon receiving any information relating to offense or suspects accused of crime, these investigating officers start the process of investigation or arrest. The general law of arrest is provided by the *Muluki* Criminal Procedure Code, 2017, apart from the special laws, including, Prevention of Corruption Act, 2002, Organized Crime Control Act, 2013, Narcotic Drugs Control Act, 1986, Human

*I would like to extend my acknowledgement to the Terai Human Rights Defenders Alliance (THRDA) for allowing me to use the case studies related to torture published in the research report *Torture In Terai 2020, Torture Is A Crime: The State Continues To Commit*, Terai Human Rights Defenders Alliance. I was also part of this research. I also would like to thank to Advocate Mohan Karna and Praveen Kumar Yadav for supporting me in doing research of case studies.

[1] CDO in Nepal has the same role as the District Magistrate in India.

Trafficking and Transportation Act, 2008, and others. In Nepal, the law of arrest has been well provisioned in the laws. However, their implementation is poor, and perpetrators are rarely punished. Due to that, the torture and killing of people in police custody has become a normal phenomenon in the name of inquiry or investigation. Over the past 3 years, since the *Muluki* Penal Code, 2017, was enforced, no perpetrator has been fined and imprisoned under the Code. Therefore, it has created doubts among the crime victims that even after the enactment *Muluki* Penal Code, the impunity may continue to prevail. The author has proposed some recommendations so that the laws can be implemented effectively, and rights of the victim are respected, protected and fulfilled.

POWER OF ARREST IN NEPAL

Section 6 (6) of the *Muluki* Criminal Procedure Code, 2017, provides power of arrest. If any person related with an offense is found committing the offense or is present before the investigating authority, such person may be arrested. If it is necessary, in the course of investigation into any offense, to immediately arrest any person, an application has to be made to the adjudicating authority for permission to issue an arrest warrant along with reasons, whereby the adjudicating authority may give permission to issue the warrant. However, if there is reasonable ground to believe that if the offender is not arrested immediately, he or she may abscond or tamper with or destroy the evidence, an urgent arrest warrant shall be issued and such arrested person be produced before the adjudicating authority for approval.[2] If any person is arrested upon the issue of an urgent arrest warrant, no further investigation proceedings relating to that offense may be conducted without obtaining approval from the adjudicating authority. If the police are not available at the time of commission of any offence, any person who is present at the time of commission of the offence or who witnesses the commission shall try to prevent the offender from running away or fleeing and hand over him or her to the nearby police office.

---

[2] This provision has been imported from Japanese Criminal Procedure Code.

For the purpose of effectuating arrest, the cause or grounds of arrest shall be informed to the person concerned. Police are authorized to use force to arrest if any person resists arrest or makes an attempt to escape. In case of women, the arrest shall be conducted by a woman police officer, with due regard to her dignity and honour.

However, Section 14 of the Code provides some checks for the police officer and has detailed out the period for taking a person into custody for investigation purposes. Any person who is arrested for investigation into any offence shall be produced before court within a period of 24 hour of such arrest. If it is necessary to hold a person in detention for a period exceeding that set forth, the investigating authority shall, through the public prosecutor, make an application to the adjudicating authority, along with reasons, who on satisfaction may issue an order to send in judicial custody for a maximum period of 25 days at once or time and again if it appears that the investigation is being conducted satisfactorily.

Despite having such checks, there are several cases of violation of the above provisions. Undue arrests, tortures in the name of inquiry or investigation are rampant in police custody, and several people have lost their lives,[3] which have been critically discussed in this article.

TORTURE IN NEPAL: FACTS AND FIGURES

The number of torture cases has decreased from conflict to post-conflict era, though the numbers and rates are still significant. The reason for decreasing incidents may be the criminalization of torture by *Muluki* Penal Code. Yet, the implementation of the law fails to prosecute acts of torture and provide victims the right to reparation. However, it remains

---

[3] *Death of Bijay Ram in Police Custody Due to Torture*, Date May 13, 2077/05/13. *available at*: https://www.onlinekhabar.com/2020/09/893305. See also the case of Sambhu Sada. On 10 June 2020, Sambhu Sada Musahar, aged 23, of Sabaila Municipality Ward Number 12, Dhanusha district, died in police custody. *Available at*: https://english.onlinekhabar.com/dhanusha-man-was-found-hanged-in-police-custody-was-it-murder-or-suicide.html and https://thewire.in/south-asia/deaths-in-custody-impunity-nepal-police

the same or has increased in the Tarai districts. In 2016, Terai Human Rights Defenders Alliance (THRDA)[4] found that 167 (24.74%) detainees out of 674 interviewed in various detention centres of 19 districts were found to be tortured by Nepal Police. Among those tortured were 9.79 per cent (66) women and 8 per cent (154) juveniles below the age of 18. Likewise, in 2017, THRDA found that 118 out of 882 detainees complained of torture including a case of custodial death in Siraha district.[5] The reports of the human rights organizations and the UN consistently exposed that torture continues in police detention of Nepal.

Evidence shows that the modus operandi of torture is diverse, and it can be difficult to track. THRDA's monitoring and documentation consists of both physical and mental torture. Kicking by boots; beating with plastic pipes, bamboo sticks wooden sticks; and butt of rifles; slapping; punching; making to jump upside down and forcing the person to do push-ups; pulling hair; burning with cigarettes; and keeping in detention without food and water, among others, are methods of physical torture. Likewise, the major forms of mental torture include threats to put under strong charge, death threats, spitting in food, vulgar words and racial slurs and humiliating words relating to the ethnicity of Madhesi and Tharus. In 2017, some cases had been reported where other co-detainees had been ordered to beat their mate detainees in the detention centres. The detainees receive threats of being indicted with serious crimes and detained for longer periods.

In its 2001 report,[6] Amnesty International reviewed the practice of torture in Nepal. The report stated that torture as a punishment was still widely perceived as acceptable. Police and local authorities have continued the historical tradition of torture and humiliation of detainees despite political changes over the last 10 years. Amnesty's report mentions:

Sometimes very gruesome forms of torture are reported. They include falanga (beatings on the soles of the feet) with bamboo sticks, iron or

---

[4] TORTURE IN TERAI 2016: VICTIMS AWAITING JUSTICE 19 (Terai Human Rights Defenders Alliance 2017).

[5] TORTURE IN THE TERAI 2016: VICTIMS AWAITING JUSTICE 7 (Terai Human Rights Defenders Alliance 2018).

[6] NEPAL: MAKE TORTURE A CRIME 2 (Amnesty International's Report 2001).

PVC pipes; belana (rolling a weighted bamboo stick or other round object along the prisoner's thighs, resulting in muscle damage); telephono (simultaneous boxing on the ears), rape, electric shock and beatings with sisnu (a plant which causes painful swellings on the skin). The latter method of torture is often inflicted on women, more particularly on their private parts.[7]

The UN Special Rapporteur, who visited Nepal in September 2005, concluded in its report that torture and ill treatment are systematically practised in Nepal. The Special Rapporteur's report states[8]:

Torture and ill-treatment are systematically practiced in Nepal by the police, armed police and the Nepal Army primarily to extract confessions and to obtain intelligence in relation to the conflict. That the Government urgently needs to send a clear and unambiguous message condemning torture and ill-treatment was made dramatically clear to the Special Rapporteur when he received repeated and disturbingly frank admissions by senior police and military officials that torture was acceptable in some instances, and was indeed systematically practiced.

The UN Office of the High Commissioner for Human Rights (OHCHR), which established a large field presence in Nepal in May 2005, was also involved in carrying out monitoring and reporting of torture. In its report to the UN Human Rights Council[9] on 18 February 2008, three different issues related to torture were cited:

1. detainees who died in detention due to torture;
2. detainees were reportedly hidden prior to OHCHR visits; and
3. the pattern of torture and certain practices of torture common during the conflict occasionally reappeared, mostly in connection with detained individuals accused of belonging to armed groups.

---

[7] *Id.*

[8] UN Commission on Human Rights, *Special Rapporteur on Torture Says Practice of Torture is Systematic in Nepal*, https://reliefweb.int/report/nepal/special-rapporteur-torture-says-practice-torture-systematic-nepal (last visited 3 March 2021).

[9] OHCHR, *Nepal Conflict Report, 2012*. An Analysis of Conflict-related Violations of International Human Rights Law and International Humanitarian Law Between February 1996 and 21 November 2006. https://www.ohchr.org/Documents/Countries/NP/OHCHR_Nepal_Conflict_Report2012.pdf

In 2008, Advocacy Forum[10] assessed the impact of Nepal's Torture Compensation Act, 1996 (CRT), over its first 12 years (1996–2008) of enactment. The findings show that only 208 cases of torture compensation were filed in 12 years; 52 victims were given compensations; and of those who got compensation, only 7 victims (13.46%) received monetary compensation. None of the perpetrators involved in these cases were brought to justice[11]. Inefficient state machinery, lack of accountability, lack of activism and entrenched impunity have all contributed to the dismal implementation of torture-related court decisions under CRT[12].

DEVELOPMENT OF LAW RELATING TO TORTURE

Torture is a heinous crime, a crime against humanity and a violation of right to live with dignity. The use of torture in crime investigation goes back to the earliest human civilizations and remains systemic in some way or the other around the world. While a small number of countries have made significant progress in preventing torture, the rest of the world is still committing serious forms of human rights violation under the guise of national security or maintaining peace and security or law and order. A review of Nepal's progress in ending torture paints a bleak picture when it comes to the state's actual prevention of torture and commitment to the justice of those responsible for inflicting physical, mental or psychological suffering on someone.[13]

In Nepali criminal justice administration, torture was and is one of the modes used by the Nepali security forces to create evidence in the process of investigating an offense or to get the confession of the accused. Therefore, in Nepal, there is a very infamous proverb or statement which gives notoriety and ironic symbolic meaning of Nepali criminal jurisprudence, *Pahile kutnus ani bujhanus* (first beat, then investigate). This gives a kind of legacy to torture in Nepal. It

---

[10] Advocacy F Advocacy Forum, *Hope and Frustration Assessing the Impact of Nepal's Torture Compensation Act - 1996*, June 26, 2008.

[11] *Id.*

[12] *Id.*

[13] *Id.*

also helps us to understand that, in Nepal, the use of torture by state agencies has become phenomenal in the last few years.

Period Before 1990

Before 1990, there were no constitutional and legal provisions relating to torture. Nepalese legal system was based on religious scriptures, *Manusmriti, Nāradsmriti, Hindu Dharmaśāstra, Rukkas, sanad and sawal.* Punishment system was based on caste and religion. The gravity of punishment was based on whether the accused was upper caste or lower caste, women or men. Punishment was torturous, barbaric and inhumane. Degradation from caste (*patiya* system), expelling the accused from villages, forcing the accused to eat excreta, burning the hands of the accused, and drowning the accused in ponds were the modes of crime punishment which were torturous and inhumane. Historically, looking back to the different dynasties of Kirat, Lichhavi, Malla, Shah and the Ranas, the practice of torture was a political recrimination. The historical literature finds that both physical and mental torture were inflicted on the accused during interrogation and to extract confession or information.[14]

Muluki Ain of 1854 was also based on religious scriptures. *Muluki Ain* of 1963 was known as Secular Ain, but it was also not free from the legacy of Hindu *Dharmaśāstra*. Several provisions of this Ain were also inconsistent with the modern principles of human rights, rule of law and established general principles of criminal law. This Ain was silent about the regulation of torture, though the existence of torture was rampant.[15]

Period from 1990 to 2006

Notably, Nepal set forth its journey of preventing torture after a major political upheaval in 1990. During the Panchayat (party-less) system,

---

[14] TULSI RAM VAIDYA AND TRI RATNA MANANDHAR, CRIME AND PUNISHMENT IN NEPAL: A HISTORICAL PERSPECTIVE (Bini Vaidya and Purna Devi Manandhar 1985).

[15] *Id.*

many political leaders were victims of torture. Those politicians who came to power in 1990 pledged their commitment to end torture. Consequently, with the restoration of multiparty democracy regime, the Constitution of the Kingdom of Nepal 1990 outlawed torture for the first time in the history. The 1990 Constitution stipulated freedom from torture as a fundamental right. Its Article 14 (4) prohibited 'physical or mental torture' and 'cruel, inhuman or degrading treatment'. It also assured that the person tortured would be compensated 'in the manner determined by the law'.

Meanwhile in 1990s, Nepal also ratified the United Nations' anti-torture conventions such as International Covenant on Civil and Political Rights (ICCPR) and its two optional protocols, the International Covenant on Economic, Social and Cultural Rights and the Convention against Torture (CAT), among others. The CRT, 1996 was enacted during this time.

Although legal developments took place in the decade, the occurrence of torture increased dramatically. Both the security forces and the Maoist rebel forces used torture to intimidate, suppress, control and punish victims. The Comprehensive Peace Accord was signed by the then mainstream political parties and the then Nepal Communist (Maoist) Party in 2006. They agreed to investigate and punish the perpetrators who were involved in torture during the conflict era. Over the decade, CRT remained the only legal recourse for torture victims. Even within the existing laws, when torture-related cases were filed at the courts, those responsible for torture were rarely brought to justice. As a result, thousands of victims of torture from the conflict era suffered injustice.

Period from 2007 to 2016

After the agreement of Comprehensive Peace Accord of 2006, the Communist Party (Maoist) of Nepal became a part of mainstream politics. The Interim Constitution of Nepal, 2007, was promulgated. The 2007 Constitution provided 'right against torture' as fundamental right and criminalized torture. It also provided compensation for victims of torture. However, the first half of this period was no better than the earlier period, though the second half created a milestone development in the history of torture from constitutional and legal perspectives. Nepal's two Constitutions—Interim Constitution of Nepal, 2007, and Constitution of Nepal (2015)—guaranteed the right against torture and stated that torture will be 'punishable by law', and 'any person so treated shall be provided compensation as determined by the law'.[16] If we compare Article 22 of 2007 Constitution with Article 22 of the Constitution of Nepal, then we do not find any substantial difference except the term 'victim' being added in Article 22 of the Constitution of Nepal.[17]

Period from 2017 to 2021

The major development of this period is the enactment of the *Muluki* Penal Code, 2017, which has criminalized torture and provides punishment for the perpetrators of torture up to 5 years of imprisonment or a fine of ₹50,000 or both. It also provides compensation to the victims of torture. *Muluki* Penal Code, 2017, entails legal provisions in line with the 2007 and 2015 Constitutions. It does not only criminalize torture, but also imposes individual responsibility on the investigating officer if found involved in torture. It has also ensured protection of the victims and witnesses. Before enactment of this Code, the State used to pay compensation for the torture committed by the State's officials, while the new law has made the perpetrators responsible to pay the compensation. Cases of torture cannot be withdrawn once they are

---

[16] Article 26 of the Interim Constitution of Nepal, 2007 provided 'Right against Torture' as follows: (1) No person who is detained during investigation or for trial or for any other reason shall be subjected to physical or mental torture or to cruel, inhuman or degrading treatment. (2) Any act referred to in Clause (1) shall be punishable by law, and any person so treated shall be provided with such compensation as may be determined by law.

[17] Article 22 of the Constitution of Nepal provides 'Right against Torture' as follows: (1) No person who is arrested or detained shall be subjected to physical or mental torture or to cruel, inhuman or degrading treatment. (2) Any act mentioned in Clause (1) shall be punishable by law, and any person who is the victim of such treatment shall have the right to obtain compensation in accordance with law.

registered at the courts. From the legal point of view, it has been a progressive change in criminal law.[18] However, the limitation to register First Information Report (FIR) within 6 months has minimized the substantial value and application of statutory provisions of this Code.[19]

CHALLENGES IN IMPLEMENTING THE *MULUKI* PENAL CODE, 2017

Three years have already passed since the passing of the Code. However, it is surprising that no perpetrator violating the Code has been prosecuted for torture, which can also be understood from the cases studies mentioned in the following respective description.[20] Several challenges are experienced by the victims of torture while perpetrators are creating number of hurdles to implement the Code properly and effectively. The challenges in implementing the Code are discussed as follows:

Refusal of First Information Report

The human rights community applauded the criminalization of torture when the Code defined torture as a punishable offense. It provided hope for the victims that incidents of torture and inhuman or degrading treatment will be investigated and prosecuted by the state. However, THRDA's monitoring and documentation found that there has not been any progress in the implementation of the new anti-torture law. This is evident from the refusal of FIRs by the police officers.[21]

---

[18] See, Section 167 of Muluki Penal Code.

[19] Section 170 (2) provides as follows: The complaint shall not be taken after the lapse of 6 months of the concerned arrested, controlled, detained or imprisoned or a person detained in preventive detention is released as provided in Section 167 and in other offenses when it was committed or known.

[20] The cases studies cited in this section have been studied mainly in the 19 districts of Madhesh region by the Team of THRDA since 2006–2020. Some of them have been also studied individually and, along with the team of THRDA, by the author of this article. Madhesh is a region where non-Nepali speaking people live, and it is the Southern part of Nepal that is attached with the four states of India, West Bengal, Bihar, Uttar Pradesh and Uttarakhand.

[21] *National Human Rights Commission of Nepal* (Harihar Bhawan, Lalitpur, Nepal Sept. 2020).

On 27 October 2019, Chai, a resident from Mayadevi Rural Municipality in Rupandehi, was arrested after police found him involved in a dispute with a person. He said he was tortured by the police in custody. THRDA reported this case to National Human Rights Commission. On 29 October 2019, Area Police Office, Lumbini refused to register FIR claiming that no torture was inflicted on Chai.

On 23 July 2019, District Police Office (DPO) of Rupandehi refused to register an FIR filed by three juveniles. Police tortured the boys accusing them of stealing a mobile phone on 18 July 2019. The DPO kept the FIR without formally registering it and told applicants that they would seek explanation from the alleged police personnel and take action.

Police officers are reluctant to register FIRs lodged by the victims of torture. Investigation into the incidents of torture can proceed only when police register FIRs. Many victims of torture are hesitant to file cases against police officers in the same police office because of fear of appraisal by the accused police officer. Likewise, THRDA human rights defenders and lawyers found that police officers, instead of registering FIR, told the applicants that they would seek explanations from the alleged police personnel and take action against them.

The challenges are in line with THRDA's experience in extrajudicial killings (EJK) cases. In the past, police refused to register FIRs filed by families of those people who were killed in fake encounters. In some cases, families of EJK victims approached the court seeking to register their FIRs and the court passed necessary orders. However, even thereafter, the concerned police officers refused to register FIRs on one or the other pretext.[22]

Procedural Hurdles

Section 5 of *Muluki* Criminal Procedure Code, 2017, provides that victims of police brutality can register FIRs against their perpetrators. As per the provision, if a concerned police office refuses to register an FIR, then it can be filed to the public prosecutor or the higher police

---

[22] *Continuing Extrajudicial Executions in The Terai*, THRD Alliance, Mar. 2014.

office who shall forward it to the concerned police office for the necessary action. Again, if the public prosecutor or the higher police office refuses to register the victims' FIR, then the victims can approach the concerned District Administration Office also or, in the alternative, the Ministry of Home Affairs too. This long process of FIR registration has created administrative hurdles delaying justice for the victims. If we compare the *Muluki* Criminal Procedure Code and CRT, it is found that seeking remedy under CRT was easier and hassle free for the victims, as they were able to file the cases directly to the courts as private matter.

Withdrawal of First Information Reports Still Continues

Before the *Muluki* Penal Code came into force, it was found that the victims were withdrawing their FIRs when they received threats from their perpetrators or offer of monetary help. There was hope that the non-withdrawal provision introduced in the *Muluki* Criminal Procedure Code, 2017, would have a positive impact. Section 116 of the Code does not allow offences mentioned under Schedules 1 and 2 to be withdrawn once they are registered in the court. However, here, the case is that the when the victim goes to the police office to register FIR, first, they are not ready to accept FIR. Even if they accept, then the police do not register. If they register, then they force, coerce or threat the victim to withdraw FIR. In some cases, police often take FIRs without registering them and put pressure on the victims threatening them that if they do not withdraw their complaints, they would frame criminal charges against them. The police allegedly offer the victims monetary incentives if they withdraw their complaints. The withdrawal of FIR continues in one or the other way. Due to these reasons, cases of torture do not proceed towards prosecution and trial. A case study related to withdrawal of FIR has been mentioned below.[23]

On 11 May 2019, Mohammad Nazir Khan, 57, of Narayanpur Rural Municipality- 1 was beaten up by APF Inspector Puran GC and Assistant Sub Inspector of Nepal Police Dirgh Bahadur Sahi for

---

[23] National Human Rights Commission of Nepal, *supra* note 21.

allegedly bringing woods from nearby forest. His left hand was broken when the police officials thrashed him severely. He also had bruises on different parts of his body. On 16 May 2019, Nazir visited the office of THRD Alliance in Nepalgunj, requesting for support. Next day, the victim, with the help of the organization, filed a FIR at the district police office, Banke, accusing the police officials of torture. However, the DPO did not register the FIR saying it contained the names of its officials. On 17 May 2019, Nazir, under pressure of police, and local political leaders, agreed to make a compromise with the police and later decided to withdraw the complaint after the police agreed to provide him medical expenses. A political representative said on condition of anonymity, the man withdrew the case as the police threatened to indict him in the criminal case that could land him in jail for 20 years.

Muluki Criminal Procedure Code, 2017: No Legal Provision for Mental Health Check-Up

The past problems with medical examination of victims have continued even though the *Muluki* Criminal Procedure Code, 2017, has included new provisions related to medical examination. Section 22 of the said Code provides for the examination of wounds of victims. It has special provision for the medical examination of torture victims. Subsection 2 provides that a victim or a third person on behalf of the victim can file an application to the court seeking physical examination of a torture victim, and the court can order for the physical examination of such person from a doctor or a medical professional prescribed by the government. Subsection 5 provides that the court shall order the alleged perpetrator to bear the cost of medical examination of the torture victim and also provides interim relief to the victim, if the court finds that the victim is tortured or beaten up in the detention centre. However, police personnel have continued to use the format of medical examination, known as Injury Examination Report, which fails to ensure a thorough examination of torture victims. There is also no examination of the detainees' mental condition simply because there is no legal provision for mental examination in the clause. Although Section 167 of the *Muluki* Penal Code has prohibited both physical and mental torture, a thorough medical report for torture cannot be prepared without an expert's examination of mental condition of torture victims. The irony is that the medical examination clauses included in the *Muluki* Criminal Procedure Code provide only for 'physical examination'. This has failed to stipulate provisions on examining the huge impact or damage caused by torture upon one's mental condition. The lack of mental health examination of detainees had led to incidents of suicides committed by the detainees in police custody. The following case study shows the situation of mental torture in a detention centre.

> Sambhu Sada Musahar, aged 23, of Sabaila Municipality Ward Number 12, Dhanusha district, died in police custody at around 2 am. He had been in detention since 26 May 2020. The detainee was found dead in the wee hours on 10 June 2020, and the facial crime scene was of suicide, according to police. The police told that the detainee hanged himself to death in the bathroom with the help of his dress (t-shirt). However, the family members of the detainee did not trust the police's claim. Three days before the incident took place, his mother and mother-in-law had met Sambhu in the detention center of APO Sabaila. According to them, the detainee looked scared and worried. He had told them that he might be killed if he was not released instantly.

No Proper Implementation of Law

The Code provides that the perpetrators of torture will be punished with 5 years of imprisonment or a fine of ₹50,000 or both. However, over the past 2 years, since the *Muluki* Penal Code was enforced, no perpetrator has been fined and imprisoned under this law. Refusal of FIRs and lack of an independent investigation have shown that this provision has no deterrent effect upon the perpetrator. Once this provision of the Code is implemented in true spirit, it will help to curb the long-standing impunity.

Justice Denied due to Statute of Limitation

The statute of limitation to file a case of torture has been increased to 6 months from 35 days, as provided by CRT. Section 170 (2) of the *Muluki* Penal Code provides that a victim of torture can file a complaint within 6 months of either the date of incident or the date of release of the person from the detention or prison. However, this extension of statute of limitation is not sufficient for the torture victims whose after-effects are seen after 6 months. This provision of the Code contradicts with the international principle of human rights and CAT itself. It is an obligation for her to respect, protect and fulfil the obligation taken under this Convention. How the law of limitation affects the victim of torture can be realized from the following case study[24]:

> On 7 April 2011, three police officers from the Rupandehi District Police Office arbitrarily arrested Mr. Pandey without giving any reasons or arrest warrant. He was brought to Lumbini Zonal Police Office and subjected to repeated interrogations, torture and severe ill-treatment, in order to extract from him a confession on his alleged involvement in the planning and execution of a bomb-explosion perpetrated on 27 March 2011, in which he always denied having any type of involvement. He was repeatedly beaten, kept constantly blindfolded and handcuffed, insulted and threatened. He was even forced to urinate on an electric heater, that left him bleeding and fainting, but never received any medical treatment or attention. Exhausted and prostrated Mr. Pandey signed a confession extorted through torture on 13 April 2011. Between 7 and 11 April 2011, he was held incommunicado. While his mother was struggling to determine his fate and where-abouts, Nepalese authorities denied having knowledge of his deprivation of liberty and deliberately concealed his whereabouts. He was allowed to communicate to the outside world only when he signed the confession paper. Newspaper articles were published and he was labeled as a terrorist and a murderer. Today, as a consequence of the severe torture endured, Mr. Pandey still suffers from depression and sexual dysfunction.

On 23 January 2013, the victim registered a writ in the Supreme Court for seeking relief and requesting to order the Rupandehi District Court that the 35-day statute of limitation provided in CRT would not be applicable in his case. However, the Supreme Court confirmed the judgement of Rupandehi District Court after 6 years. On 30 October

---

[24] *Torture in Terai 2016*, supra note 4.

2018, the Human Rights Committee issued observations following a complaint on behalf of Mr Prashanta Kumar Pandey that Nepal was responsible for the violation of his right to liberty and security, as well as fair trial. The UN Body called on Nepal to investigate the facts and prosecute those responsible for these acts.[25]

In another case,[26] the Supreme Court held that statute of limitation should not be inconsistent with the constitutional provisions and violative of human rights principles.

Immunity from Prosecution

Prashant Pandey gave his statements in the court that he was tortured. His statements were not taken seriously by the court and no order of investigation for perpetrated torture was issued. However, he had also disclosed the identity of the officers responsible, but the perpetrators were never prosecuted and punished. Mr Pandey was kept in jail during the trial period where he endured inhumane conditions of detention. On 13 June 2012, the Rupandehi District Court held that there was no evidence against Mr Pandey's involvement in the placement of the bomb. He was, however, declared responsible for the preparation of the attack and sentenced to 1 year imprisonment, which he had already spent during the trial and was, thus, released. The confession obtained through torture was considered as valid evidence. His attempts to obtain justice and redress for the harm suffered were frustrated, as Nepalese authorities refused to register his claims because he did not report the torture within 35 days from having suffered such treatment (which was impossible for him). Due to this limitation of CRT, he could not get compensation which he suffered due to torture, and no perpetrator was made responsible of his torture. The Supreme Court's decision also contradicts with the conclusion of the Human Rights Committee in response to the submission of Mr Pandey's complaint, which was facilitated by TRIAL International.

---

[25] https://trialinternational.org/latest-post/torture-and-enforced-disppearance-of-prashanta-pandey-v-nepal-in-april-2011/

[26] Advocate Om Prakash Aryal and others vs. National Human Rights Commission and others, NKP (2070), Vol. 7. DN 9029.

CONCLUSION AND RECOMMENDATION

Torture is one of the heinous forms of national as well international crime, a crime against humanity. Therefore, the United Nations has adopted CAT which criminalizes torture and obligates the States to take appropriate action. Nepal, as a member of CAT, has undertaken to fulfil its obligations under this Convention, which should be ensured. It enacted *Muluki* Penal Code, 2017, *Muluki* Criminal Procedure, 2017, and Criminal Offence (Determination of Punishment and Implementation) Act, 2017, to respect, protect and fulfil the obligation taken under international human rights laws.

However, despite these positive steps, the implementation of the new law over the years has shown that torture is yet to be realized as a criminal offence. The National Human Rights Commission (NHRC) and the UN Office of the High Commissioner for Human Rights as well as media have widely reported and documented the issues of torture and other forms of cruel, inhuman or degrading treatment. Police often resort to excessive use of force against Madhesis and Tharus. This is evident from the fact that whenever there is unrest and agitation in Madhesh, the police force deployed in the name of maintaining law and order use excessive force, causing death and serious injuries to withdraw their complaint. The long process of FIR registration has created administrative hurdles delaying justice for the victims. In some cases, police often take FIRs without registering them and put pressure on the victims threatening them to withdraw them in lieu of even money. Over the past 4 years since the *Muluki* Penal Code was enforced, no perpetrator has been fined and imprisoned under this Code. Compared to CRT, the statute of limitation to file a case of torture has been increased. However, this provision has obstructed justice in case of victims whose after-effects were seen after 6 months.

Amid challenges, human rights community is advocating for passing a separate anti-torture law compatible to the international standards. The bill for the same has been pending in the Parliament since 2014.

Based upon the findings, the following suggestions may be recommended:

- Criminalization of torture is a positive step; yet, laws that are enacted need to be properly implemented throughout the country.
- The statute of limitation related to torture should be repealed.
- An independent investigative body should be set up to investigate cases of torture and violation of law of arrest to effectively implement the provisions of *Muluki* Penal Code. Such a mechanism is necessary to prosecute and prevent such acts from occurring repeatedly.
- The anti-torture provisions should be made fully compliant with the international human rights conventions.
- NHRC, National Human Rights Unit of Police as well as the Office of the Attorney General need to collaborate with NGOs for effective and transparent monitoring of detention centres.
- HRDs should be allowed free access to detainees and respect their right to fair trial and ensure they are kept in clean, sanitary, healthy conditions in line with international prison standards.
- The Government of Nepal should investigate all allegations of torture and implement the decisions of NHRC as well as Courts to provide justice and reparations to the victims in a timely manner.
- A National Monitoring Mechanism should be formed for all detention centres to strengthen legal provisions against torture.
- Optional Protocol on CAT (OPCAT) should be ratified.

PART IV

Judicial Interventions, Legal Reforms and the Way Ahead

Chapter 15

The Footprints of Liberty

Kamaljit Singh Garewal

INTRODUCTION

Our Republic must ensure that the footprints of liberty do not stop at arrest. It is a sad fact that this is what happens when provisions of law, which protect the arrested, are violated with impunity. The judgement in *Arnab Manoranjan Goswami v. the State of Maharashtra*[1] shall, in the times to come, become the guiding beacon for judges, lawyers, prosecutors, and all those who come in contact with the criminal justice system.

The opinion of the Supreme Court in *Arnab* is set to arouse criminal courts from indolence and stop the executive from selective harassment of citizens. On liberty, the Court observed: 'Liberty survives by the vigilance of her citizens, on the cacophony of the media and in the dusty corridors of courts alive to the rule of (and not by) law'. Supreme Court expressed its expectation from criminal courts: 'It is our earnest hope that our courts will exhibit acute awareness to the need to expand the footprint of liberty and use our approach as a decision-making yardstick for future cases involving the grant of bail'. This is

---

[1] Arnab Manoranjan Goswami v. The State of Maharashtra Criminal Appeal, No. 742 of 2020 decided on 27 November 2020.

a huge and sweeping direction for the criminal courts, the criminal bar, the prosecutors and lastly, the arresting and investigating officers.

Examination of criminal procedures relating to arrests may begin with a simple illustration of the arrest of a car driver and compare it with the arrest of two famous writers. The effect of arrest on everyone's psyche is usually the same. There shall then follow an examination of various provisions of the codes of criminal procedures, and the Constitution, some broad reference to the recommendations of the Law Commissions of India, and the working of the police. Different types of arrests shall be described to show that all arrests, criminal or civil, are the same. There shall be an attempt to show that the separation of the Judiciary and the Executive is still incomplete.

THE POLICEMAN

One can meet a policeman anywhere, in the marketplace or the shopping mall or on the highway or a back lane. We must stop when stopped, co-operate with the policeman, and answer the usual questions. Where are you coming from? Where are you going? What is your name? Where do you live? These are straight questions, you give straight answers, and then move on. But you can be forgiven if your heart misses a beat on seeing a policeman blocking your way. You first look at the speedometer, check your wallet to reassure yourself that it is in your pocket with your driving license. Did you jump a traffic light? There are so many ways in which you can land in trouble. All this is a part of life, you will get off with a fine or a reprimand. These are traffic duties of our policemen, to keep us safe on the roads. You should be grateful that no traffic violation requires your arrest.

On the other hand, if you had been hit by a motorcycle and the rider had fallen or you had given a ride to a stranger or someone had used your car's registration number on his car's number plate and then committed a robbery, you may be in trouble. But don't be nervous or worried, the policeman will ask you the usual questions, and may arrest you after telling you the reason, Then, you shall be produced before a Magistrate, allowed to speak to a lawyer and to explain your story. This may cause you inconvenience but soon you will get bail and return to the comfort of your home. This is the ideal situation.

THE REALITY

There is little wonder that ordinary people fear ordinary policemen. It's the reputation which the police carry that petrifies people. The direct consequence of this is the complete lack of public co-operation in police work. No amount of convincing shall make you feel at ease at the sight of a policeman. No constitutional rights, no court judgments, no legal assurances will make you comfortable before policemen whereas our police are meant for our security and safety. If you feel our police makes you uncomfortable, you have not read about the atrocities committed by the Nazi or the Soviet police.

Sometimes things happen the other way around. You are arrested for something you have not done, and you are certain about your innocence. A policeman instead of patiently listening to your version becomes impatient, delivers a few fits of abuse and maybe a few slaps, and then marches you off to the police station. When this happens to you, rest assured that you are in for a long ride through the Indian criminal justice system. This is the typical scenario in the countryside, if not in metropolitan India where you find rude policemen, no legal help, indifferent prosecutors, and busy Magistrates. An arrested person may experience nightmares, mental agony and confusion. Welcome to criminal procedure-induced paranoia, a disease of pandemic proportions.

ARREST

The Russian writer, Alexandre Solzhenitsyn (1918–2008), spent 8 years in Stalin's prisons, then was to be exiled to a labour camp in Siberia. The order was withdrawn after Stalin's death. His crime was to criticise Stalin in a letter to a friend. Solzhenitsyn went on to write about his experiences in 'The Gulag Archipelago' (1974)[2] and was awarded the Nobel Prize for literature in 1976. Of particular interest is Solzhenitsyn's description of his arrest on the opening page of his book:

> Arrest! Need it be said that it is a breaking point in your life, a bolt of lightning which has scored a direct hit upon you? That it is an

---

[2] ALEXANDRE SOLZHENITSYN, THE GULAG ARCHIPELAGO (Harper & Row 1974).

unassimilated spiritual earthquake, not every person can cope with, as a result of which people often slip into insanity?

The Universe has as many different centers as there are living beings in it. Each of us is a center of the Universe, and that Universe is shattered when they hiss at you: You are under arrest.

If you are arrested, can anything else remain un-shattered by this cataclysm?

But the darkened mind is incapable of embracing these displacements in our universe, and both the most sophisticated and the verist simpleton among us, drawing on all life's experiences, can gasp out only: Me? What for?

On the other hand, Oscar Wilde's *De Profundis*[3] was published posthumously. He had written this work in a jail, in the form of a long letter addressed to his lover. Wilde, a celebrity writer, was the subject of a vile vendetta. He had been sentenced for 2 years for indecent behaviour (euphemism for gay) and after release died a completely broken man in Paris, 2 years later. In De Profundis he wrote:

> Many men on their release carry their prison about with them into the air, and hide it as a secret disgrace in their hearts, and at length, like poor poisoned things, creep into some hole and die. It is wretched that they should have to do so, and it is wrong, terribly wrong, of society that it should force them to do so.

To borrow astronaut Neil Armstrong's famous lines, an arrest is one small step for man, and one giant leap into a legal abyss with unforeseen consequences. The arrested person's footprints get obliterated, and his liberty gets eroded, often without him realizing where he is headed to or when he will return home. Sometimes not knowing why he has been arrested.

SECTION 46, CRPC

The footprints of liberty stop at Section 46 of the Code of Criminal Procedure, 1973 (CrPC). This Section is a peaceful and sublime means of making an arrest but in the end, gives a horrific justification

---

[3] OSCAR WILDE, DE PROFUNDIS Methuen, 1905.

for killing a person while arresting him. While making an arrest, the police officer may just touch the person to be arrested or confine him but if the person resists arrest then all means can be used. It further goes to say, in a roundabout way, that if the person to be arrested is accused of an offence punishable with death or life imprisonment, and he 'forcibly resists the endeavor to arrest him,' he can be killed. Actually, murdered in cold blood. Here lies the legal justification for all 'police encounter' deaths and extra-judicial killings by the police. Section 46(3) is the source of muscular and violent policing currently when citizens before and after arrest have well recognised rights. Can anyone believe this is still the law in India?

One first comes across Section 46 in CrPC 1898. It has surprisingly remained unchanged since the nineteenth century. This is despite revolutionary changes in the way human rights and the rights of the accused have developed worldwide. After two world wars, the Universal Declaration of Human Rights was announced on 10 December 1948[4]. Article 11 of this declaration stated:

1. Everyone charged with a penal offence has the right to be presumed innocent until proved guilty according to the law in a public trial at which he has had all the guarantees necessary for his defence.
2. No one shall be held guilty of any penal offence on account of any act or omission which did not constitute a penal offence, under national or international law, at the time when it was committed. Nor shall a heavier penalty be imposed than the one that was applicable at the time the penal offence was committed.

CRIMINAL PROCEDURE CODES

The People of India gave to themselves the Constitution on 26 January 1950. It remains an academic mystery why immediate changes were not made in the Code of Criminal Procedure, to balance the functions and powers of the judge, the prosecutor, and the investigator, for a level playing field, to try accused persons in a fair manner.

---

[4] *Universal Declaration of Human Rights*, 1948, https://www.un.org/sites/un2.un.org/files/udhr.pdf

If criminal procedures are examined, and particularly relating to arrest, one comes across provisions that have continued since the procedures developed after 1858 through various Criminal Procedure Codes 1861, 1872, 1882 and finally crystallised into CrPC 1898. These codes were meticulously drafted, and the provisions were stated with precision, administered through judges and magistrates of the Indian Civil Service. Judiciary and executive were inseparable those days. The code served the interests of the British Government to run their Indian Empire like a police state. Pakistan and Bangladesh are still following this code, though with some modifications. However, we in India changed over to a new code in 1974, yet the procedures remained much the same. And there are flaws in the way procedures are judicially administered. This leaves an impression that the quality of justice has not improved, the police state has not disappeared. There are too many pre-trial legal challenges to the system available through petitions under Section 482 CrPC and Articles 226/227 of the Constitution. In fact, the system is slowing down to a breaking point and cases are skyrocketing. If defective orders need correction even at the pre-trial stage, then there is something drastically wrong with our criminal justice system.

CONDUCT OF TRIALS

In the pre-1974 era, all trials concluded within 4–6 months of registration of FIRs. No one sought bail for fear of adverse comment by the High Court and therefore, no one challenged framing of charges or seek quashing of FIRs. Trials before a Court of Session were over in 2 days. The writer speaks from personal experience as a trial lawyer in 1972–74 and observed the transition. Adjournments of trials were unheard of. This is not so anymore, trials carry on for years before different judges. One judge examines some prosecution witnesses, another judge examines the remaining witnesses, a third judge records the defence witnesses and a fourth decides the case. Every accused person wants to have a go at filing a petition before the High Court on some pretext or other hoping to get some relief or delay the case. This is followed by SLPs before the Supreme Court. What does it speak of an accused who wants to put off a quick trial?

CODE OF CRIMINAL PROCEDURE, 1973

The present code came into force on 25 January 1974. No one can miss the irony of Republic Day eve. It was presumably to bring it in belated conformity with Articles 20, 21 and 22 of the Constitution. The emergency of June 1975, when all rights were tossed aside, was still 18 months away. The code remains a replica of the old code, therefore, an exercise in futility. The code is supposedly based on the Law Commission's voluminous Forty-First Report (1969)[5] which took into consideration earlier reports of the Commission and gave a section-wise appraisal of the code for recommending amendments. Unfortunately, the report resulted in only a few cosmetic changes but none in the real procedure to hasten fair trials. The system remained police-dominated because that was the colonial necessity and sadly remains so in republican India.

One of the main recommendations was to separate the judiciary from the executive. There is no answer to why this constitutional provision was not taken seriously by the Government at the very start, despite the specific directive in Article 50. Separation from the executive is a basic requirement of the independence of the judiciary.

Some of the other noteworthy changes were the abolition of committal proceedings; adoption of summons procedure for cases punishable up to 2 years; scope of summary trials widened for cases punishable up to 1 year; the power of revision against interlocutory orders was taken away; stoppage of proceedings when transfer applications were filed was omitted; payment of costs for adjournments; service of summons by registered post; recording of guilty plea through the post; not necessary to order re-trial if in appeal or revision any error, omission or regularity was discovered; and most importantly, facility of part-heard cases being continued by successors-in-office was extended to Courts of Session. Nothing was changed in the manner of making arrests, except the introduction of safeguards for the arrest of women in 2006 and 2009.

---

[5] *41st Report of Law Commission of India*, 1969, https://lawcommissionofindia. nic.in/1-50/Report41.pdf

COMMITTEE FOR CRIMINAL REFORMS

Currently, Committee for Reforms in Criminal Laws[6] is working to reform laws. It is doubtful if the committee will find ways to speed up criminal procedures. Looking at the history of our reforms processes and the culture of police-dominated prosecutions, there are unlikely to be improvements in the criminal justice system. The present committee was formed by the Ministry of Home, not the Ministry of Justice. The committee's report shall naturally be placed before the Ministry of Home which is heavily police-dominated. There have been important judgements of the Supreme Court giving many suggestions, and many reports of the Law Commissions of India. Justice Malimath Committee Report (2003)[7] also made many recommendations. There doesn't seem to be any reason to have the present committee for reforms in criminal laws. There are enough recommendations on the table which can be given a second look. The criminal justice system has broken and shattered; it must be rebuilt again.

THERE MUST BE CHANGE

The basic flaws in our system are only two. Too many people are sent up for a trial, too few convictions are recorded but too much valuable judicial time is spent. It should be the other way around, maximum convictions in minimum time, but convictions arrived judiciously and fairly. Only those persons should be prosecuted against whom there is strong prosecutable evidence. No one can explain why trials are not held day-to-day, as required by Section 309 CrPC. These flaws must be addressed, and procedures improved for quick and condign punishment of the accused. It seems, as the French adage goes, *plus ca change, plus c'est la meme choses* (the more things change, the more they remain the same.)

---

[6] *Committee on Reforms in Criminal Laws*, criminallawreforms.in

[7] Malimath Committee on Reforms in the Criminal Justice System, https://www.mha.gov.in/sites/default/files/criminal_justice_system.pdf

Our jurisprudence is teeming with weighty pronouncements on various aspects of the criminal justice system in general and the rights of the arrested persons in particular. Perhaps one must be told and re-told that arrested persons have to go through the entire procedure. Release on bail is an important right but bail only releases the arrested person from custody. Bail does not relieve him from the travails of the procedures, which shall take him on the road to final justice. Once a person has been arrested, he cannot get away because escape from the system is not in his hands at all but in the hands of some police officer, prosecutor, or judge. These personages are presumed to know the law; therefore, the rights of arrested persons are indeed well protected, at least that is the theory.

Law provides sufficient and more than adequate protection of rights to arrested persons. After all, every arrested person enters the criminal justice system within 24 hours of arrest and stays under a judge's umbrella till his discharge, acquittal or conviction and sentence. The period of 24 hours was fixed in the old code more than a century ago. Those days it did take 24 hours to reach the magistrate, not anymore. Within 24 hours of arrest, the arrested person begins to enjoy all protection available to him under the code and the Constitution. This is the theoretical position. In practice rights of arrested persons are often violated in the protective custody of the system run by the State with the judiciary seemingly looking the other way. No one seems to be accountable. No one is punished for violations of rights. This is the real situation in contemporary India. It may not be prevalent in metropolitan India under the gaze of watchful media. But travel to the far corners of the land, across the length and breadth of the nation, and see the real fate of arrested persons in far-flung districts.

EDUCATING INVESTIGATORS

How often do police officers get briefed on jurisprudence emanating from courts? How often do police officers read provisions of the law? How often does the conduct of police officers get castigated by courts? How many police officers understand the presumption of the arrested person's innocence until guilt is established beyond a reasonable doubt? These questions arise frequently but go unanswered. The reason, why such questions arise, is the lack of independent oversight over police investigation. The damage to individual citizens after an arrest is so severe that it can never be compensated. Law provides for compensation for the wrong arrest but no one follows up.

FLAWED INVESTIGATIONS

The constitutional requirement is to produce all arrested persons before the nearest Magistrate within 24 hours. The police habitually disobey, periods of detention without arrest stretch to many days. During this period records are fudged, evidence planted, recoveries stage-managed. All this is well known but seldom noticed, and rarely does investigation get rejected at the trial. Recording of the daily diary at the police stations is suspended, often for days. First information reports are recorded after many days and backdated. Case diaries are important to be kept updated by the investigator, but these diaries are sometimes changed to suit the police plot. Magistrates glance at the diaries in a cursory manner. Superior police officers, magistrates and judges can and must refer to them to see the conduct of the investigation. These diaries should not be kept away from the arrested/accused persons because some entries could be a useful aid in preparing a defence to wrong-foot the police investigation. Often police investigating officers get away with creating false evidence, setting up fake witnesses, and withholding evidence that will favour the defence.

Another curious feature of the police investigation is the power of officers' senior to Station House Officers (SHOs) to exercise the same investigative powers throughout the area under their charge, as is exercised by SHO within his area. This is a sweeping power that enables a senior police officer to entirely change the direction an investigation is taking and to do so without the advice of the prosecutor. Therefore, there is never finality in the investigation until the senior officers have okayed it. Scope for political interference in investigations is writ large in Section 36 CrPC 1973. Immediately on registration of FIR, politically connected persons start approaching seniors' officers for re-investigation. So how can liberty be protected if investigation decisions are taken on extraneous consideration unrelated to legal evidence?

Justice A.N. Mulla of the Allahabad High Court had made some scathing remarks about the police when he observed in *State v Mohammad Naim*[8]

> If I had felt that with my lone efforts, I could have cleaned this Augean stable, which is the police force, I would not have hesitated to wage this war singlehanded. There is not a single lawless group in the whole of the country whose record of crime comes anywhere near the record of that organised unit which is known as the Indian Police Force.

SOME LANDMARK JUDGMENTS

In *Woolmington v. Director of Public Prosecutions*[9] the House of Lords held that the presumption of innocence is the most important thing in criminal law and cannot be ignored. The burden of proof in criminal matters is that the prosecution must prove the defendant's guilt beyond a reasonable doubt. In *Liversidge v. Anderson*[10] in a dissenting speech, Lord Atkin stated his view that the majority had abdicated their responsibility to investigate and control the executive and were being 'more executive-minded than the executive'. Atkin protested that theirs was a strained construction put on words with the effect of giving an uncontrolled power of imprisonment to the minister', and went on to say: '

> In England, amidst the clash of arms, the laws are not silent. They may be changed, but they speak the same language in war as in peace. It has always been one of the pillars of freedom, one of the principles of liberty for which on the recent authority we are now fighting, that the judges are no respecters of persons, and stand between the subject and any attempted encroachments on his liberty by the executive, alert to see that any coercive action is justified in law.

---

[8] Criminal Misc. Case No. 87 of 1961 of Allahabad High Court.
[9] [1935] UKHL 1.
[10] [1941] UKHL 1.

Our Supreme Court in *Joginder Kumar v. the State of UP*[11] said that the rights of an arrested person are inherent in Articles 21 and 22(1) of the Constitution and require to be recognised and scrupulously protected. In *D.K. Basu v. State of West Bengal*[12] certain guidelines were given to the arresting officers to wear name tags, to prepare a memo of arrest signed by a witness, a friend or relative of the arrested person must be informed the name of the officer under whose custody the arrested person is, the arrested person must be examined for injuries and a memo prepared and signed by the arrested person. In *Arnesh Kumar v. the State of Bihar*[13] the court noted that

> Arrest brings humiliation, curtails freedom and cast scars forever. Lawmakers know it so also the police. There is a battle between the lawmakers and the police, and it seems that police have not learnt its lesson; the lesson implicit and embodied in the Cr.PC. It has not come out of its colonial image despite six decades of independence, it is largely considered as a tool of harassment, oppression and surely not considered a friend of public. The need for caution in exercising the drastic power of arrest has been emphasised time and again by Courts but has not yielded desired result. Power to arrest greatly contributes to its arrogance so also the failure of the Magistracy to check it. Not only this, but the power of arrest is also one of the lucrative sources of police corruption. The attitude to arrest first and then proceed with the rest is despicable. It has become a handy tool to the police officers who lack sensitivity or act with oblique motive.

ROLE OF PROSECUTORS

Once a person is arrested and his liberty taken away, the next step is to investigate and send the accused for trial. In the whole process of criminal justice, the state must engage the services of competent lawyers to present the case before the trial judge. The role of prosecutors is very crucial. They must be bold, impartial, neutral and well prepared if the prosecution is to succeed. The transformation of the case from

---

[11] (1994) 4 S.C.C. 260.

[12] (1997) 1 S.C.C. 416.

[13] (2014) 8 S.C.C. 273.

the stage of the investigation to the stage of prosecution is akin to a relay race. It requires deft handing over of the baton without dropping. But there is one difference, the investigator and the prosecutor must run the race together, strengthening their stride until the investigator drops out. Now the baton remains in the hands of the prosecutor alone until the end.

In the 14th Report of the 1st Law Commission of India M.C. Setalvad felt very strongly about the negative role of the police in prosecution and wrote,

> Police exercised too much control over the prosecution despite the latter being organically linked but theoretically independent of the former. Police did not have the legal know how to conduct prosecution and did not possess the high degree of objectivity and detachment necessary for a prosecutor. The high degree of subjectivity and attachment of the police with the case implied that the prosecutor will be more biased towards securing conviction.[14]

The above, in nutshell, gives a very dim view of the way prosecutions were conducted those days and sadly are still be conducted by giving prosecutors a subservient position. This should no more be tolerated by the State if the cause of justice is to be served and crime punished quickly.

Under CrPC 1898 continued till it was repealed by CrPC 1973. Prosecutors were then a part of the police department and were called prosecuting sub-inspectors. Under the present code, prosecutors are in chapter II (Constitution of Criminal Courts and Offices). The Parliament has deliberately placed prosecutors alongside criminal courts and recognised that prosecutors' office as a criminal office. The provisions relating to prosecutors are contained in Section 24 (Public Prosecutors), 25 (Assistant Public Prosecutors), and 25 A (Directorate of Prosecution) of CrPC 1973. Police investigators have been kept out of this chapter. Separation of prosecution from the police is theoretically complete.

---

[14] *1st Law Commission of India* (14th Report, 1958), https://lawcommissionofindia.nic.in/1-50/report14vol1.pdf

Subsequently, the Law Commission of India under the chairmanship of Mr Justice K.J. Reddy submitted the 154th report on the Code of Criminal Procedure in 1996 and recognised that the prosecution machinery has been completely separated from the investigation agency.[15] However, the Commission felt the importance of coordination between the prosecution, now an independent department, and the police.

The Law Commission had considered the National Police Commission's 4th report in detail, in which it was suggested that to improve coordination between prosecution and investigation, the Directorate of Prosecution should be made a part of the police department. This was not accepted because this would have been contrary to the law laid down in *S.B. Sahane v. the State of Maharashtra*[16]. In this case, the Supreme Court had not allowed prosecutors appointed under section 25 CrPC to function under the control of the head of the police department and freed them from its administrative and disciplinary control.

The Law Commission did recommend that the Home Department of the State Governments should prescribe guidelines to achieve the desired coordination between the Directorate of Prosecution and the investigating agency of the police for efficient investigation of cases. But it is regrettable that the following provision, designed to empower prosecution and define its functions, sadly remains unimplemented so far. This provision is as follows:

> The powers and functions of the Directorate of Prosecution and the Deputy Directors of Prosecution and the areas for which each of the Deputy Directors of Prosecution have been appointed shall be such as the State Government may, by notification, specify.[17]

The back and forth continues because the Indian State does not want to empower prosecutors. No one says there should be a

---

[15] *Law Commission of India*, 154th Report, 1996, *available at*: https://lawcommissionofindia.nic.in/101-169/Report154Vol1.pdf
[16] 1995 Supp. (3) Supreme Court Cases 37.
[17] CrPC, Section 25A (7).

Prosecutor-General fully accountable and responsible for all prosecutions, and equal in rank to the Director-General of Police. However, the Committee on reforms in the Criminal Justice System (Malimath Committee) recommended that Directors of Prosecution should be from among suitable police officers of the rank of DGP, but hedged it with withdrawing them from the police. What we need is a duly constituted All India Prosecution Service (as an All-India Service) recruited from the Bar. Prosecutors shall be competent, well trained, neutral, under careful superintendence and control of an independent Prosecutor-General, and outside the malignant influence of the police and the executive (read political masters). Today if an arrested person is denied his rights to a fair investigation and impartial prosecution, and is discharged or acquitted, where does he go for redressal of his grievance or compensation for lost years. The answer is, nowhere, because there is no one accountable for the failure of the criminal justice system. Likewise, the victims have no one to turn to.

SEPARATE JUDICIARY FROM EXECUTIVE

There have been several periodic amendments to the present code. Since this article is on arrests, which gravely impinges on personal liberty, some fundamental defects in the 'procedure established by law' need to be pointed out at this stage. Under the old code, there was no separation of the judiciary and the executive at the magisterial level. The new code introduced the concept of judicial magistrates and executive magistrates but put the subordination of executive magistrates under the district magistrate and through him, executive magistrates come under the state government. It is hard to miss the irony of this arrangement which brings executive magistrates directly under the political masters. Coupled with this the police are already under the state government. Earlier prosecution was under the police, conducted through prosecution sub-inspectors. This was a bad arrangement because it did not ensure fairness and impartiality in investigations. Right from the early days of our Republic, the Parliament has always been renegading from giving full independence to the judiciary, some power is always kept back for the executive to keep the judiciary weak. This tendency runs through our system. The habit of keeping the judiciary hamstrung by provisos and non-obstante clauses prevails in most of our law-making. First, a law is stated, giving citizens' rights then through provisos the rights are curbed. CrPC 1973, as is evident, was not required if no substantive changes were to be made in the criminal procedures. The arrangements of its provision are the same as in CrPC 1898 and so are its various sections. We could have continued with CrPC 1898 to this day.

Anyway, this principle of separation of judiciary from the executive now exists in the present code, introduced 23 years too late. Sadly, the delay has allowed wrong habits to form in the magistracy and wrong practices to develop in the police. The executive magistrate's jurisdiction extends only to Chapter VIII covering security proceedings, and Chapter X covering maintenance of public order and tranquillity. There is no reason to designate an executive magistrate a magistrate at all. Calling an executive magistrate an executive officer should be good enough. Let a judicial magistrate be the magistrate. Take back powers of Chapters VIII and X from the executive, to be exercised wholly by the judiciary through the magistracy.

There are some other provisions of law, outside CrPC, under which a person can be arrested. One is Section 67(b) of the Punjab Land Revenue Act, 1887 for recovering arrears of land revenue. In fact, this provision is frequently used to recover tax arrears and bank debts under various statutes but they involve arrest and stamping out of liberty. An arrest is a subject under the judiciary from day one and that is where it should remain because judges understand the loss of liberty and the difficulties the arrested person feels when he is arrested. The judiciary is also responsible for protecting the rights of the arrested persons. Another such provision for an arrest outside CrPC is Order 21 Rule 11 (2)(j)(iii) CPC, under which a judgment-debtor can be arrested in execution of a decree. These powers of arrest should only be exercised by a magistrate and no other officer. These arrests by a revenue officer or an executing court smack of an illiberal and conservative mindset and must be done away with to strengthen the footprints of liberty.

CONCLUSION

All 'procedures established by law' (Article 21) must remain outside the executive domain and be completed within the judiciary, limiting the role of the executive and the police to initial investigation and arrest only. Time has come to strengthen prosecution by inducting lawyers to conduct prosecutions, independent of the executive and the police. Only lawyers of high integrity and experience can take important prosecutorial decisions. The most common decisions are whom to prosecute, whom to drop, what charges are made out, and on what evidentiary basis. Prosecuting lawyers should be accountable for the failure of the prosecution. It is the right time to heed M. C. Setalvad's warning, given in 1958, about the high degree of objectivity and detachment necessary for fair prosecution which the police did not possess. Sticking to antiquated procedures, dating from the pre-constitution era, has made things from bad to worse. Liberty must be protected from its prime violators, the executive, and the police. The only way to achieve this is by scrapping the present code and re-write a new one.

Chapter 16

Arrest by Police
Judicial Mandate

R. K. Bag

INTRODUCTION

The order of the society is maintained by the implementation of the rule of law. As a law enforcement agency, the members of the police force are entrusted with the twin duties of taking preventive action after collection and analysis of secret information and carrying out an investigation after the commission of the offence, so that the guilty are punished, reformed and rehabilitated in the society through the criminal justice system.

Law has given powers to every member of the police force to arrest a person for prevention of a cognizable offence, and specific powers to the officer-in-charge of the police station to arrest in connection with the investigation of cognizable offence. The power of the officer-in-charge of the police station can be exercised by any senior officer, from the rank of Inspector of Police to the rank of Director General of Police.[1] Similarly, the police officer above the rank of constable, viz. head constable or assistant sub-inspector of police, may enjoy the powers of officer-in-charge of the police station in the absence of

---

[1] Section 36 of the Code of Criminal Procedure, 1973.

regular officer-in-charge.[2] Offences have been classified in the Code of Criminal Procedure (CrPC), 1973 in terms of the power of the police to arrest, viz. cognizable as referring to offences where police can arrest a person without a warrant and non-cognizable where the police cannot arrest any person without warrant.[3] Arrest involves taking a person in custody by words or by action. In other words, a person is taken into custody for the exercise of physical control over the said person, so that proper care and protection of his person may be taken by authority of law. If any person offers resistance or makes any attempt to do so, the police can use force to overpower the person resisting arrest and such use of force may extend even up to causing death, where the person so resisting is accused of an offence punishable with death or imprisonment for life.[4] A police officer has the power to enter any house, break open the door of the house for the purpose of arrest, if his ingress into the house is not allowed by the occupier of the house.[5] The only obligation of the police for making a forceful entry in the house for arresting a person is to notify the female occupants of the house before making entry into the house.

Any person involved in a cognizable offence of grave nature can be arrested by police on fulfilment of two conditions: first, if credible information is received by the police about such offence and second, if the police reasonably believe the commission of such offence. Similarly, any person involved in a cognizable offence punishable with imprisonment up to 7 years can be arrested by the police to prevent the commission of the further offence or to ensure fair investigation by the collection of evidence or to ensure fair trial before the court of law, if the police officer reasonably believes the commission of such offence on the basis of a reasonable complaint or credible information or reasonable suspicion.[6] The police can also arrest a person to prevent him from committing a cognizable offence, which is known as preventive arrest by the police for maintenance of order in society.[7]

---

[2] Section 2 (O) of the Code of Criminal Procedure, 1973.
[3] Sections 2 (c) and (l) of the Code of Criminal Procedure, 1973.
[4] Section 46(2) and (3) of the Code of Criminal Procedure, 1973.
[5] Section 47 of the Code of Criminal Procedure, 1973.
[6] Section 41 of the Code of Criminal Procedure, 1973.
[7] Section 151 of the Code of Criminal Procedure, 1973.

The classification of offences, manner of effecting the arrest, and the power of the police force from the lowest rank to the highest rank indicate the wide ambit of the authority given to the police by the Legislature for arresting a person. At the same time, the above parameters of arrest point out that a person cannot be arrested arbitrarily. Mere suspicion or complicity in the offence is not the pre-condition of arrest as laid down in the CrPC, 1973. However, the wide gap between the mandate of law and the perception of the police about the power to arrest is evident from arbitrary and indiscriminate arrest by police for extraneous consideration without receiving credible information and without forming an opinion of reasonable suspicion of involvement of the person in the cognizable offence.

This chapter elucidates the judicial directions given from time to time to regulate police powers and ensure the maintenance of rule of law. These guidelines are of immense importance since they outline the limits subject to which the powers must be exercised. While limits have been prescribed in the law, in many cases, they fail to capture the specific situation and/or circumstance in which the same is being exercised. For example, in cases of domestic violence or abuse by husbands, while the law clearly categorizes the offence as a cognizable one, the sensitivity of the entire situation demands that before the arrest, preferably, a preliminary enquiry is conducted to validate the allegations made. Similarly, in the case of the arrest of a judicial officer, while the law prescribes no special conditions, it is incumbent that certain procedures are followed in consonance with the independence of the judiciary. Over the years, the Courts have thus broadened the entire spectrum pertaining to arrest and detention with several guidelines which are to be adhered to by the police.

POLITICAL INTERFERENCE IN POLICE ACTION

In our country, the police machinery has not been insulated from political interference, in spite of various directions given by the Supreme Court from time to time[8] due to the apathy of the political rulers to

---

[8] Prakash Singh and Others v. Union of India and Others, (2006) 8 S.C.C. 1: (2006) 3 S.C.C. (Cri) 417.

allow the police to act independently. Since the police are bound to work under political executives and, the normal chain of command in the police force is disrupted very often at the instance of the political masters, police power is misused by the political parties to oppress and humiliate the people or class of people who may be considered as threats to the ruling party. Moreover, the power of arrest is considered as the major source of corruption in the police force of the country and the police officers who would like to indulge in corruption will keep their political bosses in good humour. As a result, the police have failed to use the discretion of arrest fairly and impartially, irrespective of status, position, and connection of the person, while investigating an offence or taking preventive action. It is pertinent to point out that the Supreme Court[9] had to intervene and evolve a new juristic principle of *"continuous mandamus"* to monitor the investigation of criminal cases. This monitoring of investigation by the High Court and the Supreme Court is not for giving any specific direction of arresting a particular person or otherwise, but to ensure that the investigating agency is insulated from political interference for investigating fairly and impartially.

JUDICIAL MANDATE FOR ARREST

An analysis of the law with regard to arrest unerringly points out that no person can be arrested in a routine manner merely on the suspicion of complicity in the cognizable offence. An arrest should be made only after arriving at a reasonable satisfaction, after undertaking an investigation as to the genuineness and *bona fides* of a complaint or information received by the police and a reasonable belief, both as to the person's complicity and as to the need of effecting arrest, to carry out further investigation and to ensure a fair trial. By quoting the third report of the National Police Commission, the Supreme Court has observed in *Joginder Kumar*[10] that a large number of arrests are unnecessary or unjustified. The clear dictum of the Court is that arrest can never be made in a mechanical manner on the mere allegation of commission

---

[9] Union of India v. Sushil Kumar Modi, (1999) S.C.C. (Cri) 84.

[10] Joginder Kumar v. State of U.P., A.I.R. 1994 S.C. 1349: (1994) 4 S.C.C. 260.

of a cognizable offence against a person, as the arrest and detention of a person in police lock-up will invariably cause incalculable harm to the reputation and self-esteem of a person. It is also pointed out that arrest can be avoided except in heinous offences, if a police officer issues notice to a person to attend the police station and not to leave the station without permission. In *Joginder Kumar*, the Supreme Court issued the following directions for enforcement of the fundamental right of a person guaranteed under Articles 21 and 22(1) of the Constitution[11]:

(i) An arrested person being held in custody is entitled ... to have one friend, relative or other person, who is known to him or likely to take an interest in his welfare, told as far as practicable that he has been arrested and the place of his detention.

(ii) The police officer shall inform the arrested person of his above right when the arrested person is brought to the police station.

(iii) An entry shall be required to be made in the diary as to who was informed of the arrest.

The above directions of the Supreme Court were subsequently amplified and elaborated in *D.K. Basu v. State of West Bengal*[12] to check arbitrary and indiscriminate arrest by police and to protect the fundamental right of the citizens guaranteed under the Constitution of India. The liberty of a person cannot be curtailed without following the procedure established by law which is just, fair and reasonable. Transparency of action and accountability are two important safeguards that the judiciary always insists upon. The gist of the guidelines given by the Supreme Court in *D. K. Basu* is[13]:

(i) The police personnel carrying out arrest and handling interrogation of the arrested person must bear accurate, visible and clear identification and name tags with designations. The particulars of all such police personnel ... must be recorded in a register.

(ii) That the police officer carrying out the arrest shall prepare a memo of arrest at the time of arrest and such memo shall be attested by at least one witness, who may either be a member of the family of

---

[11] *Id.* at 268, para. 21.

[12] D.K. Basu v. State of West Bengal, (1997) 1 S.C.C. 416: A.I.R. 1997 S.C. 610.

[13] *Id.* at 435–36, para. 35.

the arrestee or a respectable person of the locality where the arrest is made. It shall also be countersigned by the arrestee and shall contain the time and date of arrest.

(iii) A person who has been arrested or detained and is being held in custody in a police station or interrogation centre or other lock-up, shall be entitled to have one friend or relative or other person known to him or having interest in his welfare being informed, as soon as practicable, that he has been arrested and is being detained at the particular place, unless the attesting witness of the memo of arrest is himself such a friend or a relative of the arrestee.

(iv) The time and place of arrest and venue of custody of an arrestee must be notified by the police where the next friend or relative of the arrestee lives outside the district or town through the Legal Aid Organisation in the District and the police station of the area concerned telegraphically within a period of 8 to 12 hours after the arrest.

(v) The person arrested must be made aware of his right to have someone informed of his arrest and detention as soon as he is put under arrest or detention.

(vi) An entry must be made in the diary at the place of detention regarding the arrest of the person which shall also disclose the name of the next friend of the person who has been informed of the arrest and the names and particulars of the police officials in whose custody the arrestee is.

(vii) The arrestee should, where he so requests, be also examined at the time of his arrest and major and minor injuries, if any present on his/her body, must be recorded at that time. The "Inspection Memo" must be signed both by the arrestee and the police officer effecting the arrest and its copy provided to the arrestee.

(viii) The arrestee should be subjected to medical examination by trained doctor every 48 hours during his detention...

(ix) Copies of all the documents including the memo of arrest, referred to above, should be sent to the illaqa Magistrate for his record

(x) The arrestee may be permitted to meet his lawyer during inter-rogation, though not throughout the interrogation.

(xi) A police control room should be provided at all district and state headquarters, where information regarding the arrest and the place of custody of the arrestee shall be communicated by the offi-cer causing the arrest, within 12 hours of effecting the arrest and at the police control room it should be displayed on a conspicuous notice board.

The Court added that the police officer who will fail to comply with the above requirements of arrest will not only be liable for departmental action, but also for contempt of court in a proceeding to be instituted in the concerned High Court having territorial jurisdiction over the matter.

JUDICIAL INTERVENTIONS IN ABUSE OF POWERS OF ARREST

The Code of Criminal Procedure was amended by incorporating the provisions of Sections 41A–41D for implementation of the directions given by the Supreme Court in *D. K. Basu case*. The right of an arrested person to consult an advocate during interrogation, the establishment of the police control room for displaying the particulars of the arrested persons in the notice board kept outside the control room, the preparation of memo of arrest, displaying particulars of the identity of the police officer making the arrest and providing information to the arrested person about his right to inform his friend or relative about the arrest have been given statutory force by the legislature. To check arbitrary and indiscriminate arrest of a person, the statutory provision is also made for issuing notice calling upon the suspect to appear before the police officer in connection with the investigation of offence. However, the discussion of the subsequent case-laws will point out that the police power is still being misused by making arrest in a routine manner merely on the basis of allegations in the First Information Report.

The Arrest of Husband, Relatives for Dowry

The abuse of the power of arrest was brought to the notice of the Supreme Court in *Arnesh Kumar v. State of Bihar*[14] in connection with Section 498A of IPC, 1860.[15] By quoting the statistics published in National Crime Records Bureau for the year 2012, the Supreme Court observed that 197,762 persons were arrested for the offence

---

[14] Arnesh Kumar v. State of Bihar, (2014) 8 S.C.C. 273.
[15] Cruelty by Husband or relatives of the husband.

under Section 498A, IPC out of which 47,951 persons were women, that is, mother, sister and sister-in-law of the husband of the victim. The rate of filing a charge sheet in all these cases is 93.6 per cent, while the conviction rate is only 15 per cent. Thereby, about 85 per cent of the charge-sheeted accused including women were ultimately acquitted of the charge. The Supreme Court has endeavoured to ensure that the arrests are not done unnecessarily by police officers because it is lawful to arrest a person involved in a non-bailable and cognizable offence. It clarified that 'the existence of the power to arrest is one thing, the justification for the exercise of it is quite another'.[16] In order to check the arrest of a person in a routine manner on mere allegations of involvement in the cognizable and non-bailable offence, the direction was issued to the police not to arrest a person without reasonable satisfaction as to the genuineness of the allegations made against the said person. It is pertinent to point out the following directions given by the Supreme Court in *Arnesh Kumar*[17]:

(i) The police officers must satisfy themselves about the necessity for arrest under parameters flowing from Section 41 of CrPC' without arresting a person involved in the offence under section 498A of IPC in a routine manner.

(ii) 'All police officers should be provided with a checklist containing specified provisions of Section 41(1)(b)(ii) of CrPC' so that the police officer may duly fill up the checklist and furnish reasons and materials for necessitating arrest and forward the same to the Magistrate at the time of production of the arrested accused before the Magistrate.

(iii) The Magistrate shall consider the report furnished by the police for arresting the accused and record his satisfaction for authorising further detention of the accused person in custody.

(iv) The police officer will also forward to the Magistrate a report about his decision not to arrest an accused involved in the offence under Section 498A of IPC within 2 weeks from the date of institution of the case.

---

[16] Arnesh Kumar, *supra* note 14, at 277, para. 6.

[17] *Id.* at 282, para. 11.

(v) The police officer should issue one notice for the appearance of the accused in terms of Section 41A of CrPC 'within 2 weeks from the date of institution of the case, which may be extended by the Superintendent of Police ... for reasons to be recorded in writing'.

(vi) All police officers would be liable for departmental action for failure to comply with the above directions, apart from being liable for contempt of court before the concerned High Court within whose jurisdiction the criminal case was started.

In another case, the wife initiated a criminal case against the husband, parents-in-law and brothers-in-law alleging harassment and demand of dowry. The accused husband unsuccessfully moved the High Court for quashing of the criminal proceeding by invoking Section 482 CrPC 1973. The Supreme Court got the opportunity to hear both the husband and the wife when the accused husband challenged the judgment of the High Court by way of the Special Leave Petition.[18] The Supreme Court lamented how the provisions of 498A of IPC are being misused by the women for whose protection the provisions were enacted by the Legislature. The two-Judge Bench of the Supreme Court gave directions for the constitution of the Family Welfare Committee by the District Legal Services Authority and evolved the principle for settlement of the dispute by bringing into the picture the members of civil society. The directions of the Supreme Court in *Rajesh Sharma*[19] were partly affirmed, partly modified, and partly reversed by three-Judge Bench in *Social Action Forum for Manav Adhikar v. Union of India*,[20] wherein it was observed that the directions for constitution of Family Welfare Committees by the District Legal Services Authority and prescription of the duties of the committees are beyond the purview of the Code. Similarly, the directions of the Bench with regard to bail for the offence under Section 498A of IPC and the directions for settlement of the dispute in connection with

---

[18] Rajesh Sharma v. State of U.P., (2019) 1 S.C.C. (Cri) 301: (2018) 10 S.C.C. 472.

[19] *Id.*

[20] Social Action Forum for Manav Adhikar v. Union of India, (2019) 1 S.C.C. (Cri) 276: (2018) 10 S.C.C. 443.

offences under Section 498A of IPC by the involvement of the civil society are not found to be the correct expression of law. According to the Bench, the Supreme Court can give guidelines or directions to check abuse of power of arrest by the police within the framework of the Code and the power of superintendence of the authorities in the hierarchical system of investigating agency as already done by the Supreme Court in *Joginder Kumar* and *D.K. Basu*. Accordingly, the Court modified the directions in the following manner:

1. The directions in connection with the constitution of the Family Welfare Committee by the District Legal Services Authorities and the various duties to be performed by this committee were not found to be in accordance with the statutory framework of the Code of Criminal Procedure.
2. The directions with regard to the training of the investigating officers are justified so far as training of the police officers investigating offences under Section 498A of IPC with regard to the principles of arrest laid down by the Supreme Court is concerned.
3. If any settlement is arrived at in connection with offence under Section 498A of IPC, the parties can approach the High Court for quashing of the criminal proceeding by invoking Section 482 CrPC.
4. The directions with regard to the imposition of conditions for bail are justified.
5. The accused person may be granted exemption from personal appearance or permission for appearance through video conference based on the filing of an application under Section 205 of Cr.P.C. or Section 317 of Cr.P.C. depending upon the stage of the hearing.

Arrest Under SC and ST Act

The fact of abuse of the power of arrest by the police in connection with offences under the Scheduled Castes and Scheduled Tribes (Prevention of Atrocities) Act, 1989 (SC and ST Act) again came to the notice of the Supreme Court in *Subhash Kashinath Mahajan v. State of Maharashtra*,[21] when the Director of Technical Education, Maharashtra was threatened

---

[21] Subhash Kashinath Mahajan v. State of Maharashtra, (2018) 6 S.C.C. 454.

to be arrested in a mechanical manner on the basis of mere allegations against him under the provisions of the SC and ST Act, even though he only discharged his official duty as a public servant. The Supreme Court directed that no person involved in the offence under the SC and ST Act can be arrested if the said person happens to be a public servant, 'without written permission of the appointing authority' and in case of any other person, not being a public servant, 'without written permission of the Superintendent of Police of the district. Such permission must be granted for recorded reasons which must be served on the person to be arrested and forwarded to the concerned court.'[22] The further detention of such arrested person by the Court can be granted if the recorded reasons are found to be valid by the Court. Even the Supreme Court directed the police to conduct a preliminary enquiry in such cases before registration of FIR in order to avoid frivolous or motivated use of the legislation. Though the grant of anticipatory bail to the accused person involved in offences under the SC & ST Act is prohibited under Section 18 of the said Act, the Supreme Court held that exclusion of the provisions for grant of anticipatory bail in connection with an offence under the SC & ST Act will not be applicable when no prima facie case is made out or the case is patently false or malafide. Thus, limiting the exclusion of anticipatory bail in such cases is essential, according to the Supreme Court, for the protection of the fundamental right of life and liberty under Article 21 of the Constitution.

The Arrest of Judicial Officer

The fact of the arrest of a judicial officer in order to humiliate or take revenge by the police was brought to the notice of the Supreme Court by the Delhi Judicial Services Association. The Supreme Court issued guidelines to be followed by the police before arresting a judicial officer in connection with a criminal case for maintenance of the independence of the judiciary in *Delhi Judicial Services Association v. the State of Gujarat*[23]:

---

[22] *Id.* at 512, para. 77.

[23] Delhi Judicial Services Association v. State of Gujarat, (1991) 4 S.C.C. 406, at 465–66, para. 55.

(i) If a judicial officer is to be arrested for some offence, it should be done under intimation to the District Judge or the High Court as the case may be;

(ii) If the facts and circumstances necessitate immediate arrest of a judicial officer of the subordinate judiciary, a technical or formal arrest may be effected.

(iii) The fact of such arrest should be immediately communicated to the District and Sessions Judge of the concerned District and the Chief Justice of the High Court.

(iv) The judicial officer so arrested shall not be taken to the police station without prior order or directions of the District and Sessions Judge of the concerned district, if available;

(v) Immediate facilities shall be provided to the Judicial officer for communication with his family member, legal advisor and judicial officers, including the District and Sessions Judge;

(vi) No statement of a judicial officer who is under arrest be recorded nor any Panchnama be drawn up nor any medical tests be conducted except in the presence of the legal advisor of the judicial officer concerned or another judicial officer of equal or higher rank, if available;

(vii) There should be no handcuffing of a judicial officer. If however, violent resistance to arrest is offered or there is imminent need to effect physical arrest in order to avert danger to life and limb, the person resisting arrest may be overpowered and handcuffed.

The pre-condition of such physical arrest and handcuffing is that the said fact must be reported to the District and Sessions Judge and to the Chief Justice of the High Court immediately.

Arrest of Women

In *State of Maharashtra v. Christian Community Welfare Council of India*[24] 15, the Supreme Court dealt with an appeal against the judgement of Nagpur Bench of Bombay High Court, which convicted and sentenced ten police officers for offences under Sections 333, 342, 355, 34 IPC, 1860. The backdrop of conviction and sentence of the police officers

---

[24] State of Maharashtra v. Christian Community Welfare Council of India, (2003) 8 S.C.C. 546.

was the custodial death of a person whose wife was also locked up and molested by the police when she came to the police station to enquire about her husband. In this case, the direction given by the Bombay High Court with regard to the arrest of a female accused in presence of lady constable and prohibition of such arrest after sunset and before sunrise was modified by the Supreme Court in the following manner[25]:

> We think the object will be served if a direction is issued to the arresting authority that while arresting a female person, all efforts should be made to keep a lady constable present, but in the circumstances where the attesting officers are reasonably satisfied that such presence of a lady constable is not available or possible and/or the delay in arresting caused by securing the presence of a lady constable would impede the course of the investigation, such arresting officer for reasons to be recorded either before the arrest or immediately after the arrest be permitted to arrest a female person for lawful reasons at any time of the day or night depending on the circumstances of the case even without the presence of a lady constable.

Unwarranted Arrest and Compensation

In *Rini Johar v. State of Madhya Pradesh*,[26] one lady doctor and a septuagenarian lady advocate were arrested by the police of Cyber Cell, Bhopal on the allegations of committing fraud under Sections 420 and 34 IPC, 1860 and Section 66B, Information Technology Act, 2000. Both the lady accused persons were taken from Pune to Bhopal in an unreserved railway compartment and were forced to pay ₹500,000 to the DSP of Cyber Cell of Bhopal before their release from custody after 17 days of detention. When both the ladies approached the Supreme Court for compensation on the ground of unauthorised arrest by the police in violation of the fundamental right guaranteed under Article 21 of the Constitution and without following the procedure laid down in Section 41A of Cr.P.C., the Supreme Court directed the State to

---

[25] *Id.* at 549, para. 9.
[26] Rini Johar v. State of Madhya Pradesh, (2017) 1 S.C.C. (Cri) 364: (2016) 11 S.C.C. 703.

pay compensation of ₹500,000 to each of the accused persons within 3 months. In this case, the Apex Court reiterated that the investigating officer in no circumstances can flout the law laid down in Sections 41 and 41A of CrPC while investigating an offence.

A scientist of the Indian Space Research Organisation (ISRO) was arrested by a DIG who headed the Special Investigation Team investigating a criminal case started on the basis of confession of a Maldivian national who was arrested under Section 14 of the Foreigners Act, 1946. Subsequently, the State of Kerala with the consent of the Central Government handed over the investigation of this case to the Central Bureau of Investigation (CBI). The CBI ultimately submitted the final report and observed that the ISRO scientists, including Narayanan, were arrested indiscriminately without collecting any evidence against them by the Special Investigation Team. The scientist brought a writ petition before the Supreme Court which directed the State of Kerala to pay ₹5 million to the scientist as compensation for his unwanted arrest and humiliation and violation of his fundamental right guaranteed under Article 21 of the Constitution.[27]

Unauthorized Restraint in Arrest

The law does not permit the use of unnecessary restraint of a person after his arrest other than what is necessary to prevent his escape from custody. Many a time, handcuff is used after arrest on extraneous consideration like punishment by humiliation or for convenience of the escort party. The Supreme Court[28] has laid down that handcuffs can only be used by the escorting police party if the prisoner is dangerous and desperate or if the prisoner is likely to break out of the custody or play the vanishing trick. The obligation on the part of the escorting police party is to record reasons for handcuffing the

---

[27] S. Nambi Narayanan v. Siby Mathews, (2019) 1 S.C.C. (Cri) 682: (2018) 10 S.C.C. 804.

[28] Sunil Batra v. Delhi Administration, A.I.R. 1978 S.C. 1675: (1979) S.C.C. (Cri) 155: Prem Shankar Shukla v. Delhi Administration, A.I.R. 1980 S.C. 1535: (1980) S.C.C. (Cri) 815.

undertrial prisoner in extreme cases and intimate the concerned court, so that the court may consider the circumstances and issue necessary direction with regard to the use of handcuff of that particular prisoner to the escort party.

An eminent journalist wrote a letter to one of the judges of the Supreme Court disclosing the fact that seven undertrial prisoners were handcuffed and tied with a long rope to restrict their movement in Guwahati Medical College and Hospital. The Supreme Court treated the letter as an application under Article 32 of the Constitution of India and issued notice to the State of Assam. Not satisfied with the explanation, the Supreme Court[29] issued exhaustive guidelines regarding the use of handcuff after consideration of the views expressed by all the stakeholders[30]:

(i) As a rule, handcuffs or other fetters shall not be forced on undertrial prisoners or convicted persons while lodged in a jail anywhere in the country or while transporting or in transit from one jail to another or from jail to court and back.

(ii) Where the police or the jail authorities have well-grounded basis for drawing a strong inference that a particular prisoner is likely to jump from custody or break out of the custody, then the said prisoner can be produced before the concerned Magistrate and a prayer for permission to handcuff the prisoner may be made...

(iii) In all the cases where a person arrested by the police is produced before the Magistrate and remand- judicial or non- judicial- is given ..., the person concerned shall not be handcuffed unless special orders in that respect are obtained from the Magistrate at the time of grant of the remand.

(iv) When the police arrests a person in execution of a warrant of arrest obtained from a Magistrate, the person so arrested shall not be handcuffed unless the police has also obtained orders from the Magistrate for the handcuffing of the person to be so arrested.

(v) Where a person is arrested by the police without warrant, the police officer concerned may, if he is satisfied, on the basis of the

---

[29] Citizens for Democracy through its President v. State of Assam, (1995) 3 S.C.C. 743.

[30] *Id.* at 751, paras. 16–20.

guidelines ... that it is necessary to handcuff such person, he may do so till the time he is taken to the police station and thereafter his production before the Magistrate. Further use of fetters thereafter can only be done under the orders of the Magistrate....

Death in Course of Arrest and Detention

Many a time, persons are killed by fake police encounters which are done under the colour of use of force for arresting criminals involved in grave offences. The People's Union for Civil Liberty (PUCL) brought to the notice of Bombay High Court how the police misused the power of arrest by causing the death of 135 persons in about 99 encounters in Maharashtra between 1995 and 1997. The PUCL thereafter moved the apex court which issued the following guidelines to check illegal detention and death by the encounter[31]:

1. Whenever there is any intelligence or tipoff regarding the activities or movements of miscreants involved in grave offences to the police, they shall reduce it to writing without disclosing the details of the suspect and his location.

2. If any encounter takes place with the police in pursuant to such tip-off, and if any firearm is used by the police party resulting in the death of any person, an FIR to that effect must be registered and the same shall be forwarded to the Magistrate without any delay.

3. Every incident or encounter must result in an independent investigation by the Criminal Investigation Department or Police Team of another police station under the supervision of a senior police officer The investigation must seek (a) to identify the victim,... (b) to recover and preserve evidentiary material, including blood-stained earth, hair, fibres, threads, etc., (c) to identify the witnesses and obtain their statements connected with death, (d) to determine the cause, manner and location of death, time of death, (e) to ensure sending of fingerprints of the deceased for chemical

---

[31] People's Union for Civil Liberties v. State of Maharashtra, (2014) 10 S.C.C. 635, at 655, para. 31.

analysis, (f) to conduct post mortem examination of the deceased along with videography of the entire post mortem examination, (g) and to collect evidence about the weapons used in causing death and establish the cause of death.

4. A Magisterial enquiry under Section 176 CrPC must be held as it is done in case of death in police custody or death in police firing.

5. Medical aid must be provided to the injured criminal/victim and his statement must be recorded by the Magistrate or the medical officer with a certificate of fitness from the doctor.

6. The next of kin of the person killed in the encounter must be informed at the earliest opportunity.

7. After completion of the investigation, the report must be submitted before the competent court so that trial may be conducted expeditiously.

8. A half-yearly statement about such death in police encounters must be submitted before the National Human Rights Commission by the Director-General of Police.

9. The police officer causing death must surrender his weapon for forensic and ballistic analysis.

10. The disciplinary action may promptly be initiated against the police officer responsible for causing death if the killing of the person amounts to an offence under the penal law.

11. The compensation must be granted to the dependents of the person who was killed in a police encounter in terms of the provisions of Section 357A CrPC.

CONCLUSION

Over the years, an entire jurisprudence with regard to the scope of powers of arrest and detention has been evolved by the Courts. These guidelines serve as a threshold for the exercise of powers by the police and any transgressions are likely to be regarded as abuse, calling for immediate action. The power of arrest is mainly exercised by the police officers working at the level of the police station. Yet, these officers are not aware of the judicial guidelines given from time to time. No mechanism is evolved in the police administration for communication of directions of the Supreme Court with regard to preconditions of arrest, the necessity for use of restraint after arrest, principles of use of handcuff, the procedure for investigation in case of death in police encounter, etc. The various State Police Academies and the National Police Academy can play a pivotal role in the collection, compilation, and communication of these guidelines after translating the same in the regional languages, so that the police officers working at the ground level may understand and comprehend them for maintaining law and order in society. Even imparting training through online classes by the Police Training Academies may go a long way in ensuring the rule of law in the exercise of the power of arrest.

Chapter 17

Arrest and Detention
A Proposal for Reforms

Namrta Rastogi and Anurag Deep*

PERSPECTIVE

The state is held to be an organization of compulsions.[1] At the same time the state, as Dugout thinks, 'is a great public service company'.[2] It has absolute liability for causing injuries to the public or individual. Besides liability, they have the right to defend the 'life, liberty and property' of their nationals from any threat or attack, in any form. The International Covenant on Civil and Political Rights (ICCPR) recognizes the right of security of a person. Article 9(1) runs as:

> Everyone has the right to liberty and security of person. *No one shall be subjected to arbitrary arrest or detention.* No one shall be deprived of his liberty except on such grounds and in accordance with such procedure as are established by law. [Emphasis supplied]

---

* The author acknowledges the timely assistance of Ms Nivedita Chaudhary, chief student editor, ILILR and PhD-JRF research scholar at ILI.

[1] ROSCOE POUND, AN INTRODUCTION TO THE PHILOSOPHY OF LAW 160 (Yale University Press, 3rd Indian Reprint 2003).

[2] *Id.* at 98.

In the case of *William Eduardo Delgado Paez v. Colombia*,[3] it was made clear that States cannot ignore a known threat to the life of a person in its jurisdiction just because ICCPR mandates a human right against arbitrary arrest. 'States parties are under an obligation to take reasonable and appropriate measures to protect them'. Any other interpretation of Article 9 of ICCPR clipping the hands of State against known threats 'would render ineffective the guarantees of the Covenant'.[4] In *Kilic v. Turkey*,[5] a case decided by the European Court of Human Rights, it was observed that:[6]

> ...Article 2 § 1 [of the European Convention for the Protection of Human Rights and Fundamental Freedoms] enjoins the State to take appropriate steps by putting in place effective criminal law provisions to deter the commission of offences against the person, backed up by law-enforcement machinery for the prevention, suppression, and punishment of breaches of such provisions.

The aforementioned two cases answer the issue in no uncertain terms that the duty to protect its citizens does run from several international legal treaties on human rights. These treaties allow an arrest, if essential, but balance the same with the human rights of a suspect.

BALANCING POWER WITH DUTIES: FIR MANDATORY, ARREST LAST RESORT

The judiciary, especially the Supreme Court has issued various mandatory guidelines to maintain the balance between liberty and security. *Arnesh Kumar v. the State of Bihar*[7] is the latest significant development to maintain this balance in the area of FIR and arrest. Before *Arnesh Kumar* the balancing task was done in *Nandini Satpathy v. P.L. Dani*,[8]

---

[3] Case No. 195/1985, Views adopted on 12 July 1990, www.ohchr.org/Documents/Publications/DigestJurisprudenceen.pdf (last visited 5 March 2021).

[4] *Id.*

[5] ECHR, March 28, 2000 (para. 62).

[6] *Id.*

[7] (2014) 8 S.C.C. 273.

[8] (1978) 2 S.C.C. 424.

Sheela Barse v. the *State of Maharashtra,*[9] *Joginder Kumar v. the State of U.P.,*[10] and *D.K. Basu v. State of West Bengal,*[11] etc. In the case of *Amish Devgan v. Union of India,*[12] though no specific directions were issued, the Supreme Court reiterated the controlling principle that 'there has to be proper proportionality or balance between the importance of achieving the proper measure and social importance of preventing the limitation on the constitutional right'. This proportionality n balancing is the very core of a democratic state.

Therefore, a democratic state has the power as well as the duty to ensure that the country is run by the Rule of Law for which various instruments like prevention, prosecution, punishment, probation, parole, *etc.* are used. The primary requisite to apply these instruments is the registration of a first information report (FIR). If a piece of information disclosing cognizable offence is conveyed to the police officer, he is duty-bound to register a complaint (often called first information report or FIR) against the suspect under Section 154 of CrPC 1973. This is the law laid down in the case of *Lalita Kumari.*[13] However, he is not duty-bound to take that suspect into custody. An accused person is innocent so far as the guilt is concerned and s/he is a suspect so far as peace and order are concerned. Despite being a suspect once s/he is not a threat to the victim or legal process or society the person ought not to be taken into custody. The idea of liberty, freedom and dignity is not just democratic essentiality, it is a natural right and a human right.[14] In India, it has constitutional recognition in the Preamble as well as under Articles 19, 20, 21, and 22. These rights have guaranteed enforcement by the constitutional courts (the Supreme Court and the high court) which provide them with the status of fundamental rights, the strongest right codified in India. In the time-honoured *dictum* of

---

[9] A.I.R. 1983 S.C. 378.

[10] A.I.R. 1994 S.C. 1349.

[11] (1997) 1 S.C.C. 416.

[12] (2021) 1 S.C.C. 1.

[13] Lalita Kumari v. Govt. of UP, (2014) 2 S.C.C. 1. It was a unanimous opinion of the Constitution Bench.

[14] Manoj Kr. Sinha & Anurag Deep, Bail: Law and Practice in India 64 (Indian Law Institute 2019).

Maneka Gandhi v. Union of India,[15] the constitution bench reminded us that the 'procedural safeguards are the indispensable essence of liberty. The history of personal liberty is largely the history of procedural safeguards'. In the case of *Gopalanachari v. the State of Kerala*,[16] V.R. Krishna Iyer, J. leading from the full bench has rightly pointed out that Articles 21, 14 and 19 cannot 'remain symbolic and scriptural'. Instead, it is 'a shield against unjust deprivation. Law is not a mascot but a defender of the faith. Surely, if law behaves lawlessly, social justice becomes a judicial hoax'. This is the reason the police ought to be very careful before arresting a person because such custody by the police is the beginning of a long-term deprivation of liberty. In the case of *Siddharam Satlingappa Mhetre v. the State of Maharashtra*,[17] the Supreme Court also observed as under:

> The arrest should be the last option and should be restricted to those exceptional cases where arresting the accused is imperative in the facts and circumstances of that case.... Irrational and Indiscriminate arrests are gross violations of human rights.

Arnesh Kumar is a reflection of many such cases referred to above. However, the power of arrest witnesses a brazen misuse of the state authority and every year lakhs of people are arrested wrongfully. In 2001 the Law Commission of India has expressed with great disappointment (and which is true today also) which may be summarized as under[18]:

1. Code of Criminal Procedure and the Constitution contains safeguards against arbitrary arrest,
2. routine arrest is made even in civil disputes, bailable cases, non-cognizable cases,

---

[15] A.I.R. 1978 S.C. 597. It was a constitution bench.

[16] A.I.R. 1981 S.C. 674.

[17] (2011) 1 S.C.C. 694.

[18] Law Commission of India, *177th Report on Law Relating to Arrest, 2001* 188 (December 2001), https://lawcommissionofindia.nic.in/reports/177rptp2.pdf (last visited 20 February, 2021).

3. the power of arrest has become a source of extorting money,
4. in certain cases, a wrongful arrest is made 'at the instance of an enemy of the person arrested',
5. the remedy, though available under various administrative laws, the Police Act, 1861, *etc* remained pious precepts in the rule book never to be applied because the 'inhouse mechanism' is not working at all.

This gross abuse of police power owes its origin to excessive political or executive control, personal greed, a show of authority, media pressure as well as judicial neglect at the level of subordinate courts. The law to address misuse of the power of arrest, be it in the form of primary legislation, or subordinate legislation or judicial legislation, are in its place to address wrongful arrest.

WRONGFUL ARREST AND REMEDIES UNDER THE POLICE ACT, 1861

The wrongful arrest may be intentional, the result of negligent discharges of duty, or maybe a judgement error. If it is a judgement error the police must be protected and the protection against criminal activity is available under Section 76 as well as 79 of the Indian Penal Code (IPC) as well as under administrative law. If a wrongful arrest is made intentionally to harass or extort money or for any other purposes, IPC provisions can be restored. If misuse of authority is due to negligent discharge of duty, Sections 7 and 29 of the Police Act, 1861 can be used. The Law Commission of India in its 177th report rightly refers to Section 7 of the Police Act, 1861 which prescribes two remedies,[19] *viz* (a) administrative remedy like dismissal, suspension or reduction in rank 'of any police officer of the subordinate ranks whom they (the higher officials) shall think remiss or negligent in the discharge of his duties or unfit for the same' (b) a penal remedy like

> imposition of fine not exceeding one month's pay, confinement to quarters for a term not exceeding 15 days in case of a police officer of the subordinate rank performing the duties carelessly or negligently or

---

[19] *Id.* at 29.

who by any act of his own shall render himself unfit for the discharge thereof (discharge of his duty)....

Under Section 23 of the Police Act, 1861 one of the duties of police is to arrest a suspect. But the duty is not a general one. A police officer is required to arrest a suspect if *sufficient ground exists*.[20] Registration of FIR or a complaint by a person itself does not make a sufficient ground. Section 29 prescribes that

> every police-officer who shall be guilty of any violation of duty or wilful breach or neglect of any rule or regulation or lawful order made by competent authority ... shall be liable, on conviction before a Magistrate, to a penalty not exceeding three months' pay, or to imprisonment with or without hard labour, for a period not exceeding three months, or to both.[21]

Section 29 can also be used if FIR is not registered. As submitted earlier unlike FIR, an arrest is not mandatory. It is judicially recognised in many cases like *Siddharam Satlingappa Mhetre*[22] and *Joginder Kumar*[23] as referred earlier. However, the problem of wrongful arrest remained undeterred.

ARNESH KUMAR V. THE STATE OF BIHAR

One of the decisions with great precedential value on the exercise of the power of arrest and judicial discretion on custody is *Arnesh Kumar v. the State of Bihar*.[24] The Supreme Court in this case issued various mandatory directions regarding the arrest. These directions are revolutionary because it has made the police officer as well as the magistrate more accountable for arrest. This part is further divided into five sub-heads and proposes that the directions should be incorporated under CrPC or may be incorporated under a Model Arrest Manual, 2021.

---

[20] The Police Act, 1861, Section 23—Duties of police officers.
[21] The Police Act, 1861, Section 29—Penalties for neglect of duty, etc.
[22] Siddharam Satlingappa Mhetre, *supra* note 17.
[23] Joginder Kumar, *supra* note 10.
[24] Arnesh Kumar, *supra* note 7.

Background

A factual matrix may help to understand the directions. It is, therefore, desirable to refer to the facts of *Arnesh Kumar* in brief. There was a dispute between husband and wife who were married in 2007. It was alleged that the mother-in-law and father-in-law demanded eight lakh rupees, a four-wheeler, TV, AC, *etc.* It was alleged that the husband supported the demands. The case was registered under Section 498A of IPC (cruelty to wife) and Section 4 of the Dowry Prohibition Act, 1961 (Penalty for demanding dowry). As these two offences are cognizable and non-bailable, the husband was apprehending arrest. He denied these allegations but failed to secure anticipatory bail from the sessions court and the high court. He knocked on the doors of the Supreme Court. It was a special leave petition (SLP) where the two courts below had concurrent findings. Usually, the apex court does not interfere in such cases. However, the Supreme Court admitted the petition as it involved a competing claim of the fundamental right to liberty and compelling interest of the State in cases of crime against women.

Chandramauli K. Prasad, J. in *Arnesh Kumar* took judicial notice of misuse of dowry laws. He expressed great concern about Section 498A of IPC as under:

> [This section is used as a] weapon rather than shield by disgruntled wives. The simplest way to harass is to get the husband and his relatives arrested under this provision. In quite a number of cases, bed-ridden grand-fathers and grand-mothers of the husbands, their sisters living abroad for decades are arrested.

He supported the judicial presumption of misuse of dowry laws with the help of a large number of arrested persons in these cases as per records of the 'Crime in India 2012 Statistics' published by the National Crime Records Bureau (NCRB). One-fourth of the arrestees includes the mother and sisters of the husband. He also referred to the conviction rate which under Section 498A was only 15 per cent, (lowest across all heads) while charge-sheet was filed in 93.6 per cent cases. He also referred to the reports of the Law Commission of India, the Police

Commission, various judicial directions and concluded that something else needs to be done.

Directions

The directions issued by the division bench in the *Arnesh Kumar v. the State of Bihar*, case are reproduced as under for ready reference:

11.1. All the State Governments to instruct its police officers not to automatically arrest when a case under section 498-A IPC is registered but to satisfy themselves about the necessity for arrest under the parameters laid down above flowing from section 41 CrPC;

11.2. All police officers be provided with a checklist containing specified sub-clauses under section 41(1)(b)(ii);

11.3. The police officer shall forward the checklist duly filled and furnish the reasons and materials which necessitated the arrest, while forwarding/producing the accused before the Magistrate for further detention;

11.4. The Magistrate while authorising detention of the accused shall peruse the report furnished by the police officer in terms aforesaid and only after recording its satisfaction, the Magistrate will authorise detention;

11.5. The decision not to arrest an accused, be forwarded to the Magistrate within two weeks from the date of the institution of the case with a copy to the Magistrate which may be extended by the Superintendent of Police of the district for the reasons to be recorded in writing;

11.6. Notice of appearance in terms of section 41-A CrPC be served on the accused within two weeks from the date of institution of the case, which may be extended by the Superintendent of Police of the district for the reasons to be recorded in writing;

11.7. Failure to comply with the directions aforesaid shall apart from rendering the police officers concerned liable for departmental action, they shall also be liable to be punished for contempt of court to be instituted before the High Court having territorial jurisdiction.

11.8. Authorising detention without recording reasons as aforesaid by the Judicial Magistrate concerned shall be liable for departmental action by the appropriate High Court.

These directions aforesaid shall not only apply to the cases under section 498-A of the IPC or section 4 of the Dowry Prohibition Act, the case in hand, but also such cases where offence is punishable with imprisonment for a term which may be less than seven years or which may extend to seven years; whether with or without fine.

The last direction (not numbered) generalises the protective cover to all cases having maximum punishment as 7 years imprisonment. Out of these eight directions, the first, second and third directions are regarding the Police. The fourth direction is regarding judicial magistrates. The fifth and sixth direction is regarding 'not arresting a suspect'. The consequence of non-observance of these directions is mentioned in the seventh point (against the Police) and the eighth point (against the judicial officer). The Ninth direction extends the judicial rule to all cases where the prescribed punishment is up to 7 years. These directions are like judicial legislation which makes informal amendments under CrPC. The state was directed to give a checklist to the police to ensure the arrest is necessary. They are required to record reasons for arrest or non-arrest. The magistrates are required to examine the checklist and record reasons for remands. If the police or the magistrates fail to follow the directions, the consequence is departmental action as well as contempt of court. *Arnesh Kumar* has granted judicial recognition to the action under the Police Act, 1961. The consequence of contempt is something new but is natural because all directions of the court are the law of the land which is required to be followed. The judiciary is empowered to issue such directions under Article 142 of the Constitution of India if it is a matter of fundamental right, it is essential, the Parliament and the executive failed to address the problem on many occasions. This pronouncement has empowered the common person to approach the judiciary for the implementation of pre-arrest jurisprudence developed in many cases and culminated into *Arnesh Kumar*. The direction was criticised by certain experts as judicial activism which was not warranted and encroachment in the executive or Parliamentary domain. Hundred years ago, in 1921

Benjamin N. Cardozo[25] has invoked that 'I take judge-made law as one of the existing realities of life'[26] and 'the judge as the interpreter for the community of its sense of law and order must supply omissions, correct uncertainties, and harmonize results with justice through a method of free decision'.[27] The question is, should these directions be incorporated in the statutes or any secondary legislation?

Impact of Arnesh Kumar Case

The real appreciation of a judicial pronouncement is known by its subsequent application. Cardozo, J. also writes that[28]:

> In the life of the mind as in life elsewhere, there is a tendency toward the reproduction of kind. Every judgment has a generative power. It begets in its image. Every precedent, in the words of Redlich, has a 'directive force for future cases of the same or similar nature'.

Arnesh Kumar received important reference in the case of *Rini Johar v. the State of MP*,[29] where Dipak Misra, J. reproduced *Arnesh Kumar* which has imported two tests for arrest as under:

a. Is there some evidence of a reason to believe that a cognizable offence is committed? The Police must have the threshold of reason to believe which is different from Knowledge.
b. If the answer to point a. is Yes, then whether the arrest is necessary?

These tests are already mentioned under CrPC. The questions that might help the police to answer the point of the necessity of arrest may be 'why arrest? Is it required? What purpose will it serve? What object

---

[25] BENJAMIN N. CARDOZO, THE NATURE OF THE JUDICIAL PROCESS (Yale University Press 1921), https://archive.org/details/natureofthejudic008454mbp (last visited 27 February 2021).

[26] *Id.* at 10.

[27] *Id.* at 20.

[28] Redlich, *The Case Method in American Law- Schools*, BULLETIN No. 8, Carnegie Foundation, p. 37, As quoted in CARDOZO, *supra* note 25.

[29] (2016) 11 S.C.C. 703.

will it achieve?'[30] *Rini Johar* found that the Police failed to demonstrate 'fidelity to the statutory safeguards'. Two accused ladies were picked up but not presented before a magistrate. They were kept in a railway compartment in an uncomfortable situation.

> It does not require the wisdom of a seer to visualize that for some invisible reason, an attempt has been made to corrode the procedural safeguards which are meant to sustain the sanguinity of liberty. The investigating agency, as it seems, has put its sense of accountability to the law on the ventilator.

The Court ordered compensation of ₹500,000 to each, which could be recovered from erring officials. The Court declared that the dispute is of civil or contractual nature and 'no ingredient of Section 420 of IPC is remotely attracted'. The proceeding was quashed. In *Rini Johar*, the wrong was committed at multiple levels. (a) The Police registered a criminal case. (b) The judicial magistrate detected the existence of a *prima facie* case of Section 420 of IPC. (c) The necessity of arrest could not be examined carefully which was in breach of *Joginder Kumar*[31] and *Arnesh Kumar*[32] (d) The Police also dishonoured the mandate of *D. K. Basu*[33] and statutory directions. In consequence, the Court provided the remedy under constitutional tort and quashed the criminal case. What the Court missed was that the accountability mechanism could not be initiated. The facts lead to contempt of judicial precedents as mentioned above. Why were the Police authorities not summoned for contempt? Why did the Court not direct a departmental action? Both, the contempt as well as the departmental action are directions in *Arnesh Kumar*.

The second subsequent recognition of *Arnesh Kumar* may be traced in the case of *Social Action Forum for Manav Adhikar v. Union of India*.[34] *Social Action Forum for Manav Adhikar* is a full bench decision that has approved *Arnesh Kumar* which is a division bench decision. Various

---

[30] Arnesh Kumar, *supra* note 7.

[31] Joginder Kumar, *supra* note 10.

[32] Arnesh Kumar, *supra* note 7.

[33] D.K. Basu, *supra* note 11.

[34] (2018) 10 S.C.C. 443. See, paras. 33 and 38.

high courts have used *Arnesh Kumar* to interpret the power of arrest. Various high courts have also utilized the precedent of *Arnesh Kumar. Kallu Sharma v. State of Madhya Pradesh,*[35] *Aslam Quershi v. State of Uttarakhand,*[36] *Raghuveer Singh Bundela v. State of M.P.,*[37] *Shivam v. State of Madhya Pradesh*[38] and *Sarifuddin Mondal v. State*[39] are some of them.

Contempt of *Arnesh Kumar*

The copy-paste of the provisions mentioned under Section 41 of CrPC will not bring the case under 'necessary to arrest'. Many times, the Police record the reason like 'credible information received', 'matter is serious', 'allegations are grave' and so on. Such a thing will violate *Arnesh Kumar*.[40] Not only there must be some reasons but the reasons for arrest must not be vague or uncertain. In the case of *Ramadugu Omkar Varma v. Sri. Ashok Naik,*[41] the arrest was held in violation of the direction of *Arnesh Kumar* that the police officers must 'satisfy themselves about the necessity for arrest under the parameters laid down above flowing from Section 41 of CrPC 1973'.

The defining feature of *Ramadugu Omkar Varma* case is that arrest in violation of *Arnesh kumar* was declared as 'a deprivation of personal liberty by the respondent without following due process of law'. The Police officer was held to as if he 'wilfully disobeyed the judgment of the Supreme Court and is therefore, liable to be punished for Contempt of Court'. He was 'sentenced to imprisonment for four weeks'.

In 2017, the Law Commission of India in its 268th report on bail has recognised *Arnesh Kumar*[42] and suggested the incorporation of

---

[35] Decided on 23 September 2019.

[36] Writ Petition (Criminal) No. 462 of 2020.

[37] Decided on 2 December 2020.

[38] Decided on 22 November 2019.

[39] W.P. 20771(W) of 2014.

[40] Arnesh Kumar, *supra* note 7.

[41] 2020 1 A.L.D. Crl 424 (TS).

[42] Law Commission of India, *268th Report on Amendments to Criminal Procedure Code, 1973—Provisions Relating to Bail*, para 4.6, at 26 and para 11.3, at 86 (May 2017), https://lawcommissionofindia.nic.in/reports/Report268.pdf (last visited 5 March 2021).

Section 41(1A) under CrPC to recognise the directions of *Arnesh Kumar*.[43] As *Arnesh Kumar* has received wide acceptance it is desirable to incorporate the judicial directions either in the statutory provisions or in rules.

Why Should Arnesh Kumar Directions be Incorporated?

We propose to incorporate *Arnesh Kumar* directions because (a) they are essential for the protection of accused persons, (b) these directions have also been approved by a full bench decision in 2018 in the case of *Social Action Forum for Manav Adhikar v. Union of India*.[44] (c) Previous directions of the Supreme Court in *Joginder Kumar*[45] and *D. K. Basu*[46] have also been granted statutory recognition and *Arnesh Kumar* is a substantive addition in it. (d) An express recognition of judicial directions in statutes (here CrPC) adds to the spread of its educative and persuasive nature. The Police are aware that they are obliged to follow it, the citizen can insist on its enforcement and the judiciary can use the express statutory provisions for the protection of human rights. Sometimes the Police and the judicial officers, with best of the intentions may not be aware of judicial directions.

In Which Provisions Amendments Can be Proposed?

Sections 41, 41A, 57, 167 of CrPC need an amendment for statutory recognition of *Arnesh Kumar* directions. As directions of Clause 11.2

---

[43] Proposed Section (1A) The police officer making the arrest shall furnish to the Magistrate, the facts, circumstances and reasons for the arrest and it shall be the duty of the Magistrate before whom such arrested person is produced, to satisfy himself that the requirements of this sub-section have been complied with in respect of the arrested person and shall record his satisfaction in writing as to the compliance of this sub-section; and in case the Magistrate is not satisfied that the requirements of this sub-section have been complied with, the Magistrate may release the arrested person on furnishing bond with or without sureties: Provided further that non-compliance of the provisions of this sub-section shall expose the police officer or judicial officer, as the case may be, to the risk of disciplinary proceedings. The High Court may amend the rules in this regard.

[44] Social Action Forum for Manav Adhikar, *supra* note 34, at paras. 33 and 38.

[45] Joginder Kumar, *supra* note 10.

[46] D.K. Basu, *supra* note 11.

onwards in *Arnesh Kumar* need the attention of the legislature, directions 11 and 11.1 can be avoided. *Arnesh Kumar's direction* 11.2 relies on Section 41(1)(b)(ii) which provides the conditions under which an arrest can be made.

Direction 11.2 states that 'All police officers be provided with a checklist containing specified sub-clauses under section 41(1)(b)(ii)'. The Second schedule of CrPC provides various forms. After Form 2, Form 2A may be incorporated which is as under 'Schedule 2—The Second Schedule' of CrPC may incorporate *Arnesh Kumar's direction* 11.2. The Proposed amendment may be as under-

Form 2A *Check List for Police Officer Executing Arrest under Section 41(1)(b)(ii)*

Mr .... against whom a reasonable complaint has been made	Yes/No
Mr .... against whom a credible information has been received	Yes/No
Mr .... against whom a reasonable suspicion exists	Yes/No
that he has committed an offence under section ....of IPC/ special law (name the Act....................)/local law (name the Act.....................)	Yes/No
This offence is cognizable as per schedule First of CrPC or other penal law (name the law....................)	Yes/No
Punishment for the offence mentioned above is less than 7 years or 7 years	Yes/No
Punishment for the offence mentioned above is more than 7 years	Yes/No
the police officer is satisfied that such arrest is necessary–	
(a) to prevent such person from committing any further offence; or	Yes/No
(b) for proper investigation of the offence; or	Yes/No
(c) to prevent such person from causing the evidence of the offence to disappear or tampering with such evidence in any manner; or	Yes/No

(d) to prevent such person from making any inducement, threat or promise to any person acquainted with the facts of the case to dissuade him from disclosing such facts to the Court or the police officer; or	Yes/ No
(e) as unless such person is arrested, his presence in the Court whenever required cannot be ensured,	Yes/ No

Arnesh Kumar's direction 11.3 says that 'the police officer shall forward the checklist duly filled and furnish the reasons and materials which necessitated the arrest, while forwarding/producing the accused before the Magistrate for further detention'. A direction under 11.3 can be incorporated under Section 57 of CrPC 1973, which states that 'Person arrested not to be detained more than twenty-four hours' under proposed amendment Section 57 can be renumbered as 1 and 2. Clause 2 be added as under:

Section 57—Person arrested not to be detained more than twenty-four hours—

1. No police officer shall detain in custody a person arrested without a warrant for a longer period than under all the circumstances of the case is reasonable, and such period shall not, in the absence of a special order of a Magistrate under section 167, exceed twenty-four hours exclusive of the time necessary for the journey from the place of arrest to the Magistrate's Court. (already existing).
2. The police officer shall forward the checklist duly filled under Form 2A and furnish the reasons and materials which necessitated the arrest, while forwarding/producing the accused before the Magistrate for further detention.

Arnesh Kumar's direction 11.4. says that 'the Magistrate while authorising detention of the accused shall peruse the report furnished by the police officer in terms aforesaid and only after recording its satisfaction, the Magistrate will authorise detention'. Direction 11.4 can be incorporated under Section 167 which deals with 'Procedure when investigation cannot be completed in twenty-four hours'. Section 3A and 3B can be incorporated–

3A. The Magistrate while authorising detention of the accused shall peruse the report furnished by the police officer in terms section 57(2) and only after recording its satisfaction, the Magistrate will authorise detention; [*Arnesh Kumar's direction* 11.3]

3B. Authorising detention without recording reasons as aforesaid by the Judicial Magistrate concerned shall be liable for departmental action by the appropriate High Court. [*Arnesh Kumar's direction* 11.8]

Arnesh Kumar's direction 11.5 says that 'the decision not to arrest an accused, be forwarded to the Magistrate within two weeks from the date of the institution of the case with a copy to the Magistrate which may be extended by the Superintendent of Police of the district for the reasons to be recorded in writing.' This may be added as Section 41A-(5). The direction 11.6. Mandates that the 'Notice of appearance in terms of Section 41-A CrPC is served on the accused within two weeks from the date of institution of the case, which may be extended by the Superintendent of Police of the district for the reasons to be recorded in writing.' This may be added as 41A-(1A)]. Direction 11.7. prescribes that 'Failure to comply with the directions aforesaid shall apart from rendering the police officers concerned liable for departmental action, they shall also be liable to be punished for contempt of court to be instituted before the High Court having territorial jurisdiction'. This may be added as 41A-(6). Section 41A prescribes 'Notice of appearance before a police officer'. After Clause 1, Clause 1A be added as under

1A. This Notice of appearance be served on the accused within two weeks from the date of institution of the case, which may be extended by the Superintendent of Police of the district for the reasons to be recorded in writing; [*Arnesh Kumar's direction* 11.6]

Under Section 41A, Clause 5 and 6 may be added after Clause 4 as under

5. The decision not to arrest an accused, be forwarded to the Magistrate within two weeks from the date of the institution of the case with a copy to the Magistrate which may be extended by the Superintendent of Police of the district for the reasons to be recorded in writing; [*Arnesh Kumar's direction* 11.5]

6. Failure to comply with the directions under sections 41, 41A, and 57 shall apart from rendering the police officers concerned liable for departmental action, they shall also be liable to be punished for contempt of court to be instituted before the High Court having territorial jurisdiction. [*Arnesh Kumar's direction* 11.7]

These amendments, even if not incorporated, have the same force of law. The incorporation in legislative format informs the resolve of a democratic polity on codified rule of law. The codification of law brings greater certainty.

CONCLUSION

Chandramauli K. Prasad, J. deserves deep appreciation for *Arnesh Kumar's* directions on adding to pre-arrest jurisprudence which came as a relief in many cases having punishment less than 7 years especially in Section 498A of IPC which were notorious for misuse. In the case of *Rashmi Chopra v. State of Uttar Pradesh,*[47] Apex Court reiterated that 'All relatives of the husband, namely, father, mother, brother, mother's sister and husband of mother's sister have been roped'. They 'clearly indicate that application under section 156(3) of CrPC was filed with a view to *harass the applicants*'. In *Jatinder Kumar v.* the *State of Haryana,*[48] a similar reference to the tendency of 'roping in' all members in dowry cases is mentioned. In this case, many accused were not residing with the deceased. Their business, their mess was not in the same house and was away from that place. The Supreme Court quoted the high court as under[49]:

It appears that Anil Kumar, Bimla Wanti, and Atul Mittal, were falsely implicated, in the instant case, to exaggerate the number of the accused. Only Jatinder Kumar, committed the offences, punishable under sections 304-B and 498-A of the Indian Penal Code. Out of abundant caution, Anil Kumar, Bimla Wanti, and Atul Mittal, accused, are required to be given the benefit of doubt, and, thus, are entitled to acquittal.

---

[47] A.I.R. 2019 S.C. 2297. A detailed examination of this case may be read in the Anurag Deep, *Socio Economic Crimes* LV *Annual Survey of Indian Law* (Indian Law Institute 2019).

[48] A.I.R. 2020 S.C. 161.

[49] *Id.* at para. 10.

Section 498A is one provision that demonstrates the tips of the iceberg on the issue of abuse of the authority on the arrest. V.R. Krishna Iyer, J. in the case of *Gopalanachari v. State of Kerala*[50] has rightly justified judicial intervention by suggesting that the 'preventive power under section 110 [another power to arrest] were prevented from pervasive misuse by zealous judicial vigilance and interpretative strictness'. *Arnesh Kumar* is another fantastic 'judicial vigilance' of what CrPC expects in words and spirit. To address any negligence and abuse the provisions under the Police Act, 1861 especially Section 29 needs to be implemented. In case of breach of *Arnesh Kumar,* the aggrieved and the civil society ought to approach the concerned high court for contempt. As discussed earlier it was done in the case of *Ramadugu Omkar Varma*[51] where a police officer was found guilty of contempt and imprisonment ordered. Indeed, the high courts and the Supreme Court should take *suo motu* cognizance at least once a month. It will send the right signal and will act as a deterrent over negligent police officers and the magistrates.

This proposal to amend CrPC begins with the presumption that the incorporation of the Supreme Court directions in statutes is essential because the police officers, judicial officers, and advocates rely heavily on statutory provisions especially in trial courts. Sometimes, the police, judicial officers, and advocates may not know very important judicial pronouncements. There are instances that wrong provisions have been used, wrong decisions have been delivered which were corrected at a later stage. This delays the judicial process and creates confusion. Many such provisions are matters of daily affairs that should indeed be part of rules. For example, Arrest rules, remand rules, and so on. But practices indicate that the rules are not framed for years and decades. Therefore, it is safe to incorporate leading judicial pronouncements in statutes. These changes, as proposed, are mainly cosmetic. The main problem of the criminal justice system cannot be substantially addressed by these modifications. For example, unless police public ratio is increased substantially (at least to UN standard), *Prakash Singh* judgement[52] is not followed, and technology is not used aggressively, things will not improve noticeably.

---

[50] Gopalanachari, *supra* note 16.
[51] Law Commission of India, *supra* note 42.
[52] Prakash Singh v. Union of India, (2006) 8 S.C.C. 1.

Afterword

The right to liberty is an inalienable right, a natural right, but this right is not without its restrictions, and the power of arrest and detention enables state actors to arrest or detain a person under law. While Articles 21 and 22 of the Constitution provide protection in matters of arrest and detention justiciable against the state, these constitutional protections are not without their dark side since the very same provisions empower legislatures to not only have laws for arrest but also preventive detention. During the Constituent Assembly debates, Pandit Thakur Das Bhargava made an interesting remark in the context of liberty

> Fundamental Rights mean that these rights cannot be taken away by the legislature or the executive. Left to myself, I would rather be without any fundamental right, unless there is a modicum of right which ensures the liberty of the citizen.[1]

Preventive detention laws have been characterized as draconian and excessive and their efficacy questioned. However, the legitimacy of such laws has been upheld by constitutional courts in judgements like *A.K. Roy v. Union of India*[2] and *State of Madras v. VG Row*[3] holding that since the Constitution itself provides for preventive detention—though passed on the subjective satisfaction of the detaining authority without any trial, without a lawyer's assistance and without being produced before a Magistrate within 24 h of arrest, and often susceptible to misuse, they cannot be held unconstitutional on the ground that they interfere with personal liberty. Among the draconian laws of preventive detention law is the Armed Forces (Special Powers) Act (AFSPA), 1958, which gives unrestricted and unaccounted statutory power to the

---

[1] Constituent Assembly Debates, Vol. IX, 1504 (15.09.1949).

[2] A.K. Roy v. Union of India, AIR 1982 SC 710.

[3] State of Madras v. VG Row, AIR. 1952 SC 196.

forces to search, arrest and, mostly importantly, to use force once an area is declared disturbed and its constitutional validity has been upheld by the Supreme Court. The Act gives the forces license to kill 'if it is necessary to do for the maintenance of public order'. Though ostensibly, AFSPA was enacted for suppression of disorder and for restoration and maintenance of peace and public order in disturbed areas, the real purpose of this law was to prevent activities deemed secessionist and curb self-determination movements.

On the face of it, AFSPA is not just a preventive detention law; hence, it comes with even less safeguards than the preventive detention laws. Section 4(c) of AFSPA provides for arrest without warrant on mere suspicion that the arrestee was going to commit an offence. The forces are not obliged to provide for reasons of arrest; there is no body to review the arrest and to confirm it or reject it; and there is no expiry time of preventive detention under AFSPA.

A reading of the Code of Criminal Procedure (CrPC) provides ample safeguards in the matter of arrest, and the amendments to CrPC have ostensibly raised the bar for effecting arrest. However, India is a country where arrests are hasty, and it is only the interdiction of courts that can protect liberty of citizens. Unfortunately, the mandate of Section 167, CrPC, which was the crucial check on arrest and custody has become a mechanical exercise for long. With the elimination of physical presence of the accused after the first remand date, the exercise of remand through virtual court (VC) has made it still more mechanical and perfunctory. Remand (police custody or judicial custody) is not to be granted as a matter of course but requires close judicial scrutiny and must be a check on police excesses in the matter of arrest and detention. Over the past few decades, it has almost been unheard of that in any case remand was not only refused but accused was also released to liberty on account of insufficiency of material (evidence) to justify remand.

Even the constitutional courts have diluted the scrutiny of illegal custody. A stray line in *Kanu Sanyal v. District Magistrate, Darjeeling & Ors.*[4] as applied with modification in *SFIO vs. Rahul Modi*[5] to hold

---

[4] Kanu Sanyal v. District Magistrate, Darjeeling & Ors., (1974) 4 SCC 141.
[5] SFIO vs. Rahul Modi, (2019) 5 SCC 266.

that once remand is granted, habeas corpus will not lie has curtailed judicial intervention, though even in *SFIO vs. Rahul Modi*, the entire para quoted from *Kanu Sanyal* makes it clear that habeas corpus is not restricted or barred completely. What is often ignored now is the valuable phrase in *Col. Dr. Ramachandra Rao v. State of Orissa*[6] and *Kanu Sanyal* where the Supreme Court had explained lucidly that only if remand is granted by a *competent court* and it is lawful can the habeas corpus fail.

Even in the matter of bail, the libertarian eras of 1980s have been forgotten with a restrictive approach to bail and custody, with courts applying elasticity to the most tenuous of grounds pleaded in support of arrest, refusal of bail and detention of investigating agencies.

To permit an investigation agency a freehand in the matter of remand, arrest and custody, would legitimize and perpetuate illegality. In a nation governed by rule of law, this trend has to be checked before the application of draconian laws, reverse burden bail provision, dilution of the presumption of innocence becomes the norm and the right to freedom and liberty the exception.

Recently, in the case of *Munawar Faruqui*[7] who was charged with hurting Hindu sentiments and was arrested in complete violation of Section 41, CrPC, and the judgement of the Hon'ble Supreme Court in *Arnesh Kumar v. State of Bihar & Anr.*,[8] even the high court declined bail. The high court failed to consider that his freedom had been curtailed arbitrarily without compliance with procedure established by law and rejected his bail. Munawar Faruqui spent more than 30 days in jail, which was really a case of illegal detention, and was only released upon intervention by the Supreme Court[9]. Shockingly, his bail was opposed before the high court on the flimsy ground that the accused was an influential person and an 'urban naxal'.

---

[6] Col. Dr. Ramachandra Rao v. State of Orissa, (1972) 3 SCC 256.

[7] Munnawar Faruqui v. State of Madhya Pradesh, (2021) SCC OnLine MP 152, decided on 28-01-2021.

[8] Arnesh Kumar v. State of Bihar & Anr., (2014) 8 SCC 273.

[9] Munawar v. State of Madhya Pradesh, (2021) SCC OnLine SC 60.

However, the case of Munawar Faruqui is not just an isolated case, as for long, there has been a dilution of safeguards provided under CrPC and similar procedural laws on search and seizure. The practical aspect of deficiencies in investigation is made a basis to undermine statutory safeguards, more so, the condonation of the illegal and unlawful acts of investigating agencies in cases like *Pooran Mal v. Director of Inspection (Investigation)*[10] and *R.M. Malkani v. State of Maharashtra,*[11] by allowing admissibility of such illegally obtained evidence has given unbridled and unfettered powers to the investigating agencies to illegally obtain evidence with impunity and no adverse consequences. Admission of such illegally obtained evidence has allowed investigators to generate and plant evidence and undermine the rule of law and administration of justice. Every single instance of illegally obtained evidence being admitted as evidence violates the right to a fair investigation, as guaranteed under Article 21.

Constitutional safeguards with regard to arrest and detention become even more essential when it concerns juveniles in conflict with law. The Juvenile Justice Act, 2015, which was passed with the objective of protection and social re-integration of children in conflict with law is often undermined by the bodies created by the statute and the Constitutional Courts, particularly with respect to liberty. Section 12 of the Act presupposes the principle of 'bail is rule, jail is exception' unless the conditions in proviso to Section 12 are shown. However, the Juvenile Justice Boards often without a semblance of regard to procedural safeguards under the Act and Section 12 deny bail to the accused juvenile, thus defeating the very purpose why these bodies were created in the first place.

In *Miranda v. State of Arizona,*[12] the US Supreme Court guaranteed the right against self-incrimination and laid down the rights of an arrested person, which are now popularly known as Miranda rights, which include right to remain silent and right to be informed of the right to remain silent, right against self-incrimination, right to a counsel prior

---

[10] Pooran Mal v. Director of Inspection (Investigation), (1974) 1 SCC 345.

[11] R.M. Malkani v. State of Maharashtra, (1973) 1 SCC 471.

[12] Miranda v. State of Arizona, 384 US 436.

to and during interrogation, right to legal aid, right to warning that anything said can and will be used against the individual in court, etc.

The Court noted that a difficulty with interrogations is that they are *largely* 'incommunicado in a police-centric atmosphere resulting in self-incriminating statements without full warnings of constitutional rights'—a statement which best describes custodial and non-custodial interrogations in India even now.

India's own Miranda moment came in *Nandini Satpathy case*[13] when the Supreme Court relying upon Miranda came up with a set of guidelines to prevent coercion and duress on the accused. However, these guidelines were never made statutory. A few years later, certain guidelines were laid down by the Supreme Court in *D.K. Basu v. State of W.B.*,[14] which were incorporated in CrPC by the Code of Criminal Procedure (Amendment) Act, 2009, which inserted Sections 41A–41D.

The Amendments pursuant to *D. K. Basu* brought in to provide for procedural safeguards in arrest and detention. However, these are ill-conceived, incomplete and fragmented and still leave too much discretion with police officers, and this unguided discretion leads to corruption and abuse of power and political interference and has proven ineffective in preventing custodial torture, coercion and infringement of the right to remain silent.

Though Section 41D, CrPC, permits an arrestee 'to meet his lawyer during interrogation though not throughout the interrogation', there is a basis that the right has to be limited and why a lawyer must not be present throughout interrogation. The lawyer may be in sight although he may not been within hearing distance of accused and interrogator. Though *D. K. Basu* was lauded at the time, it was a dilution of *Nandini Satpathy*.

Similarly, these amendments which were brought in to provide procedural safeguards in case of arrest have completely diluted the guidelines in Nandini Satpathy.

---

[13] Nandini Satpathy case, (1978) 2 SCC 424.
[14] D.K. Basu v. State of W.B., (1997) 1 SCC 416.

Despite the lofty ideals and principles in the Constitution and often lip service to international treaties on human rights, access to basic rights during arrest and detention has been limited to judgements and has never taken form of substantial rights provided in the statute books, letting illegal arrests, custodial torture and false prosecution continue throughout the country. Seventy-five years on, Indians are still waiting for their Miranda Rights.

The concerns of the framers ring true as we remember the words of Shri H. V. Kamath in the Constituent Assembly Debates[15]:

> Before I close, I would only say that it looks to me though we are framing a short-term Constitution, we are drafting a Constitution which will last perhaps just as long as some of us hope to be in power and we do not have a long-term plan or vision. Has anybody considered how some other persons, possibly totally opposed to our ideals, to our conceptions of democracy, coming into power, might use this very Constitution against us, and suppress our rights and liberties?

It took four decades to overturn the decision in the habeas corpus case[16] by *Justice D.Y. Chandrachud* who overturned his late father's view in the privacy case.[17] While jurisprudentially this has been a great achievement, this delay in redressing the judicial wrong done during the heydays of emergency is a stark reminder of how justice is delayed.

The fact that human liberty is not as precious is seen in the onerous legislative provisions reversing the burden of innocence even at the bail stage when an accused may be handicapped due to lack of material to meet the reverse burden to prove innocence to achieve liberty.

Liberty being sacrosanct, the need to ensure strict compliance with procedural safeguards is imperative as personal liberty has been held to be the greatest of human freedoms. In *Ayya @ Ayub vs. State of UP*,[18]

---

[15] Constituent Assembly Debates, Vol. IX, 1521 (15.09.1949).
[16] ADM Jabalpur v. Shivkant Shukla, (1976) 2 SCC 521.
[17] K.S. Puttaswamy v. Union of India, (2017) 10 SCC 1.
[18] Ayya @ Ayub vs. State of UP, (1989) 1 SCC 374.

the Supreme Court had quoted Justice Douglas in the *Hamlyn Law Lectures* on *Freedom under the Law* (1949) that

> [F]aith in America is faith in her free institutions or it is nothing. The Constitution we adopted launched a daring and bold experiment. Under that compact we agreed to tolerate even the ideas we despise. We also agreed never to prosecute people merely for their ideas of beliefs....

Applying that test to India, it is time to assess whether our courts are consistently ensuring the protection of liberty and compliance with procedural safeguards or is it a case of balancing perceived notions of equity and facts against the inviolable and sacrosanct principle of liberty to be ensured through procedural safeguards and enshrined in Articles 14 and 21.

Sidharth Luthra
Sr Advocate,
Supreme Court of India

About the Editors and Contributors

EDITORS

Dipa Dube is a professor at Rajiv Gandhi School of Intellectual Property Law, Indian Institute of Technology (IIT) Kharagpur, India. She specializes in the areas of criminal laws, gender violence and victimology. She is the vice-president of Indian Society of Victimology and has been conferred the ISV Fellowship in 2020. Dr Dube has published more than 80 articles in national and international journals on victim justice, human trafficking and rape laws and has authored 7 books. She is also a member of prestigious professional bodies including World Society of Victimology, International Society of Criminology, etc.

Shruti Bedi is Professor of Law at University Institute of Legal Studies (UILS), Panjab University (PU), Chandigarh. She is the Co-ordinator for Department of Law at University School of Open Learning, PU, Director for Centre for Constitution and Public Policy, UILS, PU and also a TEDx speaker. She has authored two books and co-edited four books including a Festschrift in honour of Professor Upendra Baxi in addition to publishing numerous articles in national and international journals, blogs, books, newspapers etc. She has lectured at universities in England, Canada, Vietnam, Indonesia and Brazil.

CONTRIBUTORS

R. K. Bag (J.) was former District and Sessions Judge of Malda, Chief Judge of City and Sessions Court, Calcutta, Registrar General of the High Court, Calcutta, Director of West Bengal Judicial Academy, Judge at Calcutta High Court and Judicial Member at West Bengal Administrative Tribunal. He has taught criminal law and constitutional law to IPS officers. He is the author of three books on *Law of Medical*

Negligence and Compensation; Supreme Court on Criminal Law; and Service Laws of Government Employees.

Surja Kanta Baladhikari is a guest faculty member at WBNUJS, Kolkata. He has served as Assistant Professor of Law at Amity University, Kolkata. He has worked in different research projects including 'Assessment of the juvenile justice system in West Bengal' and 'Judicial trends in cyber law with special reference to West Bengal' involving implementation of the Information Technology Act, 2008, in the State of West Bengal.

Nirmal Kanti Chakrabarti is the vice chancellor of WBNUJS. He retired as a professor from the Department of Law at Calcutta University and served as the director of School of Law at KIIT University, Bhubaneswar. He has authored 8 books and published 80 articles and research papers (approx.) in various national and international journals. He has completed five research projects and is associated with other projects of Ministry of Law and Justice, Ford Foundation, World Justice Project of ABA-USA, UNDP, UGC, ICSSR, etc. He was conferred Fellowship in 2001 by the Indian Society of Criminology, awarded Professor. K. Chockalingam Award by Indian Society of Victimology in 2017 and awarded Research Scholarship by Max Planck Institute of Foreign and International criminal Law, Freiburg, Germany in 2017 and 2018.

R. S. Cheema is a noted Indian senior advocate and former Advocate General of Punjab. He was appointed as the Special Public Prosecutor in the 1984 Anti-Sikh Riots Case and Coalgate Scam Trials. He was also appointed as a special counsel in major cases under the Prevention of Corruption Act; *Amicus Curiae* in a number of matters including a highlighted rape case of an intellectually challenged victim; Full Bench matter dealing with Compromise—quashing in non-compoundable cases; and teachers recruitment scam in Chandigarh. He has appeared for defence in the well-known 2G trial.

Tarannum Cheema has been practising as a lawyer for over 10 years. She has appeared as part of the defence team in the 2G trial and as part of the prosecution team representing CBI in the Coal Scam cases as well as the 1984 Anti-Sikh Riot cases. She has represented various political leaders of national stature in highly contentious matters, matters of economic offences including PMLA, cases of police and executive excesses committed against conscientious dissenters and cases involving the rights of weaker and marginalized sections.

Anurag Deep is Professor at Indian Law Institute (ILI), New Delhi with LLM from BHU and PhD from Gorakhpur. His research areas are criminal law and constitutional law. He has co-edited the book *Bail: Law and Practice in India* and has authored a book on *Law of Sedition and Freedom of Expression in India*. With teaching experience of 20 years, he has over 50 publications in English and Hindi including the *Journal of Indian Law Institute, Annual Survey of Indian Law*, ISIL Yearbook, *Yojana, Pratiyogita Darpam*, LexisNexis, etc. He is the associate editor of two UGC recognized journals, *Annual Survey of Indian Law* and *ILI Law Review*.

Kamaljit Singh Garewal (J.) has served as a judge in United Nations Appeals Tribunal at New York and Geneva (2009–2012). He was elevated as a judge at Punjab and Haryana High Court in 2000 and served till 2009. He has also served as the Additional District and Sessions Judge and District and Sessions Judge in Punjab from 1986 till 2000 including registrar, Central Administrative Tribunal on deputation (1991–1995). He started his law practice at the District Courts, Ludhiana (1972–1974) and practised at the Punjab and Haryana High Court from 1975 till 1985.

Sébastien Lafrance is a prosecutor (Crown Counsel) for the Public Prosecution Service of Canada. He was a part-time professor of law at the University of Ottawa and has clerked at the Supreme Court of Canada and Quebec Court of Appeal, and has worked as in-house Counsel at the Supreme Court of Canada. He has published several book chapters and articles in Australia, Canada, France, India, Indonesia, United Kingdom and Vietnam in English, French and Vietnamese and has lectured in 21 countries. He is a hyperpolyglot.

Sidharth Luthra is a senior advocate at the Supreme Court of India. In July 2012, Sidharth Luthra was appointed as the Additional Solicitor General of India at the Supreme Court and represented the union and various state governments in matters relating to fundamental rights, electoral reforms, criminal law and policy issues. He specializes in criminal law, white-collar crimes and cyber frauds.

Nitish Nawsagaray is faculty at ILS Law College, Pune. He has a teaching experience of more than 20 years, and his areas of interest are criminal law, constitutional law and law and public policy. He has published two books and contributed articles on various legal issues in reputed law journals, newspapers and magazines. He delivered a lecture on 'Caste and Justice in India' at Harvard India Conference 2019, Harvard University. He has visited Cardiff University, UK, in 2006 for a teaching and research programme.

Kumar Askand Pandey is Associate Professor of Law and founding faculty of Dr Ram Manohar Lohiya National Law University, Lucknow. He is the coordinator of Centre for Criminal Justice Administration and project director of a UNICEF-funded mega project spread over 26 districts of Uttar Pradesh in creating and strengthening a robust child protection system. A keen researcher and prolific writer, he has published around 24 papers in national and international journals and written text/reference books on criminal law, law of evidence and juvenile justice. His current research interests include women and child rights, victimology, cybercrimes and criminal justice system.

Amira Paripurna is Assistant Professor of Faculty of Law at Universitas Airlangga, Indonesia. She is also the head of Human Rights Law Studies Center and head of undergraduate law programme at Universitas Airlangga. She obtained a PhD degree from School of Law, University of Washington, USA. She received Ford Foundation International Fellowship Program for LLM at Utrecht University, the Netherlands. In 2019, she was selected as a visiting research fellow at Asian Law Institute (ASLI), National University of Singapore.

P. Puneeth is Associate Professor of Law at Centre for the Study of Law and Governance, Jawaharlal Nehru University, New Delhi. He was a former assistant professor at ILI, honorary visiting faculty at Jindal Global Law School, guest lecturer at National Law University, Delhi, and former member of Board of Studies, Amity University, Jaipur. He has published papers in national and international journals of repute including *Journal of Indian Law Institute, Jindal Global Law Review, Delhi Law Review, CNLU Law Journal*, etc.

Namrta Rastogi is an assistant professor at Modern College of Law, Ghaziabad. She teaches criminal law and constitutional law. She has taught at Saharanpur Law College, UP, and was previously appointed as faculty in Gopeshwar Law College, Uttarakhand. For a couple of years, she practised in Haridwar district as an advocate. She was also selected as public prosecutor in Uttarakhand. Her areas of interest are criminal law and constitutional law.

Balram Prasad Raut is Associate Professor in Nepal Law Campus, Tribhuvan University. He had been a practising advocate in Nepal since 2004. He obtained PhD from South Asian University, New Delhi (2020) and is a gold medallist with specialization in criminal law. He has been awarded Nepal Bidhya Bhushan (the second highest award for a university degree) from Rt Hon Dr Rambaran Yadav, President of Nepal. He has published articles in national and international journals in the areas of criminal law, constitutional law and human rights and has recently published a text book of criminal law. Dr Raut has been a research coordinator of different governmental and non-governmental research projects.

Amiya Kumar Samanta is a retired IPS officer who served as the Director General of Intelligence Branch. He combines the dexterity of a sleuth and the acumen of a researcher in his exhaustive compilation of unpublished documents from one of the most sensational trials during the struggle for independence, when the rule of the colonial bureaucracy undermined the eulogized British ideals of law and justice. Titled, Alipore Bomb Trial (1908–1910), the work lists the statements of 206 witnesses along with 1,575 documents and materials placed before the court during the Alipore Bomb Trial or the Maniktala Conspiracy Case.

Justice A. K. Sikri is an eminent jurist and former judge of Supreme Court of India. He is presently serving as the International Judge at the Singapore International Commercial Court. He retired as the senior most puisne judge of Hon'ble Supreme Court of India on 6 March

2019. He has also served as Chief Justice of the Punjab and Haryana High Court. He is also the chairperson of News Broadcasting Standards Authority.

Kavita Singh is a professor at West Bengal National University of Juridical Sciences (WBNUJS), Kolkata. She has worked in various research projects including 'Prison Reform in India' BPRD, Government of India (2006–2007), and 'Human Rights Outreach Project' (2001–2002) organized jointly with British Council, National Law School, Bangalore and University of Warwick, UK. She has been the principal investigator of a project funded by West Bengal Judicial Academy titled, 'A Study on Adoptions in West Bengal under the Juvenile Justice (Care & Protection of Children) Act, 2000' (2014–2016). She has authored 4 books and published more than 25 articles in journals of national repute and has contributed several chapters in edited books.

Yogesh Pratap Singh is Professor of Law and Registrar at National Law University, Odisha. He received his LLM from National Law School of India University (NLSIU), Bangalore and Bachelor of Laws (LLB) from the University of Allahabad. He participated in 39th Annual Session on International Human Rights Law and CiedhU programme organized by International Institute of Human Rights (IIHR) Strasbourg, France. He has also worked as Deputy Registrar (on Deputation) in the Supreme Court of India.

Bhabani Sonowal is an assistant professor at VIT University, Chennai, Tamil Nadu. Having completed her Master of Laws (LLM) from Gauhati University, Assam, and PhD from Rajiv Gandhi School of Intellectual Property Law, IIT Kharagpur, Dr Bhabani has been engaged in teaching cyber law, criminal law, jurisprudence, women and law, law and social transformation, etc. since 2019. Her broad areas of interest include international human rights law, international humanitarian law, victimology and criminal law.

Index

Other titles in this series: